Best-Selling Chapters

ADVANCED LEVEL

15 Novels for
Teaching Literature
and Developing
Comprehension

Best-Selling Chapters

ADVANCED LEVEL

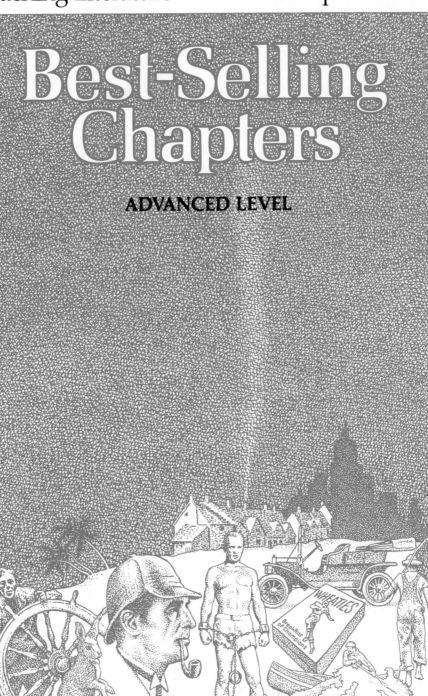

Raymond
Harris

Jamestown Publishers
Providence, Rhode Island

15 Novels for Teaching Literature
and Developing Comprehension

Best-Selling Chapters

ADVANCED LEVEL

Catalog No. 791
Catalog No. 791H, Hardcover Edition

Copyright © 1979 by
Jamestown Publishers, Inc.

Cover Design by Stephen R. Anthony
Illustrations by Mari-Ann Süvari

Printed in the United States   AL

84 85 86 87 9 8 7 6 5 4 3

ISBN 0-89061-151-3
ISBN 0-89061-319-2 Hardcover Edition

Contents

Acknowledgments

Acknowledgment is gratefully made to the following publishers for permission to reprint the works of the many authors appearing in this book:

Ragtime. From *Ragtime* by E. L. Doctorow. Copyright © 1974, 1975 by E. L. Doctorow. Reprinted by permission of Random House, Inc.

Roots. From *Roots* by Alex Haley. Copyright © 1976 by Alex Haley. Reprinted by permission of Doubleday & Company, Inc.

Hawaii. From *Hawaii* by James A. Michener. Copyright © 1959 by James A. Michener. Reprinted by permission of Random House, Inc.

Deliverance. From *Deliverance* by James Dickey. Copyright © 1970 by James Dickey. Reprinted by permission of Houghton Mifflin Company.

An American Tragedy. From *An American Tragedy* by Theodore Dreiser. Reprinted by permission of Harold J. Dies, Trustee of The Dreiser Trust.

In Cold Blood. From *In Cold Blood* by Truman Capote. Copyright © 1965 by Truman Capote. Reprinted by permission of Random House, Inc. Originally appeared in *The New Yorker* in slightly different form.

Babbitt. From *Babbitt* by Sinclair Lewis. Copyright © 1922 by Harcourt Brace Jovanovich, Inc.; renewed 1950 by Sinclair Lewis. Reprinted by permission of the publishers.

Watership Down. From *Watership Down* by Richard Adams. Copyright © 1972 by Rex Collings, Ltd. Reprinted with permission of Macmillan Publishing Company, Inc.

Lord of the Flies. From *Lord of the Flies* by William Golding. Copyright © 1954 by William Golding. Reprinted by permission of Coward, McCann & Geoghegan, Inc.

The author wishes to thank Christine Powers for her invaluable contributions to the creation of this text.

R.H.

Introduction
to the Teacher

There has been a longstanding need for a simple, direct and understandable approach to the basic elements of literature for students who are just beginning to deal with full-length novels. *Best-Selling Chapters, Advanced Level* was created to fill this need.

Best-Selling Chapters, Advanced Level grew out of an earlier text called *Chapters* which has been used successfully for more than five years to help students bridge the literary gap between brief reading selections and full-length books. While maintaining the best features of the earlier text, *Best-Selling Chapters, Advanced Level* has added many new features that make it a basic study of elements of literature, as well as a proven approach to reading improvement. Each of the 15 reading selections, consisting of one or more chapters from best-selling fiction, is accompanied by these teaching elements:

An Introduction to the Reading Selection. This short introduction sets the reading selection in its context and furnishes information a student will need to read with understanding and appreciation. A synopsis of the book, explanations of unusual ideas, foreign or dialect words, the author's intent, and some interesting background information about each author are all included in the introductions. Teachers should emphasize the importance of reading the introductions.

A Literary Lesson. Each reading selection is preceded by a simple lesson dealing with one element of literature—plot, setting, character, tone, symbolism, and so on—or with one of five genres within the realm of fiction. By reading all 15 lessons, a student may be expected to acquire a good working knowledge of the basic literary elements and an understanding of the concept of genre.

The Tasks. At the end of each lesson, students are given four "tasks" to carry with them into the reading selection that sharpen their awareness of how literary values and techniques are actually woven into a work by an author. Each task calls attention to a particular passage in the reading selection where an element taught in the lesson is clearly illustrated.

Lesson-Related Exercises. Following each reading selection there are practice exercises in which students can use what they have learned about the particular literary element or genre discussed in the lesson. Passages designated in the "tasks" are excerpted in the practice exercises, and students are asked to answer questions based on these sample passages.

Skill-Oriented Comprehension Questions. Twenty-five comprehension questions, keyed directly to specific reading and reasoning skills, are included with each unit. This was the most popular teaching tool of *Chapters* and has been retained, expanded and improved upon here. The question types are evenly distributed throughout the units to give the student ample practice in each of the twelve reading skills. All questions are labeled according to skill; the following key is provided at the end of each comprehension section for quick reference:

> Comprehension Skills: a—isolating details; b—recalling specific facts; c—retaining concepts; d—organizing facts; e—understanding the main idea; f—drawing a conclusion; g—making a judgment; h—making an inference; i—recognizing tone; j—understanding characters; k—appreciation of literary forms; l—knowledge of word meanings.

These twelve question types reflect those aspects of comprehension which we believe can be adequately sampled. We hasten to acknowledge that true comprehension does not conveniently separate into twelve independent activities—we all know that more than one skill is used in answering any one question. We have, therefore, labeled each question according to what we believe is the major or dominant skill displayed in arriving at the correct answer.

We also realize that certain question types overlap; however, we have held to certain distinctions in order to stimulate the reader to greater subtlety of thought. Fine distinctions between making a judgment and drawing a conclusion do exist, as well as between making an inference and drawing a conclusion.

Here is a detailed description of the skills measured by the twelve types of comprehension question:

Isolating Details. This skill calls upon the reader to detach or separate an individual part from among other parts.

Recalling Specific Facts. This asks the reader to bring back from memory a precise event or circumstance.

Retaining a Concept. This skill tests the reader's ability to keep in mind and recall a generalization or idea formed by mentally combining characteristics and details.

Organizing Facts. This asks the reader to form into a whole, stated, interdependent, or coordinated events or circumstances.

Understanding the Main Idea. This requires the reader to perceive clearly the writer's primary intention as interpreted in the light of important details.

Drawing a Conclusion. This requires the reader to arrive at the one decision justified by the stated evidence.

Making a Judgment. This requires the reader to arrive at a sound decision (not necessarily the only one) based on the stated evidence.

Making an Inference. This asks the reader to arrive at a deduction based on assumed premises.

Recognizing Tone. This measures the reader's ability to appreciate those qualities in an author's style which reveal his attitudes or points of view and to identify the atmosphere in which he has cast characters and events.

Understanding Characters. To do this, the reader must appreciate the aggregate of features and traits which form the individual nature of some person.

Appreciation of Literary Forms. This requires the reader to distinguish among the various types of writing and figures of speech.

Knowledge of Word Meanings. Vocabulary has not been treated as a separate entity, but has been included with comprehension where it belongs. Each word is presented contextually.

A Comprehension Skills graph is provided at the end of the book where students may make a visual record of the kinds of questions that they miss among the twelve specific skills. If a pattern emerges showing that one kind of question is missed frequently, remedial action may be indicated in this area. Jamestown's *Comprehension Skills Series* is an ideal tool to use for remediation. Booklets for each of the skills are available on both intermediate and advanced levels of difficulty.

A Comprehension Scores graph is also provided so that students can record their overall progress through the reading selections. Answer keys for self-correction can also be found in the back of the book.

Discussion Guides. Each unit contains ten discussion questions which deal with three aspects of literary criticism: analysis of the literary element or genre discussed in the lesson, interpretation of meanings and implications inherent in the selection, and analysis of the author's technique.

The Writing Exercise. The writing assignment is designed to give the student first-hand experience with the literary technique or genre discussed in the lesson. Since reading and writing improvement go hand-in-hand, the reading selections function as a springboard for broadening students' knowledge of writing techniques; in turn, the writing exercise can deepen the students' understanding and appreciation of writing styles found in their reading.

In choosing reading selections for this new text, half were taken from books that have had a long tenure on *The New York Times* best-seller list within the last decade, thus giving students a good sampling of the most popular of recent fiction. Other titles have been continuous best sellers long enough to be called modern classics—*Babbitt*, *Lord of the Flies*, and *An American Tragedy* are among these. Two selections are from all-time greats that are usually called "perfect" novels, and so must be included in any beginning study of literature; these are, of course, Dickens's *Great Expectations* and the American classic, *Huckleberry Finn*.

Among the selections used to illustrate some of the fiction genres are three classes of fiction that have long held best-reading status among students but are often unaccountably omitted from reading courses. These are humor, satire and the detective novel. So to accord these genres the honor they already hold with students, the editor has included chapters from Thurber's *My Life and Hard Times*, Vonnegut's *Breakfast of Champions* and Arthur Conan Doyle's *The Hound of the Baskervilles*.

Introduction
to the Student

When you play a record that you like, you have a pleasant emotional experience. It may be exciting or it may just put you in a quiet, sentimental mood. However it affects you, you find it enjoyable; that's why you listen, perhaps over and over again. This emotional charge is an end in itself and a principal reason for listening to music in the first place. It may be the *entire* reason that some people enjoy listening to music. Others, however, heighten their enjoyment by listening closely for such things as rhythm, melody, harmony and counterpoint, and for themes expressed either by the music or the lyrics. Still others, who have some knowledge of hi-fi equipment, analyze the music for tone, resonance and modulation, and they constantly try to increase their enjoyment of music by upgrading their audio equipment in an effort to achieve true "concert-hall" sound.

In the same way, the books you read may be read just for the emotional experience they provide. Many books become best sellers largely because of their emotional impact on readers. *The Godfather* is one of these and *Deliverance* is another—books that make your skin crawl and your pulse beat faster with the pressure of shock and suspense. *Huckleberry Finn* can make you feel nostalgic for a time you have never known, while your first reaction to *Babbitt* or *Breakfast of Champions* is amused laughter. Laughter, sentiment or spine-tingling excitement are certainly good enough reasons to read a book, and this first emotional response will greatly affect your enjoyment of it.

But there are other dimensions to books that can heighten your enjoyment of them, and make you a better reader, once you are aware that they exist and you know how to look for them. Just as song writers and composers plan every detail of a composition to achieve the precise effect they want from their music, authors spend long hours working out plots, designing settings for the story, and choosing words with the care and deliberation of a judge. They do all of this to create very specific effects. The extent to which they succeed at this will decide their success or failure in the book-writing business.

If you are able to *see* what an author has done, you will enjoy your reading more, just as you enjoy music more when you hear and understand what the composer has done. This book is a guide to understanding some of the important elements that you encounter when you read fiction. Its goal is to help you read with greater enjoyment and understanding.

TIPS FOR USING THE TEXT

1. The Introduction. Each unit begins with an introduction. Be sure to read the introduction carefully. It provides the background you need to understand the reading selection and the lesson.

2. The Lesson. Read each lesson carefully and thoughtfully. Pay close attention to the sample passages included in the lesson that are taken from the selection you will read. These illustrate the literary element under discussion. At the end of the lesson you are asked to watch for special passages in the reading selection that will further illustrate the literary element you have just learned about. Copy these directions on a piece of paper and watch for the passages as you read. You will be asked questions about them when you finish your reading.

3. The Reading Selection. Read carefully, but also read for enjoyment. Watch for elements discussed in the lesson—plot, setting, characterization, and so on. Be sure to find and note the special passages you have been asked to watch for.

4. The Comprehension Questions. The twenty-five multiple-choice questions which follow the selection test for specific reading and reasoning skills. Each question is labeled with a letter; the letter indicates which skill the question tests: (a) isolating details, (b) recalling specific facts, and so on. The key for the labels is located at the end of the questions.

To complete this section, answer the twenty-five multiple-choice questions without referring back to the selection. When you have finished, turn to the answer key at the back of the book and correct your answers. Next, turn to the graphs at the end of the book, and follow the directions given there for recording your progress throughout the text.

5. The Practice Exercises. The four exercises in this section will help you see how well you have spotted the literary technique discussed in the lesson. Each exercise consists of a passage from the selection, followed by two questions. The passages used are the ones you were asked to watch for. Complete this section by answering all questions and then correcting your answers using the key at the back of the book.

6. The Discussion Guides. Try to discuss these questions with others. If your class situation does not provide time for discussion, or if you are working alone, think about these questions carefully before going on.

7. The Writing Exercise. Each writing exercise relates to what you have read in the lesson and in the reading selection. You can often improve your writing by trying to imitate good writers. To whatever extent you can, try to imitate the author of the reading selection as you write.

Unit 1
Analyzing Setting

Ragtime

Introduction

E. L. Doctorow's *Ragtime* recreates an era in American history when a new style on the piano was breaking musical traditions and new forces on the American scene were breaking traditions that had governed how people lived, worked and played. It is about women's liberation, labor unrest, immigrants and racial prejudice. It is about a turning point in our history when America changed, for better or worse, from a rural, provincial society into the kind of world we live in today.

The novel follows the members of a family in New Rochelle, New York, through a period that roughly coincides with the emergence of ragtime music around 1900 until the United States entered World War I in 1917. The family, never identified as more than Mother, Father, Grandfather, Mother's Younger Brother and The Little Boy, lives in "a stout, three-story brown shingle with dormers, bay windows and a screened porch."

Interwoven with the lives of the family in New Rochelle are other characters, both real and fictional. Houdini, the famous magician, drives through town in his black 45 horsepower Pope-Toledo Runabout and swerves into a telephone pole in front of the family's house. Mother's Younger Brother falls in love with the beautiful actress, Evelyn Nesbit, whose name and picture have been in all the papers.

Under Doctorow's touch, actual historical figures mingle familiarly with fictional characters and with each other. J. P. Morgan, the banker, discusses reincarnation with Henry Ford, and Emma Goldman, a radical socialist and feminist, meets the beautiful actress, Evelyn Nesbit. As far as we know, these meetings never took place. But if they had, chances are they would have proceeded much as Doctorow depicts them in *Ragtime*.

Ragtime portrays a spirit in America characterized by patriotic celebrations, parades, public concerts and political picnics. Trains, steamers and trolleys moved great swarms of people from one place to another. Everyone wore white in summer, and women carried parasols. It was a time of change: America was undergoing an irrevocable transformation from rural to urban, from provincial to worldly, and never again would it display that innocence which could be both so appealing and so disturbing at the same time.

Two of the most intriguing characters in *Ragtime* are Tateh and The Little Girl. The chapters in this unit follow the progress of Tateh and The Little Girl as they leave New York City in search of a better life. Tateh (the name is a Jewish word for "Dad") is an artist who immigrated to this country from Russia. He tried to support his family by selling silhouette cut-outs on Hester Street, an immigrant Jewish neighborhood on the lower East Side of New York City. Disillusioned when his wife turns to prostitution to earn money to keep the family from starving, and when his chance friend, Evelyn Nesbit, turns out to be a prostitute of a higher social class, Tateh takes The Little Girl and leaves the city. The selection begins with their journey on a network of interurban streetcars to Lawrence, Massachusetts, where Tateh finds work in a textile mill. The mills "short pay" the workers, and a bitter, midwinter strike, organized by Big Bill Haywood (an actual historical figure) of the International Workers of the World, is the result. The selection depicts Tateh's gradual disappointment with labor unions and his eventual alienation from the working class in general.

Ragtime received enthusiastic reviews from critics for its imaginative blend of the real and the fanciful. Of this technique, E. L. Doctorow commented that "one of the governing ideas of this book is that facts are as much of an illusion as anything else. And that the line between fact and fiction is not as clearly defined as we think it is."

Doctorow lives in New Rochelle, New York, in a house built in 1906. Explaining how his house contributed inspiration for his novel, Doctorow noted, "I wrote it here—and the first line of the first draft was, 'I live in a house that was built in 1906.' With that, certain images sprang to mind: Teddy Roosevelt was President, people wore white clothes in the summertime, women carried parasols. That's how history exists in most people's minds—as sets of images. I've used some of those images and constructed a novel from them."

Analyzing Setting

Remember the last time you read a good book and tried to tell a friend about it? Chances are, you faithfully told who was in it and what happened to them, but you probably forgot to mention the setting. Setting often seems secondary to character and plot. This is because in a good story the author's choice of setting seems so right and natural. In fact, we can't imagine the action taking place anywhere else.

Though you may not be as aware of the setting as you are of the characters and plot, setting is nevertheless an extremely important part of any story. It is never an afterthought, nor is it just an author's attempt to add some local color. Rather, setting is firmly linked with the characters of a story and the conflicts which beset them. The Mississippi River is as essential to the story of Huckleberry Finn and Tom Sawyer as the gas-lit London of the Victorian era is to Sherlock Holmes. A good story cannot be uprooted and transplanted in another setting without drastically changing its nature.

Setting is simply the framework within which the author places a story. One way the author builds this framework is by presenting simple facts that put the reader in a particular time and place. The author describes the geographical location, the physical surroundings, and the historical period in which the story is set.

On another level, however, setting is more than just scenery and props. Equally important is the atmosphere, or feeling, which setting helps to create. The way you feel has a lot to do with where you are. You are more likely to feel pious in church than at a ball game. And warm, hospitable surroundings will make you feel better than a cold, strange environment. An author wants to make you feel how environment affects the characters in the story.

An author uses a variety of devices to establish setting. Some of these include sights, sounds and smells; actual historical incidents; details of architecture, clothing and transportation; and the images and impressions that characterize a certain time and place.

The following passage from *Ragtime* sets the scene for a journey. What information does this setting convey?

> The early evening was warm and all the windows of the trolley were lowered. The streets were crowded with cabs and cars and their horns blew at one another. Trolleys went along in clusters, their bells ringing, the flashes of electricity from their pantographs crackling along the overhead wires in minute intensifications of the heat lightning that flattened the sky over the darkening, sultry city.

In a few sentences, the passage above describes a city street, kinds of transportation, the time of day, the season and weather, sights and sounds of the moment, and a feeling of movement and expectation. It is a warm, humid evening, probably in midsummer when heat lightning is so common. Inside the trolley, the atmosphere is stuffy and close, and the windows have been opened. Even without being told in so many words, we know that this is a city street because of the crowds of trolleys, cabs and cars. The fact that there are these three kinds of transportation suggests a period in the early part of the century when the use of electricity was widespread, cars were already on the mass market, and trolleys were still a popular means of transportation. The reader is drawn into the sensations of the moment by the ringing of the trolley bells, the blare of car horns, and the flashes of electricity crackling along the overhead wires.

Sometimes we are made to see the setting through the eyes of one of the characters. An author may use this technique to reveal some aspect of the character as well as to describe the setting. In the following passage from *Ragtime*, E. L. Doctorow records a changing landscape through the eyes of a young girl on a journey by streetcar. What kinds of feelings are emphasized here, and what do you learn about the girl?

> Her dark eyes stared solemnly at the parades of people strolling along Broadway, the men in boaters and blue blazers and white ducks, the women in white summer frocks. The electric light bulbs of each vaudeville house rippled in a particular pattern. A ring of light spun around the rims of her pupils. Three hours later they were on a streetcar moving north along Webster Avenue in the Bronx. The moon was out, the temperature had dropped, and the trolley clipped along the broad reaches of this wide boulevard with only occasional stops. They passed grassy lots interspersed with blocks of row houses still under construction. Finally the lights disappeared entirely and the little girl realized they were traveling along the edges of a great hillside cemetery. The stones and vaults standing against the cold night sky suggested to her the fate of her mother.

The above setting conveys a feeling of movement, change and the passage of time. The scene changes from dusk to darkness, from late afternoon until well into the night, from a crowded city to lonely suburbs. Several clues establish time and place and suggest a mood characteristic of the era. The streetcar route along Broadway and through the Bronx fixes the location as New York City. The parade of people out strolling—the men decked out in boaters (straw hats) and white ducks (crisp white slacks), the ladies in white summer frocks, or dresses—suggests a more formal and leisurely time. The reference to vaudeville narrows this down to the early part of the century.

The landscape flies past the young girl's fascinated gaze in a whirl of images and impressions. The electric lights of the vaudeville house spin a ring of light around the rim of her eyes. The hillside cemetery, barely visible in the darkness, brings forth memories of her mother. Even after several hours of traveling, she cannot take her eyes off the passing scenery. To her eyes, the world is still a dazzling and exciting place.

One purpose of setting is to make the story seem more real. A good setting helps the reader visualize what is going on in the story so vividly that it almost comes to life. On the other hand, a setting that does not ring true is apt to affect the reader's acceptance of other parts of the story. In the following passage, Doctorow continues to describe the streetcar journey by listing the various stops along the way. How does this technique add to the believability of the setting?

> The streetcar went up the Post Road, along the Long Island Sound shoreline to the Connecticut border. In Greenwich, Connecticut, they transferred to another car. This took them up through the cities of Stamford, Norwalk and then to Bridgeport, the burial place of Tom Thumb . . . . At Bridgeport they transferred again. The tracks turned inland. They stopped for the night in New Haven, Connecticut . . . . A car of the Springfield Traction Company took them to New Britain and then to the city of Hartford . . . . the clapboard houses of the city seemingly close enough to reach out and touch. Then they were on the outskirts and racing along north to Springfield, Massachusetts.

In this setting, the author uses actual place names to chart the journey of the travelers from one point to another. As city after city is ticked off, the reader has the feeling of drawing a finger along a map, tracing the route of the streetcars. A reader familiar with the area would immediately recognize this route. But even readers unacquainted with the cities and towns along the way would accept them as real places. The touches of detail that describe Bridgeport as the burial place of Tom Thumb and Hartford as the city where clapboard houses back right up to the streetcar tracks catch our fancy and make the place names come alive. And the reference to The Springfield Traction Company, long since out of business, gives the reader the feeling of being back in an era when the names of the various trolley companies were as familiar to Americans as Ford, Chevrolet and General Motors are today. Details such as these help make the setting real. And when a reader accepts the setting, he or she will be more likely to accept the characters and situations as well.

Sometimes the author uses setting to develop some aspect of character or plot. For instance, the brutality of prison life might be described in order to explain personality changes in a character. Similarly, an inner city slum would be an appropriate setting for a story about social revolution. How does the following setting suggest future plot developments?

> This same winter found Tateh and his daughter in the mill town of Lawrence, Massachusetts. They had come there the previous autumn, having heard there were jobs. Tateh stood in front of a loom for fifty-six hours a week. His pay was just under six dollars. The family lived in a wooden tenement on a hill. They had no heat. They occupied one room overlooking an alley in which residents customarily dumped their garbage.

The setting described above conveys a feeling of dreariness and squalor that cannot help but affect the mood of the characters who live there. The unheated wooden tenement overlooking an alleyway filled with garbage is typical of the dwellings to which millworkers in the early part of the century returned after grueling days spent in front of a loom. The author is effectively setting the scene for a clash of some sort involving the poorly paid millworkers. Moreover, by providing this glimpse into the living conditions of the workers, the author enlists the reader's sympathy on behalf of their cause. Setting, then, is used here to explain the course of events which will follow.

Clearly, setting is more than just a rundown on the furnishings of a room or the scenery outside the window. It is used by the author to establish the proper historical and social background of the story. More importantly, setting helps create just the right atmosphere which will enable the reader to identify with the characters and understand the world in which they move. As you read the selection from *Ragtime* which follows, be aware of how setting is used to convey the sights, sounds and impressions of America in the early 1900s.

As you read these chapters:

- Notice the feeling created by the setting during the journey Tateh and the little girl took on the Worcester Electric Street Railway.

- Be aware of the setting in Lawrence when the strikers picket the mills.

- Notice your reaction when the police attack the crowd at the train station.

- Notice how the author uses the department store setting in Philadelphia.

Ragtime
E.L. Doctorow

CHAPTER 12

And what of Tateh and his little girl? After that meeting the old artist sat one night and one day in his flat and he did not eat or say anything, brooding, as he smoked endlessly his Sobrany cigarettes, on the brutal luck of his life. Every once in a while he would look at his child, and seeing the sure destruction of her incredible beauty in his continuing victimization he would clutch her to him and tears would fill his eyes. The little girl quietly prepared their simple meals in ways so reminiscent of the movements of his wife that finally he could bear the situation no longer. Throwing their few clothes in a musty suitcase whose strap had long since rotted away, he tied a piece of clothesline around the suitcase, took the girl by the hand and left the two-room flat on Hester Street forever. They walked to the corner and boarded the No. 12 streetcar for Union Square. At Union Square they transferred to the No. 8 and rode north up Broadway. The early evening was warm and all the windows of the trolley were lowered. The streets were crowded with cabs and cars and their horns blew at one another. Trolleys went along in clusters, their bells ringing, the flashes of electricity from their pantographs crackling along the overhead wires in minute intensifications of the heat lightning that flattened the sky over the darkening, sultry city. Tateh had no idea where he was going. The little girl held his hand tightly. Her dark eyes stared solemnly at the parades of people strolling along Broadway, the men in boaters and blue blazers and white ducks, the women in white summer frocks. The electric light bulbs of each vaudeville house rippled in a particular pattern. A ring of light spun around the rims of her pupils. Three hours later they were on a streetcar moving north along Webster Avenue in the Bronx. The moon was out, the temperature had dropped, and the trolley clipped along the broad reaches of this wide boulevard with only occasional stops. They passed grassy lots interspersed with blocks of row houses still under construction. Finally the lights disappeared entirely and the little girl realized they were traveling along the edges of a great hillside cemetery. The stones and vaults standing against the cold night sky suggested to her the fate of her mother. For the first time she asked her Tateh where they were going. He pulled the window shut against the cold wind whistling now through the ratcheting, rocking trolley. They were the only passengers. Sha, he said to her. Close your eyes. Distributed in his pockets and in his shoes were his life savings, some thirty dollars. He had decided to leave New York, the city that had ruined his life. There was in these days of our history a highly developed system of interurban street railway lines. One could travel great distances on hard rush seats or wooden benches by taking each line to its terminus and transferring to the next. Tateh did not know anything about the routes. He only planned to keep on going as far as each streetcar would take him.

In the early hours of the first morning of their trip they crossed the city line into Mount Vernon, New York, and there learned that the next service would not begin till daylight. They found a small park and slept in the band shell. In the morning they washed and refreshed themselves in a public facility. As the sun came up they boarded a bright red and yellow streetcar, and the conductor greeted them cheerfully. Tateh paid a nickel for himself, two cents for the child. On the wooden floor of the car, at the rear, were stacked crates filled with wet and glistening quart bottles of milk. Tateh offered to buy one. The conductor looked at him and then at the little girl and told him to take one out but did not wait to be paid for it. He pulled a cord, the trolley bell rang, and the car lurched into motion. The conductor sang. He was a robust big-bellied man with a tenor voice. He had a change-making machine strapped to his belt. A while later the streetcar entered the city of New Rochelle, New York, and slowly made its way up Main Street. Traffic was heavier now, the sun was up, and the small city was abustle. It was explained to Tateh that if he wanted to ride through he had to transfer to the Post Road Shore Line at the corner of North Avenue. This was done by paying another penny for each transfer. Tateh and the little girl got off at the corner of Main Street and North Avenue and waited for the connecting trolley. A boy and his mother passed by. The little girl looked at the boy. He was tow-headed. He wore a sailor blouse, dark blue knickers, white socks and polished white shoes. His hand was in his mother's hand and as he passed the little girl standing with her ancient father, the boy's eyes looked into hers. At this moment the Post Road streetcar appeared and Tateh holding the little girl firmly by the wrist walked into the street and stepped aboard. As the car moved off, the little girl watched the boy pass backward in her sight. She stood on the rear platform of the trolley car and watched him until she could no longer see him. His eyes had been blue and yellow and dark green, like a school globe. The streetcar went up the Post Road, along the Long Island Sound shoreline to the Connecticut border. In Greenwich, Connecticut, they transferred to another car. This took them up through the cities of Stamford, Norwalk and then to Bridgeport, the burial place of Tom Thumb. By now they knew how to tell when the end of the line was approaching. The conductor would walk back through the car and reverse the empty seats, going along the aisle and yanking the handles attached to the seat backs without breaking stride. At Bridgeport they transferred again. The tracks turned inland. They stopped for the night in New Haven, Connecticut. They slept in a rooming house and had breakfast in the landlady's dining room. Tateh furiously brushed his trousers and jacket and soft cap before going downstairs. He tied a bow tie around his frayed collar. He made sure the little girl wore her clean pinafore. It was a rooming house for university students and some of them were at the table. They wore gold spectacles and turtleneck sweaters. After breakfast the old artist and his daughter walked to the streetcar tracks and resumed their journey. A car of the Springfield Traction Company took them to New Britain and then to the city of Hartford. The car slowly swung through the narrow streets of Hartford, the clapboard houses of the city seemingly close enough to reach out and touch. Then they were on the outskirts and racing along north to Springfield, Massachusetts. The great wooden car swayed from side to side. The wind flew in their faces. They sped along the edges of open fields from which birds started and settled as they passed. The little girl saw herds of grazing cows. She saw brown horses loping in the sun. A thin layer of chalk dust settled on her face, like a mask, whitening her complexion, bringing out her large moist eyes, the redness of her mouth, and Tateh was momentarily shocked by a vision of her maturity. The car barreled along its tracks down the side of the road, and whenever it approached an intersection its air horn blew. Once it stopped and took on a load of produce. Riders crowded the aisle. The little girl could not wait for the speed to be up. Tateh realized she was happy. She loved the trip. Holding the suitcase on his lap with just one arm Tateh put the other around his child. He found himself smiling. The wind blew in his face and filled his mouth. The car threatened to jump off the tracks. It banged from side to side and everyone laughed. Tateh laughed. He saw the village of his youth going by now, some versts beyond the meadow. There was a church steeple seen above a hill. As a child he loved wagons, he loved the rides on the big tumbrils in summer moonlight, the bodies of children falling over one another in the hard bumping wagons. He looked around at the riders on the trolley and for the first time since coming to America he thought it might be possible to live here. In Springfield they bought bread and cheese and boarded a modern dark green car of the Worcester Electric Street Railway. Tateh realized now that he was going at least as far as Boston. He computed the cost of all the fares. It would come to two dollars and forty cents for him, just over a dollar for the child. The trolley hummed along the dirt roads, the sun behind it now going down in the Berkshires. Stands of fir trees threw long shadows. They passed a single oarsman in a scull on a very quiet broad stream. They saw a great dripping millwheel turning slowly over a creek. The shadows deepened. The little girl fell asleep. Tateh clutched the suitcase on his lap and kept his eyes on the tracks ahead, shining now in the single beam of the powerful electric headlamp on the front of the car.

CHAPTER 16

This same winter found Tateh and his daughter in the mill town of Lawrence, Massachusetts. They had come there the previous autumn, having heard there were jobs. Tateh stood in front of a loom for fifty-six hours a week. His pay was just under six dollars. The family lived in a wooden tenement on a hill. They had no heat. They occupied one room overlooking an alley in which residents customarily dumped their garbage. He feared she would fall victim to the low-class elements of the neighborhood. He refused to enroll her in school—it was easier here than in New York to avoid the authorities—and made her stay home when he was not there to go out with her. After work he'd walk with her for an hour through the dark streets. She became thoughtful. She held her shoulders straight and walked like a woman. He was torturing himself anticipating her maturity. At such time when the girl becomes a woman she needs a mother to instruct her. Would she have to go through this difficult change alone? Alternatively, if he found someone to marry, how would she take to the new person? It might be the worst thing in the world for her.

The dismal wooden tenements lay in endless rows. Everyone from Europe was there—the Italians, the Poles, the Belgians, the Russian Jews. The feeling was not good between the different groups. One day the biggest of the mills, American Woolen Company, gave out envelopes with short pay, and a tremor went through the workers in the plant. Several Italian workers left their machines. They ran through the mill calling for a strike. They pulled out wires and threw lumps of coal through the windows. Others followed them. The anger spread. Throughout the city people left their machines. Those who couldn't make up their minds were carried along in the momentum. In three days every textile mill in Lawrence was virtually shut down.

Tateh was overjoyed. We were going to starve to death or freeze to death, he told his daughter. Now we'll be shot to death. But people from the I.W.W. who knew how to run a strike quickly came up from New York and organized things. A strike committee was formed with every one of the races represented and the message went out to the workers: no violence. Taking the girl with him Tateh joined the thousands of pickets encircling the mill, a massive brick building that went on for blocks. They trudged under the cold gray sky. Trolley cars came down the street, the drivers peering at the sight of thousands of marchers moving silently through the snow. Overhead the telephone and telegraph wires drooped with ice. Militia with rifles nervously guarded the mill gates. The militia all had overcoats.

There were many incidents. A woman worker was shot in the street. The only ones with guns were the police and the militia, but the two strike leaders, Ettor and Giovanetti, were arrested for complicity in the shooting. They were put in jail pending their trial. Something of the sort had been expected. Tateh went down to the train station to be on hand for the arrival in Lawrence of replacements for Ettor and Giovanetti. There was an immense crowd. Out of the train stepped Big Bill Haywood, the most famous Wobbly of them all. He was a Westerner and wore a stetson which he now removed and waved. A cheer went up. Haywood raised his hands for quiet. He spoke. His voice was magnificent. There is no foreigner here except the capitalists, he said. The place went wild. Afterward everyone marched through the streets and sang the *Internationale*. The girl had never seen her Tateh so inflamed. She liked the strike because it got her out of the room. She held his hand.

But the battle went on week after week. Relief committees had set up kitchens in every neighborhood. It's not charity, a woman told Tateh when, after the child received her portion, he refused his. The bosses want you weak, therefore you have to be strong. The people who help us today will need our help tomorrow. On the picket line each cold day they wrapped their scarves around their necks and stamped their feet in the cold snow. The girl's little cloak was threadbare. Tateh volunteered for service on the strike display committee and got them off the cold streets by designing posters. The posters were very beautiful. But the man in charge told him they were not right. We don't want art, the man said. We want something to stir the anger. We want to keep the fires stoked. Tateh had drawn pickets, stark figures with their feet in snow. He had drawn families huddled in their tenements. He switched to lettering. All for one and one for all. He felt better. At night he took home scraps of paper, oak tag, pens and India ink, and to take the child's mind off their troubles he began to entertain her with silhouette drawings. He created a streetcar scene, the people getting on and off. She loved it. She leaned it against her bed pillow and looked at it from different angles. This gave him an inspiration. He did several studies of the streetcar and when he held them together and flipped the pages it appeared as if the streetcar came down the tracks from a distance and stopped so that the people could get on and off. His own delight matched the girl's. She gazed at him with such serene approval that he had a fever to create for her. He brought home more scrap paper. He imagined her on ice skates. In two nights he made a hundred and twenty silhouettes on pages not bigger than his hand. He bound them with string. She held the little book and governed the pages with her thumb and watched herself skating away and skating back, gliding into a figure eight, returning, pirouetting and making a lovely bow to her audience. Tateh held her and wept to feel her frail body, her soft lips on his face. What if the truth was that he could do nothing more for her than make pictures? What if they just went on this way in varying degrees of unrealized hope? She would grow up and curse his name.

Meanwhile the strike had become famous. Reporters arrived daily from all over the country. Support was coming in from other cities. But there was a growing weakness in the unity of the strike front. A man with children found it difficult to keep his courage and resolve. A plan was put into effect whereby children of strikers were to be sent to other cities to board with families in sympathy with the strike. Hundreds of families in Boston and New York and Philadelphia offered to take them in. Others sent money. Every family was carefully checked by the strike committee. The parents of the children had to sign permission forms. The experiment began. Wealthy women came up from New York to escort the first hundred on the train. Each child had had a medical examination and wore a new outfit of clothes. They arrived at Grand Central Station in New York like a religious army. A crowd met them and for a moment everyone held the picture of the children hand in hand staring resolutely ahead as if toward the awful fate industrial America had prepared for them. The press coverage was enormous. The mill owners in Lawrence realized that of all the stratagems devised by the workers this one, the children's crusade, was the most damaging. If it was allowed to go on, national sentiment would swing to the workingmen and the owners would have to give in. This would mean an increase in wages that would bring some workers up to eight dollars a week. They would get extra pay for overtime and for machine speed-ups. They would get off without any punishment for their strike. It was unthinkable. The mill owners knew who were the stewards of civilization and the source of progress and prosperity in the city of Lawrence. For the good of the country and the American democratic system they resolved there would be no more children's crusades.

In the meantime Tateh debated with himself: Clearly the best thing for his girl would be to have a place for a few weeks with a settled family. She would be properly fed, she would be warm, and she would get a taste of a normal home life. But he couldn't bear to part from her. The thought gave him forebodings. He went down to the relief committee, a storefront not far from the mill, and talked to one of the women there. She assured him they had more good working-class families who had volunteered to board a child than they knew what to do with. Jewish? Tateh said. You name it and we got it, the woman said. But he couldn't bring himself to sign the papers. Every family is investigated, the woman told him. Could we be careless about such things? I've been a socialist all my life, Tateh assured her. Of course, the woman said. A doctor will listen to her chest. For that alone it's worthwhile. She'll eat hot meals and know her father has friends in the world. But no one's pushing you. Look, look at the line behind you, plenty of customers.

Tateh thought Here I am in the middle of brotherhood in action and I'm thinking like some bourgeois from the *shtetl*. He signed the permission papers.

One week later he took the girl down to the railroad station. She was in a contingent of two hundred going to Philadelphia. She was wearing a new cloak and a hat that kept her ears warm. He kept stealing glances at her. She was beautiful. She had a naturally regal posture. She was enjoying her new clothes. He was casual with her and tried not to be hurt. She had accepted the idea of leaving him without one word of protest. Of course, this was good for all concerned. But if she found it so easy, what would the future bring? She had reserves of character he did not elicit from her. She attracted people. Many of the mothers stared. Tateh was proud, but frightened too. They stood in the waiting room, a pandemonium of mothers and children. Someone called Here it comes! and the crowd surged to the doors as the train slid in chuffing and hissing great clouds of steam.

A car reserved for the children was attached to the end of the train. This was the Boston and Maine line. The engine was a Baldwin 4—6—0. Everyone moved down the platform, the registered nurses from the Philadelphia Women's Committee at the head of the procession. Don't forget your manners, Tateh said as they followed along. When people ask you a question answer them. Speak up so they can hear you. Once past the corner of the station he noticed out on the street a line of militia with their blocked hats. They held their rifles across their chests. They were facing away from the platform. The procession stopped and backed up on itself. There was some sort of commotion at the front of the line. Then he heard a scream, police appeared everywhere, and suddenly the crowd was in a terrible turmoil. While amazed passengers looked out from the windows of the train the police started to separate the mothers from their children. They were dragging the mothers kicking and screaming to trucks at the end of the platform. The trucks were army Reo's with pagoda hoods and chain wheel drive. Children were being stepped on. They scattered in all directions. A woman ran by with blood coming from her mouth. Steam drifted back from the engine like patches of fog. The bell quietly rang. A woman appeared in front of Tateh. She tried to say something. She was holding her stomach. She fell. Tateh lifted his daughter bodily and swung her up on the platform of the nearest car, out of harm's way. Then he turned his attention to the fallen woman. He picked her up under the shoulders and dragged her through the crowd to a bench. As he was sitting her down he came to the attention of one of the policemen. The policeman cracked him on the shoulders and the head with his stick. What are you doing, Tateh cried. He didn't know what the maniac wanted of him. He moved back into the crowd. He was followed and beaten. He stumbled away from the crowd and was still beaten. Finally he fell.

The authority for this police action was an order issued by the city marshal prohibiting all children from leaving Lawrence, Massachusetts. It was for their own good. They were on their knees, holding the prostrate forms of their bloodied parents. Some were in hysterics. In a few minutes the police had swept the platform clean, the trucks were driven off, the militia were marched away, and only a few sobbing battered adults and weeping children remained. One was Tateh. He leaned against a pillar to regain his strength. His mind was not clear. He began to hear sounds that had been made minutes before. He heard the little girl's voice: Tateh, Tateh! At that moment it occurred to him that the station platform was unnaturally bright. The train was gone. The realization struck his heart like a chord. He was now completely alert. Still he heard the voice. Tateh, Tateh! He looked down the tracks and saw the last car of the train to Philadelphia some yards beyond the end of the station. It was not moving. He started to run. Tateh, Tateh! As he ran the train slowly began to move. He ran onto the tracks. He ran, stumbling, with his arm out. His hands caught the guardrail of the observation platform. The train was picking up speed. His feet were coming off the ground. The ties began to blur under him. He clung to the railing, finally hoisting his knees to the platform overhang and clinging there with his head pressed against the bars like a man in prison begging to be set free.

CHAPTER 17

Tateh was rescued by two conductors who lifted him by the arms and the seat of his pants onto the observation platform. First they had to pry his fingers from the railings. He found his daughter on the train and ignoring everyone around her, conductors, passengers, he gathered her in his arms and wept. Then he noticed that her new cloak was bloody. He looked at her hands. They were smeared with blood. Where are you hurt! he shouted.

Where are you hurt! She shook her head and pointed at him and he realized that the blood all over her was his own. It came from his scalp, blackening his white hair.

A doctor who happened to be on board tended Tateh's injuries and gave him an injection. After that he wasn't too clear about what happened. He slept lying on his side across two seats with his arm for a pillow. He was aware of the motion of the train and his daughter sitting in the seat facing him. She looked out the window. They were the only passengers in the special car for Philadelphia. Sometimes he heard voices but he could not bestir himself to understand what they said. At the same time he clearly saw her eyes with hills of snow proceeding slowly, in a curve, over her pupils. In this way he made the trip south to Boston, then to New Haven, through the Westchester towns of Rye and New Rochelle, through the train yards of New York, across the river to Newark, New Jersey, and then to Philadelphia.

When the train arrived the two refugees found a bench in the station and spent the night there. Tateh was not entirely himself. He had in his pockets, fortunately, that part of his week's wages he had set aside for the rent: two dollars and fifty cents. The girl sat beside him on the shiny bench and watched the patterns made by the people moving through the station. By the early morning hours there was only one porter pushing a big broom across the marble floor. As always she seemed to accept totally the situation in which she found herself. Tateh's head ached. His hands were swollen and scraped. He sat with his palms cupping his ears. He didn't know what to do. He couldn't think. Somehow they were in Philadelphia.

In the morning he picked up a discarded newspaper. On the front page was an account of the police terror in Lawrence, Massachusetts. He found his cigarettes in their box in his pocket and smoked and read the paper. An editorial called for an investigation of the outrage by the Federal Government. So that was it, the strike would be won. But then what? He heard the clacking of the looms. A salary of six dollars and change. Would that transform their lives? They would still live in that wretched room, in that terrible dark street. Tateh shook his head. This country will not let me breathe. In this mood he slowly came to the decision not to go back to Lawrence, Massachusetts. His belongings, his rags, he would leave to the landlord. What do you have with you, he said to his daughter. She showed him the contents of her small satchel—things she had taken for her trip away from home. Her underthings, her comb and brush, a hair clasp, garters, stockings, and the books he had made for her of the trolley car and the skater. From this moment, perhaps, Tateh began to conceive of his life as separate from the fate of the working class. I hate machines, he said to his daughter. He stood and she stood and took his hand and together they looked for the exit. The I.W.W. has won, he said. But what has it won? A few more pennies in wages. Will it now own the mills? No.

They cleaned and refreshed themselves in the public lavatories. They went to the station café for a breakfast of rolls and coffee and spent the day walking through the streets of Philadelphia. It was cold and the sun was shining. They looked in the windows of the stores and when their feet began to ache from the cold they walked into a department store to warm up. It was a vast emporium, every aisle crowded with shoppers. The girl noticed with interest that wire baskets swung from moving cables over the counters. They carried the money and receipts back and forth from the counters to the cashier. The sales clerks yanked on wooden-handled rope pulls to bring the baskets down and pulled on other ropes to get them back up. Mannequins, like grown-up dolls, sported satin toques and broad-brimmed hats plumed with egret feathers. One of these hats is more than a week's wages, Tateh said.

Later, on the streets again, they walked past iron-front buildings where trucks were pulled up to warehouse platforms. The windows of supply companies and wholesalers offered little of interest. But then her eye was attracted to the dirty window in which were displayed all the gimcracks of a mail-order novelty company. At this time businessmen were discovering the profit in practical jokes and parlor magic tricks. There were exploding cigars, rubber roses for the lapel that squirted water, boxes of sneezing powder, telescopes that left black eyes, exploding card decks, sound bladders for placing under chair cushions, glass paperweights with winter scenes on which snow fell when you shook them, exploding matches, punchboards, little lead liberty bells and statues of liberty, magic rings, exploding fountain pens, books that told you the meaning of dreams, rubber Egyptian belly dancers, exploding watches, exploding eggs.

Tateh stared at the window long after the girl's interest had waned. He led her into the store. Tateh removed his hat and spoke to a man in a striped shirt with sleeve garters who came forward to meet them. The man was amiable. Sure, he said, let's see it. Tateh took the girl's satchel, put it on the counter and, opening it, withdrew the book of the skater. Standing next to the proprietor he held the book at arm's length and expertly flipped the pages. The little girl skated forward and skated away, did a figure eight, came back, went into a pirouette and made a graceful bow. The man's eyebrows went up. He stuck out his lower lip. Let me try that, he said.

An hour later Tateh walked out of there with twenty-five dollars in cash and a letter of agreement which he had signed calling for four more books at twenty-five dollars each. The company—its name was the Franklin Novelty Company—would publish the books and add them to its line. For purposes of the contract they were called movie books. Come, Tateh said to his child, we'll find a boardinghouse in a good neighborhood and then we'll have ourselves a meal and a hot bath.

Unit 1

Ragtime

- Comprehension Questions
- Analyzing Setting
- Discussion Guides
- Writing Exercise

COMPREHENSION QUESTIONS

For each of the following statements and questions, select the option containing the most complete or most accurate answer.

1. The streetcar journey from New York through Connecticut and into
(k) Massachusetts allows the author to change the mood from
   □ a. cheerful to melancholy.   □ c. brooding to cheerful.
   □ b. bitter to morose.   □ d. brooding to angry.

2. Hester Street and Union Square are places in
(a) □ a. Lawrence, Massachusetts.
    □ b. New York City.
    □ c. Philadelphia, Pennsylvania.
    □ d. Hartford, Connecticut.

3. Public transportation at the turn of the century was
(f) □ a. available only to the wealthy.
    □ b. dirty and uncomfortable.
    □ c. largely undeveloped.
    □ d. both widespread and affordable.

4. The account of the trip which Tateh and the little girl took from New
(k) York City to Lawrence, Massachusetts, reads like
   □ a. a travelogue.   □ c. a letter home.
   □ b. an essay.   □ d. a sermon.

5. Although he worked in mills and sweatshops, Tateh's real talent was as
(d) □ a. a writer.   □ c. a clergyman.
    □ b. an artist.   □ d. a philosopher.

6. The lives of many immigrants in the United States at the turn of the
(e) century were generally
   □ a. isolated and lonely.   □ c. difficult and harsh.
   □ b. lawless and violent.   □ d. optimistic and happy.

7. Working conditions in factories at the turn of the century were charac-
(c) terized by
    □ a. a day's work for a day's pay.
    □ b. deliberate brutality.
    □ c. sweeping reforms.
    □ d. long hours and low pay.

8. The mill workers in Lawrence decided to strike because

(b) □ a. their wages had been cut.
　　 □ b. working conditions were poor.
　　 □ c. the I.W.W. persuaded them to.
　　 □ d. their civil rights had been violated.

9. Big Bill Haywood came to Lawrence, Massachusetts, in order to

(c) □ a. help the struggling mill owners.
　　 □ b. organize the striking mill workers.
　　 □ c. campaign for the Presidency.
　　 □ d. organize the I.W.W.

10. Which of the following choices best defines *momentum* as being used in,

(l) "Those who couldn't make up their minds were carried along in the *momentum*"?

　　 □ a. The importance of the moment
　　 □ b. The shove of the crowd
　　 □ c. The noise and the shouting
　　 □ d. The force of excitement

11. Which of the following choices best defines *inflamed* as used in this

(l) passage: "Afterward everyone marched through the streets and sang the *Internationale*. The girl had never seen Tateh so *inflamed*"?

　　 □ a. Feverish　　　　　　□ c. Proud
　　 □ b. Temperamental　　 □ d. Stirred

12. The attitude of the mill workers during the strike conveys a tone of

(i) □ a. destructive rage.　　□ c. bitter despair.
　　 □ b. mutual support.　　 □ d. mistrust and suspicion.

13. In the evenings, Tateh entertained the little girl with

(a) □ a. stories of his homeland.　□ c. silhouette drawings.
　　 □ b. folk songs.　　　　　　　□ d. socialist lectures.

14. The militia and police force of Lawrence were on the side of

(f) □ a. justice.　　　　　　　□ c. the striking workers.
　　 □ b. the mill owners.　　 □ d. the children.

15. From the time Tateh and the little girl leave New York until they leave
(d) Lawrence, Massachusetts, the seasons change from
    □ a. summer to winter.   □ c. fall to spring.
    □ b. spring to summer.   □ d. spring to fall.

16. The atmosphere at the train station when the militia tried to prevent the
(i) workers' children from leaving was one of
    □ a. excitement.   □ c. terror.
    □ b. defiance.   □ d. frustration.

17. Which of the following best defines *prostrate* as used in, "They were on
(l) their knees, holding the *prostrate* forms of their bloodied parents"?
    □ a. Lifeless   □ c. Resting
    □ b. Dying   □ d. Lying

18. The most important effect of the children's crusade on the mill workers'
(g) strike was that it
    □ a. kindled the sympathy of the outside world.
    □ b. made the mill owners aware of their mistakes.
    □ c. placed the children in good homes.
    □ d. discredited the striking workers.

19. In the end, the strikers won
(a) □ a. guarantees of job security.
    □ b. a few more pennies in wages.
    □ c. part ownership in the mills.
    □ d. significant improvements in working conditions.

20. Tateh felt that the victory won by the striking mill workers was
(h) □ a. of little consequence to anyone.
    □ b. a landmark victory for unionism.
    □ c. a good start for the union.
    □ d. a setback for everyone.

21. Tateh believed that, ideally, mills should be
(h) □ a. closed down for good.
    □ b. destroyed.
    □ c. owned by the government.
    □ d. owned by the workers.

22. The foremost consideration which governed all of Tateh's decisions was
(j) □ a. the socialist cause.   □ c. his daughter.
    □ b. art.   □ d. money.

23. Although she rarely speaks, the little girl's character is depicted as
(j) □ a. vain.   □ c. shallow.
    □ b. strong.   □ d. rebellious.

24. Tateh's idea to sell the girl's silhouette books to the Franklin Novelty
(g) Company suggests that he is
    □ a. greedy.   □ c. resourceful.
    □ b. desperate.   □ d. heartless.

25. The main theme of the chapters revolves around the
(e) □ a. indifference of government.
    □ b. plight of the immigrants.
    □ c. power of labor unions.
    □ d. progress of transportation.

Comprehension Skills: a—isolating details; b—recalling specific facts; c—retaining concepts; d—organizing facts; e—understanding the main idea; f—drawing a conclusion; g—making a judgment; h—making an inference; i—recognizing tone; j—understanding characters; k—appreciation of literary forms; l—knowledge of word meanings.

ANALYZING SETTING

Practice Exercise A

The trolley hummed along the dirt roads, the sun behind it now going down in the Berkshires. Stands of fir trees threw long shadows. They passed a single oarsman in a scull on a very quiet broad stream. They saw a great dripping millwheel turning slowly over a creek. The shadows deepened.

1. The feeling created by the setting in this passage is
   - ☐ a. lively.
   - ☐ b. peaceful.
   - ☐ c. pensive.
   - ☐ d. desolate.

2. Write three phrases from the passage which indicate the time of day.

_____

_____

_____

Practice Exercise B

Taking the girl with him Tateh joined the thousands of pickets encircling the mill, a massive brick building that went on for blocks. They trudged under the cold gray sky. Trolley cars came down the street, the drivers peering at the sight of thousands of marchers moving silently through the snow. Overhead the telephone and telegraph wires drooped with ice. Militia with rifles nervously guarded the mill gates. The militia all had overcoats.

1. The atmosphere created by this setting is one of
   - ☐ a. cold brutality.
   - ☐ b. intense hatred.
   - ☐ c. ominous tension.
   - ☐ d. numbing fatigue.

2. The bleak weather contributes to the overall atmosphere of the scene. Write four phrases or words from the above passage which indicate the weather.

_____

_____

_____

_____

Practice Exercise C

While amazed passengers looked out from the windows of the train the police started to separate the mothers from their children. They were dragging the mothers kicking and screaming to trucks at the end of the platform. The trucks were army Reo's with pagoda hoods and chain wheel drive. Children were being stepped on. They scattered in all directions. A woman ran by with blood coming from her mouth. Steam drifted back from the engine like patches of fog. The bell quietly rang. A woman appeared in front of Tateh. She tried to say something. She was holding her stomach. She fell.

1. We are told that the passengers were amazed. But the author wants the *reader* to feel something more. What is the strongest reaction created by this scene?
   - ☐ a. Shock
   - ☐ b. Dismay
   - ☐ c. Surprise
   - ☐ d. Indignation

2. The scene is full of disturbing descriptions of injured and frightened people. To heighten the reader's reaction to the people's plight, the author injects several unemotional, matter-of-fact descriptions of the physical surroundings. Underline three sentences where this is done.

Practice Exercise D

They cleaned and refreshed themselves in the public lavatories. They went to the station café for a breakfast of rolls and coffee and spent the day walking through the streets of Philadelphia. It was cold and the sun was shining. They looked in the windows of the stores and when their feet began to ache from the cold they walked into a department store to warm up. It was a vast emporium, every aisle crowded with shoppers .... Mannequins, like grown-up dolls, sported satin toques and broad-brimmed hats plumed with egret feathers. One of these hats is more than a week's wages, Tateh said.

1. The author uses the department store setting
   - ☐ a. to exhibit the fashions of the time.
   - ☐ b. to display the variety of goods within the buying power of the working class.
   - ☐ c. to compare the poverty of Tateh and the girl with the affluence of others.
   - ☐ d. to reveal a streak of vanity in the girl's character.

2. One of the ways Doctorow makes the setting believeable is by using words which were commonly used in the early 1900s but are not heard often today. Underline three words or phrases from the passage which have an "old" sound.

DISCUSSION GUIDES

Analyzing Setting

1. The novel from which these chapters are taken is set in the "ragtime" era from about 1900 through World War I. How do the settings and descriptions you have just read tend to place you in the atmosphere of the time? Would you call *Ragtime* a nostalgic look at this era? Explain.

2. Throughout the chapters, cold temperatures and raw, wintry weather chill Tateh and the little girl. How does climate contribute to the setting of this story? How does it emphasize the poverty and victimization of the characters? How would the story be different if the author had used summer instead of winter as the setting for the strike?

3. The journey which Tateh and the little girl took by trolley from New York City to Massachusetts traverses an ever-changing landscape identified by actual place names and streetcar lines. How do these elements of setting help make their journey seem authentic?

Interpreting the Chapters

4. Critics have suggested that Tateh's silhouettes are a symbol for illusions. Both a silhouette and an illusion "seem to be" but are not. The silhouettes in Tateh's movie book "seem to move," but do not. In what sense is the victory of the mill workers an illusion? the power of the I.W.W.? Can you think of any other illusions in the lives of Tateh and the little girl?

5. Why did the children's crusade succeed in forcing the mill owners to negotiate when other strike tactics, such as picketing and work stoppages, failed?

6. How does Tateh feel about the victory won by the Lawrence mill workers? How has his opinion of unions changed over the course of the strike?

7. By the end of the chapters, Tateh has disassociated himself from the working class. Why is this? What kind of role do you envision for Tateh in the future—as a capitalist, an entrepreneur, a labor leader, a politician, or what? Give reasons for your opinion.

8. "Tateh" is a Jewish word for "Dad," and the daughter is referred to simply as the little girl. Why do you suppose the author chose not to give names to these characters?

9. Big Bill Haywood, the militant leader of the I.W.W. (International Workers of the World), is an actual historical figure. Throughout *Ragtime*, the author intersperses fictional characters such as Tateh with historical personages like Big Bill Haywood. How does this technique affect the believability of the story?

10. The Novel *Ragtime* has been cited for its cinematic style. One critic felt that reading *Ragtime* was like watching a movie. What do you think the critic meant by this? How does the absence of direct conversation contribute to the cinematic effect of the story?

WRITING EXERCISE

The following setting describes a marketplace in nineteenth-century London. As you read the passage, be aware of the images and impressions which the underlined words and phrases evoke.

It was market-morning. The ground was covered, nearly ankle-deep, with filth and mire; a thick steam, perpetually rising from the reeking bodies of the cattle, and mingling with the fog, which seemed to rest upon the chimney-tops, hung heavily above. All the pens in the center of the large area, and as many temporary pens as could be crowded into the vacant space, were filled with sheep; tied up to posts by the gutter side were long lines of beasts and oxen, three or four deep. Countrymen, butchers, drovers, hawkers, boys, thieves, idlers, and vagabonds of every low grade, were mingled together in a mass; the whistling of drovers, the barking of dogs, the bellowing and plunging of oxen, the bleating of sheep, the grunting and squeaking of pigs, the cries of hawkers, the shouts, oaths, and quarrelling on all sides; the ringing of bells and roar of voices, that issued from every public-house; the crowding, pushing, driving, beating, whooping and yelling; the hideous and discordant din that resounded from every corner of the market; and the unwashed, unshaven, squalid, and dirty figures constantly running to and fro, and bursting in and out of the throng; rendered it a stunning and bewildering scene, which quite confounded the senses.

The marketplace described on the previous page is depicted as a dirty, squalid scene teeming with animals and peopled with undesirables of every kind. Replace the underlined words or rewrite the passage completely to create a setting that is pleasant and nostalgic—a marketplace such as one might picture in a quaint New England village of the same era. You may use any forms of the following words and phrases, as well as words of your own choosing.

fragrance	drifted	permeated the air
hillside	hubbub	strolling couples
passersby	ambling	street singers
artists	browsing	milling about
greetings	bartering	well groomed
delighted	crowd	hung lazily
villagers	faint aroma	excited
tumult	rowdy	melee
water trough	vendors	sightseers
clover and dandelions	high spirited	invitations
well fed	chattering	village inn
lane	laughing	tousled

Unit 2
Recognizing
Tone and Mood

Roots

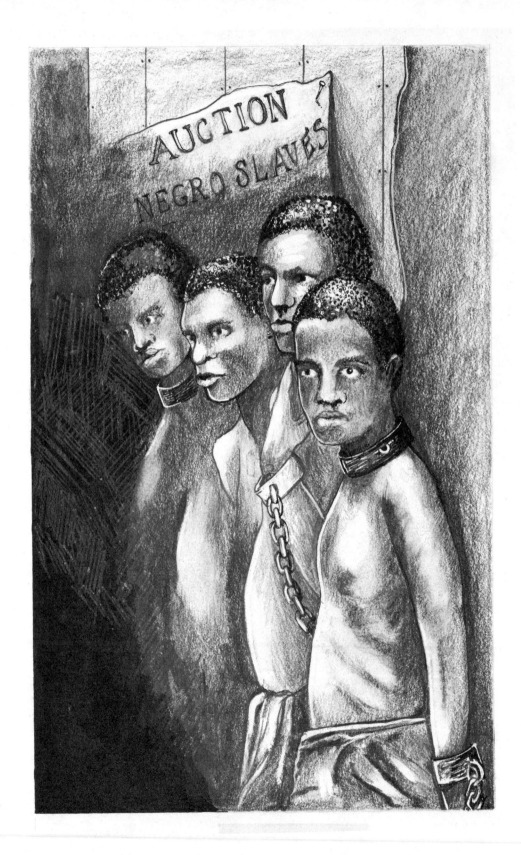

Introduction

Roots is the story of one man's family tree come to life, starting with the author's "furthest back" ancestor—an African named Kunta Kinte who was kidnapped by white slave traders while chopping wood for a drum outside his small west African village of Juffure.

The year is 1767 and, until his capture by white slave traders, Kunta Kinte was as certain as the next seventeen-year-old that disaster was something that happened to other people. Now, shackled into the hold of a slave ship, Kunta and 139 other Africans writhe in agony as the bare planks under their backs inflame the open and festering wounds left by the sadistic lashes of the ship's crew. The ship's hold offends the senses as well as the body. The men are naked and chained, and there are no toilets or water, and no lights; the stench is overwhelming, and equally distressing are the moans of those near death, overcome by pain, or unable to cope with the trauma of their ordeal.

For the first time, Kunta is forced to contemplate the reality of an unjust world and, while his faith in Allah sustains him, he is shocked to find himself in the company of others who have denounced Allah in the face of their plight. Assailed by waves of grief at being torn from his parents, younger brothers, and a future which had seemed so bright and promising, Kunta searches for an explanation of Allah's ways. There is, of course, no good reason for his suffering, and Kunta must now rest his religious convictions on the basis of simple faith—that is, belief without proof or justification.

Because of their different tribal languages, communication among the prisoners in the hold of the ship is slow and laborious. Here and there, a man might know more than one dialect and translate for the others a word or two whispered from man to man, and back again. In this way, the prisoners exchange information and speculate on their destination. For all they know, their captors could be cannibals, with a cargo destined to make soup stock. Africans had long been aware that toubob, or white men, lurked on their shores and were responsible for the mysterious disappearances of many individuals and even, occasionally, entire villages. But none, after all, had ever returned to tell his fate. It is learned in the hold that a slatee, one of the despised Blacks who assist the toubob in outfitting their ships with supplies and human cargo, is cowering somewhere in the hold. Beyond this, there is little useful information to exchange.

Even the small talk, however, serves a purpose by reminding the Blacks of their common heritage and, now, their common enemy. Inevitably, their discussions revert to talk of escape and how to kill the toubob. "Toubob fa!" they would chant up on deck when forced to "dance" for the crew. But how?

An alcala, a sort of elder counselor, directs their hatred into the selection of a leader. By a majority vote, a warrior from the Foulah tribe, well known for its vengeance in a righteous cause, is chosen to channel their waning energies into a concerted attack. But before the plan can be carried out, a lone warrior seizes his own opportunity and, in a bold and desperate move, disarms the nearest toubob and kills five whites before his head is lopped off.

The attack takes everyone by surprise, and the Foulah never gives his signal for Kunta and the others to support the assault. The Blacks are beaten down into the hold before they have a chance to capitalize on the situation, and then brought up again to witness their compatriot cut into mincemeat. The leader promises an attack the very next time they are up on deck. But that night a storm breaks, the hold is nearly flooded, and the men's wounds are excruciatingly ground into the planks under their backs as they fight the rolling of the ship. By morning, many have died, and those who are left are in no condition to fight. Most have lost the will to live, and even Kunta wonders if Allah is indeed with his faithful in the hold of this ship.

Described by the author, Alex Haley, as a work of "faction"—that is, a mixture of fact and fiction—*Roots* is an important social document that restores a lost heritage to Black Americans. Armed with only the most sketchy biographical data, Haley fleshes out his ancestors' lives with typical incidents that at once reflect the Black experience and imbue his characters with universal aspirations that transcend race and culture.

The account of Kunta Kinte's coming of age in an eighteenth-century African village is a work of popular anthropology that has won scholarly acclaim for its historical authenticity. The traditions, rituals and even the daily routines of Kunta's boyhood are based on exhaustive research and on the highly regarded oral history of tribal historians, called Griots, who still pass along the genealogy of the major African clans. Only the dialogue, thoughts and emotions of his characters were made up.

Alex Haley's odyssey into his remote ancestry is more than an expression of the Black consciousness of Afro-Americans in the 1960s and 1970s. His search sparked a popular quest among Americans of all ancestries to find their own roots from the midst of a modern culture that had long been preoccupied with the future at the expense of the past.

Recognizing
Tone and Mood

You may not be aware of it, but tone is something you use every time you speak. And you're probably quite good at using it, too. When you are unjustly accused of eating the last piece of cheesecake and you protest, "I didn't take it!" you are using a tone of indignation intended to reinforce your denial. You may use a scolding tone to a child who has forgotten his manners and a triumphant tone when you announce your victory in the tennis tournament. Without tone, we would all sound like robots.

In the same way, if you weren't good at perceiving mood, you would probably find yourself in constant trouble. If your teacher has had problems with certain classmates and is in a foul mood because of it, you know this is not the time to ask for an extension of the due date for your report. Similarly, you don't ask to borrow the family car when the mood in your household rings with tension from an argument. On the other hand, there are lighter moods in happier times when everyone is feeling good and you know that today everything is going to be just fine.

In many situations, tone and mood are made to work together. The atmosphere, or tone, in a church, for example, is quiet and solemn. It conveys a feeling of peace and puts you in a meditative mood, which is exactly what a church is designed to do. At a football game everything is noise and excitement. Bright colors, brass bands and cheer leaders are all brought together, very deliberately, to create a tone that will keep your spirits soaring and make you want to come back again next week.

Tone and mood serve much the same purpose in literature that they do in conversation and in everyday situations. In a good story, tone and mood are made to work together in such a way that you are led to recognize the author's attitude toward what is going on; you sense the atmosphere in which the characters of the story move, and you come to feel or understand the emotions that the characters feel under the circumstances that the author has created for them. It is very much as though you were there yourself, sensing the tone or atmosphere of the place and finding your mood corresponding to that of the characters.

When an author writes a story, he or she has a special attitude or feeling about the subject matter. In order for a story to succeed, the author must communicate to you the same emotions which dominated the writing of it, just as when a church is built it must be built to communicate a feeling that is appropriate for a church. Otherwise, the story will have little meaning for you and, consequently, little interest. For instance, the factual telling of the evils on board an eighteenth-century slave ship in a history book may leave a reader relatively unmoved. But when the author makes you feel his own sense of horror and anger at the plight of the Black prisoners, as Alex Haley does in *Roots*, you share his interest and want to continue reading the story. The author, then, creates a tone that communicates his own feelings as well as those of the characters in the story. Not in so many words, but simply by the way he writes the story, Haley says, "This is outrageous!" or, "I am appalled by this situation!" The tone fairly screams with outrage. You quickly sense the feeling or the mood of the moment, and you are ready to agree, "Yes, this is awful, I feel terrible about it, as you do." At this point you not only understand the tone and mood of the story, you *feel* it as well.

Tone and mood create the emotional atmosphere in which the characters of a story move. Together, they create that pervasive, yet intangible, feeling which colors a story or scene. For instance, a gloomy mood often envelops the characters of a story during a thunderstorm. A disaster is likely to create a mood of hysteria. And during a celebration, the mood is apt to be festive.

In the following passage from *Roots*, a seventeen-year-old Black youth is being whipped by white, or "toubob," slave dealers. How would you describe the tone and mood of this passage?

> A whip lashed out . . . this time at Kunta, spurring him to move ahead. The force of the blow drove him nearly to his knees and triggered an explosion of rage. With his throat ripping out almost an animal's cry, Kunta lunged off balance toward the toubob, only to fall, sprawling, dragging his shacklemate down with him, as the toubob nimbly sprang clear of them both. Men milled around them as the toubob, his eyes narrowing with hatred, brought the whip down over and over on both Kunta and the Wolof, like a slashing knife.

The tone and mood of the above passage express rage. The whip lashes bring Kunta to his knees, a degrading position which stings his pride as the whip stings his body. This sparks "an explosion of rage" as Kunta protests this uncalled-for cruelty. He cries out with "almost an animal's cry" that reflects his uncontrolled fury. And he lunges toward his tormentor in a gesture that is as futile as it is impulsive. These ungoverned outbursts of fury all contribute to the rage which dominates the scene.

Just as our moods and the tone of our own conversations change continuously, so, too, do tone and mood vary within a single story. The next passage from *Roots* reveals quite a different tone and mood from the one above. Here, the Black men in the hold of the slave ship are beginning to converse among themselves. How have the tone and mood changed?

The steady murmuring that went on in the hold whenever the toubob were gone kept growing in volume and intensity as the men began to communicate better and better with one another . . . . Sometimes men jerked upward, bumping their heads, in the double excitement of communicating with each other and the fact that it was being done without the toubob's knowledge. Muttering among themselves for hours, the men developed a deepening sense of intrigue and of brotherhood. Though they were of different villages and tribes, the feeling grew that they were not from different people or places.

The tone and mood of this scene convey a mixture of hope and excitement. The ability to communicate with one another is a tremendous source of comfort to the shackled men. Until this time each man has been alone with his thoughts and fears, unable to understand what has happened to him. Alone, each man felt hopeless and lost. But communication has given the Blacks a new-found sense of brotherhood. They are beginning to think as a group. And in the process, they are regaining their self-respect, which had been seriously eroded by the constant abuses and disdain of the toubob. The tone and mood in the hold of the ship has changed from fear and despair to hope and anticipation.

From the tone and mood of the two passages above, it is obvious that the author sympathizes with Kunta and the other Blacks. It is safe to assume, therefore, that the author disapproves of that period in our country's history when Americans kidnapped and sold Africans for use as slaves, and he is trying to make you feel the same way. Tone and mood, then, can reveal the feelings of the author as well as the feelings of the characters at any particular point in the story.

One way that an author makes you sympathetic with his feelings is by creating a tone and mood that you can identify with. In what way does the following passage create feelings that *you* may have had?

One day, Kunta nearly burst with excitement when the Wolof hastily whispered, "Is anyone here from Juffure village?" "Yes, Kunta Kinte!" he sent back breathlessly. He lay almost afraid to breathe for the hour that it took an answer to return: "Yes, that was the name. I heard the drums of his grieving village." Kunta dissolved into sobs, his mind streaming with pictures of his family around a flapping white cockerel that died on its back as the village wadanela went to spread that sad news . . . that a son of the village named Kunta Kinte now was considered gone forever.

There are actually two kinds of feelings presented in this passage—joy and grief. At first, Kunta is nearly bursting with excitement. A question whispered from man to man asks if anyone is here from the village of Juffure. Kunta is from Juffure, and he is overjoyed at the thought of meeting someone he knows. The tone and mood thus far create excitement and expectation. As it turns out, however, the other man was not from Juffure after all. He had merely heard the tribal drums announcing Kunta Kinte's disappearance. Kunta feels doubly disappointed. Not only has he failed to meet a familiar face, but the thought of the village drums announcing his own disappearance has a sound of finality to it. No longer is he a part of the village he loves. His family believes him to be dead. They will mourn his loss, but eventually they will resume their normal routine of which he will no longer be a part. Kunta "dissolves into sobs" of homesickness and loss. He has lost his family, been deprived of what promised to be a bright future, and he has been stripped of his identity as a proud Mandinka warrior.

You cannot mistake the sad tone of the story at this point or Kunta's mood which reflects an unbearable sense of grief. All of us at one time or another have had our hopes dashed and have fallen from wild elation to bitter disappointment. Because we can identify with the tone and mood, we can understand how Kunta feels and readily sympathize with his plight. We may never have experienced the same degree of suffering, but the feeling created by the tone and mood in the passage is still familiar to us.

Tone and mood, then, are literary elements that transform a straightforward report into an engrossing story. Tone and mood help you to understand the story by expressing how the characters and the author feel. They create the emotional atmosphere in which the events take place. Together, they help you to appreciate the story by placing you emotionally within the character, and they make you a part of the incidents around which the plot is constructed.

As you read the two chapters from *Roots*, be alert to the author's use of tone and mood. Notice how they contribute to your understanding of Kunta and the other Blacks. Try to imagine what it was like to travel in the hold of a slave ship. In general, be aware of how the tone and mood affect your attitude toward slavery and enhance the impact of this story.

As you read these chapters:

- Be aware of the mood when the Wolof denounces Allah.

- Notice how Kunta's feelings toward the toubob create the tone as he reflects on their moral character.

- Be aware of the tone and mood when Kunta observes the sick and broken prisoners on deck.

- Notice how descriptions of the men's physical condition during the storm help create tone and mood.

Roots
Alex Haley

CHAPTER 37

The next time the men were taken up onto the deck, Kunta made a point of looking at the man behind him in line, the one who lay beside him to the left when they were below. He was a Serere tribesman much older than Kunta, and his body, front and back, was creased with whip cuts, some of them so deep and festering that Kunta felt badly for having wished sometimes that he might strike the man in the darkness for moaning so steadily in his pain. Staring back at Kunta, the Serere's dark eyes were full of fury and defiance. A whip lashed out even as they stood looking at each other—this time at Kunta, spurring him to move ahead. The force of the blow drove him nearly to his knees and triggered an explosion of rage. With his throat ripping out almost an animal's cry, Kunta lunged off balance toward the toubob, only to fall, sprawling, dragging his shacklemate down with him, as the toubob nimbly sprang clear of them both. Men milled around them as the toubob, his eyes narrowing with hatred, brought the whip down over and over on both Kunta and the Wolof, like a slashing knife. Trying to roll away, Kunta was kicked heavily in his ribs. But somehow he and the gasping Wolof managed to stagger back up among the other men from their shelf who were shambling toward their dousing with buckets of seawater.

A moment later, the stinging saltiness of it was burning in Kunta's wounds, and his screams joined those of others over the sound of the drum and the wheezing thing that had again begun marking time for the chained men to jump and dance for the toubob. Kunta and the Wolof were so weak from their new beating that twice they stumbled, but whip blows and kicks sent them hopping clumsily up and down in their chains. So great was his fury that Kunta was barely aware of the women singing "*Toubob fa!*" And when he had finally been chained back down in his place in the dark hold, his heart throbbed with a lust to murder toubob.

Every few days the eight naked toubob would again come into the stinking darkness and scrape their tubs full of the excrement that had accumulated on the shelves where the chained men lay. Kunta would lie still with his eyes staring balefully in hatred, following the bobbing orange lights, listening to the toubob cursing and sometimes slipping and falling into the slickness underfoot—so plentiful now, because of the increasing looseness of the men's bowels, that the filth had begun to drop off the edges of the shelves down into the aisleway.

The last time they were on deck, Kunta had noticed a man limping on a badly infected leg. The chief toubob had applied grease to it, but it hadn't helped, and the man had begun to scream horribly in the darkness of the hold. When they next went on deck, he had to be helped up, and Kunta saw that the leg, which had been grayish before, had begun to rot and stink even in the fresh air. This time the man was kept up on deck when the rest were taken back below. A few days later, the women told the other prisoners in their singing that the man's leg had been cut off and that one of the women had been brought to tend him, but that the man had died that night and been thrown over the side. Starting then, when the toubob came to clean the shelves, they also dropped red-hot pieces of metal into pails of strong vinegar. The clouds of acrid steam left the hold smelling better, but soon it would again be overwhelmed by the choking stink. It was a smell that Kunta felt would never leave his lungs and skin.

The steady murmuring that went on in the hold whenever the toubob were gone kept growing in volume and intensity as the men began to communicate better and better with one another. Words not understood were whispered from mouth to ear along the shelves until someone who knew more than one tongue would send back their meanings. In the process, all of the men along each shelf learned new words in tongues they had not spoken before. Sometimes men jerked upward, bumping their heads, in the double excitement of communicating with each other and the fact that it was being done without the toubob's knowledge. Muttering among themselves for hours, the men developed a deepening sense of intrigue and of brotherhood. Though they were of different villages and tribes, the feeling grew that they were not from different peoples or places.

When the toubob next came to drive them up onto the deck, the chained men marched as if they were on parade. And when they descended again, several of those men who spoke several tongues managed to change their position in line in order to get chained at the ends of shelves, thus permitting more rapid relaying of translations. The toubob never seemed to notice, for they were either unable or unconcerned to distinguish one chained man from another.

Questions, and responses to them, had begun spreading in the hold. "Where are we being taken?" That brought a babble of bitterness. "Who ever returned to tell us?" "Because they were eaten!" The question, "How long have we been here?" brought a rash of guesses of up to a moon, until the question was translated to a man who had been able to keep a count of daylights through a small air vent near where he was chained; he said that he had counted eighteen days since the great canoe had sailed.

Because of intrusions by toubob with their food tub or their scrapers, an entire day might be used up in relaying of responses to a single statement or question. Anxious inquiries were passed along for men who might know each other. "Is anyone here from Barrakunda village?" someone asked one day, and after a time there came winging back from mouth to ear the joyous response, "I, Jabon Sallah, am here!" One day, Kunta nearly burst with excitement when the Wolof hastily whispered, "Is anyone here from Juffure village?" "Yes, Kunta Kinte!" he sent back breathlessly. He lay almost afraid to breathe for the hour that it took an answer to return: "Yes, that was the name. I heard the drums of his grieving village." Kunta dissolved into sobs, his mind streaming with pictures of his family around a flapping white cockerel that died on its back as the village wadanela went to spread that sad news among all of the people who would then come to Omoro, Binta, Lamin, Suwadu, and the baby Madi, all of them squatting about and weeping as the village drums beat out the words to inform whoever might hear them far away that a son of the village named Kunta Kinte now was considered gone forever.

Days of talking sought answers to the question: "How could the toubob of this canoe be attacked and killed?" Did anyone have or know of anything that might be used as weapons? None did. Up on the deck, had anyone noticed any carelessness or weaknesses on the part of the toubob that could be useful to a surprise attack? Again, none had. The most useful information of any sort had come from the women's singing as the men danced in their chains: that about thirty toubob were riding with them on this big canoe. There had seemed to be many more, but the women were in a better position to count them. The women said also that there had been more toubob at the beginning of the voyage, but five had died. They had been sewn inside white cloths and thrown overboard, while the white-haired chief toubob read from some kind of book. The women also sang that the toubob often fought and beat each other viciously, usually as a result of arguments over which ones would next use the women.

Thanks to their singing, not much happened up on the deck that wasn't quickly told to the men dancing in their chains, who then lay discussing it down in the hold. Then came the exciting new development that contact had been established with the men who were chained on the level yet below. Silence would fall in the hold where Kunta lay, and a question would be called out from near the hatchway: "How many are down there?" And after a time the answer would circulate on Kunta's level: "We believe about sixty of us."

The relaying of any information from whatever source seemed about the only function that would justify their staying alive. When there was no news, the men would talk of their families, their villages, their professions, their farms, their hunts. And more and more frequently there arose disagreements about how to kill the toubob, and when it should be tried. Some of the men felt that, whatever the consequences, the toubob should be attacked the next time they were taken up on deck. Others felt that it would be wiser to watch and wait for the best moment. Bitter disagreements began to flare up. One debate was suddenly interrupted when the voice of an elder rang out, "Hear me! Though we are of different tribes and tongues, remember that we are the same people! We must be as one village, together in this place!"

Murmurings of approval spread swiftly within the hold. That voice had been heard before, giving counsel in times of special stress. It was a voice with experience and authority as well as wisdom. Soon the information passed from mouth to ear that the speaker had been the alcala of his village. After some time, he spoke again, saying now that some leader must be found and agreed upon, and some attack plan must be proposed and agreed upon before there could be any hope of overcoming the toubob, who were obviously both well organized and heavily armed. Again, the hold soon filled with mutterings of approval.

The new and comforting sense of closeness with the other men made Kunta feel almost less aware of the stink and filth, and even the lice and rats. Then he heard the new fear that was circulating—that yet another slatee was believed to be somewhere on the level of men below. One of the women had sung of having been among the group of chained people whom this slatee had helped to bring, blindfolded, onto this canoe. She had sung that it was night when her blindfold was removed, but she had seen the toubob give that slatee liquor, which he drank until he stumbled about drunkenly, and then the toubob, all howling with laughter, had knocked him unconscious and dragged him into the hold. The woman sang that though she was not able to tell in any definite way the face of that slatee, he was almost surely somewhere below in chains like the rest, in terror that he would be discovered and killed, as he now knew that one slatee had been already. In the hold, the men discussed how probably this slatee, too, was able to speak some toubob words, and in hopes of saving his miserable life, he might try to warn the toubob of any attack plans he learned of.

It occurred to Kunta, as he shook his shackles at a fat rat, why he had known little of slatees until now. It was because none of them would dare to live among people in villages, where even a strong suspicion of who they were would bring about their instant death. He remembered that back in Juffure he often had felt that his own father Omoro and yet older men, when they sat around the night fires, would seem to be needlessly occupied with dark worries and gloomy speculations about dangers to which he and the other younger men privately thought they themselves would never succumb. But now he understood why the older men had worried about the safety of the village, they had known better than he how many slatees slithered about, many of them in The Gambia. The despised tan-colored sasso borro children of toubob fathers were easy to identify; but not all. Kunta thought now about the girl of his village who had been kidnaped by toubob and then escaped, who had gone to the Council of Elders just before he had been taken away, wanting to know what to do about her sasso borro infant, and he wondered what the Council of Elders had decided for her to do.

Some few slatees, he learned now from the talk in the hold, only supplied toubob canoes with such goods as indigo, gold, and elephants' teeth. But there were hundreds of others who helped toubob to burn villages and capture people. Some of the men told how children were enticed with slices of sugar cane; then bags were thrown over their heads. Others said the slatees had beaten them mercilessly during the marches after their capture. One man's wife, big with child, had died on the road. The wounded son of another was left bleeding to die from whip cuts. The more Kunta heard, the more his rage became as great for others as for himself.

He lay there in the darkness hearing the voice of his father sternly warning him and Lamin never to wander off anywhere alone; Kunta desperately wished that he had heeded his father's warnings. His heart sank with the thought that he would never again be able to listen to his father, that for the rest of whatever was going to be his life, he was going to have to think for himself.

"All things are the will of Allah!" That statement—which had begun with the alcala—went from mouth to ear, and when it came to Kunta from the man lying on his left side, he turned his head to whisper the words to his Wolof shacklemate. After a moment, Kunta realized that the Wolof hadn't whispered the words on to the next man, and after wondering for a while why not, he thought that perhaps he hadn't said them clearly, so he started to whisper the message once again. But abruptly the Wolof spat out loudly enough to be heard across the entire hold, "If your Allah wills this, give me the devil!" From elsewhere in the darkness came several loud exclamations of agreement with the Wolof, and arguments broke out here and there.

Kunta was deeply shaken. The shocked realization that he lay with a pagan burned into his brain, faith in Allah being as precious to him as life itself. Until now he had respected the friendship and the wise opinions of his older shacklemate. But now Kunta knew that there could never be any more companionship between them.

CHAPTER 38

Up on the deck now, the women sang of having managed to steal and hide a few knives, and some other things that could be used as weapons. Down in the hold, even more strongly than before, the men separated into two camps of opinion. The leader of the group that felt the toubob should be attacked without delay was a fierce-looking tattooed Wolof. On the deck, every man had seen him dancing wildly in his chains while baring his sharply filed teeth at the toubob, who clapped for him because they thought he was grinning. Those who believed in the wisdom of further watchful preparation were led by the tawny Foulah who had been beaten for choking the slatee to death.

There were a few followers of the Wolof who exclaimed that the toubob should be attacked when many of them were in the hold, where the chained men could see better than they and the element of surprise would be greatest—but those who urged this plan were dismissed as foolish by the others, who pointed out that the bulk of the toubob would still be up on the deck, and thus able to kill the chained men below like so many rats. Sometimes when the arguments between the Wolof and the Foulah would reach the point of shouting, the alcala would intervene, commanding them to be quieter lest their discussion be overheard by the toubob.

Whichever leader's thinking finally prevailed, Kunta was ready to fight to the death. Dying held no fear for him any more. Once he had decided that he would never see his family and home again, he felt the same as dead already. His only fear now was that he might die without at least one of the toubob also dead by his hand. But the leader toward whom Kunta was most inclined—along with most of the men, he felt—was the cautious, whip-scarred Foulah. Kunta had found out by now that most of the men in the hold were Mandinkas, and every Mandinka knew well that the Foulah people were known for spending years, even their entire lives if need be, to avenge with death any serious wrong ever done to them. If someone killed a Foulah and escaped, the Foulah's sons would never rest until one day they found and killed the murderer.

"We must be as one behind the leader we agree upon," the alcala counseled. There was angry muttering from those who followed the Wolof, but when it had become clear that most of the men sided with the Foulah, he promptly issued his first order. "We must examine toubob's every action with the eyes of hawks. And when the time comes, we must be warriors." He advised them to follow the counsel of the woman who had told them to look happy when they jumped on deck in their chains. That would relax the toubob's guard, which would make them easier to take by surprise. And the Foulah also said that every man should locate with his eyes any weapon-like object that he could swiftly grab and use. Kunta was very pleased with himself, for during his times up on deck, he had already spotted a spike, tied loosely beneath a space of railing, which he intended to snatch and use as a spear to plunge into the nearest toubob belly. His fingers would clutch around the handle he imagined in his hands every time he thought of it.

Whenever the toubob would jerk the hatch cover open and climb down among them, shouting and wielding their whips, Kunta lay as still as a forest animal. He thought of what the kintango had said during manhood training, that the hunter should learn from what Allah himself had taught the animals—how to hide and watch the hunters who sought to kill them. Kunta had lain for hours thinking how the toubob seemed to *enjoy* causing pain. He remembered with loathing the times when toubob would laugh as they lashed the men—particularly those whose bodies were covered with bad sores—and then disgustedly wipe off the ooze that splattered onto them. Kunta lay also bitterly picturing the toubob in his mind as they forced the women into the canoe's dark corners in the nights; he imagined that he could hear the women screaming. Did the toubob have no women of their own? Was that why they went like dogs after others' women? The toubob seemed to respect nothing at all; they seemed to have no gods, not even any spirits to worship.

The only thing that could take Kunta's mind off the toubob—and how to kill them—was the rats, which had become bolder and bolder with each passing day. Their nose whiskers would tickle between Kunta's legs as they went to bite a sore that was bleeding or running with pus. But the lice preferred to bite him on the face, and they would suck at the liquids in the corners of Kunta's eyes, or the snot draining from his nostrils. He would squirm his body, with his fingers darting and pinching to crush any lice that he might trap between his nails. But worse even than the lice and rats was the pain in Kunta's shoulders, elbows, and hips, stinging now like fire from the weeks of steady rubbing against the hard, rough boards beneath him. He

BEST-SELLING CHAPTERS

had seen the raw patches on other men when they were on deck, and his own cries joined theirs whenever the big canoe pitched or rolled somewhat more than usual.

And Kunta had seen that when they were up on the deck, some of the men had begun to act as if they were zombies—their faces wore a look that said that they were no longer afraid, because they no longer cared whether they lived or died. Even when the whips of the toubob lashed them, they would react only slowly. When they had been scrubbed of their filth, some were simply unable even to try jumping in their chains, and the white-haired chief toubob, with a look of worry, would order the others to permit those men to sit, which they did with their foreheads between their knees and the thin, pinkish fluid draining down their raw backs. Then the chief toubob would force their heads backward and into their upturned mouths pour some stuff that they would usually choke up. And some of them fell limply on their sides, unable to move, and toubob would carry them back into the hold. Even before these men died, as most of them did, Kunta knew that in some way they had willed themselves to die.

But in obedience to the Foulah, Kunta and most of the men tried to keep acting happy as they danced in their chains, although the effort was like a canker in their souls. It was possible to see, though, that when the toubob were thus made more relaxed, fewer whips fell on backs, and the men were allowed to remain on the sunlit deck for longer periods than before. After enduring the buckets of seawater and the torture of the scrubbing brushes, Kunta and the rest of the men sat resting on their haunches and watched the toubobs' every move—how they generally spaced themselves along the rails; how they usually kept their weapons too close to be grabbed away. No chained man's eye missed it whenever any toubob leaned his gun briefly against the rails. While they sat on the deck, anticipating the day when they would kill the toubob, Kunta worried about the big metal thing that showed through the barricade. He knew that at whatever cost in lives, that weapon would have to be overwhelmed and taken, for even though he didn't know exactly what it was, he knew that it was capable of some terrible act of destruction, which was of course why the toubob had placed it there.

He worried also about those few toubob who were always turning the wheel of the big canoe, a little this way, a little that way, while staring at a round brownish metal thing before them. Once, when they were down in the hold, the alcala spoke his own thought: "If those toubob are killed, who will run this canoe?" And the Foulah leader responded that those toubob needed to be taken alive. "With spears at their throats," he said, "they will return us to our land, or they will die." The very thought that he might actually see his land, his home, his family once again sent a shiver down Kunta's spine. But even if that should happen, he thought he would have to live to be very old if he was ever to forget, even a little bit, what the toubob had done to him.

There was yet another fear within Kunta—that the toubob might have the eyes to notice how differently he and the other men danced in their chains on the deck, for now they were really dancing; they couldn't help their movements from showing what was deep in their minds: swift gestures of hurling off shackles and chains, then clubbing, strangling, spearing, killing. While they were dancing, Kunta and the other men would even whoop out hoarsely their anticipation of slaughter. But to his great relief, when the dancing ended and he could again contain himself, he saw that the unsuspecting toubob only grinned with happiness. Then, one day up on the deck, the chained people suddenly stood rooted in astonishment and stared—along with the toubob—at a flight of hundreds of flying fish that filled the air above the water like silvery birds. Kunta was watching, dumfounded, when suddenly he heard a scream. Whirling, he saw the fierce, tattooed Wolof in the act of snatching a metal stick from a toubob. Swinging it like a club, he sent the toubob's brains spraying onto the deck; as other toubob snapped from their frozen positions of shock, he battered another to the deck. It was done so swiftly that the Wolof, bellowing in rage, was clubbing his fifth toubob when the flash of a long knife lopped off his head cleanly at the shoulders. His head hit the deck before his body had crumpled down, and both spurted blood from their stumps. The eyes in the face were still open, and they looked very surprised.

Amid shoutings of panic, more and more toubob scrambled to the scene, rushing out of doors and sliding like monkeys down from among the billowing white cloths. As the women shrieked, the shackled men huddled together in a circle. The metal sticks barked flame and smoke; then the big black barrel exploded with a thunderous roar and a gushing cloud of heat and smoke just over their heads, and they screamed and sprawled over each other in horror.

From behind the barricade bolted the chief toubob and his scar-faced mate, both of them screaming in rage. The huge one struck the nearest toubob a blow that sent blood spurting from his mouth, then all of the other toubob were a mass of screaming and shouting as with their lashes and knives and firesticks they rushed to herd the shackled men back toward the opened hatch. Kunta moved, not feeling the lashes that struck him, still awaiting the Foulah's signal to attack. But almost before he realized it, they were below and chained back in their dark places and the hatch cover had been slammed down.

But they were not alone. In the commotion, a toubob had been trapped down there with them. He dashed this way and that in the darkness, stumbling and bumping into the shelves, screaming in terror, scrambling up when he fell and dashing off again. His howlings sounded like some primeval beast's. *"Toubob fa!"* somebody shouted, and other voices joined him: *"Toubob fa! Toubob fa!"* they shouted, louder and louder, as more and more men joined the chorus. It was as if the toubob knew they meant it for him, and pleading sounds came from him as Kunta lay silent as if frozen, none of his muscles able to move. His head was pounding, his body poured out sweat, he was gasping to breathe. Suddenly the hatch cover was snatched open and a dozen toubob came pounding down the stairs into the dark hold. Some of their whips had slashed down onto the trapped toubob before he could make them realize he was one of them.

Then, under viciously lashing whips, the men were again unchained and beaten, kicked back up onto the deck, where they were made to watch as

BEST-SELLING CHAPTERS

four toubob with heavy whips beat and cut into a pulpy mess the headless body of the Wolof. The chained men's naked bodies shone with sweat and blood from their cuts and sores, but scarcely a sound came from among them. Every one of the toubob was heavily armed now, and murderous rage was upon their faces as they stood in a surrounding ring, glaring and breathing heavily. Then the whips lashed down again as the naked men were beaten back down into the hold and rechained in their places.

For a long while, no one dared even to whisper. Among the torrent of thoughts and emotions that assailed Kunta when his terror had subsided enough for him to think at all was the feeling that he wasn't alone in admiring the courage of the Wolof, who had died as a warrior was supposed to. He remembered his own tingling anticipation that the Foulah leader would at any instant signal an attack—but that signal hadn't come. Kunta was bitter, for whatever might have happened would have been all over now; and why not die now? What better time was going to come? Was there any reason to keep hanging onto life here in this stinking darkness? He wished desperately that he could communicate as he once did with his shacklemate, but the Wolof was a pagan.

Mutterings of anger at the Foulah's failure to act were cut short by his dramatic message: The attack, he announced, would come the next time the men on their level of the hold were on deck being washed and jumping in their chains, when the toubob seemed most relaxed. "Many among us will die," the Foulah said, "as our brother has died for us—but our brothers below will avenge us."

There was grunting approval in the murmurings that circulated now. And Kunta lay in the darkness listening to the raspings of a stolen file rubbing against chains. He knew for weeks that the file marks had been carefully covered with filth so that the toubob wouldn't see. He lay fixing in his mind the faces of those who turned the great wheel of the canoe, since their lives were the only ones to be spared.

But during that long night in the hold, Kunta and the other men began to hear an odd new sound they had never heard before. It seemed to be coming through the deck from over their heads. Silence fell rapidly in the hold and, listening intently, Kunta guessed that stronger winds must be making the great white cloths flap much harder than usual. Soon there was another sound, as if rice was falling onto the deck; he guessed after a while that it must be rain pelting down. Then he was sure that he heard, unmistakably, the muffled crack and rumble of heavy thunder.

Feet could be heard pounding on the deck overhead, and the big canoe began to pitch and shudder. Kunta's screams were joined by others' as each movement up and down, or from side to side, sent the chained men's naked shoulders, elbows, and buttocks—already festered and bleeding—grinding down even harder against the rough boards beneath them, grating away still more of the soft, infected skin until the muscles underneath began rubbing against the boards. The hot, lancing pains that shot from head to foot almost blacked him out, and it was as if from afar that he became dimly aware of the sound of water pouring down into the hold—and of shrieks amid a bedlam of terror.

The water poured more and more rapidly into the hold until Kunta heard the sound of something heavy, like some great coarse cloth, being dragged over the deck above. Moments later, the flood subsided to a trickle—but then Kunta began to sweat and gag. The toubob had covered the holes above them to shut out the water, but in so doing they had cut off all air from the outside, trapping the heat and stench entirely within the hold. It was beyond tolerance, and the men began to choke and vomit, rattling their shackles frantically and screaming in panic. Kunta's nose, throat, and then his lungs felt as if they were being stuffed with blazing cotton. He was gasping for more breath to scream with. Surrounded by the wild frenzy of jerking chains and suffocating cries, he didn't even know it when both his bladder and his bowels released themselves.

Sledgehammer waves crashed on the hull, and the timbers behind their heads strained against the pegs that held them together. The choked screams of the men down in the hold grew louder when the great canoe plunged sickeningly downward, shuddering as tons of ocean poured across her. Then, miraculously, she rose again under the torrential rains that beat down on her like hailstones. As the next mountainous broadside drove her back down again, and up again—heeling, rolling, trembling—the noise in the hold began to abate as more and more of the chained men fainted and went limp.

When Kunta came to, he was up on deck, amazed to find himself still alive. The orange lights, moving about, made him think at first they were still below. Then he took a deep breath and realized it was fresh air. He lay sprawled on his back, which was exploding with pains so terrible that he couldn't stop crying, even in front of the toubob. He saw them far overhead, ghostly in the moonlight, crawling along the crossarms of the tall, thick poles; they seemed to be trying to unroll the great white cloths. Then, turning his pounding head toward a loud noise, Kunta saw still more toubob stumbling up through the open hatchway, staggering as they dragged the limp, shackled forms of naked men up onto the deck of the canoe, dumping them down near Kunta and others already piled up like so many logs.

Kunta's shacklemate was trembling violently and gagging between moans. And Kunta's own gagging wouldn't stop as he watched the white-haired chief toubob and the huge scarred one shouting and cursing at the others, who were slipping and falling in the vomit underfoot, some of it their own as they continued to drag up bodies from below.

The great canoe was still pitching heavily, and drenching spray now and then splashed over the quarterdeck. The chief toubob had difficulty keeping his balance, now moving hurriedly, as another toubob followed him with a light. One or the other of them would turn upward the face of each limp, naked man, and the light would be held close; the chief toubob would peer closely and sometimes he would put his fingers on one wrist of that shackled man. Sometimes, then, cursing bitterly, he would bark an order and the other toubob would lift and drop the man into the ocean.

Kunta knew these men had died below. He asked himself how Allah, of whom it was said that He was in all places at all times, could possibly be here. Then he thought that even to question such a thing would make him no better than the pagan shuddering and moaning alongside him.

Unit 2

Roots

- Comprehension Questions
- Recognizing Tone and Mood
- Discussion Guides
- Writing Exercise

COMPREHENSION QUESTIONS

For each of the following statements and questions, select the option containing the most complete or most accurate answer.

1. The living conditions for the Blacks in the hold of the slave ship were
   (b) □ a. adequate but primitive.
   □ b. totally inadequate.
   □ c. humane but crowded.
   □ d. similar to the crew's quarters.

2. The prisoners had difficulty communicating with each other because
   (c) □ a. they were too sick to talk.
   □ b. they distrusted one another.
   □ c. no one felt like talking.
   □ d. they spoke different languages.

3. The white sailors treated the Blacks badly because
   (g) □ a. the captain ordered them to.
   □ b. they disliked the Black men personally.
   □ c. they regarded the Blacks as more animal than human.
   □ d. they feared the slaves would overpower them.

4. The toubob made some efforts to keep their Black prisoners alive
   (h) because they
   □ a. couldn't sell a dead slave.
   □ b. felt sorry for them.
   □ c. learned to respect the Blacks.
   □ d. were basically religious people.

5. Which of the following words is closest in meaning to *balefully* as used
   (l) in "Kunta would lie still with his eyes staring *balefully* in hatred."
   □ a. Indulgently   □ c. Vacantly
   □ b. Forlornly   □ d. Menacingly

6. Because they were kept on deck with the sailors, the Black women were
   (f) □ a. not able to communicate with the Black men.
   □ b. able to study their surroundings and captors.
   □ c. afraid to communicate with the Black men.
   □ d. not afraid to attack their white captors.

7. By constantly referring to such things as filth, rats and lice, the author
(i) seeks to create a tone that arouses a feeling of
  □ a. disgust with the dirt.
  □ b. horror at the injustice.
  □ c. squeamishness about rats and lice.
  □ 'd. relief that this happened long ago.

8. The story is told from the point of view of the
(k) □ a. women.   □ c. author.
  □ b. toubob.   □ d. Black men.

9. The most reliable information which the Blacks had about their captors
(f) came from
  □ a. the Black women's singing.
  □ b. other prisoners in the hold.
  □ c. the Black slatees.
  □ d. conversations with the toubob.

10. As a result of their conversations with each other, the Black men came
(c) to regard one another as
  □ a. enemies.   □ c. slaves.
  □ b. brothers.   □ d. animals.

11. When bitter disagreements arose among the Blacks,
(d) □ a. an elder would act as mediator.
  □ b. the slatees would report it to the toubob.
  □ c. the white men would settle the matter.
  □ d. a group would be chosen to settle the dispute.

12. Despite their intense pain and suffering, the Black men found a small
(e) measure of comfort in
  □ a. their exercise periods on deck.
  □ b. the breathtaking ocean scenery.
  □ c. their conversations with the Black women.
  □ d. their conversations with one another.

13. Black slatees were outcasts who
(a) □ a. had leprosy.   □ c. helped enemy tribes.
  □ b. helped white men.   □ d. were of a lower caste.

14. Which of the following best defines *succumb* as used in, ". . . dangers
(l) to which Kunta and the other younger men privately thought they
themselves would never *succumb*"?
   □ a. Fall victim to   □ c. Lose their fear of
   □ b. Live to tell about   □ d. Allow

15. The author describes the Black men's treatment at the hands of the
(i) toubob in such a way that you come to view the ship's crew with
   □ a. sympathy and understanding.
   □ b. objectivity.
   □ c. disgust and loathing.
   □ d. mixed feelings.

16. Kunta had great faith in
(j) □ a. Buddha.   □ c. Jesus.
   □ b. Allah.   □ d. Foulah.

17. Kunta decided he must end his friendship with his shacklemate from the
(j) Wolof tribe because
   □ a. the Wolof annoyed him with his moans.
   □ b. they spoke different languages.
   □ c. the Wolof was a slatee.
   □ d. the Wolof had denounced Allah.

18. The Foulah leader who was to plan and direct their attack on the
(a) toubob was chosen by
   □ a. the alcala.   □ c. a majority vote.
   □ b. Allah.   □ d. a committee.

19. "Kunta lay *as still as a forest animal.*" The phrase "as still as a forest
(k) animal" is an example of a simile—that is, a comparison using the words
   "like" or "as." Which of the following is also a simile?
   □ a. We must examine toubob's every action *with the eyes of hawks.*
   □ b. A flight of hundreds of flying fish filled the air above the water
       like silvery birds.
   □ c. It was *as if from afar* . . .
   □ d. It was a voice of experience and authority *as well as wisdom.*

20. "Kunta and most of the men tried to act happy as they danced in their
(h) chains, but the effort was like a canker in their souls." This suggests that
   the Blacks regarded their displays of "dancing" for the white men as a
   □ a. form of relaxation.   □ c. humiliating indignity.
   □ b. kind of religious ritual. □ d. tiresome pastime.

21. Kunta failed to join the Wolof who was decapitated in his one-man
(j) attack on the toubob because
  □ a. he was afraid to die.
  □ b. he was waiting for orders.
  □ c. he disapproved of the Wolof's actions.
  □ d. his religion forbade him to kill.

22. The prisoners' decision to stage an organized attack on the following
(d) day was thwarted by
  □ a. a violent storm.   □ c. a lack of weapons.
  □ b. a traitorous slatee.   □ d. the Blacks' fear of defeat.

23. The author seeks to instill in the reader an opinion about slavery by
(k) appealing to the reader's
  □ a. emotions.   □ c. prejudices.
  □ b. logic.   □ d. religious convictions.

24. An expression which describes a main theme of the chapters is
(e) □ a. good triumphs over evil.   □ c. the world is a just place.
    □ b. man's inhumanity to man.   □ d. all men are brothers.

25. After the storm, the captain "cursed bitterly" each time he found
(g) another dead slave. His bitterness was probably caused by
  □ a. his human feelings.
  □ b. the disgust he felt looking at the dead men.
  □ c. his anger over having been disobeyed.
  □ d. the lost value of the dead men.

Comprehension Skills: a—isolating details; b—recalling specific facts; c—retaining
concepts; d—organizing facts; e—understanding the main idea; f—drawing a
conclusion; g—making a judgment; h—making an inference; i—recognizing tone;
j—understanding characters; k—appreciation of literary forms; l—knowledge of
word meanings.

RECOGNIZING TONE AND MOOD

Practice Exercise A

"All things are the will of Allah!" That statement—which had begun with the alcala—went from mouth to ear, and when it came to Kunta from the man lying on his left side, he turned his head to whisper the words to his Wolof shacklemate. After a moment, Kunta realized that the Wolof hadn't whispered the words on to the next man . . . so he started to whisper the message once again. But abruptly the Wolof spat out loudly enough to be heard across the entire hold, "If your Allah wills this, give me the devil!"

1. The mood of the passage is reflected in the Wolof's tone of voice as he denounces Allah. What is the mood of the passage?
   ☐ a. Unemotional   ☐ c. Fearful
   ☐ b. Bitter   ☐ d. Proud

2. Underline the phrase from the above passage which indicates the tone of voice in which the Wolof spoke.

Practice Exercise B

Kunta had lain for hours thinking how the toubob seemed to *enjoy* causing pain. He remembered with loathing the times when toubob would laugh as they lashed the men—particularly those whose bodies were covered with bad sores—and then disgustedly wipe off the ooze that splattered onto them. Kunta lay also bitterly picturing the toubob in his mind as they forced the women into the canoe's dark corners in the nights; he imagined that he could hear the women screaming. Did the toubob have no women of their own? Was that why they went like dogs after others' women? The toubob seemed to respect nothing at all; they seemed to have no gods, not even any spirits to worship.

1. The tone of the above passage and Kunta's mood express
   ☐ a. pity.   ☐ c. contempt.
   ☐ b. annoyance.   ☐ d. remorse.

2. In the passage above, Alex Haley uses special words to express Kunta's feelings toward the toubob. Find these words as you do the following.

   a. In the second sentence, underline the words which describe how Kunta remembered the toubob as he lay thinking about them.

   b. Underline a phrase which Kunta uses to describe the toubob as he thinks about the way they went after the women.

Practice Exercise C

And Kunta had seen that when they were up on the deck, some of the men had begun to act as if they were zombies—their faces wore a look that said that they were no longer afraid, because they no longer cared whether they lived or died. Even when the whips of the toubob lashed them, they would react only slowly. When they had been scrubbed of their filth, some were simply unable even to try jumping in their chains, and the white-haired chief toubob, with a look of worry, would order the others to permit those men to sit, which they did with their foreheads between their knees.... And some of them fell limply on their sides, unable to move, and toubob would carry them back into the hold. Even before these men died, as most of them did, Kunta knew that in some way they had willed themselves to die.

1. The tone and mood in this passage reflect
   - ☐ a. fear.
   - ☐ b. despair.
   - ☐ c. rage.
   - ☐ d. relief.

2. In this passage, tone and mood are expressed through the attitude of the dying men. Underline one phrase from the first sentence and one from the last which describe the men's attitude and indicate the mood.

Practice Exercise D

The water poured more and more rapidly into the hold until Kunta heard the sound of something heavy, like some great coarse cloth, being dragged over the deck above. Moments later, the flood subsided to a trickle—but then Kunta began to sweat and gag. The toubob had covered the holes above them to shut out the water, but in so doing they had cut off all air from the outside, trapping the heat and stench entirely within the hold. It was beyond tolerance, and the men began to choke and vomit, rattling their shackles frantically and screaming in panic. Kunta's nose, throat, and then his lungs felt as if they were being stuffed with blazing cotton.

1. The atmosphere in the hold of the ship creates a mood of
   - ☐ a. terror.
   - ☐ b. increased discomfort.
   - ☐ c. confusion.
   - ☐ d. tension.

2. Alex Haley uses many descriptions of the men's physical condition and descriptions of physical symptoms to create the tone and mood for his story. In this passage, for example, "Kunta's nose, throat, and then his lungs felt as if they were being stuffed with blazing cotton." Underline two 3-word phrases describing physical symptoms which help create tone and mood.

Analyzing Tone and Mood

1. The *kind* of words that an author chooses and even the *sound* of the words can affect the tone of a passage. Read the two sentences that follow and compare the words that are underlined. Why do you think Alex Haley chose to use the words in the *second* sentence?

   a. The steady talking that went on in the hold whenever the white men were gone kept getting louder and louder as the men began to speak better and better with one another.

   b. The steady murmuring that went on in the hold whenever the toubob were gone kept growing in volume and intensity as the men began to communicate better and better with one another.

2. Up until the thunderstorm which took such a heavy toll on the prisoners, Kunta and the other Blacks were hopeful about their chances of taking over the ship and returning to Africa. How does the mood of Kunta and the other Blacks change as a result of the thunderstorm? How does Alex Haley prepare you for this change, beginning with the death of the Wolof on deck?

3. The author describes the incredible filth down in the hold of the ship in a tone of extreme disgust and repugnance. How does this make you feel about the Black prisoners? About their white captors?

Interpreting the Chapters

4. Some of the Blacks in the ship with Kunta had stopped believing in Allah as a result of their brutal experiences at the hands of the slave dealers. If you suffered the way these men did, would you change your mind about things you believed in? God? Humanity? Justice? Faith in yourself?

5. Is the extreme cruelty and disregard for human life seen on this slave ship something that does not happen anymore? Or is this kind of behavior an inescapable aspect of man's character? Use examples to help explain your opinion.

6. Why was it so important to the prisoners to communicate with one another? What did they gain besides information?

7. Until his capture by the slave dealers, Kunta never really believed that harm could befall him. Why do you think many young people feel this way? How should a young person act in regard to danger or risk?

8. Kunta noticed that some Blacks seemed to have lost the will to live and soon died. Is this possible, or do you think Alex Haley was exaggerating for the sake of the story?

Analyzing the Author's Technique

9. It has been said that Alex Haley was unfair to the decent white people who lived during this period in history by concentrating on bad whites. Why do you think he did this? How would the story be different if Haley tempered it with some "good" whites?

10. Even if you have a strong stomach, you soon get enough of reading about conditions in the hold of a slave ship and the suffering of the men. Why does Alex Haley virtually "rub your nose in it"? What does he accomplish by harping on sickening details?

WRITING EXERCISE

The underlined words in the following passage help create a special tone and mood. As you read the passage, be aware of the feelings which these words convey.

> . . . the white town drowsing in the sunshine of a summer's morning; the streets empty, or pretty nearly so; one or two clerks sitting in front of the Water Street stores . . . asleep; . . . two or three wood flats at the head of the wharf, but nobody to listen to the peaceful lapping of the wavelets against them; the great Mississippi, the majestic, the magnificent Mississippi, rolling its mile-wide tide alone, shining in the sun.

The mood of this paragraph is one of sleepiness and langor. Replace the underline words or rewrite the passage completely so that it conveys a lively mood. You may use forms of the following words or words of your own choosing to lend a more sprightly air to the description of this town.

rush of water	sparkling	rambunctious
alert	chatting	rowdy
working	glinting	thronging
diligently	flashing	coming to life
churning	quickening	busy
pulsating tide	scurrying	bustling
against the shore	splashing	

Unit 3
Understanding
Characterization

Great Expectations

Introduction

Great Expectations is the story of an orphan named Pip who is raised by his shrewish sister and her good-natured husband, Joe, a blacksmith. The story is written as if it is being told by Pip himself when he is grown and looking back on his life. Intelligent and sensitive by nature, Pip looked forward to working with his brother-in-law at the forge. These honest ambitions fade, however, when Pip visits the manor house of a rich old lady and her ward, Estella, a beautiful young girl about his own age. This brief glimpse of upper-class gentility spoils for him the simple pleasures of the forge, and he becomes rapidly dissatisfied with himself. Shortly thereafter, an unknown benefactor provides the money to turn Pip into an upper-class London gentleman.

In hot pursuit of his "great expectations," Pip sheds his old lifestyle, values and friends and eagerly latches onto the trappings of what he sees as "the good life." He finds out, however, that things are not necessarily what they seem. The true identity of his benefactor, who turns out to be an ex-convict, makes a mockery of his gentlemanly pretentions. And the new values in which he had put so much stock turn out to be false and shabby. When the money to support his genteel lifestyle dries up, Pip discovers what is really important to him. Picking up the pieces of his life, he starts anew on the strength of what he has learned as a result of his great expectations.

The chapter you are about to read relates that first fateful visit where Pip observes a way of life that seems so much better than his own. At the manor house, Pip meets Miss Havisham, an eccentric old lady dressed in the decaying remnants of her bridal clothes, and Estella, her beautiful young ward. In the face of Estella's undisguised scorn, Pip is made painfully aware of his coarse hands, thick boots and other homely, but honest, marks of his social class. By the end of the chapter, Pip has reached a turning point in his life. No longer can he look forward with pleasure to life at the forge.

Great Expectations was first published in 1861 in weekly installments in Charles Dickens's own literary magazine, *All the Year Round.* Since his

Pickwick Papers in 1836, Dickens had kept an enormous number of readers on the edges of their seats with his serialized novels. *Great Expectations* features this popular "pot-boiling" style which kept readers clamoring for the next installment. The novel also expresses some of his pet peeves toward English social institutions in the nineteenth century. Its highly dramatic plot contains such elements of mystery as Satis House, where Miss Havisham withdraws into a bitter world of the past; the mystery of Estella's parentage; and the startling origin of Pip's expectations. Reflecting the author's low opinion of the judicial system of the time are lawyers who mock the law and judges who dispense a different justice for rich and poor. Dickens's disapproval of the English penal system is evident in his depiction of the Hulks, or prison ships, that are moored at the marshes near Pip's village.

The period in which Dickens wrote his novels, from roughly 1836 until his death in 1870, clearly showed the effects of the Industrial Revolution. There was widespread unemployment in England; sweatshop conditions were the rule for those who found jobs in the great factories that had sprung up; and the cities, swollen by an influx from the farms, were dirty and disease-infested, with large slum areas. Dickens managed to combine this grim reality with romance, sentiment, murder and colorful characters. His sprawling plots encompassed all levels of society and exposed the vanities, virtues and villainies that were to be found in them all.

Understanding Characterization

In some primitive tribes, storytellers were regarded with the same mixture of fear and respect as were medicine men. Both possessed a certain kind of magic. Medicine men could call up spirits with the power to heal, and storytellers could create spirits with the power to entertain. And while you couldn't reach out and touch them, these imaginary figures seemed amazingly real. Listeners could "see" characters in the firelight and in the shadows that could be believed in as if they were really there.

Even today, it's not so hard to understand the admiration for those early storytellers. An author's ability to create characters that are as real to us as flesh-and-blood people still seems to be a kind of magic. This creation of imaginary persons, so believable that they exist for the reader, is called *characterization.* It is one of the most important skills of a good writer and storyteller.

There are three basic methods of characterization: 1) In the course of the story, the author may come right out and describe certain revealing elements of a character; 2) the author may show the character in action and let readers draw their own conclusions; or, 3) the character may speak directly to the reader and thus reveal what kind of person he or she is.

The first method, in which the author describes certain aspects of the character for the reader, is referred to as *direct exposition. Exposition* is simply setting forth facts. Thus, in this method, the reader is presented with facts and statements. These provide the information needed to form a first impression of a character. The facts may concern the character's looks, clothes, social status, age, background, and so on. From this information the reader can develop ideas and opinions about the character being described.

In the following passage from *Great Expectations*, the reader is introduced to Miss Havisham through the method of direct exposition. Having described the bridal finery in which Miss Havisham was dressed, Pip (the narrator) goes on to observe that there is something strange about the whole situation. What impressions do you get of Miss Havisham from this account of her appearance?

. . . I saw that everything within my view which ought to be white, had been white long ago, and had lost its luster, and was faded and yellow. I saw that the bride within the bridal dress had withered like the dress, and like the flowers, and had no brightness left but the brightness of her sunken eyes. I saw that the dress had been put upon the rounded figure of a young woman, and that the figure upon which it now hung loose, had shrunk to skin and bone.

As a result of the narrator's observations, Miss Havisham comes across as a withered, pathetic figure. You are told that she is dressed in bridal finery meant to grace the rounded figure of a young woman. Yet the wearer is an old woman who has shrunk to skin and bone. The dress, too, shows the passage of years; its whiteness has faded to yellow, and the material has lost its luster. Everything about Miss Havisham that had once been white and bright—including the lady herself—is now old, withered and yellow. The reader naturally concludes that the old, faded dress has some importance for her. Thus, we might assume that Miss Havisham is, to some extent, living in the past. The image of "skin and bone" calls up visions of ghosts and skeletons and lends a somewhat sinister aspect to the old lady. All in all, the reader gets the impression that Miss Havisham is, at best, eccentric and certainly not a character whom we are likely to regard with much warmth.

A second method of characterization is the presentation of the character in action. In this method, readers observe for themselves how the character reacts to certain situations and to other people. The author stays pretty much in the background, thus allowing the readers to draw their own conclusions about the traits this character exhibits. It is important in such cases to notice what the character does, says, and how he or she gets along with others. Does the character confront danger or run away from it? Does he alienate others when he speaks or win their respect? Does she talk like an illiterate or an educated person? All of these points reveal facets of the character's personality.

The following passage from *Great Expectations* presents Miss Havisham, whom you have just met, and Estella, a young girl in Miss Havisham's charge. What does their behavior in the following scene tell you about these two characters?

> Miss Havisham beckoned her to come close, and took up a jewel from the table, and tried its effect upon her fair young bosom and against her pretty brown hair. "Your own, one day, my dear, and you will use it well. Let me see you play cards with this boy."
> "With this boy!" Why, he is a common laboring-boy!"
> I thought I overheard Miss Havisham answer—only it seemed so unlikely—"Well? You can break his heart."

Certainly the behavior of Estella and Miss Havisham in the above scene is rude and ill-mannered. But their careless disregard for Pip's feelings suggests something more than simple bad manners. They insult Pip to his face, speak in his presence as if he is not there, or is deaf, or insensitive.

And what is the basis for their contempt? His offense seems to be his status as a "common laboring-boy." This, however, is no reflection on them, and yet they respond with a scorn that is out of all proportion to the "offense." Miss Havisham suggests to Estella that she break his heart, as if it were as good a way as any other of passing the time. Thus, we are presented with an old woman and a young girl, both of whom seem to regard other people, not as human beings, but as things to be used or played with. While the reader cannot as yet account for it, it is nonetheless evident that these two characters suffer from a defect in their personalities that warps their outlook on the world.

Sometimes the author may choose to develop characterization by having the character address the reader directly. In this technique, characters voice their most private feelings and thoughts. They reveal the impact of events or of other people upon themselves, and they tell of past incidents and emotions which influence their present actions. Thus, the reader is made to understand these characters more fully as a result of learning about the inner workings of their minds.

In the passage which follows, Pip discloses some facts about his upbringing that shed light on his character. What do you learn about Pip as a result of these remarks about himself?

> My sister's bringing up had made me sensitive. In the little world in which children have their existence, whosoever brings them up, there is nothing so finely perceived and so finely felt as injustice . . . . I had known, from the time when I could speak, that my sister, in her capricious and violent coercion, was unjust to me. I had cherished a profound conviction that her bringing me up by hand, gave her no right to bring me up by jerks. Through all my punishments, disgraces, fasts and vigils, and other penitential performances, I had nursed this assurance; and to my communing so much with it, in a solitary and unprotected way, I in great part refer the fact that I was morally timid and very sensitive.

In the above passage, Pip declares himself to be sensitive and morally timid. Moreover, he blames these feelings on his sister's method of raising him. Despite his sister's attempts to impress upon Pip his good fortune at being "brought up by hand"—as opposed to being raised in an orphanage— Pip refuses to be grateful. To his mind, he has been brought up not so much by hand as "by jerks." Thanks to his sister's stern idea of how children should be raised, his life to date has consisted—in his own mind, at least— of punishments, humiliations, going without meals, and various other small hardships. And to make matters worse, his sister is capricious—that is, changeable; there's no telling what will set her off sometimes.

Pip tells you the effect that all of this has on him. The sum total of this, he believes, has made him "sensitive and morally timid." As a result of this "confession," the reader gets a more rounded idea of Pip's character. On the one hand, he is a solitary child who spends much time feeling sorry for himself. On the other hand, such a youngster might be more considerate of other people's feelings as a result of his own sufferings. In any case, Pip's self-image is extremely fragile. And, as you shall see in the chapter which follows, it does not stand up to the ridicule of others.

In addition to choosing which method of characterization to use, storytellers also consider just how deeply they wish to develop a particular character. There are flat (two-dimensional) characters and rounded (three dimensional) characters, depending upon what the author does with them.

Flat, or two-dimensional, characters are almost always minor characters. They have only one or two striking traits, such as greediness, cruelty, cowardice or unusual goodness, kindness or understanding. Their predominant trait is not balanced by an opposite quality; they are usually all good or all bad. In the chapter which follows this lesson, Mr. Pumblechook is a flat character. He stands out in the reader's mind solely by his pompous treatment of Pip. He might possess a streak of generosity or some other redeeming quality. But, if that is so, the reader is not made aware of it. As far as we can see, Mr. Pumblechook is smug and self-satisfied, and there is no indication that he is anything else.

Such characters can be interesting or amusing in their own right, but they lack depth. Because of this, it is hard to think of them as real flesh-and-blood persons with conflicts and problems like our own. Flat characters are sometimes referred to as *static* characters because they do not change in the course of the story. The word *static* means "not moving or progressing." Static characters do not grow or progress to a better understanding of themselves or the world around them as a result of the events of the story. Things happen *to* such characters without things happening *within* them.

Major characters are almost always round, or three-dimensional. Like you and me, they have good qualities and bad qualities; they do some admirable things and some dumb things. At times they are unsure of themselves, and at times they act like they know it all. Their goals and ambitions change, and their values change. What seemed important to them at one point may seem silly later on. In short, we recognize something of ourselves in them. Thus, it's easy to feel as if you have something in common with a rounded, three-dimensional character.

One of the objectives of a storyteller is to reveal how actions and events shape major characters. A round character changes as a result of what happens to him or her. For example, a young soldier may go off to war expecting a glorious adventure and return home appalled at the pointless carnage he has witnessed. Or a young girl may enter marriage with visions of bliss, grow sadly disillusioned, and eventually come to a better understanding of both marriage and herself. A character who changes inside as a result of what happens to him is referred to in literature as a *dynamic* character. One meaning of the word *dynamic* is "changing or progressing." A dynamic character grows or progresses to a higher level of understanding in the course of a story.

In the following passage, as Pip returns home after visiting the manor house, he ponders his experiences with Estella and Miss Havisham. How does this scene establish Pip as a dynamic character, and what does the change in him consist of?

So, leaving word with the shopman on what day I was wanted at Miss Havisham's again, I set off on the four-mile walk to our forge; pondering, as I went along, on all I had seen, and deeply revolving that I was a common laboring-boy; that my hands were coarse; that my boots were thick; that I had fallen into a despicable habit of calling knaves Jacks; that I was much more ignorant than I had considered myself last night, and generally that I was in a low-lived bad way.

The passage above shows how Pip's attitude towards himself has changed in the short space of a day. The change takes place in Pip's view of himself, which has been sadly tarnished as a result of his visit at Miss Havisham's. Before, Pip had been unaware that his hands were coarse or his boots were thick. Back at the forge, all the men of Pip's acquaintance had coarse hands and thick boots. It had never occurred to him to consider himself a "common laboring-boy." Back at the forge, it was a respectable calling. And he had no way of knowing that, outside his small world at the forge, other people called jacks knaves when they played cards. As a result of all these new revelations, Pip now feels quite ignorant. And, what is more, he feels inferior. For reasons he cannot put into words, Pip has become ashamed of himself and ashamed of the life he represents.

The complexity of traits, then, that makes a character in a story seem real is called *characterization*. It can be expressed in three ways: by the author or narrator directly, through action, or in the words of the character himself. While a minor character may have only a single trait, major characters exhibit both virtues and shortcomings. And, just as we do, they grow, change and learn from their experiences. As you read the chapter which follows, try to picture in your mind's eye the characters you meet. How does the author present and develop them, and what impressions do they make on you?

As you read the chapter:

- Be aware of Mr. Pumblechook's treatment of Pip at breakfast. What does it reveal about Mr. Pumblechook's character?

- Notice how Estella's personal remarks about Pip's hands and shoes influence his opinion of himself.

- Pay attention to comments and observations made by the narrator (Pip) during the card game which suggest that Miss Havisham is weighed down by her past.

- Be aware of the scene in which Estella serves lunch to Pip and what her manners reveal about them both.

Great Expectations
Charles Dickens

CHAPTER 8

Mr. Pumblechook's premises in the High-street of the market town, were of a peppercorny and farinaceous character, as the premises of a corn-chandler and seedsman should be. It appeared to me that he must be a very happy man indeed, to have so many little drawers in his shop: and I wondered when I peeped into one or two on the lower tiers, and saw the tied-up brown paper packets inside, whether the flower-seeds and bulbs ever wanted of a fine day to break out of those jails, and bloom.

It was in the early morning after my arrival that I entertained this speculation. On the previous night, I had been sent straight to bed in an attic with a sloping roof, which was so low in the corner where the bedstead was, that I calculated the tiles as being within a foot of my eyebrows. In the same early morning, I discovered a singular affinity between seeds and corduroys. Mr. Pumblechook wore corduroys, and so did his shopman; and somehow, there was a general air and flavor about the corduroys, so much in the nature of seeds, and a general air and flavor about the seeds, so much in the nature of corduroys, that I hardly knew which was which. The same opportunity served me for noticing that Mr. Pumblechook appeared to conduct his business by looking across the street at the saddler, who appeared to transact *his* business by keeping his eye on the coachmaker, who appeared to get on in life by putting his hands in his pockets and contemplating the baker, who in his turn folded his arms and stared at the grocer, who stood at his door and yawned at the chemist. The watchmaker, always poring over a little desk with a magnifying glass at his eye, and always inspected by a group in smock-frocks poring over him through the glass of his shop-window, seemed to be about the only person in the High-street whose trade engaged his attention.

Mr. Pumblechook and I breakfasted at eight o'clock in the parlour behind the shop, while the shopman took his mug of tea and hunch of bread-and-butter on a sack of peas in the front premises. I considered Mr. Pumblechook wretched company. Besides being possessed by my sister's idea that a mortifying and penitenial character ought to be imparted to my diet—besides giving me as much crumb as possible in combination with as little butter, and putting such a quantity of warm water into my milk that it would have been more candid to have left the milk out altogether—his conversation consisted of nothing but arithmetic. On my politely bidding him Good morning, he said, pompously, "Seven times nine, boy?" And how should *I* be able to answer, dodged in that way, in a strange place, on an empty stomach! I was hungry, but before I had swallowed a morsel, he began a running sum that lasted all through the breakfast. "Seven?" "And four?" "And eight?" "And six?" "And two?" "And ten?" And so on. And after each figure was disposed of, it was as much as I could do to get a bite or a sup, before the next came; while he sat at his ease guessing nothing, and eating bacon and hot roll, in (if I may be allowed the expression) a gorging and gormandising manner.

For such reasons I was very glad when ten o'clock came and we started for Miss Havisham's; though I was not at all at my ease regarding the manner in which I should acquit myself under that lady's roof. Within a quarter of an hour we came to Miss Havisham's house, which was of old brick, and dismal, and had a great many iron bars to it. Some of the windows had been walled up; of those that remained, all the lower were rustily barred. There was a court-yard in front, and that was barred; so, we had to wait, after ringing the bell, until some one should come to open it. While we waited at the gate, I peeped in (even then Mr. Pumblechook said, "And fourteen?" but I pretended not to hear him), and saw that at the side of the house there was a large brewery. No brewing was going on in it, and none seemed to have gone on for a long time.

A window was raised, and a clear voice demanded "What name?" To which my conductor replied, "Pumblechook." The voice returned, "Quite right," and the window was shut again, and a young lady came across the court-yard, with keys in her hand.

"This," said Mr. Pumblechook, "is Pip."

"This is Pip, is it?" returned the young lady, who was very pretty and seemed very proud; "come in, Pip."

Mr. Pumblechook was coming in also, when she stopped him with the gate.

"Oh!" she said. "Did you wish to see Miss Havisham?"

"If Miss Havisham wished to see me," returned Mr. Pumblechook, discomfited.

"Ah!" said the girl; "but you see she don't."

She said it so finally, and in such an undiscussible way, that Mr. Pumblechook, though in a condition of ruffled dignity, could not protest. But he eyed me severely—as if *I* had done anything to him!—and departed with the words reproachfully delivered: "Boy! Let your behavior here be a credit unto them which brought you up by hand!" I was not free from apprehension that he would come back to propound through the gate, "And sixteen?" But he didn't.

My young conductress locked the gate, and we went across the court-yard. It was paved and clean, but grass was growing in every crevice. The brewery buildings had a little lane of communication with it; and the wooden gates of that lane stood open, and all the brewery beyond stood open, away to the high enclosing wall; and all was empty and disused. The cold wind seemed to blow colder there, than outside the gate; and it made a shrill noise in howling in and out at the open sides of the brewery, like the noise of wind in the rigging of a ship at sea.

She saw me looking at it, and she said, "You could drink without hurt all the strong beer that's brewed there now, boy."

"I should think I could, miss," said I, in a shy way.

"Better not try to brew beer there now, or it would turn out sour, boy; don't you think so?"

"It looks like it, miss."

"Not that anybody means to try," she added, "for that's all done with, and the place will stand as idle as it is, till it falls. As to strong beer, there's enough of it in the cellars already, to drown the Manor House."

"Is that the name of this house, miss?"

"One of its names, boy."

"It has more than one, then, miss?"

"One more. Its other name was Satis; which is Greek, or Latin, or Hebrew, or all three—or all one to me—for enough."

"Enough House!" said I. "that's a curious name, miss."

"Yes," she replied; "but it meant more than it said. It meant, when it was given, that whoever had this house, could want nothing else. They must have been easily satisfied in those days, I should think. But don't loiter, boy."

Though she called me "boy" so often, and with a carelessness that was far from complimentary, she was of about my own age. She seemed much older than I, of course, being a girl, and beautiful and self-possessed; and she was as scornful of me as if she had been one-and-twenty, and a queen.

We went into the house by a side door—the great front entrance had two chains across it outside—and the first thing I noticed was, that the passages were all dark, and that she had left a candle burning there. She took it up, and we went through more passages and up a staircase, and still it was all dark, and only the candle lighted us.

At last we came to the door of a room, and she said, "Go in."

I answered, more in shyness than politeness, "After you, miss."

To this, she returned: "Don't be ridiculous, boy; I am not going in." And scornfully walked away, and—what was worse—took the candle with her.

This was very uncomfortable, and I was half afraid. However, the only thing to be done being to knock at the door, I knocked, and was told from within to enter. I entered, therefore, and found myself in a pretty large room, well lighted with wax candles. No glimpse of daylight was to be seen in it. It was a dressing-room, as I supposed from the furniture, though much of it was of forms and uses then quite unknown to me. But prominent in it was a draped table with a gilded looking-glass, and that I made out at first sight to be a fine lady's dressing-table.

Whether I should have made out this object so soon, if there had been no fine lady sitting at it, I cannot say. In an arm-chair, with an elbow resting on the table and her head leaning on that hand, sat the strangest lady I have ever seen, or shall ever see.

She was dressed in rich materials—satins, and lace, and silks—all of white. Her shoes were white. And she had a long white veil dependent from her hair, and she had bridal flowers in her hair, but her hair was white. Some bright jewels sparkled on her neck and on her hands, and some other jewels lay sparkling on the table. Dresses, less splendid than the dress she wore, and half-packed trunks, were scattered about. She had not quite finished dressing, for she had but one shoe on—the other was on the table near her hand—her veil was but half arranged, her watch and chain were not put on, and some lace for her bosom lay with those trinkets, and with her handkerchief, and gloves, and some flowers, and a Prayer-book, all confusedly heaped about the looking-glass.

It was not in the first few moments that I saw all these things, though I saw more of them in the first moments than might be supposed. But, I saw that everything within my view which ought to be white, had been white long ago, and had lost its luster, and was faded and yellow. I saw that the bride within the bridal dress had withered like the dress, and like the flowers, and had no brightness left but the brightness of her sunken eyes. I saw that the dress had been put upon the rounded figure of a young woman, and that the figure upon which it now hung loose, had shrunk to skin and bone. Once, I had been taken to see some ghastly waxwork at the Fair, representing I know not what impossible personage lying in state. Once, I had been taken to one of our old marsh churches to see a skeleton in the ashes of a rich dress, that had been dug out of a vault under the church pavement. Now, waxwork and skeleton seemed to have dark eyes that moved and looked at me. I should have cried out, if I could.

"Who is it?" said the lady at the table.

"Pip, ma'am."

"Pip?"

"Mr. Pumblechook's boy, ma'am. Come—to play."

"Come nearer; let me look at you. Come close."

It was when I stood before her, avoiding her eyes, that I took note of the surrounding objects in detail, and saw that her watch had stopped at twenty minutes to nine, and that a clock in the room had stopped at twenty minutes to nine.

"Look at me," said Miss Havisham. "You are not afraid of a woman who has never seen the sun since you were born?"

I regret to state that I was not afraid of telling the enormous lie comprehended in the answer "No."

"Do you know what I touch here?" she said, laying her hands, one upon the other, on her left side.

"Yes, ma'am." (It made me think of the young man.)

"What do I touch?"

"Your heart."

"Broken!"

She uttered the word with an eager look, and with strong emphasis, and with a weird smile that had a kind of boast in it. Afterwards, she kept her hands there for a little while, and slowly took them away as if they were heavy.

"I am tired," said Miss Havisham. "I want diversion, and I have done with men and women. Play."

I think it will be conceded by my most disputatious reader, that she could hardly have directed an unfortunate boy to do anything in the wide world more difficult to be done under the circumstances.

"I sometimes have sick fancies," she went on, "and I have a sick fancy that I want to see some play. There, there!" with an impatient movement of the fingers of her right hand; "play, play, play!"

For a moment, with the fear of my sister's working me before my eyes, I had a desperate idea of starting round the room in the assumed character of Mr. Pumblechook's chaise-cart. But, I felt myself so unequal to the performance that I gave it up, and stood looking at Miss Havisham in what I suppose she took for a dogged manner, inasmuch as she said, when we had taken a good look at each other:

"Are you sullen and obstinate?"

"No, ma'am, I am very sorry for you, and very sorry I can't play just now. If you complain of me I shall get into trouble with my sister, so I would do it if I could; but it's so new here, and so strange, and so fine—and melancholy——" I stopped, fearing I might say too much, or had already said it, and we took another look at each other.

Before she spoke again, she turned her eyes from me, and looked at the dress she wore, and at the dressing-table, and finally at herself in the looking-glass.

"So new to him," she muttered, "so old to me; so strange to him, so familiar to me; so melancholy to both of us! Call Estella."

As she was still looking at the reflection of herself, I thought she was still talking to herself, and kept quiet.

"Call Estella," she repeated, flashing a look at me. "You can do that. Call Estella. At the door."

To stand in the dark in a mysterious passage of an unknown house, bawling Estella to a scornful young lady neither visible nor responsive, and feeling it a dreadful liberty so to roar out her name, was almost as bad as playing to order. But, she answered at last, and her light came along the dark passage like a star.

Miss Havisham beckoned her to come close, and took up a jewel from the table, and tried its effect upon her fair young bosom and against her pretty brown hair. "Your own, one day, my dear, and you will use it well. Let me see you play cards with this boy."

"With this boy! Why, he is a common laboring boy!"

I thought I overheard Miss Havisham answer—only it seemed so unlikely— "Well? You can break his heart."

"What do you play, boy?" asked Estella of myself, with the greatest disdain.

"Nothing but beggar my neighbour, Miss."

"Beggar him," said Miss Havisham to Estella. So we sat down to cards.

It was then I began to understand that everything in the room had stopped, like the watch and the clock, a long time ago. I noticed that Miss Havisham put down the jewel exactly on the spot from which she had taken it up. As Estella dealt the cards, I glanced at the dressing-table again, and saw that the shoe upon it, once white, now yellow, had never been worn. I glanced down at the foot from which the shoe was absent, and saw that the silk stocking on it, once white, now yellow, had been trodden ragged. Without this arrest of everything, this standing still of all the pale decayed objects, not even the withered bridal dress on the collapsed form could have looked so like grave-clothes, or the long veil so like a shroud.

So she sat, corpse-like, as we played at cards; the frillings and trimmings on her bridal dress, looking like earthy paper. I knew nothing then of the discoveries that are occasionally made of bodies buried in ancient times, which fall to powder in the moment of being distinctly seen; but, I have often thought since, that she must have looked as if the admission of the natural light of day would have struck her to dust.

"He calls the knaves, Jacks, this boy!" said Estella with disdain, before our first game was out. "And what coarse hands he has! And what thick boots!"

I had never thought of being ashamed of my hands before; but I began to consider them a very indifferent pair. Her contempt for me was so strong, that it became infectious, and I caught it.

She won the game, and I dealt. I misdealt, as was only natural, when I knew she was lying in wait for me to do wrong; and she denounced me for a stupid, clumsy laboring-boy.

"You say nothing of her," remarked Miss Havisham to me, as she looked on. "She says many hard things of you, yet you say nothing of her. What do you think of her?"

"I don't like to say," I stammered.

"Tell me in my ear," said Miss Havisham, bending down.

"I think she is very proud," I replied, in a whisper.

"Anything else?"

"I think she is very pretty."

"Anything else?"

"I think she is very insulting." (She was looking at me then with a look of supreme aversion.)

"Anything else?"

"I think I should like to go home."

"And never see her again, though she is so pretty?"

"I am not sure that I shouldn't like to see her again, but I should like to go home now."

"You shall go soon," said Miss Havisham aloud. "Play the game out."

Saving for the one weird smile at first, I should have felt almost sure that Miss Havisham's face could not smile. It had dropped into a watchful and brooding expression—most likely when all the things about her had become transfixed—and it looked as if nothing could ever lift it up again. Her chest had dropped, so that she stooped; and her voice had dropped, so that she spoke low, and with a dead lull upon her; altogether, she had the appearance of having dropped, body and soul, within and without, under the weight of a crushing blow.

I played the game to an end with Estella, and she beggared me. She threw the cards down on the table when she had won them all, as if she despised them for having been won of me.

"When shall I have you here again?" said Miss Havisham. "Let me think."

I was beginning to remind her that today was Wednesday, when she checked me with her former impatient movement of the fingers of her right hand.

"There! there! I know nothing of days of the week; I know nothing of weeks of the year. Come again after six days. You hear?"

"Yes, ma'am."

"Estella, take him down. Let him have something to eat, and let him roam and look about him while he eats. Go, Pip."

I followed the candle down, as I had followed the candle up, and she stood it in the place where we had found it. Until she opened the side entrance, I had fancied, without thinking about it, that it must necessarily be nighttime. The rush of the daylight quite confounded me, and made me feel as if I had been in the candlelight of the strange room many hours.

"You are to wait here, you boy," said Estella; and disappeared and closed the door.

I took the opportunity of being alone in the court-yard, to look at my coarse hands and my common boots. My opinion of those accessories was not favorable. They had never troubled me before, but they troubled me now, as vulgar appendages. I determined to ask Joe why he had ever taught me to call those picture-cards, Jacks, which ought to be called knaves. I wished Joe had been rather more genteelly brought up, and then I should have been so too.

She came back, with some bread and meat and a little mug of beer. She put the mug down on the stones of the yard, and gave me the bread and meat without looking at me, as insolently as if I were a dog in disgrace. I was so humiliated, hurt, spurned, offended, angry, sorry—I cannot hit upon the right name for the smart—God knows what its name was—that tears started to my eyes. The moment they sprang there, the girl looked at me with a quick delight in having been the cause of them. This gave me power to keep them back and to look at her: so, she gave a contemptuous toss—but with a sense, I thought, of having made too sure that I was so wounded—and left me.

But, when she was gone, I looked about me for a place to hide my face in, and got behind one of the gates in the brewery-lane, and leaned my sleeve against the wall there, and leaned my forehead on it and cried. As I cried, I kicked the wall, and took a hard twist at my hair; so bitter were my feelings, and so sharp was the smart without a name, that needed counteraction.

My sister's bringing up had made me sensitive. In the little world in which children have their existence, whosoever brings them up, there is nothing so finely perceived and so finely felt, as injustice. It may be only small injustice that the child can be exposed to; but the child is small, and its world is small, and its rocking-horse stands as many hands high, according to scale, as a big-boned Irish hunter. Within myself, I had sustained, from my babyhood, a perpetual conflict with injustice. I had known, from the time when I could speak, that my sister, in her capricious and violent coercion, was unjust to me. I had cherished a profound conviction that her bringing me up by hand, gave her no right to bring me up by jerks. Through all my punishments, disgraces, fasts and vigils, and other penitential performances, I had nursed this assurance; and to my communing so much with it, in a solitary and unprotected way, I in great part refer the fact that I was morally timid and very sensitive.

I got rid of my injured feelings for the time, by kicking them into the brewery-wall, and twisting them out of my hair, and then I smoothed my face with my sleeve, and came from behind the gate. The bread and meat were acceptable, and the beer was warming and tingling, and I was soon in spirits to look about me.

To be sure, it was a deserted place, down to the pigeon-house in the brewery-yard, which had been blown crooked on its pole by some high wind, and would have made the pigeons think themselves at sea, if there had been any pigeons there to be rocked by it. But, there were no pigeons in the dove-cot, no horses in the stable, no pigs in the sty, no malt in the store-house, no smells of grains and beer in the copper or the vat. All the uses and scents of the brewery might have evaporated with its last reek of smoke. In a by-yard, there was a wilderness of empty casks, which had a certain sour remembrance of better days lingering about them; but it was too sour to be accepted as a sample of the beer that was gone—and in this respect I remember those recluses as being like most others.

Behind the furthest end of the brewery, was a rank garden with an old wall: not so high but that I could struggle up and hold on long enough to look over it, and see that the rank garden was the garden of the house, and that it was overgrown with tangled weeds, but that there was a track upon the green and yellow paths, as if some one sometimes walked there, and that Estella was walking away from me even then. But she seemed to be every-where. For, when I yielded to the temptation presented by the casks, and began to walk on them, I saw *her* walking on them at the end of the yard of casks. She had her back towards me, and held her pretty brown hair spread out in her two hands, and never looked round, and passed out of my view directly. So, in the brewery itself—by which I mean the large paved lofty place in which they used to make the beer, and where the brewing utensils still were. When I first went into it, and, rather oppressed by its gloom, stood near the door looking about me, I saw her pass among the extinguished fires, and ascend some light iron stairs, and go out by a gallery high over-head, as if she were going out into the sky.

It was in this place, and at this moment, that a strange thing happened to my fancy. I thought it a strange thing then, and I thought it a stranger thing long afterwards. I turned my eyes—a little dimmed by looking up at the frosty light—towards a great wooden beam in a low nook of the building near me on my right hand, and I saw a figure hanging there by the neck. A figure all in yellow white, with but one shoe to the feet; and it hung so, that I could see that the faded trimmings of the dress were like earthy paper, and that the face was Miss Havisham's, with a movement going over the whole countenance as if she were trying to call to me. In the terror of seeing the figure, and in the terror of being certain that it had not been there a moment before, I at first ran from it, and then ran towards it. And my terror was greatest of all when I found no figure there.

Nothing less than the frosty light of the cheerful sky, the sight of people passing beyond the bars of the court-yard gate, and the reviving influence of the rest of the bread and meat and beer, could have brought me round. Even with those aids, I might not have come to myself as soon as I did, but that I saw Estella approaching with the keys, to let me out. She would have some fair reason for looking down upon me, I thought, if she saw me frightened; and she should have no fair reason.

She gave me a triumphant glance in passing me, as if she rejoiced that my hands were so coarse and my boots were so thick, and she opened the gate, and stood holding it. I was passing out without looking at her, when she touched me with a taunting hand.

"Why don't you cry?"

"Because I don't want to."

"You do," said she. "You have been crying till you are half blind, and you are near crying again now."

She laughed contemptuously, pushed me out, and locked the gate upon me. I went straight to Mr. Pumblechook's, and was immensely relieved to find him not at home. So, leaving word with the shopman on what day I was wanted at Miss Havisham's again, I set off on the four-mile walk to our forge; pondering, as I went along, on all I had seen, and deeply revolving that I was a common laboring-boy; that my hands were coarse; that my boots were thick; that I had fallen into a despicable habit of calling knaves Jacks; that I was much more ignorant than I had considered myself last night, and generally that I was in a low-lived bad way.

Unit 3

Great Expectations

- Comprehension Questions
- Understanding Characterization
- Discussion Guides
- Writing Exercise

COMPREHENSION QUESTIONS

For each of the following statements and questions, select the option containing the most complete or most accurate answer.

1. Which of the following best defines *affinity* as used in, "I discovered a
(l) singular *affinity* between seeds and corduroys"?
    □ a. Difference   □ c. Rivalry
    □ b. Relationship   □ d. Enmity

2. Which of the following best defines *acquit* as used in, "I was not at all at
(l) my ease regarding the manner in which I should *acquit* myself under
    that lady's roof"?
    □ a. Defend   □ c. Entertain
    □ b. Introduce   □ d. Behave

3. By the side of Miss Havisham's house stood a large, abandoned
(b) □ a. livery.   □ c. brewery.
    □ b. mill.   □ d. church.

4. Miss Havisham's dressing room is illuminated by
(a) □ a. candlelight.
    □ b. a crystal chandelier.
    □ c. a fireplace.
    □ d. sunlight streaming in the windows.

5. The disarray in Miss Havisham's dressing room and her appearance give
(h) the idea that she
    □ a. had been robbed many years ago.
    □ b. had forgotten what she was doing.
    □ c. had stopped in the middle of dressing.
    □ d. had been deserted by her servants many years ago.

6. By arraying Miss Havisham in bridal clothes, the author emphasizes her
(k) □ a. youthfulness.   □ c. beauty.
    □ b. old age.   □ d. innocence.

7. The author's description of Miss Havisham in her dressing room is
(i) intended to make the reader feel
    □ a. sympathetic.   □ c. puzzled.
    □ b. angry.   □ d. repulsed.

8. Pip has been instructed to go to Miss Havisham's house and

(b) □ a. play.   □ c. study.

     □ b. work.   □ d. beg.

9. Estella's tone as she speaks to Pip is

(i) □ a. formal.   □ c. insulting.

     □ b. friendly.   □ d. timid.

10. Estella ridicules Pip because he has

(b) □ a. bad manners.

     □ b. coarse hands and thick boots.

     □ c. no money.

     □ d. unpleasant features.

11. When Miss Havisham picks something up, she always

(a) □ a. puts it back exactly as it was.

     □ b. tries it on Estella before putting it down.

     □ c. shows it to Pip.

     □ d. throws it down angrily.

12. Time in the manor house seems to have

(c) □ a. flown by.   □ c. stopped.

     □ b. slowed down.   □ d. progressed at the usual rate.

13. Estella has apparently been brought up to value

(j) □ a. honesty and sincerity.

     □ b. hard work and self-sacrifice.

     □ c. honor and integrity.

     □ d. social status and stylish dress.

14. Estella seems to derive great satisfaction from

(c) □ a. winning at cards.

     □ b. making Pip cry.

     □ c. admiring herself in the mirror.

     □ d. disobeying Miss Havisham.

15. Under Miss Havisham's coaching, Estella is learning how to

(e) □ a. become a good wife and mother.

     □ b. manage a large household.

     □ c. read and write.

     □ d. break men's hearts.

16. Miss Havisham tells Pip, "I know nothing of days of the week, I know
(h) nothing of weeks of the year." This suggests that she
- a. has a poor memory for dates.
- b. wants to see Pip again soon.
- c. wants to avoid thinking about time.
- d. has servants to remind her what day it is.

17. After meeting Estella, Pip decides that he
(f) - a. is a very poor specimen of a boy.
- b. is in love with her.
- c. has led a happier life than she.
- d. never wants to see her again.

18. Estella behaves so rudely toward Pip because
(g) - a. she does not like him personally.
- b. she is at heart a mean child.
- c. he has hurt her feelings.
- d. Miss Havisham has taught her to.

19. Pip thinks of his upbringing by his sister as a series of many small
(j) - a. kindnesses.   - c. insults.
- b. injustices.   - d. cruelties.

20. From the way he behaved at the manor house, we can conclude that
(f) Pip is
- a. distrustful of people.   - c. shy.
- b. ill-mannered.   - d. spoiled.

21. Miss Havisham's eccentric life style appears to be connected with
(d) - a. Estella's arrival.
- b. her wedding day.
- c. her twenty-first birthday.
- d. a decline in the family fortune.

22. In Pip's mind, Miss Havisham is associated with images of
(k) - a. death and decay.   - c. power and wealth.
- b. youth and light.   - d. disaster and loss.

23. Pip's determination not to let Estella see him cry suggests a streak of
(j) - a. youthful vanity.   - c. personal pride.
- b. moral weakness.   - d. guile and deceit.

24. Miss Havisham's life style, plus the appearance and atmosphere of Satis
(d) House both inside and out, bring to mind a
 □ a. convent.   □ c. school.
 □ b. tomb.   □ d. bank.

25. Pip's visit to the manor house has taught him that
(e) □ a. thick boots and coarse hands are nothing to be ashamed of.
    □ b. rich people aren't that different from poor folk.
    □ c. the rich have different values from the poor.
    □ d. he'd rather be poor than rich.

Comprehension Skills: a—isolating details; b—recalling specific facts; c—retaining concepts; d—organizing facts; e—understanding the main idea; f—drawing a conclusion; g—making a judgment; h—making an inference; i—recognizing tone; j—understanding characters; k—appreciation of literary forms; l—knowledge of word meanings.

UNDERSTANDING CHARACTERIZATION

Practice Exercise A

I considered Mr. Pumblechook wretched company. Besides being possessed by my sister's idea that a mortifying and penitential character ought to be imparted to my diet—besides giving me as much crumb as possible in combination with as little butter, and putting such a quantity of warm water into my milk that it would have been more candid to have left the milk out altogether—his conversation consisted of nothing but arithmetic. On my politely bidding him Good morning, he said, pompously, "Seven times nine, boy?" And how should *I* be able to answer, dodged in that way, in a strange place, on an empty stomach! I was hungry, but before I had swallowed a morsel, he began a running sum that lasted all through the breakfast. "Seven?" "And four?" "And eight?" "And six?" "And two?" "And ten?" And so on.

1. Through Mr. Pumblechook's treatment of Pip at the breakfast table, the reader judges Pumblechook's character to be
   □ a. helpful and instructive. □ c. overbearing and stingy.
   □ b. mean and dishonest.   □ d. shy and sensitive.

2. Underline the phrase from the beginning of the paragraph which indicates the theory of child-raising that Mr. Pumblechook shared with Pip's sister.

Practice Exercise B

"He calls the knaves, Jacks, this boy!" said Estella with disdain, before our first game was out. "And what coarse hands he has! And what thick boots!"

I had never thought of being ashamed of my hands before; but I began to consider them a very indifferent pair. Her contempt for me was so strong, that it became infectious, and I caught it.

1. It is evident that what Pip caught from Estella was a
   □ a. new knowledge of himself.
   □ b. low opinion of himself.
   □ c. better opinion of himself.
   □ d. sense of pride in himself.

2. Underline two sentences that indicate a change in Pip's self-image.

Practice Exercise C

Saving for the one weird smile at first, I should have felt almost sure that Miss Havisham's face could not smile. It had dropped into a watchful and brooding expression—most likely when all the things about her had become transfixed—and it looked as if nothing could ever lift it up again. Her chest had dropped, so that she stooped; and her voice had dropped, so that she spoke low, and with a dead lull upon her; altogether, she had the appearance of having dropped, body and soul, within and without, under the weight of a crushing blow.

1. Pip's observations of Miss Havisham suggest that she has had
   - ☐ a. an unhappy experience.
   - ☐ b. a strange disease.
   - ☐ c. a physical deformity.
   - ☐ d. a poor diet.

2. On the lines provided, write the parts of Miss Havisham that seem to have "dropped."

_____

_____

Practice Exercise D

She came back, with some bread and meat and a little mug of beer. She put the mug down on the stones of the yard, and gave me the bread and meat without looking at me, as insolently as if I were a dog in disgrace. I was so humiliated, hurt, spurned, offended, angry, sorry—I cannot hit upon the right name for the smart—God knows what its name was—that tears started to my eyes. The moment they sprang there, the girl looked at me with a quick delight in having been the cause of them. This gave me power to keep them back and to look at her: so, she gave a contemptuous toss—but with a sense, I thought, of having made too sure that I was so wounded—and left me.

1. This scene emphasizes that Estella is
   - ☐ a. ignorant and untrained.
   - ☐ b. spunky and daring.
   - ☐ c. arrogant and spiteful.
   - ☐ d. educated and clever.

2. On the lines provided, write the phrase which reveals a streak of pride in Pip in response to Estella's rudeness.

_____

_____

GREAT EXPECTATIONS

DISCUSSION GUIDES

Analyzing Character

1. What impressions do you get of Pip as a child? What effect does Estella's scorn have on him? How does Pip change as a result of his visit to Satis House?

2. How is Estella developing into an instrument of Miss Havisham? Does she show any evidence of resenting this role? What kind of influence might Estella's surroundings have on her development?

3. Miss Havisham has been described as a very striking character, yet her whole personality consists of a very few outstanding traits. What are these traits? Why does this essentially two-dimensional character loom so large in Pip's and the reader's minds?

Interpreting the Chapter

4. In what ways does Satis House resemble a tomb? In what sense has Miss Havisham died?

5. All the clocks in Satis House have been stopped at twenty minutes to nine. In what other ways has time stopped in this house?

6. Pip notes that Miss Havisham's face has "a watchful and brooding expression" dating, apparently, from that time "when all the things about her had become transfixed"—that is, when the clocks, and her life, stopped. "She had the appearance of having dropped, body and soul, within and without, under the weight of a crushing blow." What do you think the "crushing blow" was in Miss Havisham's past? Where do Estella, and now Pip, fit into her present mode of existence?

7. How do you think the visits to Satis House will influence Pip's life and values? What "great expectations" might this blacksmith's son develop as a result of his exposure to Satis House?

Analyzing the Author's Technique

8. Pip is both the central character and the narrator of the story. An older, more mature Pip is telling the story, yet this chapter relates Pip's experiences as a young boy. How does this storytelling technique help bring all the characters to life?

9. Miss Havisham's dressing room, Satis House itself, the grounds and the abandoned brewery all remind you of their owner. In what ways has the author made them all resemble Miss Havisham?

10. In Pip's mind, Miss Havisham conjures up images of waxworks, skeletons, ancient mummies and phantoms swinging from gallows. Dickens uses these many images to make one larger image. What is that larger image?

WRITING EXERCISE

As you read the chapter and do the exercises, you come to know Pip, Estella and Miss Havisham rather well. But there are only hints that tell you what these characters actually look like:

Pip is young. We don't know his age exactly, but he cries easily and plays children's games.

Estella is about the same age, we are told. She is pretty and has brown hair.

Miss Havisham looks old (though we don't know how old). She is thin and has gray hair and dark eyes.

Great Expectations was made into a movie, and actors and actresses had to be chosen using just these hints *plus* what is learned about the kind of people the characters are. The problem is that each reader usually forms a picture which is different from the way other readers "see" the characters.

Pretend you are the casting director for a remake of the movie *Great Expectations.* You have to select actors to play the roles of Pip, Estella and Miss Havisham. From what you know of these characters, write a short description that tells what you think one of these characters looks like.

Unit 4
The Historical Novel

Hawaii

Introduction

Hawaii, one of James Michener's best historical novels, begins in the vast emptiness of the Pacific Ocean before the dawn of time and ends millions of years later as the Islands are about to embark on American statehood as the world's first truly pluralistic society.

Although the characters are fictional, Michener paints accurate and delicate portraits of all the Hawaiian people who have inhabited the islands over the centuries: the original Polynesians who sailed to the islands in open canoes 700 years before Columbus made his first tentative probe across the Atlantic; the whalers who came for rest and recreation and who left disease and hints of great wonders in the world beyond Hawaii; the New England missionaries who came to save the Hawaiians from the whalers and from a Christian devil they had never heard of, and who left a legacy of Yankee manners and methods; and the Chinese and Japanese who were imported as farm laborers and who stayed to become businessmen and political leaders.

In a sense, *Hawaii* is a vast genealogy that traces the descent of modern Hawaiians from the ancient kings of Bora Bora and Havaiki-of-the-North. These are the Golden Men, Michener tells us, a blend of people and cultures which produced a society influenced by both east and west, wholly modern and American yet in tune with the ancient and the Oriental.

As each new influence was thrust upon the Islands, it inevitably came in conflict with whatever culture was dominant at the time, and old cultures—the old ideas and the old ways—do not easily or willingly bow to new ways of thinking and behaving. We know this from watching the great, painful changes in the manners and morals of our own times.

The excerpt from *Hawaii* that you are about to read deals with the missionary influence on the Islands. It describes the efforts of Abner Hale and his wife, Jerusha, to convert the Hawaiians to Christianity and educate them in the ways of western civilization. At this point, they have been on the island of Lahaina for more than a year. But the success of their work has been limited by a clash of cultures. Abner unreasonably tries to remake Lahaina in the image of a New England village. He refuses to do anything the

Hawaiian way because that would be following the ways of the heathen. His stubborness in this respect is equaled by that of the kahunas, or wise men, who feel that Abner is badly in need of some of their local wisdom. Jerusha is having little better luck in her mission school. The girls eagerly embrace her code of right and wrong, but as soon as a whaling ship visits port, they drop everything—including their new dresses—and swim out to the sailors. Obviously, it takes more than sermons to change the way people live and think. Michener shows that the missionaries were, in their own way, as much the slaves of habit and superstition as the old Hawaiians.

It is hard to imagine nowadays the extent of the missionary zeal that sent young men and women on a perilous 18,000 mile voyage around Cape Horn to do God's work in a strange land. Yet New Englanders in 1820 understood sentiments like these very well. A great religious revival was sweeping the country; young people were looking for, and finding, God. In churches, meeting halls and colleges, they gathered to hear how they could spread the word of the Lord throughout the world. Some carried their good news to the American Indian tribes, some to the Africans, and some to the pagan land of Owhyhee, recently discovered by Captain Cook in 1778.

Abner Hale had experienced conversion while walking home through the fields of his father's farm. A light filled the meadow and a great shaking possessed him. "Abner Hale, are you saved?" cried a voice from nowhere, and eleven-year-old Abner Hale knew that he had found God. His pious father scrimped and saved to send him to Yale's divinity school. It was here that Abner listened to Keoki Kanakoa, a converted Christian from Owhyhee. In a moving oration, the young Hawaiian told the students how he had run away from polygamy, immorality and the worship of pagan gods who required endless human sacrifices. "Will no one go with me to save the souls of my people?" he pleaded. Abner broke down and cried, for he recognized God's call "from across the boundless deep where souls rot in evil."

Soon, Abner and other young missionaries and their new wives set sail on a mission aimed at nothing less than the complete remaking and salvation of a society. How well they succeeded is the subject of the excerpt in this unit.

A Glossary of Hawaiian Words

alii: members of the Hawaiian aristocracy

alii nui: royalty, the head of the aristocracy

aloha: the Hawaiian greeting used for both hello and goodbye

kahunas: wise men and holy men of the Islands

kapena: sailors from the whaling ships

kapu: forbidden

Makua: a title of respect (Abner Hale was called Makua Hale.)

wahine: woman

The Historical Novel

One way to learn about the past is by studying history. But the past as depicted in history books is apt to seem remote and impersonal. This is because the people and the events you read about in history books are described in terms of cold, factual data—dates, policies, wars, treaties, and so on. Perhaps the book will reproduce an old painting showing an immense, grim-faced monarch dressed in some outlandish costume and mounted on an ornate throne. But this in no way gives the reader a clue as to what kind of person this monarch was or what it was like to live in his kingdom.

But there's another way to learn about the past that takes up where history books leave off, and that is the *historical novel*. As the name implies, it is a novel—that is, fiction—but it is history, too. An historical novel is set in the past, but it is less concerned with battles, kings and conquests than with the story *behind* the facts. Why did the king act as he did? What kind of person was he, and what kinds of influences shaped his policy decisions? Was he a happy man? An historical novel presents the human-interest side of history without sacrificing historical authenticity. This is achieved by creating fictional characters who mingle with real people or representations of real people out of history. The fictional characters participate in actual historical events and show the reader what it was really like to live at that particular time and place.

A typical historical novel does three things: 1) It tells about an age when a culture is changing—something is dying and something else is being born; 2) it introduces fictional characters into this unsettled atmosphere; and 3) it recreates a feeling for the spirit of the age.

1. Conflict and Change. Social conflict and change can take a variety of forms and usually involve a challenge to established ways of thinking and doing things. For instance, an historical novel set in Puritan New England might center around the clash of religious and worldly interests. The southern plantations were the scene of another classic conflict in which slave-owning cotton growers fought to save their gracious but doomed way

of life. Both of these conflicts involved challenges to established customs and institutions. Inevitably, the old ways must yield to the new. In the process, heroes arise, fortunes are made or lost, and new ways must be found to live and cope with life. Historical novels are rich in the excitement which accompanies these great struggles and changes.

The following passage from *Hawaii* involves conflict. The time is 1824. Abner is a Christian missionary, and the kahunas are the traditional holy men of the island. A new church is to be built. What cultural conflict is being expressed in this scene?

> ... the kahunas merely listened, and when it came time for them to speak they said, "Now when Kane, that is God, wishes a church to be built, he supervises it. He always did when we built our temples . . . ."
>
> "But God is not Kane," Abner patiently repeated.
>
> The men nodded sagely and continued: "Now, since Kane is concerned about this church, and since we have always loved Kane, we thought it proper to advise you that this door . . ."
>
> "The door will be where it now is," Abner explained, "because that is where the door to a church has always been. In Boston the door would be here. In London it would be here."
>
> "But in Lahaina, Kane would not like it to be here," the Kahunas argued.
>
> "Kane is not God," Abner stubbornly repeated.
>
> "We understand, Makua Hale," the kahunas politely agreed, "but since God and Kane are the same idea . . ."
>
> "No," Abner insisted, "God and Kane are not the same."
>
> "Of course," the kahunas agreed heartily, "their names are different, but we know that Kane would not like this door here."
>
> "The door has to be here," Abner explained.

The passage above illustrates a typical conflict between old and new religions. In this case, Abner represents the new and the kahunas the old. Each have their own beliefs which they consider sacred and indisputable. Each side secretly believes that the other is superstitious and stubborn.

The issue in point is the location of the door for the new church. Abner insists that the door should face in the same direction it would in Boston, London or any other western city. The kahunas, on the other hand, have always faced their temples in another direction. But behind their disagreement about the church door lies a deeper conflict. The kahunas profess to worship Abner's God. Yet at heart they are still worshipping their own god and merely calling him by a different name. Abner recognizes this and, in his determination to root out the old religion, he refuses to compromise with the kahunas on even the smallest matters. This confrontation illustrates a basic struggle that reappears throughout the reading selection: the slow and difficult process of changing the way people think and live.

2. Fictional and Historic Characters. Any history book, of course, includes accounts of conflicting ideas as well as stories of battles. This is because it is often disagreements like the one between Abner and the kahunas that start wars. But, unlike the history books, the historical novel introduces fictional characters who participate in the historical events and move among real people or representations of real people from history. For instance, an author writing an historical novel set during the Civil War might have fictional characters who talk with Abraham Lincoln and fight in the battle of Gettysburg. Similarly, an historical novel set during the American Revolution might feature a patriot who crosses the Delaware with George Washington or spreads the alarm with Paul Revere.

Fictional characters serve two important functions in an historical novel. First, they are the means by which an author expresses the impact which historical events had upon the people living through them. Second, fictional characters add a sense of drama to the action. The reader comes to identify with these fictional characters, and this makes the whole sequence of events seem more real and personal. When the reader discovers that people of another age were pretty much like people today, history no longer seems so remote.

In the following passage from *Hawaii*, Abner, the missionary, and Kelolo, who represents the husband of a Hawaiian queen, are walking home in the night when they hear the tramping of footsteps behind them. When they turn around, however, there is no one there. To Kelolo, they are the footsteps of spirits—"night marchers." Abner, however, does not believe in ghosts. Here, again, is the conflict between the old religion and the new. But this time the struggle is being enacted on the more personal level of Kelolo's fear. How does Kelolo's encounter with the night marchers enhance your understanding of this struggle? (The *alii* which Kelolo mentions are Hawaiian kings out of the island's distant past.)

"It is the night marchers!" Kelolo whispered, his lips quivering in horror.

"Who are they?" Abner whispered back, pulling Kelolo's hand from his mouth.

"The great alii of the past." Kelolo trembled. "I am afraid they are coming for me."

"Ridiculous!" Abner grunted, trying to break free. But his captor held him pinioned in the ditch, and he could feel the awful tenseness of the big man's muscles. Kelolo was terrified.

"Why are they coming for you?" Abner whispered.

"No one knows," Kelolo replied, his teeth chattering. "Perhaps because I gave the land of Kane for your church."

...(Kelolo) pressed himself into the ditch, hiding Abner beneath his ample form, and the missionary could hear the man praying, "Oh, Pele, save me now; I am your child, Kelolo, and I do not want to die tonight."

In the above episode, an ancient Hawaiian legend has caught Kelolo in its cold grip of terror. Kelolo had earlier embraced the Christian religion which Abner brought to the islands, but his conversion, it turns out, is only skin-deep. In moments of panic like the one above, he reverts to his former beliefs and appeals to the ancient Hawaiian goddess Pele to save him from the ghostly night marchers.

Outwardly, the island and its inhabitants are promising converts to Christianity. But the traditional beliefs lie just below the surface, barely suppressed, and are called up by basic instincts and emotions that no amount of reasoning can dispel. This is no textbook problem. To Kelolo it is a matter of life and death. Thus, through the characters the author brings home to the reader, better than any explanation could, what it must have felt like to be torn between two cultures in nineteenth-century Hawaii.

3. **Authenticity and Spirit.** Like serious historians, historical novelists have a responsibility to get facts straight and to present an honest picture of the age being described. The characters' clothing, their pastimes, the slang they use, and the fads they embrace should accurately reflect that point in history. So, too, should the architecture, transportation, industries and landscape mirror the time and the place.

Naturally, if an actual battle figures in the course of the novel, you would expect the dates of the battle and the outcome to be accurately reported. More than that, however, the historical novelist also has an obligation to represent the spirit of the time. If, for instance, the soldiers who participated in a battle were dirty, hungry and tired to the bone or if they disliked their leader and disapproved of their country's involvement in that war, then these feelings should be conveyed to the reader. Similarly, in an age marked by revolution, the historical novel should recapture the restlessness, uncertainty and excitement that characterize such an era.

The following passage from *Hawaii* portrays the arrival of a whaling ship at the Hawaiian port of Lahaina in 1824. What impressions do you get of the island from reading this passage?

Then, when it seemed as if the mission were gaining control of Lahaina, the whaler *John Goodpasture*, out of New Bedford, put in with a record tonnage of oil from the recently discovered Off-Japan whaling grounds, and Jerusha's school for girls was suddenly interrupted by the excited cry from the road: "Kelamoku! Too many sailors inside boat! Come right away here!"

Since the *John Goodpasture* was well and favorably known in Lahaina from previous visits, the intelligence created much excitement, especially among the four daughters of Pupali, who spent the next few minutes darting significant glances at one another. Finally, they rose as a team and marched out of class. When Jerusha tried to stop them, the oldest girl explained that their youngest sister felt ill: "Poor Iliki head all come sore," and amid loud giggles they disappeared.

At first Jerusha did not appreciate what had happened, but later when one of her students blurted out, "Kapena aloha Iliki. She swim ship, see kapena," it became obvious that the mission's moral teaching had been outraged, and Jerusha dismissed class. Wrapping a light shawl about her shoulders and placing her poke bonnet firmly on her brown locks, she marched down to the waterfront in time to see the four girls, largely naked, climbing eagerly aboard the *John Goodpasture*, where sailors who had known them before greeted them with cheers.

From the above passage it is clear that Lahaina was both an exotic island and a busy whaling port. Ships came frequently into the harbor, where the sailors received a warm welcome from the native girls. Lately, however, a new element had entered the picture—the missionaries, from whom the girls learned a dialect of pidgin English that was part English and part Hawaiian. So now the waterfront, where the town activity was clearly centered, displayed a missionary or two like Jerusha. Dressed in their heavy New England clothes, they completed a picture of contrasts alongside the heavily muscled sailors and the naked Hawaiian girls. As a result of these different influences that were at work, the reader gets a picture of Lahaina in 1824 as an island that was partly primitive, partly corrupted, and partly civilized, and wholly caught up in the bustle of modern times, whatever and however they turned out to be.

A good historical novel, then, is true to the times in both fact and spirit. An historical novel zeroes in on the challenges that rocked established ways of living and thinking. The fictional characters reflect the thoughts and feelings that were typical of people who lived at that time. The setting is authentic in detail, and the events faithful to history. And when the reader puts the book down, he should have a clearer understanding of the forces that shaped an era.

As you read the following selection from James A. Michener's *Hawaii*, be aware of the many ways in which the clash of old and new is depicted on this Hawaiian island in 1824.

As you read the selection:

- Pay attention to the scene in which Kelolo pleads with Abner to listen to the advice of the kahunas.

- Notice the discussion between Abner and Jerusha after Iliki runs off to the whaling ship.

- Pay special attention to the scene in which Abner informs Malama that the sailors laugh about Hawaii.

- Be aware of the passage in which Malama asks Abner what should be done to control the sailors from whaling ships and the Hawaiian girls.

Hawaii
James A. Michener

III FROM THE FARM OF BITTERNESS

In 1823, when the building of the church was two thirds completed, Kelolo approached Abner one evening with his final plea. "We can still change the entrance," he argued, "Then the evil spirits will be sure to keep away."

"God keeps evil from His churches," Abner replied coldly.

"Will you come with me to the grounds?" Kelolo begged.

"Everything has been arranged," Abner snapped.

"I want to show you a simple way . . ." Kelolo began.

"No!" Abner cried.

"Please," the tall chief insisted. "There is something you must know."

Against his better judgment, Abner threw down his pen and grudgingly walked in the night air to the church grounds, where a group of elderly men sat on their haunches, studying his church. "What are they doing?" Abner asked.

"They are my praying kahunas," Kelolo explained.

"No!" Abner protested, drawing back. "I do not want to argue with kahunas about a church of the Lord."

"These men love the Lord," Kelolo insisted. "Ask them. They know the catechism. They want the church to be built strong."

"Kelolo," Abner explained patiently, drawing near to the solemn kahunas, "I understand perfectly that in the old days these kahunas accomplished much that was good. But God does not require kahunas."

"Makua Hale," Kelolo pleaded, "we have come to you as friends who love this church. Please do not keep the door where it is. Every kahuna knows that that is wrong for the spirits of this location."

"God is the supreme spirit!" Abner argued, but since the night was pleasant, with a pale crescent moon in the west and occasional clouds sweeping in from the roads, he sat with the kahunas and talked with them about religion. He was surprised at how much of the Bible they knew, and at the skill with which they could accommodate it to their ancient beliefs. One old man explained, "We believe you are correct in what you say, Makua Hale. There is only one God, and we used to call Him Kane. There is a Holy Ghost, and we called Him Ku. There is Jesus Christ, and He is Lono. And there is the king of the underworld, and he is Kanaloa."

"God is not Kane," Abner reasoned, but the kahunas merely listened, and when it came time for them to speak they said, "Now when Kane, that is God, wishes a church to be built, he supervises it. He always did when we built our temples."

"God does not personally supervise the building of this church," Abner explained.

"Kane did."

"But God is not Kane," Abner patiently repeated.

The men nodded sagely and continued: "Now, since Kane is concerned about this church, and since we have always loved Kane, we thought it proper to advise you that this door . . ."

"The door will be where it now is," Abner explained, "because that is where the door to a church has always been. In Boston the door would be here. In London it would be here."

"But in Lahaina, Kane would not like it to be here," the kahunas argued.

"Kane is not God," Abner stubbornly repeated.

"We understand, Makua Hale," the kahunas politely agreed, "but since God and Kane are the same idea . . ."

"No," Abner insisted, "God and Kane are not the same."

"Of course," the kahunas agreed heartily, "their names are different, but we know that Kane would not like this door here."

"The door has to be here," Abner explained.

"If it is, Kane will destroy the church," the kahunas said sorrowfully.

"God does not go about destroying his own churches," Abner assured the men.

"But we know that Kane does, if they are built wrong, and since Kane and God mean the same thing . . ."

The solemn kahunas never lost their tempers with the stubborn little stranger who did not quite understand religion, so far as they could judge, and Abner had learned not to lose his, so the argument about the door lasted for several hours, until the moon had vanished from the west and only low dark clouds scudded across the mysterious and silent sky. With nothing agreed, but with the kahunas feeling very sorry for their misguided friend who insisted upon building a doomed church for Kane, the meeting broke up and Kelolo said, "After I bid the kahunas good night I will walk back home with you."

"I can find my way alone," Abner assured him.

"On a night like this . . ." Kelolo said speculatively, looking at the low clouds over the coconut palms, "it would be better, perhaps . . ." And he bade the kahunas a hasty farewell so that he could hurry down the dusty road and overtake the missionary, but they had progressed only a few hundred yards when Abner heard the kahunas walking behind them, and he said, "I don't want to argue with them any more," but when Kelolo turned to tell the kahunas so, he saw nothing. There were no kahunas. There were no walking men. There was only an ominous echo under the scudding

BEST-SELLING CHAPTERS

clouds, and suddenly Kelolo grabbed Abner in a vise of death and muttered in horror, "It is the night marchers! Oh, God! We are lost!" And before Abner could protest, Kelolo had caught him about the waist and had swept him precipitately over a hedge and thrown him into a ditch, where foul water drenched him. When he tried to rise, Kelolo's mighty arm pinned him to the wet earth, and he could feel that the huge alii was trembling in terror.

"What is it?" Abner sputtered, but Kelolo's giant hand clasped his mouth, accidentally forcing grass and mud into his lips.

"It is the night marchers!" Kelolo whispered, his lips quivering in horror.

"Who are they?" Abner whispered back, pulling Kelolo's hand from his mouth.

"The great alii of the past." Kelolo trembled. "I am afraid they are coming for me."

"Ridiculous!" Abner grunted, trying to break free. But his captor held him pinioned in the ditch, and he could feel the awful tenseness of the big man's muscles. Kelolo was terrified.

"Why are they coming for you?" Abner whispered.

"No one knows," Kelolo replied, his teeth chattering. "Perhaps because I gave the land of Kane for your church."

With the greatest circumspection he lifted his huge head until it was even with the top of the hedge, looked for a moment up the dark path, and shuddered. "They are marching toward us!" he gasped. "Oh, Makua Hale, pray to your god for me. Pray! Pray!"

"Kelolo!" Abner grunted, smothered by the pressure on his chest. "There is nothing out there. When alii die they remain dead."

"They are marching," Kelolo whispered. And in the silence of the night, with only wind rustling through dead palm leaves, there was indeed a sound of feet. "I can see them coming past the church," Kelolo reported. "They carry torches and feathered staves. They wear their golden robes and feather helmets. Makua Hale, they are coming for me."

The giant alii pressed himself into the ditch, hiding Abner beneath his ample form, and the missionary could hear the man praying, "Oh, Pele, save me now; I am your child, Kelolo, and I do not want to die tonight."

The sound grew louder and Kelolo engaged in violent actions, almost smothering Abner, who mumbled, "What are you doing?"

"Undressing!" Kelolo grunted. "You cannot speak to the gods with clothes on." When he was completely naked he resumed praying in an agitated voice, but suddenly he grew calm and Abner heard him say, "The little man I am hiding is Makua Hale. He is a good man and he brings learning to my people. He doesn't know enough to throw off his clothes, so please excuse him." There was a long silence, after which Kelolo said, "I know the little man preaches against you, Woman of Whiteness, but even so he is a good man." There was another protracted silence, and then the sound of imminent feet, and Kelolo trembled as if a great wind tormented him and then he spoke. "Thank you, Pele, for having told the marchers I am your child."

The wind subsided. Only fitful sounds came from the topmost crowns of the coconut palms, and there was no echo of marching feet. It could have been the kahunas going home, Abner thought. It could have been a group of dogs. Or wind along the dusty footpath. Now there was no sound; the low scudding clouds were gone, and the stars shone.

"What was it?" Abner asked, as he wiped the mud from his mouth.

"They were marching to take me away," Kelolo explained.

"Whom were you speaking to?" Abner inquired, spitting the gravel from his teeth.

"Pele. Didn't you hear her tell the marchers that we were her children?"

Abner did not reply. He brushed the sand from his clothes and wondered how he would get the muddy portions of his clothing cleaned, and he was brushing his knees when Kelolo grabbed him and spun him around, demanding, "You did hear Pele, didn't you? When she protected you?"

"Did she mention my name?" Abner asked quietly.

"You heard her!" Kelolo cried. "Makua Hale, it is a very good sign when Pele protects a man. It means . . ." But his joy at having been saved from the revengeful night marchers was so great that he could not express his gratitude, either for her aid in saving him or for her unprecedented benevolence in protecting the little missionary. "You are my brother," Kelolo said passionately. "Now you see that it would have been foolish for me to have torn down my platform to the gods. Suppose Pele had not come to help us tonight!"

"Did you see the night marchers?" Abner pressed.

"I saw them," Kelolo replied.

"Did you see Pele?" the missionary continued.

"I often see her," Kelolo assured him. Then in a burst of passion he caught Abner by the hands and pleaded: "It is for these reasons, Makua Hale, that I beg you not to keep the door where it is."

"That door . . ." Abner began. But he did not bother to finish his sentence, and when he reached home and Jerusha cried,"Abner, what have you been doing?" he replied simply, "It was dark and I fell in a ditch." And the door was built where he intended.

Then, when it seemed as if the mission were gaining control of Lahaina, the whaler *John Goodpasture*, out of New Bedford, put in with a record tonnage of oil from the recently discovered Off-Japan whaling grounds, and Jerusha's school for girls was suddenly interrupted by the excited cry from the road: "Kelamoku! Too many sailors inside boat! Come right away here!"

Since the *John Goodpasture* was well and favorably known in Lahaina from previous visits, the intelligence created much excitement, especially among the four daughters of Pupali, who spent the next few minutes darting significant glances at one another. Finally, they rose as a team and marched out of class. When Jerusha tried to stop them, the oldest girl explained that their youngest sister felt ill: "Poor Iliki head all come sore," and amid loud giggles they disappeared.

At first Jerusha did not appreciate what had happened, but later when one of her students blurted out, "Kapena aloha Iliki. She swim ship, see kapena," it became obvious that the mission's moral teaching had been outraged, and Jerusha dismissed class. Wrapping a light shawl about her shoulders and placing her poke bonnet firmly on her brown locks, she marched down to the waterfront in time to see the four girls, largely naked, climbing eagerly aboard the *John Goodpasture*, where sailors who had known them before greeted them with cheers.

Running up to an elderly American sailor who was scrimshawing a whalebone beside Kamehameha's old brick palace, she cried, "Row me out to that boat!" But the sailor continued carving the whalebone and drawled, "Ma'am, it's best if you don't fight the laws of nature."

"But Iliki is only a child!" Jerusha protested.

"First law of the sea, ma'am. If they're big enough, they're old enough," and he looked into the channel, where the girls' pleased squeals filled the air.

Appalled by this indifference, Jerusha ran over to an old Hawaiian woman who sat on a rock guarding the four mission dresses which the girls had discarded. "Aunty Mele," Jerusha pleaded, "how can we get those girls back?"

"You stop one time. Bimeby ship go," Aunty Mele assured her. "Wahine come back, same like always."

In frustration, Jerusha grabbed at the besmirched mission dresses, as if to take them home with her, away from the contaminated waterfront, but Aunty Mele held onto them grimly, saying, "Hale Wahine! Bimeby wahine come back, I make ready dress for dem." And like the good friend she was, she remained on the rock, holding the girls' apparel until such time as they might need it once more for resumption of their missionary lessons.

That night it was a gloomy mission household that reviewed the day's defeats. "I cannot understand these girls," Jerusha wept. "We give them the best of everything. Iliki in particular knows what good and evil are. Yet she runs off to the whaling ship."

"I brought the matter up with Malama," Abner reported in deep confusion, "and she said merely, 'The girl is not an alii. She can go to the ships if she likes.' So I asked Malama, 'Then why were you so angry when the three sailors tried to take Noelani to their ship?' And Malama replied, 'Noelani is kapu alii.' As if that explained everything."

"Abner, I shudder to think of the evil that flourishes in Lahaina," Jerusha replied. "When I left the waterfront, where nobody would do anything, I went into the town to ask for help, and at Murphy's grog shop I heard a concertina. And girls laughing. And I tried to go in to stop whatever was happening, and a man said, 'Don't go in there, Mrs. Hale. The girls have no clothes on. They never do when the whalers are in port.' Abner! What is happening to this town?"

"For some time I have known it to be the modern Sodom and Gomorrah."

"What are we going to do about it?"

"I haven't decided," he replied.

"Well, I have," Jerusha said firmly. And that very night she marched down to Malama's palace and said in her able Hawaiian, "Alii Nui, we must stop the girls from going out to the whaling ships."

"Why?" Malama asked. "The girls go because they want to. No harm is done."

"But Iliki is a good girl," Jerusha insisted.

"What is a good girl?" Malama asked.

"Girls who do not swim out to ships," Jerusha replied simply.

"I think you missionaries want to stop all fun," Malama countered.

"Iliki is not engaging in fun," Jerusha argued. "She is engaging in death." And this Malama knew to be true.

"But she has always gone out to the ships," she said sadly.

"Iliki has an immortal soul," Jerusha said firmly. "Exactly as you and I."

"You mean to claim that Iliki . . . wahine i Pupali . . . like you or me?"

"Exactly like you, Malama. Exactly like me."

"I cannot believe it," Malama said. "She has always gone to the ships."

"It is our job to stop her. To stop all the girls."

Malama would do nothing that night, but on the next day she assembled the alii then in residence, and Reverend and Mrs. Hale presented their arguments, with Jerusha pleading: "You can tell a good town by the way it protects its babies and young girls. You can tell a good alii by the way in which he protects women. You are not good alii if you permit your own daughters to go out to the ships. In London the good alii try to stop such things. In Boston, too."

Kelolo contradicted this assertion by pointing out: "Kekau-ike-a-ole sailed on a whaler and he got to both London and Boston and he has often told us of how there were special houses filled with girls. Everywhere he went there were such houses."

"But the good alii in all cities try to control this vice," Jerusha argued bitterly.

It was Abner, however, who delivered the aching blow. "Do you know what happens if you alii of Lahaina permit your girls to be debauched in this way?" he asked ominously.

"What happens, Makua Hale?" Malama asked, for she trusted him.

"When the ships sail back home, the men laugh at Hawaii."

There was a long silence as this ugly accusation was digested, for the alii of Hawaii were proud people, desperately hungry for the world's approval. Finally, Malama asked cautiously, "Would the alii of Boston allow their girls to swim out to a Hawaiian ship?"

"Of course not," Kelolo snapped. "The water is too cold."

There was no laughter, for this was an honest observation, and Abner quickly added, "Kelolo is correct. The water in Boston is not so sweet and warm as here, but even if it were, no girls would be allowed to swim out to Hawaiian ships. The alii of Boston would be ashamed if that happened."

Malama asked quietly, "Do you think the sailors laugh at us, Makua Hale?"

"I know they do, Malama. Do you remember the whaler *Carthaginian* when it was here? I was aboard the *Carthaginian* on the whaling grounds, and the sailors were laughing about Honolulu."

"Ah, but Honolulu is known to be an evil place," Malama admitted. "That is why I will not live there. That's why the king keeps his capital here at Lahaina."

"And they laughed at Lahaina," Abner insisted.

"That is bad," Malama frowned. After a while she asked, "What should we do?"

Abner replied, "You should build a fort, by the roads, and each night at sunset a drum should beat, and any sailor who is ashore should then be arrested and kept in the fort till morning. And any girl who swims out to ships should be put in jail, too."

"Such laws are too harsh," Malama said, and she dismissed the meeting, but when the other alii had gone she took Jerusha aside and asked querulously, "Do you think the sailors laugh at us, because of the girls?"

"I laugh at you!" Jerusha said firmly. "To think of people debauching their own daughters!"

"But they are not alii," Malama insisted.

"You are the conscience of the people," Jerusha replied.

That night the Hales argued long as to whether the daughters of Pupali should be admitted back into the mission school, and Abner was for dismissing them permanently, but Jerusha held that they should be given another chance, and when the *John Goodpasture* left the roads, the four delinquent girls, dressed neatly in new dresses, came penitently back. The more Jerusha preached to them about the miserableness of their sin, the more heartily they agreed. But when, some weeks later, a child heralded the arrival of the whaler *Vashti* with the exciting cry, "*Vashti* iron hook fall now, plenty kelamoku," the four girls bolted again, and that night Abner insisted that the older three at least be expelled. They were, and since these were the years when whalers came to Lahaina with increasing frequency—seventeen were to arrive in 1824—the three older daughters of Pupali did a good business. They no longer had to go out to ships, for they became the dancers at Murphy's grog shop and kept little rooms aft of the small dance floor, where they were permitted to keep half of the coins they earned.

Iliki, the fairest of the daughters, was allowed to stay in the mission school, and under Jerusha's most careful guidance grew to understand the Bible and to forswear whaling ships. She was slim for a Hawaiian girl, with very long hair and flashing eyes. When she smiled, her handsome white teeth illuminated her face, and Jerusha could appreciate why it was that men wanted her. "When she is twenty," Jerusha said, "we will marry her to some Christian Hawaiian, and you mark my words, Abner, she'll be the best wife in the islands."

When Jerusha spoke thus, Abner was not listening, for he had erected for himself, out of rough ends of timber gathered here and there—for nothing in Lahaina was more precious than wood—a small table upon which papers were spread in seven or eight neat piles, each with a sea shell placed on it to preserve order. For he had begun, in co-operation with the other missionaries throughout the islands, the work which would be his most lasting contribution to Hawaii. He was translating the Bible into Hawaiian and sending his pages as they were finished to the printer in Honolulu, where they were being published a little at a time.

Nothing that Abner applied himself to in these years gave him greater pleasure, for he kept before him his Greek and Hebrew texts, Cornelius Schrevelius' *Greek-Latin Lexicon*, plus those versions of the Bible he had studied at Yale. He was happy, like a plowman who turns furrows in a field without stones, or a fisherman who sets his nets for known returns.

Usually he worked with Keoki, laboring over every passage with the most minute attention, and as the years passed he reached those two books of the Bible which he cherished most. The first was Proverbs, which seemed to him a distillation of all the knowledge man could hope to know. It was especially appropriate for Hawaii, since its crystallizations were in simple language, easily understood and long remembered, and when he came to the glorious closing pages in which King Lemuel describes the ideal woman, his pen truly flew along the ruled pages, for it seemed to him that Lemuel spoke specifically of Jerusha Bromley: "Who can find a virtuous woman? For her price is far above rubies. The heart of her husband doth safely trust in her, so that he shall have no need of spoil. . . . She is like the merchants' ships; she bringeth her food from afar. . . . She stretcheth out her hand to the poor; yea, she reacheth forth her hands to the needy. . . . Strength and honor are her clothing; . . . Many daughters have done virtuously, but thou excellest them all."

When he finished translating Proverbs he left the last pages exposed, so that Jerusha might read them, and he was disappointed that she did not take notice of them, for she had learned not to interfere with his Biblical studies; so at last he was forced to hand her the pages of King Lemuel's conclusions, and she read them quietly, saying only, "A woman would do well to mark those pages." He was constrained to cry, "They were written about you, Jerusha!" but he said nothing, and put them along with the rest and forwarded them to Honolulu.

Unit 4

Hawaii

- Comprehension Questions
- The Historical Novel
- Discussion Guides
- Writing Exercise

COMPREHENSION QUESTIONS

For each of the following statements and questions, select the option containing the most complete or most accurate answer.

1. Kelolo and the kahunas are upset about
(a) ☐ a. the size of the proposed church.
   ☐ b. the location of the church door.
   ☐ c. who will be allowed to enter the church.
   ☐ d. their role in the new church.

2. Kelolo and the kahunas believe that Abner's religion is
(f) ☐ a. the one, true religion.
   ☐ b. false and corrupt.
   ☐ c. for white men only.
   ☐ d. a lot like their own.

3. The tone of the argument between Abner and the kahunas is
(i) ☐ a. patient but unyielding.
   ☐ b. wild and frenzied.
   ☐ c. angry and bitter.
   ☐ d. congenial and harmonious.

4. The low, dark clouds scudding across the night sky as Kelolo and Abner
(i) walk home create an atmosphere that is
   ☐ a. sad and depressing.
   ☐ b. pleasant and inviting.
   ☐ c. ominous and mysterious.
   ☐ d. wistful and nostalgic.

5. As they walk home, Abner and Kelolo hear footsteps behind them
(a) which Kelolo says belong to
   ☐ a. the kahunas.
   ☐ b. Hawaiian kings of the past.
   ☐ c. robbers.
   ☐ d. ancient Hawaiian gods.

6. Which of the following best defines *circumspection* as used in, "With the
(l) greatest *circumspection* he lifted his huge head until it was even with the top of the hedge, looked for a moment up the dark path, and shuddered"?
   ☐ a. Speed   ☐ c. Prudence
   ☐ b. Ease   ☐ d. Relief

7. Kelolo tells Abner that
(b) □ a. Pele spoke to him.
     □ b. he saw Pele stop the marchers.
     □ c. only he can hear Pele.
     □ d. he has never seen Pele.

8. The footsteps which Abner and Kelolo both heard as they walked
(d) home in the night
     □ a. were made by the night marchers.
     □ b. were figments of their imaginations.
     □ c. were made by the kuhunas.
     □ d. were never explained.

9. Kelolo believes that he and Abner were saved from the night marchers
(d) by Pele. This incident served to reinforce Kelolo's belief in
     □ a. the Christian God.   □ c. magic.
     □ b. Hawaiian gods.   □ d. the Holy Ghost.

10. Abner's decision to build the church according to his original plans
 (j) suggests that he is
     □ a. stubborn.   □ c. open-minded.
     □ b. smarter than the kahunas. □ d. very religious.

11. Abner's treatment of the native Hawaiians suggests that he regards
(h) them as
     □ a. children.   □ c. rivals.
     □ b. equals.   □ d. brothers.

12. Jerusha's school for the native girls is disrupted by
(b) □ a. the entrance of Malama.
     □ b. a tropical storm.
     □ c. the arrival of a whaling ship.
     □ d. the footsteps of the night marchers.

13. Jerusha's visits to the docks, to Murphy's grog shop, and finally to
 (j) Malama's palace to end the prostitution of Hawaiian girls emphasize
     this character's
     □ a. fearless determination.   □ c. timid personality.
     □ b. moral cowardice.   □ d. uncertain loyalties.

14. Abner Hale calls Lahaina "the modern Sodom and Gomorrah." This
(k) Biblical allusion is used to stress the island's
☐ a. popularity.   ☐ c. godliness.
☐ b. antiquity.   ☐ d. sinfulness.

15. When the missionaries try to convince Malama to outlaw the prosti-
(h) tution of Hawaiian girls, their most potent argument centers on
☐ a. the risk of disease.
☐ b. the fact that foreigners laugh at Hawaii.
☐ c. the unhappy lives of half-breed children.
☐ d. the fear of punishment after death.

16. Malama's leadership qualities are probably best illustrated by
(g) ☐ a. her belief that she is better than those she rules.
☐ b. her indifference to the health of Hawaiian girls.
☐ c. her concern for Hawaii's image among nations.
☐ d. her tolerance of Murphy's grog shop.

17. The daughters of Pupali continue to swim out to the whaling ships
(e) despite Jerusha's stern lectures forbidding it. This shows that
☐ a. it is hard to change old customs overnight.
☐ b. Jerusha was not well-liked by the Hawaiians.
☐ c. the daughters of Pupali were extremely wicked.
☐ d. the missionaries' labors had achieved nothing.

18. Abner's decision to expel Iliki's three sisters from the missionary school
(g) was
☐ a. vindictive.   ☐ c. predictable.
☐ b. weak.   ☐ d. irrational.

19. The following two similes are used to describe how Abner feels while
(k) translating the Bible into Hawaiian: "...like a plowman who turns
furrows in a field without stones, or a fisherman who sets his nets for
known returns." This figurative language is used to express Abner's
☐ a. weariness at his task.   ☐ c. discouragement at his task.
☐ b. satisfaction in his task.   ☐ d. indifference to his task.

20. Which of the following best defines *distillation* as used in, "The first
(l) was Proverbs, which seemed to him a *distillation* of all the knowledge
man could hope to know"?
☐ a. A history   ☐ c. The essence
☐ b. A litany   ☐ d. The source

21. Abner feels that the Biblical book of Proverbs is especially appropriate
(c) for the Hawaiians because of its
- a. simplicity.
- c. predictions.
- b. warnings.
- d. frankness.

22. Abner's behavior as he translates King Lemuel's description of the ideal
(j) woman indicates that he
- a. is overproud.
- b. is jealous of Jerusha.
- c. approves of Malama's leadership.
- d. admires Jerusha.

23. The arrival of missionaries and whaling ships in Hawaii resulted in a
(e) - a. Hawaiian civil war.
- b. native revolt against the newcomers.
- c. native revolt against the Hawaiian royalty.
- d. gradual exchange of old ways for new.

24. In addition to bringing Christianity to the islands, the missionaries also
(c) brought
- a. industrialization.
- c. the wisdom of the Far East.
- b. western civilization.
- d. scientific farming methods.

25. The building of a church, the enactment of laws, the education of
(f) Hawaiian children and the translation of the Bible into Hawaiian indicate
that the missionaries were concerned with
- a. making lasting changes.
- b. taking over the islands.
- c. learning Hawaiian culture.
- d. displaying their power over the Hawaiians.

Comprehension Skills: a—isolating details; b—recalling specific facts; c—retaining concepts; d—organizing facts; e—understanding the main idea; f—drawing a conclusion; g—making a judgment; h—making an inference; i—recognizing tone; j—understanding characters; k—appreciation of literary forms; l—knowledge of word meanings.

THE HISTORICAL NOVEL

Practice Exercise A

Against his better judgment, Abner threw down his pen and grudgingly walked in the night air to the church grounds, where a group of elderly men sat on their haunches, studying his church. "What are they doing?" Abner asked.

"They are my praying kahunas," Kelolo explained.

"No!" Abner protested, drawing back. "I do not want to argue with kahunas about a church of the Lord."

"These men love the Lord," Kelolo insisted. "Ask them. They know the catechism. They want the church to be built strong."

"Kelolo," Abner explained patiently, drawing near to the solemn kahunas, "I understand perfectly that in the old days these kahunas accomplished much that was good. But God does not require kahunas."

"Makua Hale," Kelolo pleaded, "we have come to you as friends who love this church. Please do not keep the door where it is. Every kahuna knows that that is wrong for the spirits of this location."

"God is the supreme spirit!" Abner argued . . . .

1. Abner doesn't want to discuss the new church with the kahunas because
   ☐ a. he is afraid of them.
   ☐ b. they represent the "old ways."
   ☐ c. they don't really know the catechism.
   ☐ d. they want to sabotage his church.

2. On the lines provided, copy two statements made by Abner that best point to the changing role of the kahunas in the island's religious affairs.

   _____

   _____

   _____

   _____

   _____

Practice Exercise B

That night it was a gloomy mission household that reviewed the day's defeats. "I cannot understand these girls," Jerusha wept. "We give them the best of everything. Iliki in particular knows what good and evil are. Yet she runs off to the whaling ship."

"I brought the matter up with Malama," Abner reported in deep confusion," and she said merely, 'The girl is not an alii. She can go to the ships if she likes.' So I asked Malama, 'Then why were you so angry when the three sailors tried to take Noelani to their ship?' And Malama replied, 'Noelani is kapu alii.' As if that explained everything."

1. The passage above shows that
   □ a. Malama has no sense of right and wrong.
   □ b. Hawaiian society is without law and structure.
   □ c. Abner and Jerusha are still baffled by Hawaiian customs.
   □ d. Abner and Jerusha are, by custom, not allowed to argue with Hawaiian royalty.

2. On the lines provided, write the two sentences that explain the social difference between Iliki and Noelani.

_____

_____

_____

_____

Practice Exercise C

Malama would do nothing that night, but on the next day she assembled the alii then in residence, and Reverend and Mrs. Hale presented their arguments, with Jerusha pleading: "You can tell a good town by the way it protects its babies and young girls. You can tell a good alii by the way in which he protects women .... In London the good alii try to stop such things. In Boston, too ...."

It was Abner, however, who delivered the aching blow. "Do you know what happens if you alii of Lahaina permit your girls to be debauched in this way?" he asked ominously.

"What happens, Makua Hale?" Malama asked, for she trusted him.

"When the ships sail back home, the men laugh at Hawaii."

There was a long silence as this ugly accusation was digested, for the alii of Hawaii were proud people, desperately hungry for the world's approval.

1. From the passage above it is clear that the Hawaiian royalty at this time were gravely concerned with
   □ a. the conversion of the islands to Christianity.
   □ b. the morality of their young people.
   □ c. the economic well-being of the islands.
   □ d. their emerging image as a nation among nations.

2. On the lines provided, copy the sentence which indicates a concern of the Hawaiian royalty at this time.

   _____

   _____

   _____

   _____

   _____

Practice Exercise D

"And they laughed at Lahaina," Abner insisted.

"That is bad," Malama frowned. After a while she asked, "What should we do?"

Abner replied, "You should build a fort, by the roads, and each night at sunset a drum should beat, and any sailor who is ashore should then be arrested and kept in the fort till morning. And any girl who swims out to ships should be put in jail, too."

"Such laws are too harsh," Malama said, and she dismissed the meeting, but when the other alii had gone she took Jerusha aside and asked querulously, "Do you think the sailors laugh at us, because of the girls?"

"I laugh at you!" Jerusha said firmly. "To think of people debauching their own daughters!"

"But they are not alii," Malama insisted.

"You are the conscience of the people," Jerusha replied.

1. This passage shows that Malama
   □ a. is undecided about what to do.
   □ b. has decided to reject the methods of white people.
   □ c. has decided that some girls may swim to the ships but not others.
   □ d. is angry with Jerusha because of her interference.

2. On the lines provided, write the sentence which shows that Malama still feels that certain conduct is all right for some people but not for others.

_____

_____

DISCUSSION GUIDES

Analyzing the Historical Novel

1. In one sense, the fictional characters of an historical novel are both imaginary and real. In an introductory note to *Hawaii*, the author states that the characters which you met in your reading selection are imaginary. In what respects, however, are they also real? What actions, emotions, or traits of character could also have been true of their historical counterparts?

2. In the selection which you have just read, which detail, scene or incident do you think best expresses the spirit of Hawaii in 1824? Explain.

3. An historical novel, as you have learned, often deals with the clash of two forces, one dying out and the other being born. These forces might be opposing armies, cultures, lifestyles, philosophies or social movements. If at some future date an author were to write an historical novel set in your own lifetime, what conflict might an author choose as representative of this period? Why?

Interpreting the Selection

4. Both Abner and the kahunas have definite ideas about where the door of the new church should be located. Unfortunately, their opinions do not coincide. Do you find this scene humorous in any way? Explain.

5. When Malama asks, "What is a good girl?" Jerusha replies simply, "Girls who do not swim out to ships." Why may this definition have been confusing and unsatisfactory to Malama?

6. Jerusha told Malama, "You are the conscience of the people." What did she mean by this? In what ways do we expect *our* leaders to be the conscience of the people?

7. Were missionaries like Abner and Jerusha Hale wrong in trying to convert the Hawaiians and change their ways of living and worshipping? Explain your opinion.

8. Abner and Jerusha were bitterly disappointed when the young girl Iliki swam out to the whaling ship in spite of being taught otherwise. What do you think of their reaction to this event?

Analyzing the Author's Technique

9. Why doesn't the author reveal who or what made the sounds that both Abner and Kelolo heard and that Kelolo insisted were the night marchers?

10. This novel is written from the point of view of an omniscient author— that is, the attitudes and feelings of all the characters are explained by a person who can see and understand everything that is going on from all sides. How does this technique give the reader a balanced view of the missionaries and the Hawaiians? How might the story be different if it were written solely from the point of view of Abner Hale?

WRITING EXERCISE

The American Wild West in the last half of the nineteenth century attracted several different groups of people, who were usually at odds with one another. Among these groups were the cowboys who drove cattle across the range, the settlers who wanted to fence in the open range, the railroad barons who were buying up huge areas of land and laying tracks across it, and the Indians to whom all these groups represented a threat to their survival.

This page and the next contain a partially completed outline for an historical novel set during this period. Fill in the blanks using your knowledge of the elements of an historical novel plus your own imagination. Choose *any* *two* of the above groups as the basis for your outline—that is, cowboys versus Indians, or railroad barons versus Indians, and so on.

The American West in the Last Half of the Nineteenth Century

I. The clash of cultures
   A. Two groups are in conflict with each other. (Name them.)

   1. _____

   2. _____

   B. Each has different feelings about the use or ownership of land.
      1. The first group feels that:

      _____

      _____

      2. The second group believes:

      _____

      _____

C. A confrontation develops. The two groups come to blows over a specific incident. That incident is:

_____

_____

II. The characters (These may be real or imaginary.)
   A. Two people from group 1 are (name and brief description):

     1. _____

     2. _____

   B. Two people from group 2 are (name and brief description):

     1. _____

     2. _____

   C. They all have one thing in common:

_____

_____

III. The setting and spirit of the time
   A. The action takes place in (name town and describe it):

_____

_____

   B. The atmosphere of this setting is:

_____

_____

   C. As a result of the conflict between these two groups and the natural march of progress, the place is changing (describe the changes):

_____

_____

Unit 5
Analyzing Conflict

Deliverance

Introduction

Most of us will never have to prove ourselves in a life and death conflict. We amble through life using our bodies at about half capacity and can only speculate about how we would perform in a crisis situation. It's probably just as well because who can predict whether one will rise to the occasion or fall apart?

In James Dickey's novel, *Deliverance*, four middle-aged men embark on a whitewater canoe trip down a wild river in North Georgia. It should have been no more than a memorable adventure. However, before the weekend is over, a life and death conflict pitting man against man, man against nature, and man against himself will mercilessly expose the inner faces of these men. One of them will die, one will be the victim of a homosexual assault, and two of them will become killers. The survivors, however, will come away with a new awareness of their own mortality, a clearer understanding of their limits and capabilities, and a sobering insight into the dark forces which lurk deep within mankind and nature.

It's interesting to speculate about how we would survive if a nuclear holocaust suddenly blasted us back into the Stone Age. Lewis Medlock was the kind of man who not only anticipated such a calamity, he was fully prepared for it. He was into weight-lifting, bow hunting and canoeing, each of which he pursued with the enthusiasm of a fanatic. His friend Ed Gentry, who regarded Lewis with a mixture of good-natured tolerance and open admiration, remarks that he has never seen such a male body in his life. "I could not even begin to conceive how many sit-ups and leg raises—and how much dieting—had gone into bringing [those veins and muscles] into view."

It is Lewis who organizes their ill-fated canoe trip down the wild Cahulawassee River. A dam which is already under construction will submerge the entire valley by the following spring. "But right now it's wild," declares Lewis with characteristic zest, "and I *mean* wild; it looks like something up in Alaska." Besides Ed, Lewis cajoles Bobby Trippe and Drew Ballinger into coming along. Bobby, who is pleasantly cynical, notes that this kind of urge "gets hold of middle class householders every once in a while. But most of them just lie down until the feeling passes." Mild-mannered Drew points out that they have no business up in those mountains where "we don't really know what we're getting into." But when Lewis casually asks each of them how they had planned to spend the afternoon, they contemplate the sales meetings, mutual funds and ad agency layouts that consume their energies. In this light, the river comes to symbolize a kind of deliverance from the humdrum tedium of their middle-class lives.

The outing begins innocently enough. They go skinny dipping in the river, Drew strums his guitar by the campfire, and Ed tracks a deer early the next morning and just misses it with his bow and arrow.

But soon the nightmare starts. Ed and Bobby, in one canoe, pull off the river for a break and find themselves in the clutches of two armed hillbillies. While one of them holds the gun, the other rapes Bobby. Just as it is Ed's turn, an arrow zings out of nowhere and lodges in the armed man's chest, killing him. His companion runs into the woods as Ed grabs the rifle and Lewis steps into the clearing, his bow in hand. Faced with a dead body and involvement in a murder, Drew is all for going to the police. The other three, however, have their doubts about the justice they would receive from a local jury packed with the dead man's relatives. Over Drew's objections, the body is lugged into the woods and buried. As Lewis points out, soon the whole area will be hundreds of feet underwater, and something buried *under* a lake is about as buried as it can get.

There is no way out except downriver, so the trip proceeds. But their exuberance has given way to a grim desire to simply get off the river and back home. The selection in this unit begins as they are heading toward Aintree, some twenty miles downriver, where their car is waiting. They are unaware that the dead man's companion is stalking them. Lewis is in his glory, calling upon his superbly conditioned body and disciplined mind to deliver his friends to safety. But in the course of the trip, Lewis is seriously injured and the burden of leadership falls to Ed, a very average man who is challenged to the limits of his physical and mental endurance.

Analyzing Conflict

When two rival gangs have a brawl, that's conflict. When a blizzard threatens the life of a mountain climber, that's conflict, too. When a spirited young woman wants to lead a life that is different from that of most other young women, she will probably come into conflict with some elements of society that do not approve of her. And when a politician is torn between representing the will of the people and gratifying a lust for power, he will probably experience an inner conflict until the problem is resolved.

Conflict, therefore, is not just a fight to the death between good guys and bad guys. It is also the day-to-day business of making choices, coping with problems, and accepting—or defying—the consequences of our actions. It is the many ways of dealing with the big and little problems that confront us every day.

Discussing problems and how we deal with them is the very basis of story-telling. At the heart of storytelling is conflict. Conflict is the essence of fiction. It creates plot. If the families of Romeo and Juliet had been friends instead of enemies, there would have been no reason for the young lovers to hide their feelings, elope and die; and there would have been no reason to write a play about them either because without the element of conflict there would be no suspense and no interest in the story.

"There are eight million stories in the Naked City," a popular television show used to tell us. This was simply a way of saying that there is conflict, and thus a story, in the lives of each of New York City's eight million people—which is quite true. There are countless stories that arise from the conflicts in which people become involved. In the context of fiction, however, the conflicts we encounter can usually be identified as one of four kinds: conflict with other people, conflict with nature, conflict with society, and internal conflict (a battle with the inner self).

1. **Conflict with Other People.** Conflict that pits one person against another is interesting and exciting. This is why we like to watch a good fight or a football game, and this is why we devour page after page of a book until we find out if Sherlock Holmes can get the best of the evil Dr. Moriarity.

But finding out who will win is only half the interest created by conflict. We also want to know how a character reacts to the stress of conflict. The quarterback who is Mr. Nice Guy in the locker room becomes a clawing animal on the playing field. The Congresswoman who is all charm and friendliness at lunch becomes cold steel in the committee room. These kinds of changes make good reading, whether in a newspaper or in a good book, because we ask ourselves, "How would I act under the same circumstances?" We share feelings and identify with the person experiencing the conflict.

The following passage from *Deliverance* illustrates conflict with people. A group of men are on a wilderness canoe trip on an isolated river. The adventure has become a nightmare. They have been molested by two strangers and are forced to kill one of them. One of the canoeists has been killed in revenge. Now, two of the adventurers, Bobby and Ed, find they must try to kill the second stranger who is stalking them. What conflict emerges in this passage, and what do you learn about Bobby and Ed from their reactions to it?

> [Bobby] "What you mean is . . ."
> [Ed] "What I mean is like they say in the movies, especially on Saturday afternoon. It's either him or us. We've killed a man. So has he. Whoever gets out depends on who kills who. It's just that simple."
> "Well," he said, "all right. I don't want to die."
> "If you don't, help me figure. We've got to figure like he's figuring, up there. Everything depends on that."
> "I don't have any idea what he's figuring."
> "We can start out with the assumption that he's going to kill us."
> "I got that far."
> "The next thing is when. He can't do anything until it gets light. So that means we've got till morning to do whatever we're going to do."

The passage deals with one of the most elemental human conflicts—kill or be killed. Under the stress of the conflict, the two men have changed significantly. Back home they were law-abiding citizens who could scarcely have conceived of killing anyone. If you had described this situation to them, they surely would have suggested any number of "sensible" alternatives for dealing with their pursuer. But to go after him with the express intention of killing him would have been unthinkable. And yet here they are, calmly discussing his murder. Thus, the conflict has brought about a dramatic change in the two men.

The author's use of conflict also gives the reader greater insight into the characters of the two men. We see that Ed is a natural leader in times of crisis. It is he who outlines the situation in all its grim reality and suggests a course of action. All Bobby knows is that he doesn't want to die. But he is incapable of either assessing their situation or responding to it. He merely allows himself to be swept along in the wake of Ed's more forceful personality.

The conflict clearly moves the plot along because it creates expectation in the reader's mind. What will happen in the morning? What will the killer do? When will he strike? Will Ed be able to outguess him? All of these questions compel the reader to turn the page and find out what happens.

2. Conflict with Nature. A human being is the highest form of life on earth. No other creature has the same capacity to love, to worship and to create. Thus it always comes as a rude shock to find out that such a magnificent being can be snuffed out by something as elemental as nature. If an earthquake strikes, we are at its mercy. Hurricanes, tornadoes and blizzards are all oblivious to our well-being. A run-in with the forces of nature is always humbling because it demonstrates just how fragile human life really is.

In literature, conflict with nature is a popular theme. On the one hand, it expresses the insignificance of a single human life in the cosmic scheme of things. Anyone who feels invincible has only to get lost in a blizzard to learn otherwise. On the other hand, a run-in with nature tests the limits of a person's strength and will to live. It is a sobering experience, and anyone who survives usually emerges a wiser person because of it. On still another level, most people derive a kind of chilling pleasure from the terror of storms and other cataclysms.

The following passage from *Deliverance* is a good example of conflict with nature. On a whitewater canoe trip down a wild river in North Georgia, the canoe in which Ed is traveling overturns, and Ed is pitched into the surging current. What does Ed learn about himself and the forces of nature as a result of his spill in the river?

> The river took me in . . . . My life jacket brought me up, and Lewis' canoe was on top of me like a whale, rising up on the current. It hit me in the shoulder, driving me down where the rocks swirled like marbles, and something, probably a paddle, thrust into the side of my head as Lewis or Bobby fended me off like a rock. I kicked at the rushing stones and rose up . . . . A rock hit me and I felt some necessary thing—a muscle or bone—go in my leg. I kicked back with both feet and caught something solid. I must have been upside down, for there was no air. I opened my eyes but there was nothing to see. I threw my head, hoping I would be throwing it clear of the water, but it did not clear. I was not breathing and was being beaten from all sides, being hit and hit at and brushed by in the most unlikely and unexpected places in my body, rushing forward to be kicked and stomped by everything in the river.
>
> I turned over and over. I rolled, I tried to crawl along the flying bottom. Nothing worked. I was dead. I felt myself fading out into the unbelievable violence and brutality of the river, joining it. This is not such a bad way to go, I thought; maybe I'm already there.

The passage stresses Ed's helplessness in the face of the "unbelievable violence and brutality of the river." Ed becomes a passive victim of the river.

The river "took me in," he tells us. He is hit, hit at, brushed by, kicked and stomped by everything in the river, and there is not a thing he can do about it; he is at its mercy. Ultimately, he succumbs to it: "I felt myself fading out into . . . the river, joining it." He has accepted the river's superior power and is content to give himself up and merge with this formidable force. It's "not such a bad way to go," he decides.

This canoe trip was planned as a lark, but these men find they are strictly outclassed by the elements. They are faced with the supreme test of their lives, and if they survive, they will never be the same again.

3. Conflict with Society. Sometimes a person's values, beliefs and actions result in conflict with just about everyone. Such an individual may hold no personal grievance against anyone in particular. Rather, it is the values and customs which everyone else lives by that are being challenged. This person becomes a social outcast, a loner whose only consolation lies in the stubborn certainty of being proved right in the end.

The story of Robin Hood is a good example of a man in conflict with society. In stealing from the rich to give to the poor, he challenges the status quo—that is, the existing state of affairs—of society. This is generally very unpopular since those who are in positions of power are usually quite satisfied with things the way they are. The sheriff and his men are after Robin Hood simply because stealing is against the law, regardless of Robin Hood's motives. Thus, in challenging the unequal distribution of wealth in the English economy, Robin Hood is forced to live as an outlaw.

As in other kinds of conflict, sparks fly when people clash with society. A character may come to an untimely end as a result of his or her convictions. The character may, on the other hand, bring others around to a sympathetic point of view, or it may be decided that society was right after all. But whatever the outcome, a character's conflict with society provokes suspense and excitement and serves as a telling commentary upon the character.

4. Internal Conflict. Not all conflict involves other people. Sometimes people are their own worst enemies. We have all experienced occasions when two conflicting elements have struggled within us for mastery. For instance, you might be taking an important exam when the opportunity to cheat arises. You are torn between your sense of right and wrong, and your desire to get a good grade. In another case, a woman may want very much to work hard and be a success in business, but she has been programmed to believe that a woman's place is in the home. Thus she is torn between the desire to live up to society's expectations and the wish to play a successful role in the business world.

An internal conflict is a good test of a character's values. Does he succumb to temptation or rise above it? Does she demand the most from herself or settle for something less? Does she even bother to struggle? The internal conflicts of a character and how they are resolved are good clues to the character's inner strength.

In the following passage from *Deliverance*, Ed is climbing up a sheer face of rock. Notice that there are two conflicts here. The first, a conflict against nature, triggers a second conflict. What is the conflict taking place inside Ed at this point?

I became aware of the sound of my breath, whistling and humming crazily into the stone: the cliff was steepening, and I was laboring backbreakingly for every inch. My arms were tiring and my calves were not so much trembling as jumping. I knew now that not looking down or back—the famous advice to people climbing things—was going to enter into it. Panic was getting near me. Not as near as it might have been, but near. I concentrated everything I had to become ultrasensitive to the cliff, feeling it more gently than before, though I was shaking badly. I kept inching up. With each shift to a newer and higher position I felt more and more tenderness toward the wall.

Despite everything, I looked down.

In the passage above, Ed's instinct for survival is being undermined by fear and fatigue. At this point, his ascent up the cliff has become a psychological, as well as a physical, challenge. Ed does not want to die, but he is almost paralyzed with fear. "Panic was getting near me," he says. The combination of fear and fatigue is making the muscles of his arms and legs twitch, further imperiling his climb. And though he knows on a purely intellectual level that people climbing things should not look down, he looks down anyway.

Clearly, Ed will conquer this cliff only if he first overcomes the emotional obstacles that are thwarting his will to live. The outcome of this conflict within himself will reveal either courage and mental discipline, or a fatal flaw that will plunge him to his death.

Conflict in literature, then, can take several forms. A character may struggle against another person, against nature, against society, and against self. Often, more than one kind of conflict is taking place at the same time. As we have seen, Ed's ascent up the cliff is a struggle against nature—the cliff—as well as against himself. In every case, however, the existence of conflict enhances the reader's understanding of a character and creates the suspense and interest that make you want to continue reading.

As you read the selection:

- Be aware of the scene in which Ed steps back into the river and looks up at the cliff that he must challenge and overcome.

- Notice the conflict that develops when Bobby objects to Ed's plan to scale the cliff.

- Be aware of the point at which the rock face becomes perpendicular during Ed's ascent up the cliff.

- Pay special attention to the superhuman powers that Ed calls upon in the final phase of his climb.

DELIVERANCE

Deliverance
James Dickey

SEPTEMBER 15TH

We moved well for the better part of an hour. Lewis was keeping up, too, driving the almost-buried canoe forward with an effort I could not even guess at. He liked to take things on himself and, because he could, do more than anyone else. And I was glad to see that in an emergency his self-system didn't fold up on him, but carried on the same, or even stronger.

But I was also very glad that Drew and I were light and maneuverable. There were no rapids, but the river seemed to be moving faster. There was an odd but definite sensation of going downhill in a long curving slant like a ramp. I noticed this more and more, and finally it occurred to me that the feeling was caused by what the land on both sides was doing. At first it had lifted into higher banks, the left higher than the right, and now it was going up raggedly and steadily, higher and higher, changing the sound of the river to include a kind of deep beating noise, the tone coming out more and more as the walls climbed, shedding their trees and all but a few bushes and turning to stone. Most of the time the sides were not vertical, but were very steep, and I knew we would be in real trouble if we spilled. I prayed that there would be no rapids while we were in the gorge, or that they would be easy ones.

We pulled and pulled at the river. Drew was hunched forward in a studious position like a man at a desk, and at every stroke the old GI shirt he wore took a new hold across his shoulders, one which was the old hold as well.

I looked back. We had opened up a little distance on the other canoe; it was about thirty yards behind us. I thought I heard Lewis holler to us, probably to slow down, but the voice, thinly floating through the boom of wall-sound, had no authority and very little being at all.

The walls were at least 150 feet high on both sides of us now. The cross-reverberation seemed to hold us on course as much as the current did; it was part of the same thing—the way we had to move to get through the gorge.

I looked around again, and Lewis and Bobby had gained a little. They were too close to us for running rapids, but there was nothing I could do about it; as far as I was concerned they were going to have to take their chances.

As we cleared each turn, before Drew swung across in front of me I kept looking for white water, and when I'd checked for that I looked along both banks as far downriver as I could see, to try to tell if either of them was lowering. There was no white water, and the walls stayed like they were, gray and scrubby, limestonish, pitted and scabby.

But the sound was changing, getting deeper and more massively frantic and authoritative. It was the old sound, but it was also new, it was a fuller one even than the reverberations off the walls, with their overtones and undertones; it was like a ground-bass that was made of all the sounds of the river we'd heard since we'd been on it. God, God, I thought, I know what it is. If it's a falls we're gone.

The sun fell behind the right side of the gorge, and the shadow of the bank crossed the water so fast that it was like a quick step from one side to the other. The beginning of darkness was thrown over us like a sheet, and in it the water ran even faster, frothing and near-foaming under the canoe. My teeth were chattering; I felt them shaking my skull, as though I had already been in the river and now had to suffer in the stone shade of the bank. We seemed to leap, and then leap from that leap to another down the immense ditch, like flying down an underground stream with the ceiling ripped off.

We couldn't make it to Aintry by dark; I knew that now. And we couldn't survive on the river, even as it was here, without being able to see. The last place I wanted to be was on the river in the gorge in the dark. It might be better to pull over while there was still light and find a flat rock or a sandbar to camp on, or get ready to sleep in the canoes.

We came around one more bend, and at the far end of it the river-bed began to step down. There was a succession of small, rough rapids; I couldn't tell how far they went on. About the only thing I had learned about canoeing was to head into the part of the rapids that seemed to be moving the fastest, where the most white water was. There was not much light left, and I had already made up my mind to get through this stretch of water and pull over to the bank, no matter what Lewis and Bobby decided to do.

The water was throwing us mercilessly. We came out in a short stretch between rapids, but we were going too fast to get out of the middle of the river before the next rocks. I didn't want to risk getting the canoe broadside to the river and then be sucked into the rocks. That would not only spill us, but would probably wedge the canoe on the rocks, and the force of water against it would keep it there. And we couldn't make it downriver with four of us in one canoe, as low in the water and hard to turn as it would be. I tried to hold Drew centered on the white water, to line him up and shoot him through the rocks; if I could get him through, I'd be with him.

"Give me some speed, baby," I hollered.

Drew lifted his paddle and started to dig in long and hard.

Something happened to him. It looked at first—I can see it in my mind in three dimensions and slow motion and stop action—as if something, a puff of wind, but much more definite and concentrated, snatched at some of the hair at the back of his head. For a second I thought he had just shaken his head, or had been jarred by the canoe in some way I hadn't felt, but at the same instant I saw this happen I felt all control of the canoe go out of it. The river whirled the paddle from Drew's hand as though it had never been there. His right arm shot straight out, and he followed it, turning the whole canoe with him. There was nothing I could do; I rolled with the rest.

In a reflex, just before my head smashed face-first into the white water with the whole river turning around in midair and beginning to swing upside down, I let go the paddle and grabbed for the bow at my feet, for even in panic I knew I would rather have a weapon than the paddle, as dangerous as it would be to have the naked broadheads near me in such water.

The river took me in, and I had the bow. My life jacket brought me up, and Lewis' canoe was on top of me like a whale, rising up on the current. It hit me in the shoulder, driving me down where the rocks swirled like marbles, and something, probably a paddle, thrust into the side of my head as Lewis or Bobby fended me off like a rock. I kicked at the rushing stones and rose up. Downstream, the green canoe drove over the broadside other one, reared nearly straight up, and Bobby and Lewis pitched out on opposite sides. A rock hit me and I felt some necessary thing—a muscle or bone—go in my leg. I kicked back with both feet and caught something solid. I must have been upside down, for there was no air. I opened my eyes but there was nothing to see. I threw my head, hoping I would be throwing it clear of the water, but it did not clear. I was not breathing and was being beaten from all sides, being hit and hit at and brushed by in the most unlikely and unexpected places in my body, rushing forward to be kicked and stomped by everything in the river.

I turned over and over. I rolled, I tried to crawl along the flying bottom. Nothing worked. I was dead. I felt myself fading out into the unbelievable violence and brutality of the river, joining it. This is not such a bad way to go, I thought; maybe I'm already there.

My head came out of the water, and I actually thought of putting it under again. But I got a glimpse of the two canoes, and that interested me enough to keep me alive. They were together, the green one buckled, rolling over and over each other like logs. Something was nailing one of my hands, the left one, to the water. The wooden canoe burst open on a rock and disappeared, and the aluminum one leapt free and went on.

Get your feet forward of you, boy, I said, with my mouth dragging through the current. Get on your back.

I tried, but every time I came up with my feet I hit a rock either with my shins or thighs. I went under again, and faintly I heard what must have been the aluminum canoe banging on the stones, a ringing, distant, beautiful sound.

I got on my back and poured with the river, sliding over the stones like a creature I had always contained but never released. With my life preserver the upper part of my body drew almost no water. If I could get my feet—my heels—over the stones I slid over like a moccasin, feeling the moss flutter lightly against the back of my neck before I cascaded down into the next rapids.

Body-surfing and skidding along, I realized that we could never have got through this stretch in canoes. There were too many rocks, they were to haphazardly jumbled, and the water was too fast; faster and faster. We couldn't have portaged, either, because of the banks, and we couldn't have got out and walked the canoes through. We would have spilled one way or the other, and strangely I was just as glad. Everything told me that the way I was doing it was the only way, and I was doing it.

It was terrifyingly enjoyable, except that I hurt in so many places. The river would shoot me along; I'd see a big boulder looming up, raise my feet and slick over, crash down in a foaming pool, pick up speed and go on. I got banged on the back of the head a couple of times until I learned to bend forward as I was coming down off the rock, but after that nothing new hurt me.

I was already hurt, I knew. But I was not sure where. My left hand hurt pretty bad, and I was more worried about it than anywhere else, for I couldn't remember having hit it with anything. I held it up and saw that I had hold of the bow by the broadheads and was getting cut in the palm every time I flinched and grabbed. The bow was also clamped under my left arm, and now I took it out and swung the heads away from me, just before I went over another rock. As I slid down I saw calm water below, through another stretch of rapids: broad calm, then more white water farther down, far off into evening. I relaxed again, not even touching the stones of the passage this time, but riding easily along through the flurrying cold ripples into the calm water, cradling the bow.

I was floating, not flowing anymore. Turning idly in the immense dark bed, I looked up at the gorge side rising and rising. My legs were killing me, but I could kick them both, and as far as I could tell neither was broken. I lifted my hand from the water; it was nicked and chopped a little in places, but not as badly as it might have been; there was a diagonal cut across the palm, but not a deep one—a long slice.

I floated on, trying to recover enough to think what to do. Finally I started to struggle weakly around to look upstream for the others. My body was heavy and hard to move without the tremendous authority of the rapids to help it and tell it what to do.

Either upstream or down, there was nobody in the river but me. I kept watching the last of the falls, for I had an idea that I might have passed the others, somewhere along. There had probably been several places where the water split and came down through the rocks in different ways; all three of them might be back there somewhere, dead or alive.

As I thought that, Bobby tumbled out of the rapids, rolling over and over on the slick rocks, and then flopped belly-down into the calm. I pointed to the bank and he began feebly to work toward it. So did I.

"Where is Lewis?" I yelled.

He shook his head, and I stopped pulling on the water and turned to wait in midstream.

After a minute or two Lewis came, doubled-up and broken-looking, one hand still holding his paddle and the other on his face, clasping something intolerable. I breaststroked to him and lay beside him in the cold coiling water under the falls. He was writhing and twisting uselessly, caught by something that didn't have hold of me, something that seemed not present.

"Lewis," I said.

"My leg's broke," he gasped. "It feels like it broke off."

The water where we were did not change. "Hold on to me," I said.

He moved his free hand through the river and fixed the fingers into the collar of my slick nylon outfit, and I moved gradually crossways on the water toward the big boulders under the cliff. The dark came on us faster and faster as I hauled on the crossgrain of the current with Lewis' choking weight dragging at my throat.

From where we were the cliff looked something like a gigantic drive-in movie screen waiting for an epic film to begin. I listened for interim music, glancing now and again up the pale curved stone for Victor Mature's stupendous image, wondering where it would appear, or if the whole thing were not now already playing, and I hadn't yet managed to put it together.

As we neared the wall, I saw that there were a few random rocks and a tiny sand beach where we were going to come out; where Bobby was, another rock. I motioned to him, and he unfolded and came to the edge of the water, his hands embarrassing.

He gave me one of them, and I dragged us out. Lewis hopped up onto a huge placid stone, working hard, and then failed and crumpled again. The rock, still warm with the last of the sun that had crossed the river on its way down, held him easily, and I turned him on his back with his hand still over his face.

"Drew was shot," Lewis said with no lips. "I saw it. He's dead."

"I'm not sure," I said, but I was afraid that's what it was. "Something happened to him. But I don't know. I don't know."

"Let's take his pants down," I said to Bobby.

He looked at me.

"*Damn* phraseology," I said. "We're in another bag, now, baby. Get his pants off him and see if you can tell how bad he's hurt. I've got to try to get that damned canoe, or we'll stay here."

I turned back to the river. I waded in, feeling the possibility of a rifle shot die with the very last light, moving back into the current like an out-of-shape animal, taking on the familiar weight and lack-of-weight of water. Very clear-headed, I sank down.

The depth came to me, increasing—no one can tell me different—with the darkness. The aluminum canoe floated palely, bulging half out of the total dark, making slowly for the next rapids, but idly, and unnaturally slowed and stogged with calm water. Nearly there, I ran into a thing of wood that turned out to be a broken paddle. I took it on.

I swam slow-motion around the canoe, listening for the rifle shot I would never hear if it killed me; that I had not heard when it killed Drew, if it did. Nothing from that high up could see me, and I knew it, though it might see the canoe. Even that was doubtful, though, and the conviction enlarged on me that I could circle the canoe all night, if I chose, in the open.

The calm was deep; there was no place to stand to dump the water out. I hung to the upside-down gunwale, tipping it this way and that, trying to slip the river out of the factory metal. Finally it rolled luckily, and the stream that had been in it began to flow again; the hull lightened and climbed out of the water, and was mostly on top of it. I pushed on the sharp stern, keeping it going with excruciating frog legs. The current went around me, heading into the darkness downstream. I could see a little white foaming, but it was peacefully beyond, another problem for another time. I turned to the cliff and called softly out to Bobby, and he answered.

I looked up and could barely make out his face. The canoe went in to him, guided by the same kind of shove I gave Dean when he was first learning to walk. He waded and drew it up onto the sand by the bow rope, and we beached it under the overhang.

I moved onto land, not saying anything.

"For God's sake," Bobby said, "don't be so damned quiet. I'm flipping already."

Though my mouth was open, I closed it against the blackness and moved to Lewis, who was now down off the rock and lying in the sand. His bare legs were luminous, and the right leg of his drawers was lifted up to the groin. I could tell by its outline that his thigh was broken; I reached down and felt of it very softly. Against the back of my hand his penis stirred with pain. His hair gritted in sand, turning from one side to the other.

It was not a compound fracture; I couldn't feel any of the bone splinters I had been taught to look for in innumerable compulsory first-aid courses, but there was a great profound human swelling under my hand. It felt like a thing that was trying to open, to split, to let something out.

"Hold on, Lew," I said. "We're all right now."

It was all-dark. The river-sound enveloped us as it never could have in light. I sat down beside Lewis and motioned to Bobby. He crouched down as well.

"Where is Drew?" Bobby asked.

"Lewis says he's dead," I said. "Probably he is. He may have been shot. But I can't really say. I was looking right at him, but I can't say."

Lewis' hand was pulling at me from underneath. I bent down near his face. He tried to say something, but couldn't. Then he said, "It's you. It's got to be you."

"Sure it's me," I said. "I'm right here. Nothing can touch us."

"No. That's not ..." The river had the rest of what he said, but Bobby picked it up.

"What are we going to do?" he made the dark say; night had taken his red face.

"I think," I said, "that we'll never get out of this gorge alive."

Did I say that? I thought. Yes, a dream-man said, you did. You did say it, and you believe it.

"I think he means to pick the rest of us off tomorrow," I said out loud, still stranger than anything I had ever imagined. When do the movies start, Lord?

"What ...?"

"That's what I'd do. Wouldn't you?"

"I don't ..."

"If Lewis is right, and I think he is, that toothless bastard drew down on us while we were lining up to go through the rapids, and before we were going too fast. He killed the first man in the first boat. Next would have been me. Then you."

"In other words, it's lucky we spilled."

"Right. Lucky. Very lucky."

It was an odd word to use, where we were. It was a good thing that we couldn't see faces. Mine felt calm and narrow-eyed, but it might not have been. There was something to act out.

"What are we going to do?" Bobby said again.

"The question is, what is *he* going to do?"

Nothing came back. I went on.

"What can he lose now? He's got exactly the same thing going for him that we had going for us when we buried his buddy back in the woods. There won't be any witnesses. There's no motive to trace him by. As far as anybody else knows, he's never seen us and we've never seen him. If all four of us wind up in the river, that'll just even things out. Who in the hell cares? What kind of search party could get up into these rapids? A helicopter's not going to do any good, even if you could see into the river from one, which you can't. You think anybody's going to fly a helicopter down into this gorge, just on the chance that he *might* see something? Not a chance in the world. There might be an investigation, but you can bet nothing will come of it. This is a wild damn river, as you might know. What is going to happen to us, if he kills us, is that we are going to become a legend. You bet, baby: one of those unsolved things."

"You think he's up there? Do you really?"

"I'm thinking we better believe he's up there."

"But then what?"

"We're caught in this gorge. He can't come down here, but the only way out of this place for us is down the river. We can't run out of here at night, and when we move in the morning he'll be up there somewhere."

"Jesus Christ Almighty."

"Yes," I said. "You might say that. As Lewis might say, 'Come on, Jesus boy, walk on down to us over that white water. But if you don't, we've got to do whatever there is to do.' "

"But listen, Ed," he said, and the pathetic human tone against the river-sound made me cringe, "you got to be sure."

"Sure of what?"

"Sure you're right. What if you're wrong? I mean, we may not really be in any danger, at all, from anybody up . . . up there." He gestured, but it was lost.

"You want to take a chance?"

"Well, no. Not if I don't have to. But what . . .?"

"*What* what?"

"What can we do?"

"We can do three things," I said, and some other person began to tell me what they were. "We can just sit here and sweat and call for our mamas. We can appeal to the elements. Maybe we can put Lewis back up on the rock and do a rain dance around him, to cut down the visibility. But if we got rain, we couldn't get out through it, and Lewis would probably die of exposure. Look up yonder."

I liked hearing the sound of my voice in the mountain speech, especially in the dark; it sounded like somebody who knew where he was and knew what he was doing. I thought of Drew and the albino boy picking and singing in the filling station.

There was a pause while we looked up between the wings of cliff and saw that the stars were beginning there, and no clouds at all.

"And then what?" Bobby said.

"Or somebody can try to go up there and wait for him on top."

"What you mean is . . ."

"What I mean is like they say in the movies, especially on Saturday afternoon. It's either him or us. We've killed a man. So has he. Whoever gets out depends on who kills who. It's just that simple."

"Well," he said, "all right. I don't want to die."

"If you don't, help me figure. We've got to figure like he's figuring, up there. Everything depends on that."

"I don't have any idea what he's figuring."

"We can start out with the assumption that he's going to kill us."

"I got that far."

"The next thing is when. He can't do anything until it gets light. So that means we've got till morning to do whatever we're going to do."

"I still don't know what that is."

"Just let me go on a minute. My feeling is this. You can't hear a gunshot that far off, with all this damn noise down here. After he shot Drew, he might have shot at us some more, and we'd never have known it unless another one of us was hit. I don't have any idea how well he can see from where he is. But I think it's reasonable to suppose that he saw well enough to know that he hit Drew, and that the canoes turned over. He might believe that the rest of us drowned, but I don't believe he'd want to take a chance that we did. That's awful rough water, but the fact that you and Lewis and I got out of it proves that it can be done, and I'm thinking he probably knows it. Again, maybe the reason he didn't nail the rest of us was that by the time we got down here where we are now, we'd been carried a good ways past him, and also it was too dark. That's our good luck; it means we've got at least a couple of advantages, if we can figure how to work them."

"*Advantages?* Some advantages. We've got a hurt man. We've got a water-logged canoe with the bottom stove in. We've got two guys who don't know the first thing about the woods, who don't even know where in the hell they are. He's got a rifle, and he's up above us. He knows where we are and can't help being, and we don't have the slightest notion of where he is, or even who he is. We haven't got a damn chance, if you and Lewis are right. If he's up there and wants to kill us, he can kill us."

"Well now, it hasn't happened yet. And we've got one big card."

"What?"

"He thinks we can't get at him. And if we can, we can kill him."

"How?"

"With either a knife or a bow. Or with bare hands, if we have to."

"We?"

"No. One of us."

"I can't even shoot a bow," he said. He was saved for a little while.

"That narrows it down, sure enough," I said. "You see what I mean about solving our problems? If you just do a little figuring."

It was a decision, and I could feel it set us apart. Even in the dark the separation was obvious.

"Ed, level with me. Do you really think you can get up there in the dark?"

"To tell the truth, I don't. But we haven't got any other choice."

"I still think that maybe he's just gone away. Suppose he has?"

"Suppose he hasn't?" I said. "Do you want to take the chance? Look, if I fall off this cliff, it's not going to hurt you any. If I get shot, it's not going to be you getting shot. You've got two chances to live. If he's gone away, or if for some reason or other he doesn't shoot, or if he misses enough times for the canoe to get away downriver, you'll live. Or if I get up there and kill him, you'll live. So don't worry about it. Let me worry."

"Ed . . ."

"Shut up and let me think some more."

I looked up at the gorge side but I couldn't tell much about it, except that it was awfully high. But the lower part of it, at least, wasn't quite as steep as I had thought at first. Rather than being absolutely vertical, it was more of a very steep slant, and I believed I could get up it at least part of the way, when the moon came up enough for me to see a little better.

"Come here, Bobby. And listen to everything I tell you. I'm going to make you go back over it before I leave, because the whole thing has got to be done right, and done right the first time. Here's what I want you to do."

"All right. I'm listening."

"Keep Lewis as warm and comfortable as you can. When it gets first light—and I mean just *barely* light: light enough for you to see where you're going—get Lewis into the canoe and move out. The whole business is going to have to be decided right there."

I was the one. I walked up and down a little on the sandbar, for that should have been my privilege. Then for some reason I stepped into the edge of the river. In a way, I guess, I wanted to get a renewed feel of all the elements present, and also to look as far up the cliff as I could. I stood with the cold water flowing around my calves and my head back, watching the cliff slant up into the darkness. More stars had come out around the top of the gorge, a kind of river of them. I strung the bow.

I ran my right hand over the limbs, feeling for broken pieces and splinters of fiber glass. Part of the upper limb seemed a little rougher than it should have, but it had been that way before. I took out the arrows I had left. I had started with four but had wasted two on the deer. One of the remaining ones was fairly straight; I spun it through my fingers as Lewis had taught me to do, feeling for the passing tick and jump a crooked aluminum arrow has when it spins. It may have been a little bent up in the crest, just under the feathers, but it was shootable, and at short range it ought to be accurate. The other arrow was badly bent, and I straightened it as well as I could with my hands, but there was not much I could do in the dark. Holding it at eye level and pointing it toward the best of the light places in the sky, I could not see even well enough to tell exactly where and how badly it was bent. But the broadhead was all right.

I walked back to Bobby and leant the bow against the spur of stone that overhung the canoe. Bobby stepped over to me as I paid out and recoiled the thin rope that had been at my waist the whole time. I had made a lucky buy—considering that a cliff I had not counted on being involved *was* involved, and a rope was a good thing to have in such a situation—and I had a brief moment of believing that the luck would run through the other things that were coming. I ran the rope over and over my left thumb and elbow until I had a tight ring. I tied the ends and passed the belt that held the big knife through the coil.

"Don't go to sleep," I said to Bobby.

"Not likely," he said. "O God."

"Now listen. If you go at first light, you'll make a damned hard target from the top of the gorge. You should be safe as long as you're running these little rapids along here. If I'm going to get on top of the cliff, I'll be there by then, and the odds will be evened out a little, if our man the Human Fly really does find a way to climb up there. I'll do everything I can to see that he doesn't crack down on you. From the little I was able to tell about the cliff before it got dark, it's rough as hell up there, and if he misses you at one place—or if you can slip by him without his seeing you—he won't be able to keep up with you; all you have to do is get by him and get around one turn and you're home free."

"Ed, will you tell me one thing? Have you ever thought there might be more than one?"

"Yes, I've thought of it. I must say I have."

"What if there is?"

"Then we're likely to die, early tomorrow morning."

"I believe you."

"I don't believe, though, that there's more than one man. I'll tell you why. It's not a good idea to involve somebody else in a murder if you don't have to. That's one thing. The other is that I don't think there's been time for him to go and get anybody else. He's got all the advantages; he doesn't need anybody to help him."

"I sure hope you're right."

"We'll have to figure I am. Anything else?"

"Yes, I've got to say it. I don't think we're going about this the right way. We may have the whole thing wrong."

"I'm staking my life on being right. Lewis would do it. Now I'm going to have to. Let me get going."

"Listen," Bobby said, grabbing at me weakly, "I can't do it. I won't make a sitting duck out of myself so you can go off in the woods and leave us to be shot down. I can't. I just can't."

"Listen, you son of a bitch. If you want to go up that cliff, you go right ahead. There it is; it's not going away. But if I go up it we're going to play this my way. And I swear to God that if you don't do exactly what I say I'll kill you myself. It's just that damned simple. And if you leave Lewis on this rock I'll do the same thing."

"Ed, I'm not going to leave him. You know I wouldn't do that. It's just that I don't want to go out there in plain sight of some murderous hillbilly and set myself up to be killed like Drew."

"If everything works right—and if you do what I tell you to do—you won't get killed. Just *listen* to me. I'm going through this one more time, and it's got to stick. I'm going to tell you what to do no matter what should happen."

"All right," he said at last.

"Number one, move out as soon as you can see the river well enough to get through the next set of rapids. It'll probably still be too dark to shoot from the top. Even if it isn't he doesn't stand much chance of hitting you when you're in the rapids. Whenever you're in calm water, pull like hell for a while, then slack off; don't hit a constant speed. If he does shoot at you, try your damndest to get to the next set of rapids, or around the next turn. If you see you can't possibly get away—that is, if you see he's got you brack-eted, and the shots are coming closer and closer—dump the canoe and let it go. Try to get Lewis out, then stay with him and wait for a day, and I'll try to bring back help. If nothing happens by that time, you'll know I didn't make it. Then leave Lewis and try to get downriver the best way you can, even if you have to swim part of the way. Take all three life jackets and float yourself down. We can't be more than fifteen miles from a highway bridge. If you have to do that, though, for God's sake remember where you left Lewis. If you don't remember, he's going to die. And that's for sure."

He looked at me, and for the first time since the sun had gone down I could see his eyes; they had some points of light in them.

"That's about it, then," I said. I picked up the bow and went over to the canoe near where Lewis was lying, tirelessly grinding the back of his head into the sand. I crouched down beside him; he was shaking in a certain matter-of-fact way, with the false cold of pain, and some of it came into me as he reached up and touched me on the front of the shoulder.

"Do you know what you're doing?"

"No, creature," I said. "I'm going to try to make it up as I go along."

"Don't let him see you," he said. "And don't have any mercy. Not any."

"I won't if I can help it."

"Help it."

I held my breath.

"Kill him," Lewis said with the river.

"I'll kill him if I can find him," I said.

"Well," he said, lying back, "here we are, at the heart of the Lewis Medlock country."

"Pure survival," I said.

"This is what it comes to," he said. "I told you."

"Yes. You told me."

Everything around me changed. I put my left arm between the bowstring and the bow and slid the bow back over my shoulder with the broadheads turned down. Then I walked to the gorge side and put a hand on it, the same hand that had been cut by the arrow in the river, as though I might be able to feel what the whole cliff was like, the whole problem, and hold it in my palm. The rock was rough, and a part of it fell away under my hand. The river sound loudened as though the rocks in the channel had shifted their positions. Then it relaxed and the extra sound died or went away again into the middle distance, the middle of the stream.

I knew that was the sign, and I backed off and ran with a hard scramble at the bank, and stretched up far enough to get an elbow over the top side of the first low overhang. Scraping my sides and legs, I got up on it and stood up. Bobby and Lewis were directly beneath me, under a roof of stone, and might as well not have been there. I was standing in the most entire aloneness that I had ever been given.

My heart expanded with joy at the thought of where I was and what I was doing. There was a new light on the water; the moon was going up and up, and I stood watching the stream with my back to the rock for a few minutes, not thinking of anything, with a deep feeling of nakedness and helplessness and intimacy.

I turned around with many small foot movements and leaned close to the cliff, taking on its slant exactly. I put my cheek against it and raised both hands up into the darkness, letting the fingers crawl independently over the soft rock. It was this softness that bothered me more than anything else; I was afraid that anything I would stand on or hold to would give way. I got my right hand placed in what felt like a crack, and began to feel with my left toes for something, anything. There was an unevenness—a bulge—in the rock and I kicked at it and worried it to see how solid it was, then put my foot on it and pulled hard with my right arm.

I rose slowly off the top of the overhang, the bow dropping back further over my left shoulder—which made it necessary to depend more on my right arm than my left—got my right knee and then my foot into some kind of hole. I settled as well as I could into my new position and began to feel upward again. There was a bulge to the left, and I worked toward it, full of wonder at the whole situation.

The cliff was not as steep as I had thought, though from what I had been able to tell earlier, before we spilled, it would probably get steeper toward the top. If I had turned loose it would have been a slide rather than a fall back down to the river or the overhang, and this reassured me a little—though not much—as I watched it happen in my mind.

I got to the bulge and then went up over it and planted my left foot solidly on it and found a good hold on what felt like a root with my right hand. I looked down.

The top of the overhang was pale now, ten or twelve feet below. I turned and forgot about it, pulling upward, kneeing and toeing into the cliff, kicking steps into the shaly rock wherever I could, trying to position both hands and one foot before moving to a new position. Some of the time I could do this, and each time my confidence increased. Often I could only get one handhold and a foothold, or two handholds. Once I could only get one handhold, but it was a strong one, and I scrambled and shifted around it until I could get a toe into the rock and pull up.

The problem-interest of it absorbed me at first, but I began to notice that the solutions were getting harder and harder: the cliff was starting to shudder in my face and against my chest. I became aware of the sound of my breath, whistling and humming crazily into the stone: the cliff was steepening, and I was laboring backbreakingly for every inch. My arms were tiring and my calves were not so much trembling as jumping. I knew now that not looking down or back—the famous advice to people climbing things—was going to enter into it. Panic was getting near me. Not as near as it might have been, but near. I concentrated everything I had to become ultrasensitive to the cliff, feeling it more gently than before, though I was shaking badly. I kept inching up. With each shift to a newer and higher position I felt more and more tenderness toward the wall.

Despite everything, I looked down. The river had spread flat and filled with moonlight. It took up the whole of space under me, bearing in the center of itself a long coiling image of light, a chill, bending flame. I must have been seventy-five or a hundred feet above it, hanging poised over some kind of inescapable glory, a bright pit.

I turned back into the cliff and leaned my mouth against it, feeling all the way out through my nerves and muscles exactly how I had possession of the wall at four random points in a way that held the whole thing together.

It was about this time that I thought of going back down, working along the bank and looking for an easier way up, and I let one foot down behind me into the void. There was nothing. I stood with the foot groping for a hold in the air, then pulled it back to the place on the cliff where it had been. It burrowed in like an animal, and I started up again.

I caught something—part of the rock—with my left hand and started to pull. I could not rise. I let go with my right hand and grabbed the wrist of the left, my left-hand fingers shuddering and popping with weight. I got one toe into the cliff, but that was all I could do. I looked up and held on. The wall was giving me nothing. It no longer sent back any pressure against me. Something I had come to rely on had been taken away, and that was it. I was hanging, but just barely. I concentrated all my strength into the fingers of my left hand, but they were leaving me. I was on the perpendicular part of the cliff, and unless I could get over it soon I would just peel off the wall. I had what I thought of as a plan if this should happen; this was to kick out as strongly as I could from the cliff face and try to get clear of the overhang and out into the river, into the bright coiling of the pit. But even if I cleared the rocks, the river was probably shallow near the bank where I would land, and it would be about as bad as if I were to hit the rocks. And I would have to get rid of the bow.

I held on. By a lot of small tentative maneuvers I swapped hands in the crevice and touched upward with my left hand, weighted down by the bow hanging over my shoulder, along the wall, remembering scenes in movies where a close-up of a hand reaches desperately for something, through a prison grate for a key, or from quicksand toward someone or something on solid ground. There was nothing there. I swapped hands again and tried the wall to my right. There was nothing. I tried the loose foot, hoping that if I could get a good enough foothold, I could get up enough to explore a little more of the wall with my hands, but I couldn't find anything there either, though I searched as far as I could with the toe and the knee, up and down and back and forth. The back of my left leg was shaking badly. My mind began to speed up, in the useless energy of panic. The urine in my bladder turned solid and painful, and then ran with a delicious sexual voiding like a wet dream, something you can't help or be blamed for. There was nothing to do but fall. The last hope I had was that I might awaken.

I was going, but anger held me up a little longer. I would have done something desperate if I had had a little more mobility, but I was practically nailed in one position; there was nothing desperate I could do. Yet I knew that if I were going to try something, I had better do it now.

I hunched down into what little power was left in my left leg muscles and drove as hard as it was possible for me to do; harder than it was possible. With no holds on the cliff, I fought with the wall for anything I could make it give me. For a second I tore at it with both hands. In a flash inside a flash I told myself not to double up my fists but to keep my hands open. I was up against a surface as smooth as monument stone, and I still believe that for a space of time I was held in the air by pure will, fighting an immense rock.

Then it seemed to spring a crack under one finger of my right hand; I thought surely I had split the stone myself. I thrust in other fingers and hung and, as I did, I got the other hand over, feeling for a continuation of the crack; it was there. I had both hands in the cliff to the palms, and strength from the stone flowed into me. I pulled up as though chinning on a sill and swung a leg in. I got the middle section of my body into the crevice as well, which was the hardest part to provide for, as it had been everywhere else. I wedged into the crack like a lizard, not able to get far enough in. As I flattened out on the floor of the crevice, with all my laborious verticality gone, the bow slid down my arm and I hooked upward just in time to stop it with my wrist. I pulled it into the cliff with me, the broadheads at my throat.

Unit 5

Deliverance

- Comprehension Questions
- Analyzing Conflict
- Discussion Guides
- Writing Exercise

COMPREHENSION QUESTIONS

For each of the following statements and questions, select the option containing the most complete or most accurate answer.

1. As the four men proceed downstream in their canoes, the sounds made
(a) by the river become
    ☐ a. gentle and lapping.
    ☐ b. familiar and even friendly.
    ☐ c. deeper and more threatening.
    ☐ d. weaker and distant.

2. As the men paddle down the river, the banks on either side gradually
(a) ☐ a. show signs of civilization.   ☐ c. flatten out.
    ☐ b. become steeper.   ☐ d. recede.

3. In their everyday lives back home, these men were probably
(h) ☐ a. middle-class office workers.
    ☐ b. upper-class, wealthy executives.
    ☐ c. blue-collar working people.
    ☐ d. outdoorsmen—farmers, foresters, and so on.

4. The purpose of this trip was probably
(f) ☐ a. to escape from the police.
    ☐ b. to look for trouble.
    ☐ c. to flirt with death.
    ☐ d. to get away from it all.

5. The single most important item which Ed is determined to save when
(a) their canoe spills is
    ☐ a. his rope.   ☐ c. the canoe.
    ☐ b. his bow.   ☐ d. his knife.

6. Which of the following best defines *stogged* as used in, "The aluminum
(l) canoe floated palely, bulging half out of the total dark, making slowly
for the next rapids, but idly, and unnaturally slowed and *stogged* with
calm water"?
    ☐ a. Bogged down   ☐ c. Buoyed up
    ☐ b. Flooded   ☐ d. Buffeted

7. Lewis says that Drew was
(b) □ a. shot by a bow and arrow.
   □ b. wounded with a slingshot.
   □ c. killed by a bullet.
   □ d. struck by lightning.

8. Bobby is the kind of man who reacts to stress by
(j) □ a. making the best of things.
   □ b. going to pieces.
   □ c. rising to meet the challenge.
   □ d. assuming a leadership role.

9. Ed's decision to scale the cliff in the darkness and take the killer by
(g) surprise using his bow and arrow was probably
   □ a. an excuse to live out a boyhood fantasy.
   □ b. a veiled death wish.
   □ c. an escape from an intolerable and hopeless situation.
   □ d. the only rational response to a desperate situation.

10. Ed's assumption that the killer would be lying in wait for them on top
(h) of the cliff was based on a
   □ a. desperate bluff.   □ c. logical deduction.
   □ b. lucky guess.   □ d. known fact.

11. Ed is scaling a cliff with the intention of taking another man's life. His
(j) attitude toward his mission is best described as
   □ a. cold and matter-of-fact.   □ c. guilt-ridden and reluctant.
   □ b. eager and expectant.   □ d. unfeeling and unconcerned.

12. "When do the movies start, Lord?" said Ed to himself in a tone that
(i) expressed his
   □ a. optimism.   □ c. disbelief at their situation.
   □ b. loss of faith.   □ d. anger at their situation.

13. Bobby protests against Ed's going up the cliff because he
(b) □ a. would rather go up himself.
   □ b. is afraid for his own life.
   □ c. is afraid for Ed's life.
   □ d. has a better idea.

DELIVERANCE

14. Which of the following best defines *cringe* as used in, " 'But listen, Ed,'
(l) he said, and the pathetic human tone against the river-sound made me
cringe, 'you got to be sure' "?
   ☐ a. Feel disgust   ☐ c. Feel sympathy
   ☐ b. Feel fear   ☐ d. Feel anger

15. The predominant tone that pervades the account of Ed's ascent up the
(i) cliff is one of
   ☐ a. detachment.   ☐ c. annoyance.
   ☐ b. anger.   ☐ d. suspense.

16. The course of Ed's progress up the cliff indicates that the face of the
(d) gorge
   ☐ a. is uniformly vertical.
   ☐ b. gets smoother and steeper as one ascends.
   ☐ c. has a consistent angle of incline.
   ☐ d. leans out over the river.

17. In his description of his ascent up the cliff, Ed says ". . . I still believe
(g) that for a space of time I was held in the air by pure will . . ." and ". . . I
thought surely I had split the stone myself." These phrases indicate
that Ed's perceptions of reality became
   ☐ a. keener.   ☐ c. dangerously unreliable.
   ☐ b. totally inaccurate.   ☐ d. exaggerated.

18. In three different similes, Ed compares himself to an animal. Body-
(k) surfing down the rapids, he feels "like a creature I had always contained
but never released." Climbing the cliff, he wedged into a crack "like a
lizard," and he moves about in the river "like an out-of-shape animal."
These three similes show that Ed was coming to feel more like
   ☐ a. an athlete.   ☐ c. an impartial observer.
   ☐ b. God.   ☐ d. a part of nature.

19. Time and again the author compares Ed's situation to something out of
(k) the movies: ". . . the cliff looked something like a gigantic drive-in
movie screen waiting for an epic film to begin" and ". . . like they say in
the movies, especially on Saturday afternoon. It's either him or us."
And again, ". . . remembering scenes in movies where a close-up of a
hand reaches desperately for something . . . ." The author uses the
movies as a symbol to express the
   ☐ a. unreal, storylike quality of their situation.
   ☐ b. glamor and romance of their situation.
   ☐ c. risk and danger in their situation.
   ☐ d. good time they were enjoying.

20. During the course of the selection, the role of leadership changes hands
(d) from
    ☐ a. Drew to Bobby.   ☐ c. Lewis to Ed.
    ☐ b. Bobby to Ed.   ☐ d. Ed to Lewis.

21. The key to surviving in the wilderness is to have
(f) ☐ a. faith in God.   ☐ c. high moral values.
    ☐ b. faith in oneself.   ☐ d. a superior education.

22. In *Deliverance*, nature is depicted as being
(c) ☐ a. wild and untamed.   ☐ c. serene and beautiful.
    ☐ b. bountiful and idyllic.   ☐ d. cruel and destructive.

23. In the backwoods country where these men have strayed, human life is
(c) more
    ☐ a. innocent.   ☐ c. vulnerable.
    ☐ b. rewarding.   ☐ d. dignified.

24. Up in the mountains where these men have ventured, justice is often
(e) arrived at
    ☐ a. through traditional rituals.
    ☐ b. by reasonable compromises.
    ☐ c. with a rational discussion.
    ☐ d. outside the law.

25. One point which the selection makes is that a man's true character is
(e) revealed by the way he
    ☐ a. copes with everyday demands.
    ☐ b. responds to challenges.
    ☐ c. handles an awkward situation.
    ☐ d. reacts to change.

Comprehension Skills: a—isolating details; b—recalling specific facts; c—retaining concepts; d—organizing facts; e—understanding the main idea; f—drawing a conclusion; g—making a judgment; h—making an inference; i—recognizing tone; j—understanding characters; k—appreciation of literary forms; l—knowledge of word meanings.

ANALYZING CONFLICT

Practice Exercise A

I was the one. I walked up and down a little on the sandbar, for that should have been my privilege. Then for some reason I stepped into the edge of the river. In a way, I guess, I wanted to get a renewed feel of all the elements present, and also to look as far up the cliff as I could. I stood with the cold water flowing around my calves and my head back, watching the cliff slant up into the darkness. More stars had come out around the top of the gorge, a kind of river of them. I strung the bow.

1. In the passage above, Ed's actions may be compared to a boxer
   □ a. struggling against his inner fear.
   □ b. preparing to throw a fight.
   □ c. sizing up his opponent.
   □ d. anticipating the monetary reward regardless of the outcome of the fight.

2. Ed says, "I was the one." The one what? or who? On the lines provided, finish this sentence to explain Ed's train of thought at this point.

   _____

   _____

Practice Exercise B

"Listen," Bobby said, grabbing at me weakly, "I can't do it. I won't make a sitting duck out of myself so you can go off in the woods and leave us to be shot down. I can't. I just can't."

"Listen, you son of a bitch. If you want to go up that cliff, you go right ahead. There it is; it's not going away. But if I go up it we're going to play this my way. And I swear to God that if you don't do exactly what I say I'll kill you myself. It's just that damned simple. And if you leave Lewis on this rock I'll do the same thing."

1. The conflict between Bobby and Ed expressed in the above passage reveals a side of Bobby's character that is
   □ a. weak and cowardly.   □ c. supportive and helpful.
   □ b. strong and cruel.   □ d. spiteful and vengeful.

2. Circle the sentence above that *best* illustrates the fact that Ed becomes dictatorial and ruthless under pressure.

Practice Exercise C

I caught something—part of the rock—with my left hand and started to pull. I could not rise. I let go with my right hand and grabbed the wrist of the left, my left-hand fingers shuddering and popping with weight. I got one toe into the cliff, but that was all I could do. I looked up and held on. The wall was giving me nothing. It no longer sent back any pressure against me. Something I had come to rely on had been taken away, and that was it. I was hanging, but just barely. I concentrated all my strength into the fingers of my left hand, but they were leaving me. I was on the perpendicular part of the cliff, and unless I could get over it soon I would just peel off the wall.

1. In the passage above, the scaling of the cliff represents a conflict primarily against
   ☐ a. another man.   ☐ c. himself.
   ☐ b. nature.   ☐ d. society.

2. Circle the sentence above that *best* illustrates the "attitude" of the wall as Ed's opponent in this conflict.

Practice Exercise D

I was going, but anger held me up a little longer. I would have done something desperate if I had had a little more mobility, but I was practically nailed in one position; there was nothing desperate I could do. Yet I knew that if I were going to try something, I had better do it now.

I hunched down into what little power was left in my left leg muscles and drove as hard as it was possible for me to do; harder than it was possible. With no holds on the cliff, I fought with the wall for anything I could make it give me. For a second I tore at it with both hands. In a flash inside a flash I told myself not to double up my fists but to keep my hands open. I was up against a surface as smooth as monument stone, and I still believe that for a space of time I was held in the air by pure will, fighting an immense rock.

1. In this phase of Ed's ascent up the mountain, two conflicting feelings are struggling within him. These are
   ☐ a. determination versus apathy.
   ☐ b. fatigue versus a fear of death.
   ☐ c. pride versus a subconscious wish to die.
   ☐ d. a feeling of impending doom versus anger at the cliff.

2. Circle one phrase and one sentence from the excerpt above that illustrate the superhuman powers which Ed summoned in his struggle against the cliff.

DISCUSSION GUIDES

Analyzing the Use of Conflict

1. How does a wild setting help to depict raw human conflict? What kinds of conflict might take place in a sleepy rural town? in a big city?

2. Ed and Bobby are friends, but there is conflict between them. What is the conflict?

Interpreting the Selection

3. Ed plots the murder of their pursuer with a clear and rational mind and proceeds to scale the cliff as part of the job he has to do. Does this make him a cold-blooded murderer? How does the murder that Ed is about to commit affect your personal opinion of him?

4. As he is about to scale the cliff in pursuit of a killer, Ed says, "My heart expanded with joy at the thought of where I was and what I was doing." What kind of satisfaction could Ed possibly be getting out of such a grueling and lawless mission?

5. What do you think Lewis meant when he told Ed, "Well, here we are at the heart of Lewis Medlock country"? Are you ever likely to encounter Lewis Medlock country?

6. What skills and character traits are most valuable for survival in the wilderness? for survival in civilization?

7. What are some things that might have motivated these men to go on a wilderness canoe trip? What reasons would prompt you to "get away from it all" in this manner?

8. Why do you think the author called this book *Deliverance?* Whose deliverance is he referring to, and from what?

Analyzing the Author's Technique

9. Like the selection which you read, the whole book is without significant female characters. Why do you think the author chose not to include women in this wilderness odyssey? Could the story be rewritten effectively with four female characters?

10. It may be said that the author uses the river and the cliff as "characters" in the story. In what ways are these two inanimate objects "characters"?

WRITING EXERCISE

In the story "The Outcasts of Poker Flat" by Bret Harte, the citizens of Poker Flat form a secret committee and decide to rid the settlement of all "low and vulgar persons." The "collected wickedness" of Poker Flat is escorted to the edge of the settlement by armed men. The "undesirable citizens" include Mr. Oakhurst (a professional gambler), The Duchess, Mother Shipton (an older lady) and Uncle Billy (the town drunkard and suspected claim robber).

As the party crosses the Sierra Mountains, they meet an innocent young boy and girl who have eloped and hope to get married. The two groups make camp together. During the night, the drunkard steals all the supplies and horses leaving the others to their fate in the rugged mountains.

The gambler, the two women of questionable reputation, and the young couple are soon trapped in a blizzard with meager shelter and very little food. At one point, Mr. Oakhurst alone remains sober, quietly watching the group. He does not drink, but remains cool and alert. The reader is left to wonder if leaving his weaker companions and ensuring his own survival has occurred to him.

Step One

"The Outcasts of Poker Flat" contains four kinds of conflict. Find the four examples of conflict in the summary above, one of each type, and list them. Correct your answers using the answer key at the back of the book before going on to step two.

A. Conflict with Society

_____ versus _____

B. Conflict with Other People

_____ versus _____

C. Conflict with Nature

_____ versus _____

D. Internal Conflict (Mr. Oakhurst)

_____ versus _____

Step Two

Decide how you would develop and resolve conflicts C and D and end the story. Express your ideas by completing the summary begun above.

Unit 6
**Analyzing
Plot Structure
and Development**

An American Tragedy

Introduction

Poor boy meets rich uncle and goes to work in his uncle's factory. Soon he is promoted to assistant foreman. More promotions follow. He wins the hand of a rich girl, inherits his uncle's business, and lives happily ever after. This was an American Dream, the kind that most people in the 1920s believed in. After all, some of the most famous fortunes had been made by poor boys who were now household names—Andrew Carnegie, John D. Rockefeller and Henry Ford. Horatio Alger's stories about the poor boys who made good by dint of luck, hard work and the will to succeed had become a sort of national myth.

An American Tragedy is Theodore Dreiser's version of the American Dream in a disturbingly warped variation of the Horatio Alger theme. The main character in the book is Clyde Griffiths, the son of streetcorner evangelists who were as poor as they were pious. At the age of fifteen, Clyde finds work as a bellhop in an opulent Kansas City hotel. Its lavish furnishings and glamorous clientele were intoxicating to a poor boy, and the small change he received in tips seemed "Aladdinish" to him—as if wealth were descending on him by magic. The atmosphere of riches and power cast a spell over Clyde from which he would never recover. But Book I ends on a note of disaster: A reckless escapade with other bellhops in a "borrowed" car ends in a child's death, and Clyde is forced to flee Kansas City in a boxcar to escape the scandal.

Three years later, while working as a bellhop in the exclusive Union League Club in Chicago, Clyde meets his rich uncle, Samuel Griffiths, who is visiting on business. Impressed with Clyde's pleasant manners, he offers him a job in his factory in Lycurgus, New York. It is the opportunity Clyde has been waiting for, and he accepts without hesitation. Once in Lycurgus, however, Clyde's wealthy relatives pointedly exclude him from their social circle. He is, after all, just a poor nephew.

Clyde works hard (as in the American Dream), and he is soon promoted to assistant foreman in the stamping department. It is here that he meets

Roberta Alden, one of the factory girls under his supervision. Like Clyde, Roberta is poor but anxious to better herself. They are immediately attracted to one another and their relationship blossoms.

Then, by a quirk of fate, Clyde unexpectedly gains access to that upper-class society which he has yearned for all his life. He meets and falls in love with Sondra Finchley, a beautiful and wealthy girl. Soon, she is inviting Clyde to her parties, and she persuades her friends to include him in their activities also. Eventually, the Griffiths themselves are obliged to treat Clyde as one of the family. With high hopes of marrying Sondra Finchley, Clyde resolves to break off his now faltering relationship with Roberta when a bombshell drops—Roberta is pregnant.

Desperately, Clyde stalls for time. Everything he has dreamed of all his life, and which he is now on the verge of attaining, is in jeopardy. With Roberta threatening to expose him if he does not marry her, Clyde happens to read a newspaper article about a young couple who drowned while canoeing on a lake. The man's body was never found. What if *he* could arrange such an "accident"? Roberta, whom he knows cannot swim, would drown while he would swim away to freedom and to Sondra. It is a terrible plan, but as time runs out, Clyde is driven to it as a last resort.

Such is the situation as the chapter in this unit begins. Proposing a sort of honeymoon trip before their marriage, Clyde has lured Roberta to a remote lake resort area in upstate New York. The chapter describes the nightmarish outing in detail.

Theodore Dresier calls Clyde's plight an "American tragedy" because it is so deeply rooted in the American Dream. All his life Clyde has succumbed to its allure. Like the hero in Horatio Alger stories, Clyde has clawed his way upwards. In a society focused on the acquisition of money and the things it can buy, Clyde has made its values his values. And now, having swallowed the American Dream whole, it is his unenviable fate to act out an American tragedy.

Like his hero Clyde Griffiths, Theodore Dreiser grew up in an atmosphere of poverty and religious fanaticism. He, too, longed for the material pleasures in life and left home at any early age to pursue the American Dream. Dreiser became a skillful journalist and editor, and his reporter's eye for detail and documentation is evident throughout *An American Tragedy*, especially in Book III in which Clyde is arrested, tried and convicted of premeditated murder. Dreiser once remarked that "most men and women are haunted by poverty, and all are helpless in the clutch of a relentless fate." Dreiser never outgrew his sympathy for those individuals who are always on the outside of society looking in.

BEST-SELLING CHAPTERS

Analyzing
Plot Structure
and Development

All fiction—whether it's a novel, short story or play—is based on conflict, and this conflict is presented in a structured format called a *plot*. Plot is the most natural way of telling a story because it presents the information a reader needs to know in an orderly and logical fashion. Plot structure is not something that gets in the way of a story. Rather, a well-knit plot builds a story so that each incident grows out of preceding incidents. The total effect is one of movement towards what seems to be an inevitable conclusion.

No two stories are alike, and some ways of telling a story seem radically different from others. But all successful fiction has a basic construction consisting of five elements: 1) exposition, 2) complication, 3) crisis, 4) climax, and 5) resolution.

1. Exposition. The *exposition* is simply the introductory material which gives the setting, creates the tone, presents the characters, and supplies other facts necessary for understanding the story.

The exposition allows the reader to become oriented in the world which the author has created. Often, the exposition will give background information about the main character or establish an atmosphere that will pervade the entire story. In all cases, the exposition contributes to the reader's understanding of the complication that will come further on.

The chapter from *An American Tragedy* found in this unit is about a murder. Clyde Griffiths, a poor boy who aspires to high society, has gotten a factory girl pregnant. Roberta Alden insists that Clyde marry her, but Clyde is determined to marry a rich girl named Sondra Finchley. He takes Roberta on a so-called honeymoon to a remote lake where he plans to have a boating accident in which she will drown and he will swim away. As the chapter begins, Clyde and Roberta have just arrived at Grass Lake. How does the information presented in these opening paragraphs "set the stage" for the reader?

> And then, as planned that night between them—a trip to Grass Lake
> the next morning in separate cars, but which, upon their arrival and

to his surprise, proved to be so much more briskly tenanted than he anticipated. He was very much disturbed and frightened by the evidence of so much active life up here. For he had fancied this, as well as Big Bittern, would be all but deserted . . . . And Roberta at once exclaiming:

"Now, there, isn't that cute? Why couldn't we be married over there by the minister of that church?"

And Clyde, puzzled and shaken by this sudden and highly unsatisfactory development, at once announced: "Why, sure— I'll go over after a bit and see," yet his mind busy with schemes for circumventing her. He would take her out in a boat after registering and getting settled and remain too long. Or should a peculiarly remote and unobserved spot be found . . . but no, there were too many people here. The lake was not large enough, and probably not very deep. It was black or dark like tar, and sentineled to the east and north by tall, dark pines—the serried spears of armed and watchful giants, as they now seemed to him— ogres almost—so gloomy, suspicious and fantastically erratic was his own mood in regard to all this.

These introductory paragraphs create a gloomy atmosphere which is an appropriate backdrop for the coming murder. They also provide the reader with an insight into Clyde's mental state as he plots Roberta's death.

The setting is presented through Clyde's eyes. He sees Grass Lake as a busy place; but then, for his purposes, even one other person on the lake is a crowd. The tall, dark pines around the lake which other people might find scenic seem like watchful giants or ogres to Clyde. Clyde's mood of fitful apprehension is already apparent. From the moment of their arrival, his plan to murder Roberta runs into complications he had not foreseen. He is puzzled and shaken by the way things are developing, and he has no very clear idea of what he will do next. Altogether, this exposition has sketched an unlucky beginning for an enterprise that turns out to be a gruesome exercise in frustration.

2. Complication. In the *complication* of a plot, the author develops the conflict upon which the plot is based, and proceeds to entangle the characters in the web of this conflict.

Conflict is the essence of all fiction. If there is no conflict, then there is no story. The development of the conflict, in the complication phase of the plot, creates a feeling of movement. Things are starting to happen. The character faced with the conflict is being forced to react in some way, and this character's reactions set into motion a chain of events which proceed to "snowball," generating suspense as it gathers momentum.

The following passage from *An American Tragedy* represents the complication of Clyde's plans. What conflict is expressed here, and how does it create suspense?

> . . . he walked here and there, making strained and yet admiring comments on the beauty of the scene—the pines and the curve of

this small bay, yet thinking—thinking, thinking of the island farther on and the bay below that again somewhere, where somehow, and in the face of a weakening courage for it, he must still execute this grim and terrible business before him—not allow this carefully planned opportunity to go for nothing—if—if—he were to not really run away and leave all that he most desired to keep.

And yet the horror of this business and the danger, now that it was so close at hand—the danger of making a mistake of some kind—if nothing more, of not upsetting the boat right—of not being able to—to—oh, God! And subsequently, maybe, to be proved to be what he would be—then—a murderer. Arrested! Tried. (He could not, he would not, go through with it. No, no no!)

There are two kinds of conflict in this chapter. There is the obvious conflict between Clyde and Roberta as expressed by his intention to kill her. But the conflict from which the complication grows and upon which the story moves is within Clyde himself. As the above passage relates, Clyde is torn by his desire to be free of Roberta at any cost and his fear that he is not equal to the task at hand. Clyde worries that he doesn't have the courage to overturn the boat when the time comes or that he might be caught and exposed as a murderer. This conflict creates suspense because the reader is anxious to learn which side of Clyde proves to be the stronger—the killer or the coward.

3. Crisis. The conflict which is developed in the complication of the plot comes to a head in the *crisis*. The crisis is the turning point of a story. At this point, the opposing forces of the conflict interlock. This is the moment toward which the story has been building.

In regard to the chapter in this unit, the crisis provides the answer to the question, "Will Clyde murder Roberta, or won't he?" How does the following scene answer this question?

At this cataclysmic moment, and in the face of the utmost, the most urgent need of action, a sudden palsy of the will—of courage—of hate or rage sufficient; and with Roberta from her seat in the stern of the boat gazing at his troubled and then suddenly distorted and fulgurous, yet weak and even unbalanced face—a face of a sudden, instead of angry, ferocious, demoniac—confused and all but meaningless in its registration of a balanced combat between fear . . . and a harried and restless and yet self-repressed desire to do—to do—to do—yet temporarily unbreakable here and now—a static between a powerful compulsion to do and yet not to do.

This moment of crisis reveals Clyde's inability to act. A sudden palsy, or paralysis, of will has rendered him incapable of carrying out his plan. He is caught in a "static"—a kind of twilight zone marked by frustration and generated by an unbreakable tension between the compulsion to do and yet not to do. Something must happen now. We are approaching the climax of the episode.

4. Climax. The *climax*, in turn, grows out of the crisis. It is the high point of the story for the reader. It is the moment of highest interest and greatest emotional response on the reader's part.

In a typical mystery story, the conflict between the detective and his unknown quarry builds to a crisis which culminates in a climactic scene where the detective unmasks the criminal. In a cowboy film, the climax may come in a dramatic shootout or with the arrival of the cavalry in the nick of time. There is usually a high point of excitement at the moment of climax. The tension is great and you are on the edge of your seat waiting to see how things will work out.

In the passage above which reveals the crisis, Clyde has reacted to his inner conflict by *not acting*. It is less a decision than a surrender of will. Still, here he is in the boat with Roberta. Something must happen. But what?

Roberta, noticing the strange look that has come over Clyde's face in his moment of crisis, gets up from her seat in the boat and moves toward him. Clyde strikes out with his arm in rejection of the comfort she is offering. Quite unintentionally, he hits her. Roberta is thrown off balance and the boat overturns, pitching them both into the lake. In the following scene, Clyde listens to Roberta's cries for help as she flounders helplessly in the water. In what sense is this scene the emotional high point for the reader? In what sense is it a logical extension of the crisis?

> "Help! Help!
> "Oh, my God, I'm drowning, I'm drowning. Help! Oh, my God!
> "Clyde, Clyde!"
>
> And then the voice at his ear!
>
> "But this—this—is not this that which you have been thinking and wishing for this while—you in your great need? And behold! For despite your fear, your cowardice, this—this—has been done for you. An accident—an accident—an unintentional blow on your part is now saving you the labor of what you sought, and yet did not have the courage to do! But will you now, and when you need not, since it is an accident, by going to her rescue, once more plunge yourself in the horror of that defeat and failure which has so tortured you and from which this now releases you? You might save her. But again you might not! For see how she strikes about. She is stunned. She herself is unable to save herself and by her erratic terror, if you draw near her now, may bring about your own death also. But you desire to live! And her living will make your life not worth while from now on. Rest but a moment—a fraction of a minute! Wait—wait—ignore the pity of that appeal. And then—then— But there! Behold. It is over. She is sinking now. You will never, never see her alive any more—ever.

The above scene is emotionally moving because it is a human drama rather than the purely psychological drama that took place in Clyde's mind moments before. What reader can resist the image of poor Roberta crying out for Clyde's help while he lets her drown in front of his very eyes? It is pitiful to contemplate, and this scene moves the reader more than Clyde's personal crisis. We want to scream with Roberta, we want to save her. But she drowns in front of our eyes, and we are appalled and repelled by Clyde's cold-blooded heartlessness.

5. Resolution. The *resolution*, also called the *denouement*, of a plot serves to round out the action and bring the reader down from the climactic high. The action is concluded.

In a murder mystery, the resolution may consist of an explanation of the murderer's motives. The tightly knit plot is unraveled for the benefit of the reader, and this is the point where the reader usually slaps his forehead and exclaims, "Of course! He was the only one with both motive and opportunity!"

In the chapter from *An American Tragedy* which you are about to read, how does this final paragraph effectively conclude the action?

> The dusk and silence of a closing day. A concealed spot in the depths of the same sheltering woods where alone and dripping, his dry bag near, Clyde stood, and by waiting, sought to dry himself. But in the interim, removing from the side of the bag the unused tripod of his camera and seeking an obscure, dead log farther in the woods, hiding it. Had any one seen? Was any one looking? Then returning and wondering as to the direction! He must go west and then south. He must not get turned about! But the repeated cry of that bird—harsh, nerve shaking. And then the gloom, in spite of the summer stars. And a youth making his way through a dark, uninhabited wood, a dry straw hat upon his head, a bag in his hand, walking briskly and yet warily—south—south.

This concluding paragraph winds up the action at the lake with Clyde striding furtively away from the scene of the crime. The gloomy mood and the harsh, nerve-shaking cry of the bird seem to mock Clyde's pathetic attempts to conceal the traces of his presence. In the final sentence, the author has retreated to an impersonal distance and Clyde becomes, simply, "a youth." The reader's last view is of a nameless figure in an unlikely get-up of wet clothes and a dry straw hat, making his way south. It is an ominous end to an undertaking that seemed doomed from the start.

It is clear that plots are constructed in a logical and orderly fashion. This format involves five elements in the following sequence: exposition, complication, crisis, climax and resolution.

Along the way, however, a good plot must also fulfill certain conditions. It must be *selective*—that is, the author selects only those details that point to a certain end. A good plot is *unified;* it has an organizing principle to which all of its parts are related. In the chapter from *An American Tragedy*, that organizing principle is Clyde, the main character. Other organizing principles might just as easily be a theme, a setting or even an atmosphere that pervades the story. The ever-present lakes, trees and water, for example, also act as a unifying force in the reading selection. A good plot is also *believable*. The characters behave with a fitting degree of probability, and the ending seems inevitable. This is not to say that it is the only possible ending. Rather, the reader should finish a story feeling that, given these particular characters and that set of circumstances, this is probably the best conclusion. Above all, a good plot leaves a reader feeling satisfied, not cheated. Life itself may seem incomprehensible at times, but a good plot makes a neat package out of an untidy world.

As you read the chapter:

- Notice the bus trip through the woods which Clyde and Roberta take on their way to Big Bittern.

- Observe the scene at the boathouse platform as Clyde and Roberta step into the boat.

- Pay attention to the scene in the boat when the actual opportunity to carry out his plan presents itself to Clyde.

- Think about the scene in which the boat capsizes and Roberta and Clyde are pitched into the water.

An American Tragedy
Theodore Dreiser

CHAPTER 47

And then, as planned that night between them—a trip to Grass Lake the next morning in separate cars, but which, upon their arrival and to his surprise, proved to be so much more briskly tenanted than he anticipated. He was very much disturbed and frightened by the evidence of so much active life up here. For he had fancied this, as well as Big Bittern, would be all but deserted. Yet here now, as both could see, it was the summer seat and gathering place of some small religious organization or group—the Winebrennarians of Pennsylvania—as it proved with a tabernacle and numerous cottages across the lake from the station. And Roberta at once exclaiming:

"Now, there, isn't that cute? Why couldn't we be married over there by the minister of that church?"

And Clyde, puzzled and shaken by this sudden and highly unsatisfactory development, at once announced: "Why, sure—I'll go over after a bit and see," yet his mind busy with schemes for circumventing her. He would take her out in a boat after registering and getting settled and remain too long. Or should a peculiarly remote and unobserved spot be found . . . but no, there were too many people here. The lake was not large enough, and probably not very deep. It was black or dark like tar, and sentineled to the east and north by tall, dark pines—the serried spears of armed and watchful giants, as they now seemed to him—ogres almost—so gloomy, suspicious and fantastically erratic was his own mood in regard to all this. But still there were too many people—as many as ten on the lake.

The weirdness of it.

The difficulty.

But whisper:—one could not walk from here through any woods to Three Mile Bay. Oh, no. That was all of thirty miles to the south now. And besides this lake was less lonely—probably continually observed by members of this religious group. Oh, no—he must say—he must say—but what—could he say? That he had inquired, and that no license could be procured here? Or that the minister was away, or that he required certain identifications which he did not have—or—or, well, well—anything that would serve to still Roberta until such hour tomorrow, as the train south from here left for Big Bittern and Sharon, where, of course, they would surely be married.

Why should she be so insistent? And why, anyhow, and except for her crass determination to force him in this way, should he be compelled to track here and there with her—every hour—every minute of which was torture—an unending mental crucifixion really, when, if he were but rid of her! Oh, Sondra, Sondra, if but now from your high estate, you might bend down and aid me. No more lies! No more suffering! No more misery of any kind!

But instead, more lies. A long and aimless and pestilential search for water-lilies, which because of his own restless mood, bored Roberta as much as it did him. For why, she was now thinking to herself as they rowed about, this indifference to this marriage possibility, which could have been arranged before now and given this outing the dream quality it would and should have had, if only—if only he had arranged for everything in Utica, even as she had wanted. But this waiting—evasion—and so like Clyde, his vacillating, indefinite, uncertain mood, always. She was beginning to wonder now as to his intentions again—whether really and truly he did intend to marry her as he had promised. Tomorrow, or the next day at most, would show. So why worry now?

And then the next day at noon, Gun Lodge and Big Bittern itself and Clyde climbing down from the train at Gun Lodge and escorting Roberta to the waiting bus, the while he assured her that since they were coming back this way, it would be best if she were to leave her bag here, while he, because of his camera as well as the lunch done up at Grass Lake and crowded into his suitcase, would take his own with him, because they would lunch on the lake. But on reaching the bus, he was dismayed by the fact that the driver was the same guide whom he had heard talk at Big Bittern. What if it should prove now that this guide had seen and remembered him! Would he not at least recall the handsome Finchley car—Bertine and Stuart on the front seat—himself and Sondra at the back—Grant and that Harley Baggott talking to him outside?

At once that cold perspiration that had marked his more nervous and terrified moods for weeks past, now burst forth on his face and hands. Of what had he been thinking, anyhow? How planning? In God's name, how expect to carry a thing like this through, if he were going to think so poorly? It was like his failing to wear his cap from Lycurgus to Utica, or at least getting it out of his bag before he tried to buy that straw hat; it was like not buying the straw hat before he went to Utica at all.

Yet the guide did not remember him, thank God! On the contrary he inquired rather curiously, and as of a total stranger: "Goin' over to the lodge at Big Bittern? First time up here?" And Clyde, enormously relieved and yet really tremulous, replied: "Yes," and then in his nervous excitement asked: "Many people over there today?" a question which the moment he had propounded it, seemed almost insane. Why, why, of all questions, should he ask that? Oh, God, would his silly, self-destructive mistakes never cease?

So troubled was he indeed, now, that he scarcely heard the guide's reply, or, if at all, as a voice speaking from a long way off. "Not so many. About seven or eight, I guess. We did have about thirty over the Fourth, but most o' them went down yesterday."

The stillness of these pines lining this damp yellow road along which they were traveling; the cool and the silence; the dark shadows and purple and gray depths and nooks in them, even at high noon. If one were slipping away at night or by day, who would encounter one here? A blue-jay far in the depths somewhere uttered its metallic shriek; a field sparrow, tremulous upon some distant twig, filled the silver shadows with its perfect song. And Roberta, as this heavy, covered bus crossed rill and thin stream, and then rough wooden bridges here and there, commented on the clarity and sparkle of the water: "Isn't that wonderful in there? Do you hear the tinkling of that water, Clyde? Oh, the freshness of this air!"

And yet she was going to die so soon!

God!

But supposing now, at Big Bittern—the lodge and boathouse there—there were many people. Or that the lake, peradventure, was literally dotted with those that were there—all fishermen and all fishing here and there, each one separate and alone—no privacy or a deserted spot anywhere. And how strange he had not thought of that. This lake was probably not nearly as deserted as he had imagined, or would not be today, any more than Grass Lake had proved. And then what?

Well, flight then—flight—and let it go at that. This strain was too much—hell—he would die, thinking thoughts like these. How could he have dreamed to better his fortunes by any so wild and brutal a scheme as this anyhow—to kill and then run away—or rather to kill and pretend that he and she had drowned—while he—the real murderer—slipped away to life and happiness. What a horrible plan! And yet how else? How? Had he not come all this way to do this? And was he going to turn back now?

And all this time Roberta at his side was imagining that she was not going to anything but marriage—tomorrow morning sure; and now only to the passing pleasure of seeing this beautiful lake of which he had been talking—talking, as though it were something more important and delectable than any that had as yet been in her or his life for that matter.

But now the guide was speaking again, and to him: "You're not mindin' to stay over, I suppose. I see you left the young lady's bag over there." He nodded in the direction of Gun Lodge.

"No, we're going on down tonight—on that 8:10. You take people over to that?"

"Oh, sure."

"They said you did—at Grass Lake."

But now why should he have added that reference to Grass Lake, for that showed that he and Roberta had been there before coming here. But this fool with his reference to "the young lady's bag"! And leaving it at Gun Lodge. The Devil! Why shouldn't he mind his own business? Or why should he have decided that he and Roberta were not married? Or had he so decided? At any rate, why such a question when they were carrying two bags and he had brought one? Strange! The effrontery! How should he know or guess or what? But what harm could it do—married or unmarried? If she were not found—"married or unmarried" would make no difference, would it? And if she were, and it was discovered that she was not married, would that not prove that she was off with some one else? Of course! So why worry over that now?

And Roberta asking: "Are there any hotels or boarding houses on the lake besides this one we're going to?"

"Not a one, miss, outside o' the inn that we're goin' to. There was a crowd of young fellers and girls campin' over on the east shore, yesterday, I believe, about a mile from the inn—but whether they're there now or not, I dunno. Ain't seen none of 'em today."

A crowd of young fellows and girls! For God's sake! And might not they now be out on the water—all of them—rowing—or sailing—or what? And he here with her! Maybe some of them from Twelfth Lake! Just as he and Sondra and Harriet and Stuart and Bertine had come up two weeks before—some of them friends of the Cranstons, Harriets, Finchleys or others who had come up here to play and who would remember him, of course. And again, then, there must be a road to the east of this lake. And all this knowledge and their presence there now might make this trip of his useless. Such silly plotting! Such pointless planning as this—when at least he might have taken more time—chosen a lake still farther away and should have—only so tortured had he been for these last many days, that he could scarcely think how to think. Well, all he could do now was to go and see. If there were many he must think of some way to row to some real lonely spot or maybe turn and return to Grass Lake—or where? Oh, what could or would he do— if there were many over here?

But just then a long aisle of green trees giving out at the far end as he now recalled upon a square of lawn, and the lake itself, the little inn with its pillared verandah, facing the dark blue waters of Big Bittern. And that low, small red-roofed boathouse to the right on the water that he had seen before when he was here. And Roberta exclaiming on sight, "Oh, it is pretty, isn't it—just beautiful." And Clyde surveying that dark, low island in the distance, to the south, and seeing but few people about—none on the lake itself—exclaiming nervously, "Yes, it is, you bet." But feeling half choked as he said it.

And now the host of the inn himself appearing and approaching—a medium-sized, red-faced, broad-shouldered man who was saying most intriguingly, "Staying over for a few days?"

But Clyde, irritated by this new development and after paying the guide a dollar, replying crustily and irritably, "No, no—just came over for the afternoon. We're going on down tonight."

"You'll be staying over for dinner then, I suppose? The train doesn't leave till eight-fifteen."

"Oh, yes—that's so. Sure. Yes, well, in that case, we will." . . . For, of course, Roberta on her honeymoon—the day before her wedding and on a trip like this, would be expecting her dinner. Damn this stocky, red-faced fool, anyway.

"Well, then, I'll just take your bag and you can register. Your wife'll probably be wanting to freshen up a bit anyway."

He led the way, bag in hand, although Clyde's greatest desire was to snatch it from him. For he had not expected to register here—nor leave his bag either. And would not. He would recapture it and hire a boat. But on top of that, being compelled "for the register's sake," as Boniface phrased it, to sign Clifford Golden and wife—before he could take his bag again.

And then to add to the nervousness and confusion engendered by all this, thoughts as to what additional developments or persons, even, he might encounter before leaving on his climacteric errand—Roberta announcing that because of the heat and the fact that they were coming back to dinner, she would leave her hat and coat—a hat in which he had already seen the label of Braunstein in Lycurgus—and which at the time caused him to meditate as to the wisdom of leaving or extracting it. But he had decided that perhaps afterwards—afterwards—if he should really do this—it might not make any difference whether it was there or not. Was she not likely to be identified anyhow, if found, and if not found, who was to know who she was?

In a confused and turbulent state mentally, scarcely realizing the clarity or import of any particular thought or movement or act now, he took up his bag and led the way to the boathouse platform. And then, after dropping the bag into the boat, asking of the boathouse keeper if he knew where the best views were, that he wanted to photograph them. And this done—the meaningless explanation over, assisting Roberta (an almost nebulous figure, she now seemed, stepping down into an insubstantial rowboat upon a purely ideational lake), he now stepped in after her, seating himself in the center and taking the oars.

The quiet, glassy, iridescent surface of this lake that now to both seemed, not so much like water as oil—like molten glass that, of enormous bulk and weight, resting upon the substantial earth so very far below. And the lightness and freshness and intoxication of the gentle air blowing here and there, yet scarcely rippling the surface of the lake. And the softness and furry thickness of the tall pines about the shore. Everywhere pines—tall and spearlike. And above them the humped backs of the dark and distant Adirondacks beyond. Not a rower to be seen. Not a house or cabin. He sought to distinguish the camp of which the guide had spoken. He could not. He sought to distinguish the voices of those who might be there—or any voices. Yet, except for the lock-lock of his own oars as he rowed and the voice of the boathouse keeper and the guide in converse two hundred, three hundred, five hundred, a thousand feet behind, there was no sound.

"Isn't it still and peaceful?" It was Roberta talking. "It seems to be so restful here. I think it's beautiful, truly, so much more beautiful than that other lake. These trees are so tall, aren't they? And those mountains. I was thinking all the way over how cool and silent that road was, even if it was a little rough."

"Did you talk to any one in the inn there just now?"

"Why, no; what makes you ask?"

"Oh, I thought you might have run into some one. There don't seem to be very many people up here today, though, does there?"

"No, I don't see anyone on the lake. I saw two men in that billiard room at the back there, and there was a girl in the ladies' room, that was all. Isn't this water cold?" She had put her hand over the side and was trailing it in the blue-black ripples made by his oars.

"Is it? I haven't felt it yet."

He paused in his rowing and put out his hand, then resumed. He would not row directly to that island to the south. It was—too far—too early. She might think it odd. Better a little delay. A little time in which to think—a little while in which to reconnoiter. Roberta would be wanting to eat her lunch (her lunch!) and there was a charming looking point of land there to the west about a mile further on. They could go there and eat first—or she could—for he would not be eating today. And then—and then——

She was looking at the very same point of land that he was—a curved horn of land that bent to the south and yet reached quite far out into the water and combed with tall pines. And now she added:

"Have you any spot in mind, dear, where we could stop and eat? I'm getting a little hungry, aren't you?" (If she would only not call him *dear*, here and now!)

The little inn and the boathouse to the north were growing momentarily smaller,—looking now, like that other boathouse and pavilion on Crum Lake the day he had first rowed there, and when he had been wishing that he might come to such a lake as this in the Adirondacks, dreaming of such a lake—and wishing to meet such a girl as Roberta—then—— And overhead was one of those identical woolly clouds that had sailed above him at Crum Lake on that fateful day.

The horror of this effort!

They might look for water-lilies here today to kill time a little, before— to kill time . . . to kill, (God)—he must quit thinking of that, if he were going to do it at all. He needn't be thinking of it now, at any rate.

At the point of land favored by Roberta, into a minute protected bay with a small, curved, honey-colored beach, and safe from all prying eyes north or east. And then he and she stepping out normally enough. And Roberta, after Clyde had extracted the lunch most cautiously from his bag, spreading it on a newspaper on the shore, while he walked here and there, making strained and yet admiring comments on the beauty of the scene— the pines and the curve of this small bay, yet thinking—thinking, thinking of the island farther on and the bay below that again somewhere, where some- how, and in the face of a weakening courage for it, he must still execute this grim and terrible business before him—not allow this carefully planned opportunity to go for nothing—if—if—he were to not really run away and leave all that he most desired to keep.

And yet the horror of this business and the danger, now that it was so close at hand—the danger of making a mistake of some kind—if nothing more, of not upsetting the boat right—of not being able to—to—oh, God! And subsequently, maybe, to be proved to be what he would be—then— a murderer. Arrested! Tried. (He could not, he would not, go through with it. No, no, no!)

And yet Roberta, sitting here with him now on the sand, feeling quite at peace with all the world as he could see. And she was begining to hum a little, and then to make advisory and practical references to the nature of their coming adventure together—their material and financial state from now on—how and where they would go from here—Syracuse, most likely—since Clyde seemed to have no objection to that—and what, once there, they would do. For Roberta had heard from her brother-in-law, Fred Gabel, of a new collar and shirt factory that was just starting up in Syracuse. Might it not be possible for Clyde, for the time being at least, to get himself a position with that firm at once? And then later, when her own worst trouble was over, might not she connect herself with the same company, or some other? And temporarily, since they had so little money, could they not take a small room together, somewhere in some family home, or if he did not like that, since they were by no means so close temperamentally as they once had been, then two small adjoining rooms, maybe. She could still feel his unrelenting opposition under all this present show of courtesy and consideration.

And he was thinking, Oh, well, what difference such talk now? And whether he agreed or whether he did not. What difference since he was not going—or she either—that way. Great God! But here he was talking as though tomorrow she would be here still. And she would not be.

If only his knees would not tremble so; his hands and face and body continue so damp.

And after that, farther on down the west shore of this small lake in this little boat, to that island, with Clyde looking nervously and wearily here and there to see that there was no one—no one—not anywhere in sight on land or water—no one. It was so still and deserted here, thank God. Here—or anywhere near here might do, really,—if only he had the courage so to do now, which he had not,—yet. Roberta trailing her hand in water, asking him if he thought they might find some water-lilies or wild flowers somewhere on shore. Water-lilies! Wild flowers! And he convincing himself as he went that there were no roads, cabins, tents, paths, anything in the form of a habitation among these tall, close, ranking pines—no trace of any little boat on the widespread surface of this beautiful lake on this beautiful day. Yet might there not be some lone, solitary hunter and trapper or guide or fisherman in these woods or along these banks? Might there not be? And supposing there were one here now somewhere? And watching!

Fate!

Destruction!

Death! Yet no sound and no smoke. Only—only—these tall, dark, green pines—spear-shaped and still, with here and there a dead one—ashen pale in the hard afternoon sun, its gaunt, sapless arms almost menacingly outstretched.

Death!

And the sharp metallic cry of a blue-jay speeding in the depths of these woods. Or the lone and ghostly tap-tap-tap of some solitary woodpecker, with now and then the red line of a flying tanager, the yellow and black of a yellow-shouldered blackbird.

"Oh, the sun shines bright in my old Kentucky home."

It was Roberta singing cheerfully, one hand in the deep blue water.

And then a little later—"I'll be there Sunday if you will," one of the popular dance pieces of the day.

And then at last, after fully an hour of rowing, brooding, singing, stopping to look at some charming point of land, reconnoitering some receding inlet which promised water-lilies, and with Roberta already saying that they must watch the time and not stay out too long,—the bay, south of the island itself—a beautiful and yet most funereally pine-encircled and land delimited bit of water—more like a smaller lake, connected by an inlet or passage to the larger one, and yet itself a respectable body of water of perhaps twenty acres of surface and almost circular in form. The manner in which to the east, the north, the south, the west, even, except for the passage by which the island to the north of it was separated from the mainland, this pool or tarn was encircled by trees! And cat-tails and water-lilies here and there— a few along its shores. And somehow suggesting an especially arranged pool or tarn to which one who was weary of life and cares—anxious to be away from the strife and contentions of the world, might most wisely and yet gloomily repair.

And as they glided into this, this still dark water seemed to grip Clyde as nothing here or anywhere before this ever had—to change his mood. For once here he seemed to be fairly pulled or lured along into it, and having encircled its quiet banks, to be drifting, drifting—in endless space where was no end of anything—no plots—no plans—no practical problems to be solved—nothing. The insidious beauty of this place! Truly, it seemed to mock him—this strangeness—this dark pool, surrounded on all sides by those wonderful, soft, fir trees. And the water itself looking like a huge, black pearl cast by some mighty hand, in anger possibly, in sport or fantasy maybe, into the bosom of this valley of dark, green plush—and which seemed bottomless as he gazed into it.

And yet, what did it all suggest so strongly? Death! Death! More definitely than anything he had ever seen before. Death! But also a still, quiet, unprotesting type of death into which one, by reason of choice or hypnosis or unutterable weariness, might joyfully and gratefully sink. So quiet—so shaded—so serene. Even Roberta exclaimed over this. And he now felt for the first time the grip of some seemingly strong, and yet friendly sympathetic, hands laid firmly on his shoulders. The comfort of them! The warmth! The strength! For now they seemed to have a steadying effect on him and he liked them—their reassurance—their support. If only they would not be removed! If only they would remain always—the hands of this friend! For where had he ever known this comforting and almost tender sensation before in all his life? Not anywhere—and somehow this calmed him and he seemed to slip away from the reality of all things.

To be sure, there was Roberta over there, but by now she had faded to a shadow or thought really, a form of illusion more vaporous than real. And while there was something about her in color, form that suggested reality— still she was very insubstantial—so very—and once more now he felt strangely alone. For the hands of the friend of firm grip had vanished also.

And Clyde was alone, so very much alone and forlorn, in this somber, beautiful realm to which apparently he had been led, and then deserted. Also he felt strangely cold—the spell of this strange beauty overwhelming him with a kind of chill.

He had come here for what?

And he must do what?

Kill Roberta? Oh, no!

And again he lowered his head and gazed into the fascinating and yet treacherous depths of that magnetic, bluish, purple pool, which, as he continued to gaze, seemed to change its form kaleidoscopically to a large, crystalline ball. But what was that moving about in this crystal? A form! It came nearer—clearer—and as it did so, he recognized Roberta struggling and waving her thin white arms out of the water and reaching toward him! God! How terrible! The expression on her face! What in God's name was he thinking of anyway? Death! Murder!

And suddenly becoming conscious that his courage, on which he had counted so much this long while to sustain him here, was leaving him, and he instantly and consciously plumbing the depths of his being in a vain search to recapture it.

Kit, kit, kit, Ca-a-a-ah!

Kit, kit, kit, Ca-a-a-ah!

Kit, kit, kit, Ca-a-a-ah!

(The weird, haunting cry of that unearthly bird again. So cold, so harsh! Here it was once more to startle him out of his soul flight into a realization of the real or unreal immediate problem with all of its torturesome angles that lay before him.)

He must face this thing! He must!

Kit, kit, kit, Ca-a-a-ah!

Kit, kit, kit, Ca-a-a-ah!

What was it sounding—a warning—a protest—condemnation? The same bird that had marked the very birth of this miserable plan. For there it was now upon that dead tree—that wretched bird. And now it was flying to another one—as dead—a little farther inland and crying as it did so. God!

And then to the shore again in spite of himself. For Clyde, in order to justify his having brought his bag, now must suggest that pictures of this be taken—and of Roberta—and of himself, possibly—on land and water. For that would bring her into the boat again, without his bag, which would be safe and dry on land. And once on shore, actually pretending to be seeking out various special views here and there, while he fixed in his mind the exact tree at the base of which he might leave his bag against his return—which must be soon now—must be soon. They would not come on shore again together. Never! Never! And that in spite of Roberta protesting that she was getting tired; and did he not think they ought to be starting back pretty soon? It must be after five, surely. And Clyde, assuring her that presently they would—after he had made one or two more pictures of her in the boat with those wonderful trees—that island and this dark water around and beneath her.

His wet, damp, nervous hands!
And his dark, liquid, nervous eyes, looking anywhere but at her.

And then once more on the water again—about five hundred feet from shore, the while he fumbled aimlessly with the hard and heavy and yet small camera that he now held, as the boat floated out nearer the center. And then, at this point and time looking fearfully about. For now—now—in spite of himself, the long evaded and yet commanding moment. And no voice or figure or sound on shore. No road or cabin or smoke! And the moment which he or something had planned for him, and which was now to decide his fate at hand! the moment of action—of crisis! All that he needed to do now was to turn swiftly and savagely to one side or the other—leap up— upon the left wale or right and upset the boat; or, failing that, rock it swiftly, and if Roberta protested too much, strike her with the camera in his hand, or one of the oars at his right. It could be done—it could be done—swiftly and simply, were he now of the mind and heart, or lack of it— with him swimming swiftly away thereafter to freedom—to success—of course—to Sondra and happiness—a new and greater and sweeter life than any he had ever known.
Yet why was he waiting now?
What was the matter with him, anyhow?
Why was he waiting?
At this cataclysmic moment, and in the face of the utmost, the most urgent need of action, a sudden palsy of the will—of courage—of hate or rage sufficient; and with Roberta from her seat in the stern of the boat gazing at his troubled and then suddenly distorted and fulgurous, yet weak and even unbalanced face—a face of a sudden, instead of angry, ferocious, demoniac—confused and all but meaningless in its registration of a balanced combat between fear (a chemic revulsion against death or murderous brutality that would bring death) and a harried and restless and yet self-repressed desire to do—to do—to do—yet temporarily unbreakable here and now—a static between a powerful compulsion to do and yet not to do.
And in the meantime his eyes—the pupils of the same growing momentarily larger and more lurid; his face and body and hands tense and contracted—the stillness of his position, the balanced immobility of the mood more and more ominous, yet in truth not suggesting a brutal, courageous power to destroy, but the imminence of trance or spasm.
And Roberta, suddenly noticing the strangeness of it all—that something of eerie unreason or physical and mental indetermination so strangely and painfully contrasting with this scene, exclaiming: "Why, Clyde! Clyde! What is it? Whatever is the matter with you anyhow? You look so—so strange—so—so— Why, I never saw you look like this before. What is it?" And suddenly rising, or rather leaning forward, and by crawling along the even keel, attempting to approach him, since he looked as though he was

about to fall forward into the boat—or to one side and out into the water. And Clyde, as instantly sensing the profoundness of his own failure, his own cowardice or inadequateness for such an occasion, as instantly yielding to a tide of submerged hate, not only for himself, but Roberta—her power— or that of life to restrain him in this way. And yet fearing to act in any way—being unwilling to—being willing only to say that never, never would he marry her—that never, even should she expose him, would he leave here with her to marry her—that he was in love with Sondra and would cling only to her—and yet not being able to say that even. But angry and confused and glowering. And then, as she drew near him, seeking to take his hand in hers and the camera from him in order to put it in the boat, he flinging out at her, but not even then with any intention to do other than free himself of her—her touch—her pleading—consoling sympathy—her presence forever—God!

Yet, (the camera still unconsciously held tight) pushing at her with so much vehemence as not only to strike her lips and nose and chin with it, but to throw her back sidewise toward the left wale which caused the boat to careen to the very water's edge. And then he, stirred by her sharp scream, (as much due to the lurch of the boat, as the cut on her nose and lip), rising and reaching half to assist or recapture her and half to apologize for the unintended blow—yet in so doing completely capsizing the boat—himself and Roberta being as instantly thrown into the water. And the left wale of the boat as it turned, striking Roberta on the head as she sank and then rose for the first time, her frantic, contorted face turned to Clyde, who by now had righted himself. For she was stunned, horror-struck, unintelligible with pain and fear—her lifelong fear of water and drowning and the blow he had so accidentally and all but unconsciously administered.

"Help! Help!

"Oh, my God, I'm drowning, I'm drowning. Help! Oh, my God!

"Clyde, Clyde!"

And then the voice at his ear!

"But this—this—is not this that which you have been thinking and wishing for this while—you in your great need? And behold! For despite your fear, your cowardice, this—this—has been done for you. An accident—an accident—an unintentional blow on your part is now saving you the labor of what you sought, and yet did not have the courage to do! But will you now, and when you need not, since it is an accident, by going to her rescue, once more plunge yourself in the horror of that defeat and failure which has so tortured you and from which this now releases you? You might save her. But again you might not! For see how she strikes about. She is stunned. She herself is unable to save herself and by her erratic terror, if you draw near her now, may bring about your own death also. But you desire to live! And her living will make your life not worth while from now on. Rest but a moment— a fraction of a minute! Wait—wait—ignore the pity of that appeal. And then— then— But there! Behold. It is over. She is sinking now. You will never, never see her alive any more—ever. And there is your own hat upon the water—as you wished. And upon the boat, clinging to that rowlock a veil belonging to her. Leave it. Will it not show that this was an accident?"

And apart from that, nothing—a few ripples—the peace and solemnity of this wondrous scene. And then once more the voice of that weird, contemptuous, mocking, lonely bird.

Kit, kit, kit, Ca-a-a-ah!
Kit, kit, kit, Ca-a-a-ah!
Kit, kit, kit, Ca-a-a-ah!

The cry of that devilish bird upon that dead limb—the wier-wier.

And then Clyde, with the sound of Roberta's cries still in his ears, that last frantic, white, appealing look in her eyes, swimming heavily, gloomily and darkly to shore. And the thought that, after all, he had not really killed her. No, no. Thank God for that. He had not. And yet (stepping up on the nearby bank and shaking the water from his clothes) had he? Or, had he not? For had he not refused to go to her rescue, and when he might have saved her, and when the fault for casting her in the water, however accidentally, was so truly his? And yet—and yet—

The dusk and silence of a closing day. A concealed spot in the depths of the same sheltering woods where alone and dripping, his dry bag near, Clyde stood, and by waiting, sought to dry himself. But in the interim, removing from the side of the bag the unused tripod of his camera and seeking an obscure, dead log farther in the woods, hiding it. Had any one seen? Was any one looking? Then returning and wondering as to the direction! He must go west and then south. He must not get turned about! But the repeated cry of that bird,—harsh, nerve shaking. And then the gloom, in spite of the summer stars. And a youth making his way through a dark, uninhabited wood, a dry straw hat upon his head, a bag in his hand, walking briskly and yet warily—south—south.

Unit 6

An American Tragedy

- Comprehension Questions
- Analyzing Plot Structure and Development
- Discussion Guides
- Writing Exercise

COMPREHENSION QUESTIONS

For each of the following statements and questions, select the option containing the most complete or most accurate answer.

1. Clyde goes on the outing with Roberta in order to
(d) ☐ a. kill Roberta and then himself.
  ☐ b. talk Roberta out of marrying him.
  ☐ c. kill Roberta and swim away.
  ☐ d. stage a phony marriage ceremony.

2. Clyde is worried that the lake resort which he and Roberta are visiting
(b) is too
  ☐ a. expensive.   ☐ c. lonely.
  ☐ b. crowded.   ☐ d. tacky.

3. The remote bay surrounded by tall trees which Clyde chooses as the
(i) scene of Roberta's murder projects an aura of
  ☐ a. hypnotic serenity.   ☐ c. eager anticipation.
  ☐ b. hustle and bustle.   ☐ d. fear and dread.

4. Clyde's mood throughout the ordeal is one of
(i) ☐ a. calm resolution.   ☐ c. careless nonchalance.
  ☐ b. listless apathy.   ☐ d. nervous anxiety.

5. Clyde's actions and behavior throughout this episode suggest that
(f) ☐ a. everything has been carefully planned.
  ☐ b. murder is a profoundly disturbing experience.
  ☐ c. murder is nothing new to him.
  ☐ d. he is unaffected by the whole situation.

6. Roberta is
(g) ☐ a. a scheming woman.   ☐ c. a social climber.
  ☐ b. an innocent victim.   ☐ d. a social misfit.

7. Which of the following best defines *vacillating* as used in, "But this
(l) waiting—evasion—and so like Clyde, his *vacillating*, indefinite, uncertain
  mood, always"?
  ☐ a. Mistrustful   ☐ c. Wavering
  ☐ b. Disagreeable   ☐ d. Menacing

8. Throughout the chapter, Roberta's mood seems
(g) □ a. happy and tranquil.   □ c. picky and annoyed.
     □ b. reserved and undecided. □ d. suspicious and fearful.

9. Roberta's only concern seems to be
(c) □ a. making sure she wasn't seen.
     □ b. getting away from Clyde.
     □ c. persuading Clyde to like her.
     □ d. marrying Clyde.

10. The term "dramatic irony" refers to a situation in which a character in a
(k) story is blind to facts known to the reader. An example of this in the
     chapter is
     □ a. the reader's knowledge of Roberta's impending death.
     □ b. Roberta's knowledge of Clyde's lack of affection for her.
     □ c. the reader's awareness of the setting.
     □ d. Clyde's reluctance to marry Roberta.

11. On the lake with Roberta, Clyde decided not to row directly out to the
(c) island because
     □ a. he wanted to save his strength.
     □ b. he was afraid it would make her suspicious.
     □ c. there were too many people on the island.
     □ d. it was beginning to get dark.

12. Clyde imagines the trees to be monsters and the bird that goes "kit, kit,
(k) kit, Ca-a-ah!" to be contemptuous and mocking. These are both
     examples of a literary device referred to as
     □ a. hyperbole (exaggeration).
     □ b. meiosis (understatement).
     □ c. personification (ascribing human traits to animals or objects).
     □ d. metaphor (comparison).

13. Clyde's decision to murder Roberta was probably arrived at out of
(h) □ a. spite.   □ c. boredom.
     □ b. revenge.   □ d. desperation.

14. Clyde is experiencing a conflict between
(j) □ a. his desire to be free of Roberta versus his reluctance to commit
            murder.
     □ b. his love for Roberta versus his love for Sondra.
     □ c. his impatience to carry out his plan versus his difficulty in finding
            a suitable spot.
     □ d. his desire to do right by Roberta versus his inability to support a
            family.

15. Clyde's plans depend a good deal on
    (h) ☐ a. having many people remember seeing him.
    ☐ b. establishing an alibi with the guide.
    ☐ c. not being seen or remembered.
    ☐ d. Roberta's playing her part well.

16. It could be said of Clyde's plans that
    (e) ☐ a. they were working out pretty well.
    ☐ b. they were working out in spite of Clyde.
    ☐ c. Clyde really had no plan.
    ☐ d. Clyde was making things up as he went along.

17. Trees are mentioned several times in the story. They are
    (a) ☐ a. birch and willows.   ☐ c. pine and fir trees.
    ☐ b. fruit trees.   ☐ d. beech and maple.

18. Clyde's inability to carry out his scheme is due to a
    (c) ☐ a. change of heart.   ☐ c. guilty conscience.
    ☐ b. lack of courage.   ☐ d. change of plans.

19. Clyde comes to despise himself because of
    (f) ☐ a. his inability to carry out his plan.
    ☐ b. his cruel treatment of Roberta.
    ☐ c. the murder which he had plotted.
    ☐ d. the way people were talking about him.

20. As she rises from her seat in the boat and moves toward Clyde, Roberta
    (a) is struck by
    ☐ a. Clyde's fist.   ☐ c. a sail.
    ☐ b. an oar.   ☐ d. his camera.

21. Which of the following best defines *vehemence* as used in, "Yet . . .
    (l) pushing at her with so much *vehemence* as not only to strike her lips
    and nose and chin with [the camera], but to throw her back sidewise
    toward the left wale which caused the boat to careen to the very water's
    edge"?
    ☐ a. Fear   ☐ c. Violence
    ☐ b. Difficulty   ☐ d. Rapidity

22. Listed below in random order are five details surrounding Roberta's
(d) death:

    1. The boat capsizes.
    2. Roberta moves toward Clyde.
    3. Clyde moves toward Roberta.
    4. Clyde's face becomes distorted with an ugly emotion.
    5. Roberta is struck in the face.

    Their proper sequence is
    □ a. 2, 4, 5, 3, 1.   □ c. 2, 4, 3, 1, 5.
    □ b. 3, 4, 5, 2, 1.   □ d. 4, 2, 5, 3, 1.

23. In the end, the responsibility for Roberta's death lay with
(g) □ a. Roberta because of her inability to swim.
    □ b. Clyde because of his refusal to rescue her.
    □ c. neither of them because the boat overturned accidentally.
    □ d. both of them equally.

24. After swimming to shore, Clyde tries to
(b) □ a. rationalize his role in Roberta's death.
    □ b. forget about Roberta.
    □ c. recover the body.
    □ d. turn himself in to the police.

25. The major question the reader is left with is:
(e) □ a. Did Clyde really love Roberta?
    □ b. Will Clyde now reject Sondra, too?
    □ c. Was it murder or an accident?
    □ d. Were there any witnesses?

Comprehension Skills: a—isolating details; b—recalling specific facts; c—retaining
concepts; d—organizing facts; e—understanding the main idea; f—drawing a
conclusion; g—making a judgment; h—making an inference; i—recognizing tone;
j—understanding characters; k—appreciation of literary forms; l—knowledge of
word meanings.

ANALYZING PLOT STRUCTURE AND DEVELOPMENT

Practice Exercise A

The stillness of these pines lining this damp yellow road along which they were traveling; the cool and the silence; the dark shadows and purple and gray depths and nooks in them, even at high noon. If one were slipping away at night or by day, who would encounter one here? A blue-jay far in the depths somewhere uttered its metallic shriek; a field sparrow, tremulous upon some distant twig, filled the silver shadows with its perfect song. And Roberta, as this heavy, covered bus crossed rill and thin stream, and then rough wooden bridges here and there, commented on the clarity and sparkle of the water: "Isn't that wonderful in there? Do you hear the tinkling of that water, Clyde? Oh, the freshness of this air!"

And yet she was going to die so soon!

God!

1. In the passage above, the author sets the stage for the ensuing conflict by contrasting
   - ☐ a. the beauty of the setting with the ugly crime about to take place.
   - ☐ b. the stillness of the pines with the noise of the birds.
   - ☐ c. dark colors with light colors.
   - ☐ d. Roberta's chatter with Clyde's silence.

2. Circle the sentence which shows that Clyde views their surroundings only in terms of his terrible scheme.

Practice Exercise B

In a confused and turbulent state mentally, scarcely realizing the clarity or import of any particular thought or movement or act now, he took up his bag and led the way to the boathouse platform. And then, after dropping the bag into the boat, asking of the boathouse keeper if he knew where the best views were, that he wanted to photograph them. And this done—the meaningless explanation over, assisting Roberta (an almost nebulous figure, she now seemed, stepping down into an insubstantial rowboat upon a purely ideational lake), he now stepped in after her, seating himself in the center and taking the oars.

1. The growing conflict within Clyde is reflected in his mental state, which might be likened to a
   - ☐ a. daydream.
   - ☐ b. state of shock.
   - ☐ c. hypnotic trance.
   - ☐ d. childhood fantasy.

2. Circle the phrase which suggests that Roberta is becoming less real to Clyde.

Practice Exercise C

And then once more on the water again—about five hundred feet from shore, the while he fumbled aimlessly with the hard and heavy and yet small camera that he now held, as the boat floated out nearer the center. And then, at this point and time looking fearfully about. For now—now—in spite of himself, the long evaded and yet commanding moment. And no voice or figure or sound on shore. No road or cabin or smoke! And the moment which he or something had planned for him, and which was now to decide his fate at hand! The moment of action—of crisis!

1. As the moment of crisis draws near, Clyde becomes increasingly
   □ a. eager and impatient.   □ c. murderous and enraged.
   □ b. calm and self-assured.   □ d. nervous and fretful.

2. On the lines provided, write the sentence which suggests that Clyde has not been looking forward to his moment of crisis.

   _____

   _____

Practice Exercise D

And then, as she drew near him, seeking to take his hand in hers and the camera from him in order to put it in the boat, he flinging out at her, but not even then with any intention to do other than free himself of her . . . .

Yet (the camera still unconsciously held tight) pushing at her with so much vehemence as not only to strike her lips and nose and chin with it, but to throw her back sidewise toward the left wale which caused the boat to careen to the very water's edge. And then he, stirred by her sharp scream . . . rising and reaching half to assist or recapture her and half to apologize for the unintended blow—yet in so doing completely capsizing the boat—himself and Roberta being as instantly thrown into the water.

1. In this climactic scene, the author strives to emphasize
   □ a. Clyde's anger and violent temper.
   □ b. Clyde's innocent role in upsetting the boat.
   □ c. Roberta's attempts to provoke an incident.
   □ d. Clyde's actual deliberate execution of his plan.

2. Circle the phrase that shows a softening of Clyde's attitude toward Roberta.

DISCUSSION GUIDES

Analyzing Plot

1. Book III of *An American Tragedy*, which follows the chapter in which Roberta drowns, is devoted to Clyde's arrest and trial for Roberta's murder. Based on the single chapter you have read, what do you think is the "inevitable" conclusion of this book? What hints does Dreiser drop to prepare the reader for Clyde's eventual fate?

2. In what sense are the lakes which Clyde and Roberta visit a unifying element in the plot?

3. In a review of *An American Tragedy*, Irving Howe said that "the action of the novel moves like a series of waves, each surging forward to a peak of tension and then receding into quietness." What are the surges and peak of tension in the chapter you have read?

Interpreting the Chapter

4. Do you find Clyde a tragic figure in any way? What character traits or circumstances tend to make you at least a little bit sympathetic toward Clyde?

5. If *An American Tragedy* were set in the present instead of in the 1920s, in what ways would the entire situation be different? Consider both Clyde's feelings and Roberta's attitude.

6. If Clyde had been wealthy instead of poor, would his predicament have been quite so desperate? Explain.

7. If you were on a jury deciding on Clyde's guilt or innocence in Roberta's death, how would you rule? Be prepared to justify your verdict.

Analyzing the Author's Technique

8. Why do you think the author concentrates almost exclusively on Clyde's thoughts and emotions instead of Roberta's in this account of her drowning?

9. As the critical moment draws near when Clyde must put his plan into action, the author presents Clyde's thoughts in a "stream of consciousness" style. "Stream of consciousness" refers to the continual, rather than the interrupted, flow of thoughts in the mind, in which the most trivial as well as the most significant thoughts of a character are related. Why is this technique particularly effective at this point in the story?

10. *An American Tragedy* was inspired by a real-life case: the drowning of Grace Brown by Chester Gillette in Herkimer County, New York, in 1906. In what respects is this novel a documentary—that is, non-fiction? In what respects is it fiction?

WRITING EXERCISE

Robert Redwick is legislative assistant to Congressman Brooks Algood. At the Congressman's suggestion, they are taking a two week vacation hiking in the mountains of a remote part of Idaho.

Algood has just announced that he will run for the Senate in November, an office he has aspired to all of his life. It will be a hard race, but he thinks he can win. There is one difficulty. He has accepted special favors from a lady named Jeanette Aramco who is on the payroll of a powerful lobbying group. If this becomes known, Algood will have no chance of being elected. He could even be censured in the House for his actions.

Neither the lobbying group nor Jeanette will talk about it because their actions were illegal and they could be sent to jail. But Robert Redwick also knows about the affair, and Congressman Algood is not entirely certain of Redwick's loyalty.

Step One

Following is a list of events that occur just before and during the trip to Idaho. Create a plot outline by arranging the events in the proper order. Indicate your answers by writing numbers on the lines provided. The first event has been indicated for you.

_____ a. On the plane to Idaho, Congressman Algood thinks about his chances of winning the senatorial election in November. He is concerned about his dealings with Jeanette Aramco and becomes increasingly worried about the fact that Robert Redwick knows about it.

_____ b. Algood is arrested for murder when an old prospector arrives to report that he saw the Congressman strike Redwick.

_____ c. On their hike through the mountains, Algood and Redwick come to a lonely mountain stream. It is in full flood and raging.

__1__ d. Congressman Algood calls Robert Redwick into his office.

_____ e. At a general store in Idaho, Congressman Algood buys a stout hiking stick. He is considering using it on Redwick.

_____ f. Redwick protests against crossing a raging mountain stream. Algood insists they cross.

_____ g. Algood returns to the nearest town to report an "accident."

_____ h. Plans are made for a hiking vacation in Idaho.

_____ i. In midstream Redwick loses his footing. At the same moment he sees Algood raise his stick to strike him.

_____ j. As he leaves the office, Redwick tells the Congressman that Jeanette Aramco has been calling. "I assume you don't want to see her again," he says.

_____ k. At a general store in Idaho, Congressman Algood sees in a newspaper that Jeanette Aramco is under investigation for her unusual lobbying activities.

_____ l. Algood beats Redwick into unconsciousness and Redwick is swept away by the stream.

_____ m. On the way to Idaho, Congressman Algood discusses Jeanette Aramco with Redwick. "If there is an investigation, how will you testify?" the Congressman asks. Answering honestly, Redwick says, "I don't know. But don't worry, Congressman; it won't come up before November."

Step Two

By writing the letter of each event on the appropriate line, tell which category of plot each event falls into. Correct your answers using the answer key at the back of the book before going on to step three.

Exposition (setting the stage): _____

Complication (development of the conflict): _____

Crisis (conflict comes to a head): _____

Climax (high point of the story): _____

Resolution (conclusion of the action): _____

Step Three

Write the story from your plot outline.

Unit 7
The Detective Novel

The Hound of the Baskervilles

Introduction

Many American Presidents have been avid readers of detective fiction. Abraham Lincoln read and re-read Edgar Allan Poe's detective stories; Woodrow Wilson publicly praised his own personal favorite, *The Middle Temple Murder*, by J. S. Fletcher; Franklin D. Roosevelt provided the plot for a detective novel entitled *The President's Mystery Story*, and John F. Kennedy was a James Bond fan. But the detective novel has never needed the endorsement of Presidents to enhance its popularity. Since the first detective story, Poe's *Murders in the Rue Morgue*, hit the bookstores in 1841, this form of literature has had widespread appeal. Mystery fiction has come to be called "the greatest escape literature of all time," and it's not hard to understand why.

The true detective story challenges the reader to a mental contest to solve the crime. The temptation to play "armchair detective" is irresistible, and from the safety of that armchair the reader can enjoy the crime and participate in solving the mystery. Reader involvement by itself, however, could hardly account for the fanatical devotion of the average mystery story fan. Equally compelling is the personal mystique of the detective. The most famous fictional detectives all have their little eccentricities that endear them to their readers. Indeed, long after the details of the crime have been forgotten, the personality of the detective lingers on in the minds of devoted fans.

The most famous detective of them all is Sherlock Holmes, a fictional character who is so real to the reading public that fans still mail letters to him requesting his assistance. What makes Sherlock Holmes seem more lifelike than any of the others is that we know so many of the intimate details of his life. He lived in cluttered rooms at 221B Baker Street; he played the violin to calm his nerves and help him think; he loaded his pipe from tobacco kept in the toe of a slipper; he used cocaine for a time to relieve his boredom; and he had but one good friend—his faithful companion and biographer, Dr. John Watson. There is a Sherlock Holmes museum where you can actually see the Baker Street apartment as it was when the detective "lived" there. And, on both sides of the Atlantic, there are Sherlock Holmes fan clubs, called "The Baker Street Irregulars," named after a band of street urchins whom the detective sometimes employed in his investigations.

The Hound of the Baskervilles is perhaps the most well known of all the "little problems" which Holmes has looked into for his clients. The case involves a wealthy English nobleman named Sir Charles Baskerville who is frightened to death one night by a hound from hell. Or so it would seem. Because, you see, an ancient curse has hung over the Baskerville line for generations. One of Sir Charles's ancestors, Hugo Baskerville, called upon the devil's assistance in one of his evil deeds. The devil came, all right, in the form of a gigantic black hound that proceeded to chomp upon Hugo's throat. Ever since then, according to the family legend, Baskervilles have met strange and violent deaths. Sir Charles fully expected to meet a similarly unhappy end. And when he does, his close friend, Dr. Mortimer, enlists the aid of Sherlock Holmes in protecting the last remaining Baskerville, a young man named Henry, from the same gruesome fate.

But even the world's greatest consulting detective (as Holmes immodestly referred to himself) would seem to be out of his league when it comes to taking on the devil himself. The reading selection which follows consists of Chapters 2 and 3 from *The Hound of the Baskervilles*. Here, the mysterious circumstances surrounding the death of Sir Charles are presented. Was it the devil? Or was it murder? As you shall see, Sherlock Holmes has already formed his own opinion on the matter and is in hot pursuit of the forces of evil, whatever shape they may take. Since it is a mortal sin to reveal the ending of any detective story, you will have to read the rest of this short novel on your own to discover "whodunit."

The author of the Sherlock Holmes tales, Sir Arthur Conan Doyle, set up practice as an eye doctor after graduating from Edinburgh University in 1881. When the expected patients never came, he turned to writing. The first story featuring Sherlock Holmes, *A Study in Scarlet*, appeared in 1887. The Holmes stories literally "took off," and each new story or installment of a novel was as anxiously awaited as any of Charles Dickens's popular potboilers.

Sir Arthur himself was one of the few persons in the civilized world who did not hold Sherlock Holmes in high esteem. In fact, at one point he killed off his famous hero in "The Final Problem" only to be besieged by outraged letters of protest from angry fans. Fortunately for us, Doyle later resurrected Holmes for another series of adventures.

Sir Arthur was knighted by the Queen of England, not for his creation of Sherlock Holmes, but for his defense of the British cause in a book titled *The Great Boer War*. He wished to be remembered as a scholarly historian, but it is the great Sherlock Holmes who made him famous.

The Detective Novel

The detective novel is, essentially, a puzzle story. The reader is presented with a crime, a handful of clues, a cast of suspects, and a detective. The object of the game is to beat the detective to the solution of the crime.

The detective novel has been called "a fictional celebration of the scientific method." The scientific method, as you may recall, involves formulating a hypothesis, or theory, based on the observation and examination of available data, and then proving the theory with hard facts. In a detective novel, your data consists of clues to a crime, and your hypothesis is arrived at by observing and examining these clues. In the end, they should reveal a telltale pattern, a glaring inconsistency, or the proverbial "smoking pistol"—the hard facts that unmask the murderer. It is an exercise in logic fleshed out with characters, a setting, and a conflict. This conflict will seem to defy rational explanation. But the solution, as Sherlock Holmes once observed, is simple: "When you have eliminated the impossible, whatever remains, however improbable, must be the truth."

The appeal—and the frustration—of the detective novel lies in the fact that the solution is so puzzling as the story unfolds, and then so obvious when explained by the detective. The author must supply us with the necessary clues to arrive at the solution on our own, without actually giving away the ending. A falling off in either direction will result in a dissatisfied reader. These restrictions have resulted in a set of unwritten rules governing the construction of a detective story.

Rule 1: The Detective Must Be Memorable. Naturally, we expect a famous detective to be clever. But fictional detectives are expected to be both shrewd *and* a little bit out of the ordinary. They must have some small eccentricity—an unusual style of dress, perhaps; a passion for antiques; or a gourmet's appreciation of fine foods and wines—anything that sets them apart from the crowd. It is this distinctive touch that makes a detective memorable in the minds of readers.

Agatha Christie's Belgian detective, Hercule Poirot, for instance, is noted for his dapper appearance—from his carefully waxed mustache down to his patent leather shoes. Nero Wolfe is fat; Charlie Chan is Chinese. Miss Jane Marple is an elderly spinster, and Hildegarde Withers likes outlandish hats. Lieutenant Columbo wears a rumpled raincoat, and Kojak is bald and sucks lollipops. All of our favorite detectives have some such distinguishing traits.

The chapters in this unit are from Arthur Conan Doyle's *The Hound of the Baskervilles*. Its hero, Sherlock Holmes, is probably the most famous of all detectives. You probably already connect him with his clay pipe, plaid deerstalker cap, and magnifying glass. But you may be surprised to learn that he used opium for a time, played the violin, and occasionally decorated the walls of his apartment with bullet holes during target practice. Dr. Watson, who shared rooms with Holmes, was severely tried by his roommate's unconventional habits. These included irregular hours, foul-smelling chemical experiments, and a strong brand of shag tobacco that regularly polluted the atmosphere at 221B Baker Street, as in the following scene:

> My first impression as I opened the door was that a fire had broken out, for the room was so filled with smoke that the light of the lamp upon the table was blurred by it. As I entered, however, my fears were set at rest, for it was the acrid fumes of strong coarse tobacco which took me by the throat and set me coughing. Through the haze I had a vague vision of Holmes in his dressing-gown coiled up in an arm-chair with his black clay pipe between his lips.

To true fans of the detective novel, these little glimpses into the private life of their favorite sleuth are as important as the cases which he solves.

Rule 2: The Crime Must Be Significant. Traditionally, the detective novel is constructed around a murder. This is not because of the American reader's supposed taste for blood and gore. Rather, murder is the one crime which cannot be reversed or made amends for. We as readers feel that we have some small stake in unmasking the murderer because we want to see such a criminal punished. Robbery, blackmail and other lesser crimes just do not arouse our sense of justice—and our natural desire to avenge the victim—like murder does. Thus, it is the only crime worth a reader's trouble to unravel.

The Hound of the Baskervilles is no exception. In the following excerpt, how does the murder of Sir Charles Baskerville evoke both your sympathy and your interest?

> "On the night of Sir Charles's death Barrymore the butler, who made the discovery, sent Perkins the groom on horseback to me, and as I was sitting up late I was able to reach Baskerville Hall within an hour of the event . . . . Sir Charles lay on his face, his arms out, his fingers dug into the ground, and his features convulsed with some strong emotion to such an extent that I could hardly have sworn to his identity. There was certainly no physical injury of any kind. But one false statement was made by

Barrymore at the inquest. He said that there were no traces upon the ground round the body. He did not observe any. But I did— some little distance off, but fresh and clear.

"Footprints?"

"Footprints."

"A man's or a woman's?"

Dr. Mortimer looked strangely at us for an instant, and his voice sank almost to a whisper as he answered:—

"Mr. Holmes, they were the footprints of a gigantic hound!"

In the passage above, the author paints a vivid picture of Sir Charles's corpse, its face almost unrecognizable in the grip of some dreadful emotion. But as if that weren't bad enough, it appears that Sir Charles's death was not only lamentable but downright unnatural. If his friend is to be believed, Sir Charles glimpsed "a gigantic hound" just before his death. This fact, together with the fascinating family legend that we learn about in the story, is enough to enlist our mental energies in pursuit of whoever—or whatever—drove Sir Charles to his untimely end.

Rule 3: The Murderer Must Be a Worthy Opponent. In real life, most murders are committed by unimaginative people of low intelligence. They kill their victims in a fit of passion or rage, or in the course of a routine hold-up. Their crimes are not planned, and bringing such murderers to justice is largely a matter of luck or tip-offs from informants.

In the true detective novel, of course, this would never do. If detectives are to display their considerable skills, they must match wits with adversaries of equal cunning. For this reason, the criminal in a detective story usually possesses a decided flair for crime. The conflict between the detective and the criminal thus becomes a battle of minds, with each side trying to outwit the other. The mind of the murderer may well be the intellectual equal of the detective's, and in such cases the reader cannot help but admire the bad guy as well as the good guy.

Rule 4: All the Suspects, Including the Murderer, Must Be Presented Early in the Story. It goes without saying that the reader can cry, "Foul!" if a new character introduced on Page 224 is revealed as the murderer on Page 225. This is because there are actually two conflicts in every detective mystery: The obvious conflict is the one between the detective and the murderer. But the reader is waging a conflict, too, against the author by trying to guess the ending. And half the fun of reading a novel of detection comes from this mental contest between the reader and the author. Since the author presents the material, he or she holds all the cards in this game, so to speak. Thus, this rule evens out the odds for the reader. The reader can safely assume that the murderer is one of the main characters in the story.

In *The Hound of the Baskervilles*, the main characters, including the murderer, are introduced by the end of the second chapter. The following passage is spoken by Dr. James Mortimer, who has brought Sir Charles's death to Sherlock Holmes's attention. How does Dr. Mortimer's statement narrow down the field of suspects right from the start?

"The moor is very sparsely inhabited, and those who live near each other are thrown very much together. For this reason I saw a good deal of Sir Charles Baskerville. With the exception of Mr. Frankland, of Lafter Hall, and Mr. Stapleton, the naturalist, there are no other men of education within many miles . . . .

"Within the last few months it became increasingly plain to me that Sir Charles's nervous system was strained to the breaking point . . . .

"It was at my advice that Sir Charles was about to go to London . . . . I thought that a few months among the distractions of town would send him back a new man. Mr. Stapleton, a mutual friend who was much concerned at his state of health, was of the same opinion. At the last instant came this terrible catastrophe.

"On the night of Sir Charles's death Barrymore the butler, who made the discovery, sent Perkins the groom on horseback to me, and as I was sitting up late I was able to reach Baskerville Hall within an hour of the event. I checked and corroborated all the facts which were mentioned at the inquest.

Dr. Mortimer's statement, presented at a very early stage of the book, includes most of the suspects upon whom the investigation will hinge. There is Mr. Frankland of Lafter Hall; Mr. Stapleton, the naturalist; Barrymore, the butler (nowadays, it should be added, it is considered in very poor taste to have the victim done in by the butler); Perkins the groom; and Dr. James Mortimer himself, who was among the first to examine the body. A good mystery writer provides each of the main characters with both convincing alibis and incriminating secrets.

Rule 5: All Clues Discovered by the Detective Must Be Made Available to the Reader. This is another "fair play" rule that helps even up the odds for the armchair detective who is reading the book. In essence, it prohibits a situation like the following: "Arriving at the scene of the crime, the eminent detective got down on his hands and knees on the thick shag carpet and soon found what he had been looking for. Without a word, he slipped the item into his jacket pocket." And so much for the unknown item until the last chapter, when it turns out to have been the telltale piece of evidence which wraps up the case. The reader must be given the same opportunity to solve the crime as the detective, and this means getting the same evidence at the same time it is made available to the detective.

Naturally, the author is not obliged to thrust the clues under our very noses. An important clue may be tossed off by a character in the course of a casual conversation, and vital evidence might be contained in an innocent description of the setting. Indeed, an author may deliberately mislead the reader, *as long as the detective is similarly deceived.*

The following excerpts from Dr. Mortimer's statement in *The Hound of the Baskervilles* all contain clues to the mysterious death of Sir Charles Baskerville. How many of these potential clues might *you* have missed in a casual reading?

Sir Charles, as is well known, made large sums of money in South African speculation.

•

It is understood that the next-of-kin is Mr. Henry Baskerville, if he be still alive, the son of Sir Charles Baskerville's younger brother.

•

The third [brother], Rodger, was the black sheep of the family. He came of the old masterful Baskerville strain, and was the very image, they tell me, of the family picture of old Hugo. He made England too hot to hold him, fled to Central America, and died there in 1876 of yellow fever.

•

The moor is very sparsely inhabited, and those who live near each other are thrown very much together.

•

I think it unlikely that he waited at the moor-gate every evening. On the contrary, the evidence is that he avoided the moor. That night he waited there. It was the night before he made his departure for London.

As in any well-written story, there is no irrelevant information in a good detective novel. The author presents the reader with just the facts necessary to tell the story. And in the end, the little tidbits of information like the ones above will fit into place like the pieces of a puzzle.

Rule 6: The Solution Must Appear Obvious when the Detective Explains How He Fingered the Murderer. The last chapter of every detective novel is devoted to the detective's explanation of how he solved the crime. It is at this point that we want to kick ourselves for not having noticed the pattern of events, or vital clue, that points to the murderer. But oddly enough, the more completely we have been fooled, the better we like it. The story is best if it seems as if the culprit has been staring us in the face all along. When we are confronted with the solution, we must be left with the conviction that if we had not failed to take notice of a piece of evidence when it was given to us, or if we had reasoned properly from the available data, we would have achieved the solution on our own. And it is this tantalizing possibility— that we, too, could solve a crime if we only put our minds to it—that makes detective novels so addictive.

These then, are the classic elements of the detective novel: a memorable detective, a murder, a worthy opponent, a cast of suspects, a set of clues, and a dismayingly obvious solution. And the formula hasn't changed much since Sir Arthur Conan Doyle wrote his Sherlock Holmes stories in the late nineteenth century. In recent years, detective novels have become more realistic—the murders are depicted more vividly, and the detectives have become more human. They're more likely to be professional policemen solving crimes using authentic police methods—informants, luck and pounding the pavement. But while the detective's habitat may have changed and the glamorous image brought down a peg or two, the appeal of the chase is as strong as ever.

As you read the chapters:

- Notice what is revealed in Holmes's discussion about the old manuscript at the beginning of the selection.

- Determine how the newspaper article helps the author meet the requirements of a good detective novel.

- Be aware of Holmes's views on the true nature of the murderer.

- Find the "hidden" clues in Dr. Mortimer's discussion of the Baskerville heirs.

The Hound of
the Baskervilles
A. Conan Doyle

CHAPTER 2
THE CURSE OF THE BASKERVILLES

"I have in my pocket a manuscript," said Dr. James Mortimer.

"I observed it as you entered the room," said Holmes.

"It is an old manuscript."

"Early eighteenth century, unless it is a forgery."

"How can you say that, sir?"

"You have presented an inch or two of it to my examination all the time that you have been talking. It would be a poor expert who could not give the date of a document within a decade or so. You may possibly have read my little monograph upon the subject. I put that at 1730."

"The exact date is 1742." Dr. Mortimer drew it from his breast-pocket. "This family paper was committed to my care by Sir Charles Baskerville, whose sudden and tragic death some three months ago created so much excitement in Devonshire. I may say that I was his personal friend as well as his medical attendant. He was a strong-minded man, sir, shrewd, practical, and as unimaginative as I am myself. Yet he took this document very seriously, and his mind was prepared for just such an end as did eventually overtake him."

Holmes stretched out his hand for the manuscript and flattened it upon his knee.

"You will observe, Watson, the alternative use of the long *s* and the short. It is one of several indications which enabled me to fix the date."

I looked over his shoulder at the yellow paper and the faded script. At the head was written: "Baskerville Hall," and below, in large, scrawling figures: "1742."

"It appears to be a statement of some sort."

"Yes, it is a statement of a certain legend which runs in the Baskerville family."

"But I understand that it is something more modern and practical upon which you wish to consult me?"

"Most modern. A most practical, pressing matter, which must be decided within twenty-four hours. But the manuscript is short and is intimately connected with the affair. With your permission I will read it to you."

Holmes leaned back in his chair, placed his fingertips together, and closed his eyes, with an air of resignation. Dr. Mortimer turned the manuscript to the light and read in a high, crackling voice the following curious, old-world narrative:—

Of the origin of the Hound of the Baskervilles there have been many statements, yet as I come in a direct line from Hugo Baskerville, and as I had the story from my father, who also had it from his, I have set it down with all belief that it occurred even as is here set forth. And I would have you believe, my sons, that the same Justice which punishes sin may also most graciously forgive it, and that no ban is so heavy but that by prayer and repentance it may be removed. Learn then from this story not to fear the fruits of the past, but rather to be circumspect in the future, that those foul passions whereby our family has suffered so grievously may not again be loosed to our undoing.

"Know then that in the time of the Great Rebellion (the history of which by the learned Lord Clarendon I most earnestly commend to your attention) this Manor of Baskerville was held by Hugo of that name, nor can it be gainsaid that he was a most wild, profane, and godless man. This, in truth, his neighbors might have pardoned, seeing that saints have never flourished in those parts, but there was in him a certain wanton and cruel humor which made his name a byword through the West. It chanced that this Hugo came to love (if, indeed, so dark a passion may be known under so bright a name) the daughter of a yeoman who held lands near the Baskerville estate. But the young maiden, being discreet and of good repute, would ever avoid him, for she feared his evil name. So it came to pass that one Michaelmas this Hugo, with five or six of his idle and wicked companions, stole down upon the farm and carried off the maiden, her father and brothers being from home, as he well knew. When they had brought her to the Hall the maiden was placed in an upper chamber, while Hugo and his friends sat down to a long carouse, as was their nightly custom. Now, the poor lass upstairs was like to have her wits turned at the singing and shouting and terrible oaths which came up to her from below, for they say that the words used by Hugo Baskerville, when he was in wine, were such as might blast the man who said them. At last in the stress of her fear she did that which might have daunted the bravest or most active man, for by the aid of the growth of ivy which covered (and still covers) the south wall she came down from under the eaves, and so homeward across the moor, there being three leagues betwixt the Hall and her father's farm.

"It chanced that some little time later Hugo left his guests to carry food and drink—with other worse things, perchance—to his captive, and so found the cage empty and the bird escaped. Then, as it would seem, he became as one that hath a devil, for, rushing down the stairs into the dining-hall, he sprang upon the great table, flagons and trenchers flying before him, and he cried aloud before all the company that he would that very night render his body and soul to the Powers of Evil if he might but overtake the wench. And while the revellers stood aghast at the fury of the man, one more wicked or, it may be, more drunken than the rest, cried out that they should put the hounds upon her. Whereat Hugo ran from the house, crying to his grooms that they should saddle his mare and unkennel the pack, and giving the hounds a kerchief of the maid's, he swung them to the line, and so off full cry in the moonlight over the moor.

"Now, for some space the revellers stood agape, unable to understand all that had been done in such haste. But anon their bemused wits awoke to the nature of the deed which was like to be done upon the moorlands. Everything was now in an uproar, some calling for their pistols, some for their horses, and some for another flask of wine. But at length some sense came back to their crazed minds, and the whole of them, thirteen in number, took horse and started in pursuit. The moon shone clear above them, and they rode swiftly abreast, taking that course which the maid must needs have taken if she were to reach her own home.

"They had gone a mile or two when they passed one of the night shepherds upon the moorlands, and they cried to him to know if he had seen the hunt. And the man, as the story goes, was so crazed with fear that he could scarce speak, but at last he said that he had indeed seen the unhappy maiden, with the hounds upon her track. 'But I have seen more than that,' said he, 'for Hugo Baskerville passed me upon his black mare, and there ran mute behind him such a hound of hell as God forbid should ever be at my heels.' So the drunken squires cursed the shepherd and rode onwards. But soon their skins turned cold, for there came a galloping across the moor, and the black mare, dabbled with white froth, went past with trailing bridle and empty saddle. Then the revellers rode close together, for a great fear was on them, but they still followed over the moor, though each, had he been alone, would have been right glad to have turned his horse's head. Riding slowly in this fashion they came at last upon the hounds. These, though known for their valor and their breed, were whimpering in a cluster at the head of a deep dip or goyal, as we call it, upon the moor, some slinking away and some, with starting hackles and staring eyes, gazing down the narrow valley before them.

"The company had come to a halt, more sober men, as you may guess, than when they started. The most of them would by no means advance, but three of them, the boldest, or it may be the most drunken, rode forward down the goyal. Now, it opened into a broad space in which stood two of those great stones, still to be seen there, which were set by certain forgotten peoples in the days of old. The moon was shining bright upon the clearing, and there in the center lay the unhappy maid where she had fallen, dead of fear and of fatigue. But it was not the sight of her body, nor yet was it that of the body of Hugo Baskerville lying near her, which raised the hair upon the heads of these three daredevil roysterers, but it was that, standing over Hugo and plucking at his throat, there stood a foul thing, a great, black beast, shaped like a hound, yet larger than any hound that ever mortal eye has rested upon. And even as they looked the thing tore the throat out of Hugo Baskerville, on which, as it turned its blazing eyes and dripping jaws upon them, the three shrieked with fear and rode for dear life, still screaming, across the moor. One, it is said, died that very night of what he had seen, and the other twain were but broken men for the rest of their days.

"Such is the tale, my sons, of the coming of the hound which is said to have plagued the family so sorely ever since. If I have set it down it is because that which is clearly known hath less terror than that which is but hinted at and guessed. Nor can it be denied that many of the family have been unhappy in their deaths, which have been sudden, bloody, and mysterious. Yet may we shelter ourselves in the infinite goodness of Providence, which would not forever punish the innocent beyond that third or fourth generation which is threatened in Holy Writ. To that Providence, my sons, I hereby commend you, and I counsel you by way of caution to forbear from crossing the moor in those dark hours when the powers of evil are exalted.

"(This from Hugo Baskerville to his sons Rodger and John, with instructions that they say nothing thereof to their sister Elizabeth.)"

When Dr. Mortimer had finished reading this singular narrative he pushed his spectacles up on his forehead and stared across at Mr. Sherlock Holmes. The latter yawned and tossed the end of his cigarette into the fire.

"Well?" said he.

"Do you not find it interesting?"

"To a collector of fairy tales."

Dr. Mortimer drew a folded newspaper out of his pocket.

"Now, Mr. Holmes, we will give you something a little more recent. This is the *Devon County Chronicle* of May 14th of this year. It is a short account of the facts elicited at the death of Sir Charles Baskerville which occurred a few days before that date."

My friend leaned a little forward and his expression became intent. Our visitor readjusted his glasses and began: —

"The recent sudden death of Sir Charles Baskerville, whose name has been mentioned as the probable Liberal candidate for Mid-Devon at the next election, has cast a gloom over the county. Though Sir Charles had resided at Baskerville Hall for a comparatively short period his amiability of character and extreme generosity had won the affection and respect of all who had been brought into contact with him. In these days of *nouveaux riches* it is refreshing to find a case where the scion of an old county family which has fallen upon evil days is able to make his own fortune and to bring it back with him to restore the fallen grandeur of his line. Sir Charles, as is well known, made large sums of money in South African speculation. More wise than those who go on until the wheel turns against them, he realized his gains and returned to England with them. It is only two years since he took up his residence at Baskerville Hall, and it is common talk how large were those schemes of reconstruction and improvement which have been interrupted by his death. Being himself childless, it was his openly expressed desire that the whole countryside should, within his own lifetime, profit by his good fortune, and many will have personal reasons for bewailing his untimely end. His generous donations to local and county charities have been frequently chronicled in these columns.

"The circumstances connected with the death of Sir Charles cannot be said to have been entirely cleared up by the inquest, but at least enough has been done to dispose of those rumors to which local superstition has given rise. There is no reason whatever to suspect foul play, or to imagine that death could be from any but natural causes. Sir Charles was a widower, and a man who may be said to have been in some ways of an eccentric habit of mind. In spite of his considerable wealth he was simple in his personal tastes, and his indoor servants at Baskerville Hall consisted of a married couple named Barrymore, the husband acting as butler and the wife as housekeeper. Their evidence, corroborated by that of several friends, tends to show that Sir Charles's health has for some time been impaired, and points especially to some affection of the heart, manifesting itself in changes of color, breathlessness, and acute attacks of nervous depression. Dr. James Mortimer, the friend and medical attendant of the deceased, has given evidence to the same effect.

"The facts of the case are simple. Sir Charles Baskerville was in the habit every night before going to bed of walking down the famous Yew Alley of Baskerville Hall. The evidence of the Barrymores shows that this had been his custom. On the 4th of May Sir Charles had declared his intention of starting next day for London, and had ordered Barrymore to prepare his luggage. That night he went out as usual for his nocturnal walk, in the course of which he was in the habit of smoking a cigar. He never returned. At twelve o'clock Barrymore, finding the hall door still open, became alarmed, and, lighting a lantern, went in search of his master. The day had been wet, and Sir Charles's footmarks were easily traced down the Alley. Half-way down this walk there is a gate which leads out on to the moor. There were indications that Sir Charles had stood for some little time here. He then proceeded down the Alley, and it was at the far end of it that his body was discovered. One fact which has not been explained is the statement of Barrymore that his master's footprints altered their character from the time that he passed the moor-gate, and that he appeared from thence onwards to have been walking upon his toes. One Murphy, a gypsy horse-dealer, was on the moor at no great distance at the time, but he appears by his own confession to have been the worse for drink. He declares that he heard cries, but is unable to state from what direction they came. No signs of violence were to be discovered upon Sir Charles's person, and though the doctor's evidence pointed to an almost incredible facial distortion—so great that Dr. Mortimer refused at first to believe that it was indeed his friend and patient who lay before him—it was explained that that is a symptom which is not unusual in cases of dyspnoea and death from cardiac exhaustion. This explanation was borne out by the post-mortem examination, which showed long-standing organic disease, and the coroner's jury returned a verdict in accordance with the medical evidence. It is well that this is so, for it is obviously of the utmost importance that Sir Charles's heir should settle at the Hall and continue the good work which has been so sadly interrupted.

Had the prosaic finding of the coroner not finally put an end to the romantic stories which have been whispered in connection with the affair, it might have been difficult to find a tenant for Baskerville Hall. It is understood that the next-of-kin is Mr. Henry Baskerville, if he be still alive, the son of Sir Charles Baskerville's younger brother. The young man when last heard of was in America, and inquiries are being instituted with a view to informing him of his good fortune."

Dr. Mortimer refolded his paper and replaced it in his pocket.

"Those are the public facts, Mr. Holmes, in connection with the death of Sir Charles Baskerville."

"I must thank you," said Sherlock Holmes, "for calling my attention to a case which certainly presents some features of interest. I had observed some newspaper comment at the time, but I was exceedingly preoccupied by that little affair of the Vatican cameos, and in my anxiety to oblige the Pope I lost touch with several interesting English cases. This article, you say, contains all the public facts?"

"It does."

"Then let me have the private ones." He leaned back, put his finger-tips together, and assumed his most impassive and judicial expression.

"In doing so," said Dr. Mortimer, who had begun to show signs of some strong emotion, "I am telling that which I have not confided to anyone. My motive for withholding it from the coroner's inquiry is that a man of science shrinks from placing himself in the public position of seeming to endorse a popular superstition. I had the further motive that Baskerville Hall, as the paper says, would certainly remain untenanted if anything were done to increase its already rather grim reputation. For both these reasons I thought that I was justified in telling rather less than I knew, since no practical good could result from it, but with you there is no reason why I should not be perfectly frank.

"The moor is very sparsely inhabited, and those who live near each other are thrown very much together. For this reason I saw a good deal of Sir Charles Baskerville. With the exception of Mr. Frankland, of Lafter Hall, and Mr. Stapleton, the naturalist, there are no other men of education within many miles. Sir Charles was a retiring man, but the chance of his illness brought us together, and a community of interests in science kept us so. He had brought back much scientific information from South Africa, and many a charming evening we have spent together discussing the comparative anatomy of the Bushman and the Hottentot.

"Within the last few months it became increasingly plain to me that Sir Charles's nervous system was strained to the breaking point. He had taken this legend which I have read you exceedingly to heart—so much so that, although he would walk in his own grounds, nothing would induce him to go out upon the moor at night. Incredible as it may appear to you, Mr. Holmes, he was honestly convinced that a dreadful fate overhung his family, and certainly the records which he was able to give of his ancestors were not encouraging. The idea of some ghastly presence constantly haunted him, and on more than one occasion he has asked me whether I had on my medical journeys at night ever seen any strange creature or heard the baying of a hound. The latter question he put to me several times, and always with a voice which vibrated with excitement.

"I can well remember driving up to his house in the evening, some three weeks before the fatal event. He chanced to be at his hall door. I had descended from my gig and was standing in front of him, when I saw his eyes fix themselves over my shoulder, and stare past me with an expression of the most dreadful horror. I whisked round and had just time to catch a glimpse of something which I took to be a large black calf passing at the head of the drive. So excited and alarmed was he that I was compelled to go down to the spot where the animal had been and look around for it. It was gone, however, and the incident appeared to make the worst impression upon his mind. I stayed with him all the evening, and it was on that occasion, to explain the emotion which he had shown, that he confided to my keeping that narrative which I read to you when first I came. I mention this small episode because it assumes some importance in view of the tragedy which followed, but I was convinced at the time that the matter was entirely trivial and that his excitement had no justification.

"It was at my advice that Sir Charles was about to go to London. His heart was, I knew, affected, and the constant anxiety in which he lived, however chimerical the cause of it might be, was evidently having a serious effect upon his health. I thought that a few months among the distractions of town would send him back a new man. Mr. Stapleton, a mutual friend who was much concerned at his state of health, was of the same opinion. At the last instant came this terrible catastrophe.

"On the night of Sir Charles's death Barrymore the butler, who made the discovery, sent Perkins the groom on horseback to me, and as I was sitting up late I was able to reach Baskerville Hall within an hour of the event. I checked and corroborated all the facts which were mentioned at the inquest. I followed the footsteps down the Yew Alley, I saw the spot at the moor-gate where he seemed to have waited, I remarked the change in the shape of the prints after that point, I noted that there were no other footsteps save those of Barrymore on the soft gravel, and finally I carefully examined the body, which had not been touched until my arrival. Sir Charles lay on his face, his arms out, his fingers dug into the ground, and his features convulsed with some strong emotion to such an extent that I could hardly have sworn to his identity. There was certainly no physical injury of any kind. But one false statement was made by Barrymore at the inquest. He said that there were no traces upon the ground round the body. He did not observe any. But I did—some little distance off, but fresh and clear."

"Footprints?"

"Footprints."

"A man's or a woman's?"

Dr. Mortimer looked strangely at us for an instant, and his voice sank almost to a whisper as he answered:—

"Mr. Holmes, they were the footprints of a gigantic hound!"

CHAPTER 3
THE PROBLEM

I confess that at these words a shudder passed through me. There was a thrill in the doctor's voice which showed that he was himself deeply moved by that which he told us. Holmes leaned forward in his excitement and his eyes had the hard, dry glitter which shot from them when he was keenly interested.

"You saw this?"

"As clearly as I see you."

"And you said nothing?"

"What was the use?"

"How was it that no one else saw it?"

"The marks were some twenty yards from the body and no one gave them a thought. I don't suppose I should have done so had I not known this legend."

"There are many sheep-dogs on the moor?"

"No doubt, but this was no sheep-dog."

"You say it was large?"

"Enormous."

"But it had not approached the body?"

"No."

"What sort of night was it?"

"Damp and raw."

"But not actually raining?"

"No."

"What is the Alley like?"

"There are two lines of old yew hedge, twelve feet high and impenetrable. The walk in the centre is about eight feet across."

"Is there anything between the hedges and the walk?"

"Yes, there is a strip of grass about six feet broad on either side."

"I understand that the yew hedge is penetrated at one point by a gate?"

"Yes, the wicket-gate which leads on to the moor."

"Is there any other opening?"

"None."

"So that to reach the Yew Alley one either has to come down it from the house or else to enter it by the moor-gate?"

"There is an exit through a summer-house at the far end."

"Had Sir Charles reached this?"

"No; he lay about fifty yards from it."

"Now, tell me, Dr. Mortimer—and this is important—the marks which you saw were on the path and not on the grass?"

"No marks could show on the grass."

"Were they on the same side of the path as the moor-gate?"

"Yes; they were on the edge of the path on the same side as the moor-gate."

"You interest me exceedingly. Another point. Was the wicket-gate closed?"

"Closed and padlocked."

"How high was it?"

"About four feet high."

"Then anyone could have got over it?"

"Yes."

"And what marks did you see by the wicket-gate?"

"None in particular."

"Good Heaven! Did no one examine?"

"Yes, I examined myself."

"And found nothing?"

"It was all very confused. Sir Charles had evidently stood there for five or ten minutes."

"How do you know that?"

"Because the ash had twice dropped from his cigar."

"Excellent! This is a colleague, Watson, after our own heart. But the marks?"

"He had left his own marks all over that small patch of gravel. I could discern no others."

Sherlock Holmes struck his hand against his knee with an impatient gesture.

"If I had only been there!" he cried. "It is evidently a case of extraordinary interest, and one which presented immense opportunities to the scientific expert. That gravel page upon which I might have read so much has been long ere this smudged by the rain and defaced by the clogs of curious peasants. Oh, Dr. Mortimer, Dr. Mortimer, to think that you should not have called me in! You have indeed much to answer for."

"I could not call you in, Mr. Holmes, without disclosing these facts to the world, and I have already given my reasons for not wishing to do so. Besides, besides——"

"Why do you hesitate?"

"There is a realm in which the most acute and most experienced of detectives is helpless."

"You mean that the thing is supernatural?"

"I did not positively say so."

"No, but you evidently think it."

"Since the tragedy, Mr. Holmes, there have come to my ears several incidents which are hard to reconcile with the settled order of Nature."

"For example?"

"I find that before the terrible event occurred several people had seen a creature upon the moor which corresponds with this Baskerville demon, and which could not possibly be any animal known to science. They all agreed that it was a huge creature, luminous, ghastly, and spectral. I have cross-examined these men, one of them a hard-headed countryman, one a farrier, and one a moorland farmer, who all tell the same story of this dreadful apparition, exactly corresponding to the hell-hound of the legend. I assure you that there is a reign of terror in the district and that it is a hardy man who will cross the moor at night."

"And you, a trained man of science, believe it to be supernatural?"

"I do not know what to believe."

Holmes shrugged his shoulders.

"I have hitherto confined my investigations to this world," said he. "In a modest way I have combated evil, but to take on the Father of Evil himself would, perhaps, be too ambitious a task. Yet you must admit that the foot-mark is material."

"The original hound was material enough to tug a man's throat out, and yet he was diabolical as well."

"I see that you have quite gone over to the supernaturalists. But now, Dr. Mortimer, tell me this. If you hold these views, why have you come to consult me at all? You tell me in the same breath that it is useless to investigate Sir Charles's death, and that you desire me to do it."

"I did not say that I desired you to do it."

"Then, how can I assist you?"

"By advising me as to what I should do with Sir Henry Baskerville, who arrives at Waterloo Station"—Dr. Mortimer looked at his watch—"in exactly one hour and a quarter."

"He being the heir?"

"Yes. On the death of Sir Charles we inquired for this young gentleman, and found that he had been farming in Canada. From the accounts which have reached us he is an excellent fellow in every way. I speak not as a medical man but as a trustee and executor of Sir Charles's will."

"There is no other claimant, I presume?"

"None. The only other kinsman whom we have been able to trace was Rodger Baskerville, the youngest of three brothers of whom poor Sir Charles was the elder. The second brother, who died young, is the father of this lad Henry. The third, Rodger, was the black sheep of the family. He came of the old masterful Baskerville strain, and was the very image, they tell me, of the family picture of old Hugo. He made England too hot to hold him, fled to Central America, and died there in 1876 of yellow fever. Henry is the last of the Baskervilles. In one hour and five minutes I meet him at Waterloo Station. I have had a wire that he arrived at Southampton this morning. Now, Mr. Holmes, what would you advise me to do with him?"

"Why should he not go to the home of his fathers?"

"It seems natural, does it not? And yet, consider that every Baskerville who goes there meets with an evil fate. I feel sure that if Sir Charles could have spoken with me before his death he would have warned me against bringing this the last of the old race, and the heir to great wealth, to that deadly place. And yet it cannot be denied that the prosperity of the whole poor, bleak country-side depends upon his presence. All the good work which has been done by Sir Charles will crash to the ground if there is no tenant of the Hall. I fear lest I should be swayed too much by my own obvious interest in the matter, and that is why I bring the case before you and ask for your advice."

Holmes considered for a little time.

"Put into plain words, the matter is this," said he. "In your opinion there is a diabolical agency which makes Dartmoor an unsafe abode for a Baskerville—that is your opinion?"

"At least I might go the length of saying that there is some evidence that this may be so."

"Exactly. But surely, if your supernatural theory be correct, it could work the young man evil in London as easily as in Devonshire. A devil with merely local powers like a parish vestry would be too inconceivable a thing."

"You put the matter more flippantly, Mr. Holmes, than you would probably do if you were brought into personal contact with these things. Your advice, then, as I understand it, is that the young man will be as safe in Devonshire as in London. He comes in fifty minutes. What would you recommend?"

"I recommend, sir, that you take a cab, call off your spaniel who is scratching at my front door, and proceed to Waterloo to meet Sir Henry Baskerville."

"And then?"

"And then you will say nothing to him at all until I have made up my mind about the matter."

"How long will it take you to make up your mind?"

"Twenty-four hours. At ten o'clock tomorrow, Dr. Mortimer, I will be much obliged to you if you will call upon me here, and it will be of help to me in my plans for the future if you will bring Sir Henry Baskerville with you."

"I will do so, Mr. Holmes." He scribbled the appointment on his shirt cuff and hurried off in his strange, peering, absent-minded fashion. Holmes stopped him at the head of the stair.

"Only one more question, Dr. Mortimer. You say that before Sir Charles Baskerville's death several people saw this apparition upon the moor?"

"Three people did."

"Did any see it after?"

"I have not heard of any."

"Thank you. Good morning."

Holmes returned to his seat with that quiet look of inward satisfaction which meant that he had a congenial task before him.

"Going out, Watson?"

"Unless I can help you."

"No, my dear fellow, it is at the hour of action that I turn to you for aid. But this is splendid, really unique from some points of view. When you pass Bradley's would you ask him to send up a pound of the strongest shag tobacco? Thank you. It would be as well if you could make it convenient not to return before evening. Then I should be very glad to compare impressions as to this most interesting problem which has been submitted to us this morning."

I knew that seclusion and solitude were very necessary for my friend in those hours of intense mental concentration during which he weighed every particle of evidence, constructed alternative theories, balanced one against the other, and made up his mind as to which points were essential and which immaterial. I therefore spent the day at my club and did not return to Baker

Street until evening. It was nearly nine o'clock when I found myself in the sitting-room once more.

My first impression as I opened the door was that a fire had broken out, for the room was so filled with smoke that the light of the lamp upon the table was blurred by it. As I entered, however, my fears were set at rest, for it was the acrid fumes of strong coarse tobacco which took me by the throat and set me coughing. Through the haze I had a vague vision of Holmes in his dressing-gown coiled up in an arm-chair with his black clay pipe between his lips. Several rolls of paper lay around him.

"Caught cold, Watson?" said he.

"No, it's this poisonous atmosphere."

"I suppose it *is* pretty thick, now that you mention it."

"Thick! It is intolerable."

"Open the window, then! You have been at your club all day, I perceive."

"My dear Holmes!"

"Am I right?"

"Certainly, but how——?"

He laughed at my bewildered expression.

"There is a delightful freshness about you, Watson, which makes it a pleasure to exercise any small powers which I possess at your expense. A gentleman goes forth on a showery and miry day. He returns immaculate in the evening with the gloss still on his hat and his boots. He has been a fixture therefore all day. He is not a man with intimate friends. Where, then, could he have been? Is it not obvious?"

"Well, it is rather obvious."

"The world is full of obvious things which nobody by any chance ever observes. Where do you think that I have been?"

"A fixture also."

"On the contrary, I have been to Devonshire."

"In spirit?"

"Exactly. My body has remained in this armchair, and has, I regret to observe, consumed in my absence two large pots of coffee and an incredible amount of tobacco. After you left I sent down to Stamford's for the Ordnance map of this portion of the moor, and my spirit has hovered over it all day. I flatter myself that I could find my way about."

"A large scale map, I presume?"

"Very large." He unrolled one section and held it over his knee. "Here you have the particular district which concerns us. That is Baskerville Hall in the middle."

"With a wood round it?"

"Exactly. I fancy the Yew Alley, though not marked under that name, must stretch along this line, with the moor, as you perceive, upon the right of it. This small clump of buildings here is the hamlet of Grimpen, where our friend Dr. Mortimer has his head-quarters. Within a radius of five miles there are, as you see, only a very few scattered dwellings. Here is Lafter Hall, which was mentioned in the narrative. There is a house indicated here which may be the residence of the naturalist—Stapleton, if I remember right, was his name. Here are two moorland farm-houses, High Tor and Foulmire. Then fourteen miles away the great convict prison of Princetown. Between and around these scattered points extends the desolate, lifeless moor. This, then, is the stage upon which tragedy has been played, and upon which we may help to play it again."

"It must be a wild place."

"Yes, the setting is a worthy one. If the devil did desire to have a hand in the affairs of men——"

"Then you are yourself inclining to the supernatural explanation."

"The devil's agents may be of flesh and blood, may they not? There are two questions waiting for us at the outset. The one is whether any crime has been committed at all; the second is, what is the crime and how was it committed? Of course, if Dr. Mortimer's surmise should be correct, and we are dealing with forces outside the ordinary laws of Nature, there is an end of our investigation. But we are bound to exhaust all other hypotheses before falling back upon this one. I think we'll shut that window again, if you don't mind. It is a singular thing, but I find that a concentrated atmosphere helps a concentration of thought. I have not pushed it to the length of getting into a box to think, but that is the logical outcome of my convictions. Have you turned the case over in your mind?"

"Yes, I have thought a good deal of it in the course of the day."

"What do you make of it?"

"It is very bewildering."

"It has certainly a character of its own. There are points of distinction about it. That change in the footprints, for example. What do you make of that?"

"Mortimer said that the man had walked on tiptoe down that portion of the Alley."

"He only repeated what some fool had said at the inquest. Why should a man walk on tiptoe down the Alley?"

"What then?"

"He was running, Watson—running desperately, running for his life, running until he burst his heart and fell upon his face."

"Running from what?"

"There lies our problem. There are indications that the man was crazed with fear before ever he began to run."

"How can you say that?"

"I am presuming that the cause of his fears came to him across the moor. If that were so, and it seems most probable, only a man who had lost his wits would have run *from* the house instead of towards it. If the gypsy's evidence may be taken as true, he ran with cries for help in the direction where help was least likely to be. Then, again, whom was he waiting for that night, and why was he waiting for him in the Yew Alley rather than in his own house?"

"You think that he was waiting for someone?"

"The man was elderly and infirm. We can understand his taking an evening stroll, but the ground was damp and the night inclement. Is it natural that he should stand for five or ten minutes, as Dr. Mortimer, with more practical sense than I should have given him credit for, deduced from the cigar ash?"

"But he went out every evening."

"I think it unlikely that he waited at the moor-gate every evening. On the contrary, the evidence is that he avoided the moor. That night he waited there. It was the night before he made his departure for London. The thing takes shape, Watson. It becomes coherent. Might I ask you to hand me my violin, and we will postpone all further thought upon this business until we have had the advantage of meeting Dr. Mortimer and Sir Henry Baskerville in the morning."

Unit 7

The Hound of
the Baskervilles

- Comprehension
  Questions
- The Detective Novel
- Discussion Guides
- Writing Exercise

COMPREHENSION QUESTIONS

For each of the following statements and questions, select the option containing the most complete or most accurate answer.

1. Dr. Mortimer states that, for some time before his death, Sir Charles
   (e) Baskerville had been greatly troubled by
   - ☐ a. the theft of several household items.
   - ☐ b. his lonely life at Baskerville Hall.
   - ☐ c. an old family legend.
   - ☐ d. his dwindling fortune.

2. Some two hundred years earlier, Hugo Baskerville had offered his soul
   (b) to the devil in exchange for
   - ☐ a. a large fortune.
   - ☐ b. the capture of a girl he had kidnapped.
   - ☐ c. eternal life.
   - ☐ d. the death of his rival for a young girl's love.

3. The devil appeared in the form of a fierce hound that
   (a) ☐ a. savagely attacked and killed Hugo Baskerville.
   - ☐ b. savagely attacked and killed the girl.
   - ☐ c. obeyed Hugo Baskerville's every command.
   - ☐ d. terrorized the entire countryside.

4. Since Hugo Baskerville first called upon the hound from hell, generations
   (a) of Baskervilles have
   - ☐ a. ordered the hound to kill their enemies.
   - ☐ b. been killed by a terrible hound.
   - ☐ c. made their own pacts with the devil.
   - ☐ d. died violent or mysterious deaths.

5. Dr. Mortimer and Sir Charles were on friendly terms because of their
   (b) mutual interest in
   - ☐ a. Baskerville Hall. ☐ c. science.
   - ☐ b. legends and magic. ☐ d. music.

6. One of the main questions raised by Sir Charles's death might be
   (e) expressed as
   - ☐ a. "How did Sir Charles *really* acquire that fortune?"
   - ☐ b. "Did Henry Baskerville have anything to do with his uncle's death?"
   - ☐ c. "Is the Baskerville legend true?"
   - ☐ d. "Who would Sir Charles have been running against in the upcoming election?"

7. Dr. Mortimer has brought Sir Charles's death to Sherlock Holmes's
(b) attention because he
    □ a. questions the identity of the arriving heir to the Baskerville fortune.
    □ b. fears for the personal safety of the new heir.
    □ c. is convinced that Sir Charles was murdered.
    □ d. believes that Sherlock Holmes is the only man who can take on the
        devil himself.

8. The tone in Dr. Mortimer's voice when he informs Sherlock Holmes that
(i) he found the footprints of a gigantic hound near Sir Charles's body is
    □ a. nervous and excited.   □ c. sinister and threatening.
    □ b. casual and offhand.   □ d. disbelieving and unimpressed.

9. Dr. Mortimer describes himself as a man of science—practical and
(j) unimaginative. His attitude towards the strange events at Baskerville
    Hall, however, suggest that Dr. Mortimer is also
    □ a. devious and cunning.   □ c. superstitious.
    □ b. selfish.   □ d. meddlesome.

10. Which of the following best defines *trivial* as used in, "I was convinced
(l) at the time that the matter was entirely *trivial* and that his excitement
    had no justification"?
    □ a. Understandable   □ c. Suspicious
    □ b. Significant   □ d. Unimportant

11. A possible motive that might account for the murder of Charles
(g) Baskerville is
    □ a. his criminal record.   □ c. an old love affair.
    □ b. his large fortune.   □ d. his political intentions.

12. The old document, the newspaper story, and Dr. Mortimer's statement
(k) are all narrative devices used to
    □ a. add local color to the story.
    □ b. create suspense.
    □ c. present the story from different points of view.
    □ d. display Sherlock Holmes's crime-solving techniques.

13. From the tone of the newspaper account of Sir Charles's death, one
(f) might conclude that the newspaper wanted
    □ a. to put an end to the rumors surrounding Sir Charles's death.
    □ b. to provoke an investigation into the rumors surrounding his death.
    □ c. to discourage his heir from taking up residence at Baskerville Hall.
    □ d. to protect Sir Charles's murderer.

14. The worsening condition of Sir Charles's mental state due to anxiety
(d) over the Baskerville demon dated from
  □ a. a lifelong obsession with the family legend.
  □ b. his South African days.
  □ c. his arrival at Baskerville Hall some two years earlier.
  □ d. the last few months before his death.

15. Which of the following best defines *flippantly* as used in, "You put the
(l) matter more *flippantly*, Mr. Holmes, than you would probably do if you
  were brought into personal contact with these things"?
  □ a. Seriously   □ c. Lightly
  □ b. Concisely   □ d. Gravely

16. Judging by his remark that "A devil with merely local powers like a
(g) parish vestry would be too inconceivable a thing," Sherlock Holmes's
  brand of humor might be described as
  □ a. slapstick.   □ c. whimsical.
  □ b. dry.   □ d. corny.

17. Sherlock Holmes seems to believe that the gigantic hound whose foot-
(f) prints Dr. Mortimer saw was
  □ a. the devil's servant.
  □ b. a lie fabricated by Dr. Mortimer.
  □ c. a figment of Dr. Mortimer's imagination.
  □ d. a device used by the murderer.

18. Sherlock Holmes's first step in solving the mystery is
(d) □ a. to study a detailed map of Devonshire County.
  □ b. to consult with Scotland Yard.
  □ c. to take the first train to Baskerville Hall.
  □ d. to discuss the case with Dr. Watson.

19. Holmes's conclusion that Watson had spent the day at his club was
(c) arrived at through
  □ a. a lucky guess.
  □ b. the process of deduction.
  □ c. trial and error.
  □ d. his familiarity with Watson's habits.

20. Holmes credits his success as a detective to
(c) □ a. experience.
  □ b. sophisticated laboratory techniques.
  □ c. an ability to notice the obvious.
  □ d. his network of informants.

21. Sherlock Holmes is the kind of man who has great respect for
(j) □ a. reason and logic.   □ c. neatness.
    □ b. physical strength.   □ d. wealth and lineage.

22. Dr. Watson helps Sherlock Holmes by being
(h) □ a. an intellectual equal with whom Holmes can brainstorm.
    □ b. a rival detective with whom Holmes can compete.
    □ c. a sounding board for testing Holmes's theories and ideas.
    □ d. an errand boy.

23. The original 1742 document regarding the hound of the Baskervilles was
(h) based on an account made by two drunken revelers at least three genera-
    tions removed from the author of the document. Thus, it might be
    inferred that
    □ a. a certain amount of exaggeration had already crept into the story.
    □ b. the beast was probably even more dreadful than the document
         claims.
    □ c. the document may be taken as a rational, eye-witness account.
    □ d. the document was a forgery.

24. A *metaphor* is a figure of speech which implies a comparison between
(k) two unlike things, such as "love is a rose" or "The whole world is a
    stage." Of the following quotations, which one *is not* a metaphor?
    □ a. ". . . the gravel page upon which I might have read so much . . . ."
    □ b. "This, then, is the stage upon which tragedy has been played."
    □ c. "[Hugo] found the cage empty and the bird escaped."
    □ d. "He made England too hot to hold him."

25. At the end of the selection, Holmes says, "The thing takes shape,
(i) Watson. It becomes coherent. Might I ask you to hand me my violin,
    and we will postpone all further thought upon this business . . . ."
    Though the reader wishes to do anything but "postpone" hearing
    Holmes's thoughts on the case, Holmes himself is remarkably
    □ a. tired and indifferent.   □ c. sad and confused.
    □ b. calm and controlled.   □ d. frustrated and nervous.

Comprehension Skills: a—isolating details; b—recalling specific facts; c—retaining
concepts; d—organizing facts; e—understanding the main idea; f—drawing a
conclusion; g—making a judgment; h—making an inference; i—recognizing tone;
j—understanding characters; k—appreciation of literary forms; l—knowledge of
word meanings.

Practice Exercise A

"I have in my pocket a manuscript," said Dr. James Mortimer.

"I observed it as you entered the room," said Holmes.

"It is an old manuscript."

"Early eighteenth century, unless it is a forgery."

"How can you say that, sir?"

"You have presented an inch or two of it to my examination all the time that you have been talking. It would be a poor expert who could not give the date of a document within a decade or so. You may possibly have read my little monograph upon the subject. I put that at 1730."

"The exact date is 1742."

1. Which of the rules for detective stories is followed in the passage above?
   ☐ a. The detective must be memorable.
   ☐ b. The crime must be significant.
   ☐ c. All suspects must be presented early.
   ☐ d. The solution to the murder must appear obvious.

2. On the lines provided, write a sentence which shows how little time and how little evidence Holmes required to deduce the date of the manuscript.

   _____

   _____

   _____

   _____

Practice Exercise B

". . . Sir Charles was a widower, and a man who may be said to have been in some ways of an eccentric habit of mind. In spite of his considerable wealth he was simple in his personal tastes, and his indoor servants at Baskerville Hall consisted of a married couple named Barrymore, the husband acting as butler and the wife as housekeeper. Their evidence, corroborated by that of several friends, tends to show that Sir Charles's health has for some time been impaired, and points especially to some affection of the heart, manifesting itself in changes of color, breathlessness, and acute attacks of nervous depression. Dr. James Mortimer, the friend and medical attendant of the deceased, has given evidence to the same effect . . . .

One Murphy, a gypsy horse-dealer, was on the moor at no great distance at the time, but he appears by his own confession to have been the worse for drink. He declares that he heard cries, but is unable to state from what direction they came . . . .

It is understood that the next-of-kin is Mr. Henry Baskerville, if he be still alive, the son of Sir Charles Baskerville's younger brother. The young man when last heard of was in America, and inquiries are being instituted with a view to informing him of his good fortune."

1. The excerpt above from the newspaper account of the death of Sir Charles serves mainly
   □ a. to heighten the suspense.
   □ b. to point out the cleverness of the murderer.
   □ c. to increase the importance of the crime.
   □ d. to round out the list of possible suspects.

2. Besides Sir Charles, six characters are mentioned in the passage above. On the lines provided, list them and tell who they are.

   _____

   _____

   _____

   _____

   _____

   _____

THE HOUND OF THE BASKERVILLES

Practice Exercise C

[Holmes] "If I had only been there!" he cried. "It is evidently a case of extraordinary interest, and one which presented immense opportunities to the scientific expert . . . ."

[Mortimer] "I could not call you in, Mr. Holmes, without disclosing these facts to the world, and I have already given my reasons for not wishing to do so. Besides, besides—"

"Why do you hesitate?"

"There is a realm in which the most acute and most experienced of detectives is helpless."

"You mean that the thing is supernatural?"

"I did not positively say so."

"No, but you evidently think it . . . ."

"I do not know what to believe."

Holmes shrugged his shoulders.

"I have hitherto confined my investigations to this world," said he. "In a modest way I have combated evil, but to take on the Father of Evil himself would, perhaps, be too ambitious a task. Yet you must admit that the footmark is material."

"The original hound was material enough to tug a man's throat out, and yet he was diabolical as well."

1. The passage above indicates that
   □ a. the detective is memorable.
   □ b. the murderer is a worthy opponent.
   □ c. an important clue has been revealed.
   □ d. the solution to the murder is obvious.

2. Dr. Mortimer tends toward the view that the murderer is a supernatural being, though as a scientist he can't admit it. Sherlock Holmes, on the other hand, seems to feel that the murderer is human. On the lines provided, write two sentences which suggest their two points of view concerning the nature of the murderer.

_____

_____

_____

_____

Practice Exercise D

"...The only other kinsman whom we have been able to trace was Rodger Baskerville, the youngest of three brothers of whom poor Sir Charles was the elder. The second brother, who died young, is the father of this lad Henry. The third, Rodger, was the black sheep of the family. He came of the old masterful Baskerville strain, and was the very image, they tell me, of the family picture of old Hugo. He made England too hot to hold him, fled to Central America, and died there in 1876 of yellow fever. Henry is the last of the Baskervilles.

1. Although he isn't aware of it, Dr. Mortimer's statement includes some potential clues. One important consideration that Dr. Mortimer failed to make in his investigation of Sir Charles Baskerville's heirs is the possibility that
   ☐ a. Rodger Baskerville may have had children by a marriage in Central America.
   ☐ b. Henry may yet marry and continue the Baskerville line.
   ☐ c. Henry may not wish to carry on his uncle's plans for the reconstruction and improvement of Baskerville Hall.
   ☐ d. Sir Charles was not really older than Rodger Baskerville.

2. On the lines provided, write a sentence which suggests that the evil influence of Hugo Baskerville may have been passed down through the family for many generations.

   _____

   _____

   _____

DISCUSSION GUIDES

Analyzing the Detective Novel

1. A "cliff-hanger" is an event or other device used to make you want to read the next chapter of a novel or buy the next episode of a serial. Analyze the cliff-hangers in the selection you have read.

2. Assuming that Sir Charles Baskerville was not the victim of a supernatural hound, how does the method of his murder suggest that Sherlock Holmes is facing a worthy adversary?

3. When reading a detective novel, most people tend to identify with the detective. How does this add to the fun of reading? In what ways would you like to be like Sherlock Holmes?

4. At one point Dr. Mortimer gets up to leave. As he is going out the door, Holmes says, "Only one more question, Dr. Mortimer," and he asks two questions. Many modern detectives, notably Lieutenant Columbo, also do this. What does this device accomplish?

Interpreting the Chapters

5. How do you get the impression that Holmes is superior to most people? Give examples from the reading selection which suggest this.

6. No precise date is given in the old manuscript for the time when Hugo Baskerville was supposedly killed by a supernatural hound. Re-read the manuscript and decide how you can determine the date of this event within a few years.

7. Dr. Mortimer says, in speaking of young Henry Baskerville, "And yet, consider that every Baskerville who goes there meets an evil fate." What does this line contribute to the story?

Analyzing the Author's Technique

8. Sometimes providing the necessary background for a detective novel results in tedious reading. You may have found this with the old Baskerville manuscript and the newspaper account of the murder. How does Arthur Conan Doyle pick up the pace right after this? (Look at the end of one chapter and the beginning of the next.)

9. Holmes says at the outset that the tale of the hound was a "fairy tale." Every reader knows that there are no supernatural hounds. How does the author get you to feel that *maybe* there *was* a hound after all?

10. Arthur Conan Doyle uses Watson as a foil for Holmes—that is, he uses Watson to make Holmes look good. How does he do this? Point to some examples in the story that demonstrate this.

WRITING EXERCISE

The great detective Peter Elliot has been called in to solve a murder. Set up a format for a typical detective story by writing a few sentences about each of the following topics.

1. Describe some peculiar characteristic of Detective Elliot that will make him memorable for the reader.

2. Describe the murder.

3. Make a brief list of some possible suspects. Tell which of them will turn out to be the murderer. Tell why this character is a worthy opponent for Peter Elliot.

4. Make a brief list of clues that you will include at the beginning of your story. These may be facts, such as a business connection of the victim, as well as physical evidence, such as the murder weapon.

Unit 8
**Psychological Aspects
in Literature**

In Cold
Blood

Introduction

In mid-November, 1959, Herbert Clutter, his wife Bonnie, a daughter Nancy and a son Kenyon were brutally murdered by two ex-convicts, Perry Smith and Richard Hickock, in what Truman Capote later called "a psychological accident." Perry and Dick went to the Clutter farm in a small Kansas community looking for a safe that they had been told contained a lot of money. There was no safe and very little money. After taking about fifty dollars, a radio and a pair of binoculars, the two men tied the Clutters with rope and killed them with a shotgun. The murders were done without spite, as if they were the inevitable end of a psychodrama that had begun many years before.

Following fanciful ideas that never could materialize, the murderers drifted down to Mexico, came back to Kansas, went to Florida, then west again in what Perry called "a race without a finish line." The race was not with the law, however. They were certain that having left no witnesses there was no way to connect them with the crime. There was only the nagging doubt which kept haunting them, "that anyone can get away with a thing like that."

They didn't get away with it. They made mistakes and unwittingly left a broad trail to follow. Patient, methodical police work resulted in their arrest in less than eight weeks. The evidence was overwhelming, and both men made full, free confessions. Five and a half years later, after exhausting all avenues of appeal, the two men were hanged in a warehouse at the Kansas State Prison.

In Cold Blood is a true account of the mass killing of the Clutter family and how it affected all of the people involved: the murderers themselves, their families, the people of the small farm community, the police officers who worked on the case, the lawyers, judges and jailers. The book, which has been called one of the finest crime books ever written in America, represents six years of intense research by the author. During that time, Truman Capote spent many hours interviewing the condemned men and the many "plain people" of Kansas who were, in one way or another, touched by the murders and their consequences.

The events of the chapters in this unit occur within two weeks or so after the murders. Dick and Perry have arrived in Mexico and are heading south toward Mexico City and beyond. Perry's head is filled with foolish notions of making a fortune skin-diving for treasure (though he doesn't swim), operating a deep-sea fishing boat (he has never so much as paddled a canoe), or driving stolen cars to South America (he has read somewhere you can get $500 a car for this). Dick, a bit more realistic, is satisfied to get what money he can through petty swindles and by passing bad checks, and to spend it as fast as he can on women and whiskey. Someday he will get a good job working on cars and save a lot of money; no one, right now, is paying wages that are high enough to suit him. Memories of the murders flit in and out of their consciousness like a bad dream.

The chapters are short. Leaving Dick and Perry in Mexico for a moment, the author takes us back to Hartman's Café in Holcomb, Kansas, where he gives us an intimate glimpse of how the murders have affected the townspeople. It is late November; with crops in and pheasant season over, people have little to do but "sit around and scare each other," Mrs. Hartman says. We can see, however, that feelings created by the murder run deeper than that. The once close-knit community is now ridden with suspicion. People are truly frightened, and some of them feel compelled to leave.

Back in Mexico once more, Dick and Perry are enjoying one of the few high points of their trip. They have fallen in with a rich vacationing German who takes them on daily fishing trips. "This is finally it. The way it ought to be." But we learn later in the book that this is the first, last and only fulfilling experience in lives that are otherwise warped and deprived.

After writing the book, Truman Capote said that he had created a new kind of book—a nonfiction novel. Many people are inclined to agree with him. While the book is a true account of a mass murder and its consequences (thus, nonfiction), the actions and conversations are reconstructed as the author imagined they happened, as is the case in a novel. The result is an incisive and revealing look at the minds and feelings of people who are capable of doing murder and at the minds and feelings of people who become caught up in the aftermath of a brutal act.

In Cold Blood is not a psychological novel in the strictest sense of the word (since there is considerable doubt that it is even a novel in the strictest sense of the word). But it uses many of the techniques of a psychological novel, as you will see, to penetrate the innermost thoughts and feelings of the characters. And although you know the crime, the "whodunnit," and the inevitable outcome of the chase, there is still a tension, suspense and excitement that is found only in the best-written crime novels. It is quite certain that most of you who are meeting Dick and Perry for the first time will not be able to rest until you have read the full account of their miserable existence and extinction. The book, one critic said when it first appeared, both "chills the blood and exercises the intelligence." *In Cold Blood* does just that.

Psychological Aspects
in Literature

A long-forgotten comedian used to say, "People are funnier than anybody." As is so often the case with things said in jest, this little sentence nicely sums up a much larger and more serious truth about human beings: People are unpredictable. You never know what someone is liable to do from one moment to the next, and you can never cease to be amazed at the variety of things—often bizarre things—that people can think of to do.

Because we are thinking creatures, we constantly ask ourselves *why* we do the things we do, why we feel as we do, why we react as we do to life's situations. We have, in fact, developed a science, which we call psychology, to look into just these questions.

Psychology is not limited to textbooks and doctors' offices, however. The whys and wherefores of human feelings and behavior are also subjects for hallway gossip and confidential conversations among friends. It appears in newspaper and magazine columns, plays, poems and in popular novels. We love to analyze ourselves and others. It seems natural, then, that the feelings and motives of people make absolutely fascinating subjects for literature.

Many authors reveal the feelings of major characters and give reasons for their characters' actions. Sometimes the author simply gives the impression of searching for answers and allows the reader to make a final analysis. When the internal analysis of character—the search for inner feelings and motives—becomes as important as the action, we are usually dealing with a *psychological novel*.

Psychology in literature is not a new thing. While the term is fairly new, a psychological study of a character is not new. Many of Shakespeare's plays, for example, deal heavily with the thoughts of characters and the reasons behind their actions. *Hamlet* and *King Lear* are two of his best known plays in this vein. And long before Shakespeare, the ancient Greek tragedians were taking hard, searching looks into the minds of their characters.

Closer to our own time, Charles Dickens examines the inside as well as the outside of his major characters in such books as *Great Expectations* and

Dombey and Son so that readers get to know the real reasons behind their actions and emotions. Today, we have become so aware of the things that influence our feelings and behavior that we expect authors to delve into the minds of their characters, and we are disappointed when they don't.

There are basically three ways that an author brings us into contact with the innermost being of the characters. First, the author may comment directly on the character's background and personality. Second, the author may let the reader observe the actions of the characters or eavesdrop on revealing conversations. And third, the author may take the reader inside the character's mind to "see" or "hear" what's going on there.

1. The Author's Comments. Frequently, when people discuss the actions of acquaintances, the question will arise, "Why do you suppose Dorothy, or Tom, acted that way?" Someone who knows the families well may suggest that Dorothy was spoiled as a child by permissive parents, or Tom had become cynical after an unhappy romance, and a detailed account of how their character defects developed may follow. "Yes," the company may agree, "that certainly could account for the rude way they acted at the party!"

An author, in a sense, may act as one of a group of people engaged in the discussion of an acquaintance. An action has occurred, and everyone wants to know why the person in question has behaved in a particular way. So the author, who knows the character intimately, presents some pertinent facts to enlighten us.

When preparing to write *In Cold Blood,* Truman Capote spent many hours with the two young men who were on death row in a Kansas prison, convicted of a brutal murder. He came to know them intimately. As he reconstructed their story, he frequently played the role of an intimate acquaintance of the murderers, Dick and Perry. In this way, he made interesting comments about their backgrounds and states of mind. What do you find out about Dick and Perry from the author's comments in the following passage?

> Though as a child he had attended church, Dick had never "come near" a belief in God, nor was he troubled by superstitions. Unlike Perry, he was not convinced that a broken mirror meant seven years' misfortune, or that a young moon if glimpsed through glass portended evil. But Perry, with his sharp and scratchy intuitions, had hit upon Dick's one abiding doubt. Dick, too, suffered moments when that question circled inside his head: Was it possible—were the two of them "honest to God going to get away with doing a thing like that?" Suddenly, he said to Perry, "Now, just shut up!"

Perry, according to the author, is superstitious. Dick is not. Dick had been taken to church as a child, but religion or a belief in God had never meant much to him. Things supernatural are not much of a factor in controlling the way he thinks or acts. Still, Perry's "scratchy intuitions" are able to penetrate Dick's mental armor. He is beginning to worry that there may indeed be a God who will not let them get away with murder.

BEST-SELLING CHAPTERS

2. The Reader's Observations. The things people say and do are not always reliable indicators of how they really feel or what they are really like. The face that a person presents to the world is not always the same face that is presented at home in the midst of family. But if, by chance, you catch someone off guard in a revealing moment, you may get a glimpse that teaches a great deal about the person.

In literature, where the psychology of characters is important, the author arranges for you to see the characters in revealing moments. It is the same with conversations between characters that you are privileged to "overhear." The conversations are carefully designed by the author to provide revealing moments of deep insight into a character's personality.

In Cold Blood is a true account of a mass murder. It was designed to provide insight into the characters of real murderers. It describes the effects the murders had on real people in a real town in Kansas. Still, the author, Truman Capote, was not with the murderers right after they killed four people in the Clutter family, nor was he in Holcomb to witness the immediate effects of the murder on the town's residents. He had to reconstruct actions and conversations as they may have occurred based on what he learned from his research, from talking to the murderers in jail and from talking to the townspeople of Holcomb.

Truman Capote knew, for example, that in an effort to win Dick's admiration, Perry told a lie about killing a Black man he had known in Las Vegas. Then, knowing the kind of men he was dealing with and the warped racial attitudes they must have grown up with, Capote could guess that Perry's and Dick's conversation would probably have taken place in just the objectionable manner in which he recorded it in his book:

> "Or did you? Kill him like you said?" Dick asked . . . . "Sure I did. Only—a nigger. It's not the same."

Thus the actions and conversations are partly real and partly reconstructions. They have certainly been carefully selected to provide intimate glimpses of how the characters are thinking. In the following scene from *In Cold Blood*, Capote allows you to "overhear" a conversation between Mrs. Ashida and Mrs. Hartman, owner of Hartman's Café in Holcomb. Mrs. Ashida and her husband, longtime residents of the community, are going to leave it. What do you learn about the psychological impact of the murder on the people of Holcomb from "overhearing" Mrs. Ashida's conversation.

> "Gosh, you think I want to leave?" Mrs. Ashida said. "Far as people go, this is the nicest place we ever lived. But Hideo, he's the man, and he says we can get a better farm in Nebraska. And I'll tell you something, Bess." Mrs. Ashida attempted a frown, but her plump, round, smooth face could not quite manage it. "We used to argue about it. Then one night I said, 'O.K., you're the boss, let's go.' After what happened to Herb and his family, I felt something around here had come to an end. I mean personally. For me. And so I quit arguing. I said O.K." She dipped a hand into

Bruce's box of Cracker Jack. "Gosh, I can't get over it. I can't get it off my mind. I *liked* Herb. Did you know I was one of the last to see him alive?

Holcomb, Kansas, is an isolated town of 270 people. Everyone knows everybody else, just like an overlarge family. Four people of this community have been brutally murdered for no apparent reason. Mrs. Ashida's exclamation, "Gosh, I can't get over it," pretty well sums up the impact the murders have had on the townspeople. The people have developed new attitudes towards one another which includes deep suspicion. The family feeling is gone. When Herb Clutter and his family died, something "had come to an end."

"Far as people go," Mrs. Ashida assures us, "this is the nicest place we ever lived. But ...." The *but* becomes "But Hideo, he's the man ...." But we, as the reading psychologists in the case, get a feeling that she really means, "*but* we don't trust these people anymore." There is a deep abiding fear in Holcomb, and some people are leaving because of it.

3. **The Character's Inner Thoughts.** There are several techniques that authors use to take a reader right inside a character's mind to reveal his or her innermost thoughts. A very old technique is the soliloquy which is best known from the way Shakespeare used it in his tragedies. A character— Hamlet or Macbeth or Othello—will appear on stage alone and speak as if to himself, thus revealing his innermost thoughts and feelings to the audience.

In a novel this technique may become what is called an *interior monologue.* Through an interior monologue, the reader "hears" what is going on in a character's mind. In one form of interior monologue the author may seem to disappear, leaving you alone with the stream of thoughts and images that are going through the character's mind. Sometimes the author may choose to drop in and out of a character's train of thought to offer important comments that guide us through the thinking. Other times, the author uses a combination of techniques or develops new ones to get readers involved in a character's most private self.

In the following passage from *In Cold Blood,* Truman Capote uses a very interesting technique. He takes us inside Dick's thoughts to reveal information about *Perry.* What do you find out about both Dick and Perry by eavesdropping on Dick's thoughts?

"There's got to be something wrong with somebody who'd do a thing like that," Perry said.

"Deal me out, baby, "Dick said. "I'm a normal." And Dick meant what he said. He thought himself as balanced, as sane as anyone—maybe a bit smarter than the average fellow, that's all. But Perry—there *was,* in Dick's opinion, "something wrong" with Little Perry. To say the least. Last spring, when they had celled together at Kansas State Penitentiary, he'd learned most of Perry's lesser peculiarities: Perry could be "such a kid," always wetting his bed and crying in his sleep ("Dad, I been looking everywhere,

where you been, Dad?"), and often Dick had seen him "sit for hours just sucking his thumb and pouring over them phony damn treasure guides." Which was one side; there were others. In some ways old Perry was "spooky as hell."

Notice how the author's presence is felt strongly at the beginning of the passage but becomes less and less apparent as the reading goes along until you are not sure when the author is intruding and when you are alone with Dick's thoughts.

Dick insists he is normal. As reader-psychologists, we are likely to disagree. A "normal" doesn't feel quite so strongly about convincing himself and others of his normalcy. And, of course, there are the brutal murders that Perry keeps bringing up to contradict Dick's claims of being normal.

From Dick's memories of the time he shared a cell with Perry, we learn that Perry has some serious disturbances left over from his childhood: bed wetting, thumb sucking and crying out for his father. Truly, here is a man badly in need of psychiatric counseling. But this is Dick's friend, traveling companion and cohort in a senseless murder. The reader must wonder about a "normal" person who chooses and clings to such a companion. Perhaps in dwelling on Perry's peculiarities Dick is really questioning whether there is "something wrong" with him, too.

As an element of storytelling, psychological analysis is here to stay. An author may comment directly on a character's state of mind, make us observers of a character's actions or conversations, or place us where we can "hear" a character's innermost thoughts. But however it is done, these private glimpses into the working of a mind add immeasurably to the appreciation and enjoyment of a good book. As you read the chapters from *In Cold Blood*, try to be aware of the different ways that Truman Capote helps you see and understand the thoughts and feelings of all the people who are caught in the shadow of a brutal murder.

As you read the chapters:

- Notice the paragraph in which Perry thinks about the members of his family.

- Think about the episode in which Dick kills an old dog. Try to decide what Dick wishes to prove by this action.

- Observe how a talkative English woman, Mrs. Archibald William Warren-Browne, reveals her state of mind after the murder in a long-winded monologue.

- Pay close attention to what the author tells us about Perry in the episode in which a friend is making sketches of him.

IN COLD BLOOD

In Cold Blood
Truman Capote

II PERSONS UNKNOWN

The car was parked on a promontory where Perry and Dick had stopped to picnic. It was noon. Dick scanned the view through a pair of binoculars. Mountains. Hawks wheeling in a white sky. A dusty road winding into and out of a white and dusty village. Today was his second day in Mexico, and so far he liked it fine—even the food. (At this very moment he was eating a cold, oily tortilla.) They had crossed the border at Laredo, Texas, the morning of November 23, and spent the first night in a San Luis Potosi brothel. They were now two hundred miles north of their next destination, Mexico City.

"Know what I think?" said Perry. "I think there must be something wrong with us. To do what we did."

"Did what?"

"Out there."

Dick dropped the binoculars into a leather case, a luxurious receptacle initialed H.W.C. He was annoyed. Annoyed as hell. Why the hell couldn't Perry shut up? What damn good did it do, always dragging the damn thing up? It really was *annoying*. Especially since they'd agreed, sort of, not to talk about the damn thing. Just forget it.

"There's got to be something wrong with somebody who'd do a thing like that," Perry said.

"Deal me out, baby," Dick said. "I'm a normal." And Dick meant what he said. He thought himself as balanced, as sane as anyone—maybe a bit smarter than the average fellow, that's all. But Perry—there *was*, in Dick's opinion, "something wrong" with Little Perry. To say the least. Last spring, when they had celled together at Kansas State Penitentiary, he'd learned most of Perry's lesser peculiarities: Perry could be "such a kid," always wetting his bed and crying in his sleep ("Dad, I been looking everywhere, where you been, Dad?"), and often Dick had seen him "sit for hours just sucking his thumb and poring over them phony damn treasure guides." Which was one side; there were others. In some ways old Perry was "spooky as hell." Take, for instance, that temper of his. He could slide into a fury "quicker than ten drunk Indians." And yet you wouldn't know it. "He might be ready to kill you, but you'd never know it, not to look at or listen to," Dick once said. For however extreme the inward rage, outwardly Perry remained a cool young tough, with eyes serene and slightly sleepy. The time had been when Dick had thought he could control, could regulate the temperature of these sudden cold fevers that burned and chilled his friend. He had been mistaken, and in the aftermath of that discovery, had grown very unsure of Perry, not at all certain what to think—except that he felt he ought to be afraid of him, and wondered really why he wasn't.

"Deep down," Perry continued, "way, way rock bottom, I never thought I could do it. A thing like that."

"How about the nigger?" Dick said. Silence. Dick realized that Perry was staring at him. A week ago, in Kansas City, Perry had bought a pair of dark glasses—fancy ones with silver-lacquered rims and mirrored lenses. Dick disliked them; he'd told Perry he was ashamed to be seen with "anyone who'd wear that kind of flit stuff." Actually, what irked him was the mirrored lenses; it was unpleasant having Perry's eyes hidden behind the privacy of those tinted, reflecting surfaces.

"But a nigger," said Perry. "That's different."

The comment, the reluctance with which it was pronounced, made Dick ask, "Or did you? Kill him like you said?" It was a significant question, for his original interest in Perry, his assessment of Perry's character and potentialities, was founded on the story Perry had once told him of how he had beaten a colored man to death.

"Sure I did. Only—a nigger. It's not the same." Then Perry said, "Know what it is that really bugs me? About the other thing? It's just I don't believe it—that anyone can get away with a thing like that. Because I don't see how it's possible. To do what we did. And just one hundred percent get away with it. I mean, that's what bugs me—I can't get it out of my head that something's got to happen."

Though as a child he had attended church, Dick had never "come near" a belief in God; nor was he troubled by superstitions. Unlike Perry, he was not convinced that a broken mirror meant seven years' misfortune, or that a young moon if glimpsed through glass portended evil. But Perry, with his sharp and scratchy intuitions, had hit upon Dick's one abiding doubt. Dick, too, suffered moments when that question circled inside his head: Was it possible—were the two of them "honest to God going to get away with doing a thing like that?" Suddenly, he said to Perry, "Now, just shut up!" Then he gunned the motor and backed the car off the promontory. Ahead of him, on the dusty road, he saw a dog trotting along in the warm sunshine.

Mountains. Hawks wheeling in a white sky.

When Perry asked Dick, "Know what I think?" he knew he was beginning a conversation that would displease Dick, and one that, for that matter, he himself would just as soon avoid. He agreed with Dick: Why go on talking about it? But he could not always stop himself. Spells of helplessness occurred, moments when he "remembered things"—blue light exploding in a black room, the glass eyes of a big toy bear—and when voices, a particular few words, started nagging his mind: "Oh, no! Oh, please! No! No! No! No! Don't! Oh, please don't, please!" And certain sounds returned—a silver dollar rolling across a floor, boot steps on hardwood stairs, and the sounds of breathing, the gasps, the hysterical inhalations of a man with a severed windpipe.

When Perry said, "I think there must be something wrong with us," he was making an admission he "hated to make." After all, it was "painful" to imagine that one might be "not just right"—particularly if whatever was wrong was not your own fault but "maybe a thing you were born with." Look at his family! Look at what had happened there! His mother, an alcoholic, had strangled to death on her own vomit. Of her children, two sons and two daughters, only the younger girl, Barbara, had entered ordinary life, married, begun raising a family. Fern, the other daughter, jumped out of a window of a San Francisco hotel. (Perry had ever since "tried to believe she slipped," for he'd loved Fern. She was "such a sweet person," so "artistic," a "terrific" dancer, and she could sing, too. "If she'd ever had any luck at all, with her looks and all, she could have got somewhere, been somebody." It was sad to think of her climbing over a window sill and falling fifteen floors.) And there was Jimmy, the older boy—Jimmy, who had one day driven his wife to suicide and killed himself the next.

Then he heard Dick say, "Deal me out, baby. I'm a normal." Wasn't that a horse's laugh? But never mind, let it pass. "Deep down," Perry continued, "way, way rock bottom, I never thought I could do it. A thing like that." And at once he recognized his error: Dick would, of course, answer by asking, "How about the nigger?" When he'd told Dick that story, it was because he'd wanted Dick's friendship, wanted Dick to "respect" him, think him "hard," as much "the masculine type" as he had considered Dick to be. And so one day after they had both read and were discussing a *Reader's Digest* article entitled "How Good a Character Detective Are You?" ("As you wait in a dentist's office or a railway station, try studying the give-away signs in people around you. Watch the way they walk, for example. A stiff-legged gait can reveal a rigid, unbending personality; a shambling walk a lack of determination"), Perry had said "I've always been an outstanding character detective, otherwise I'd be dead today. Like if I couldn't judge when to trust somebody. You never can much. But I've come to trust you, Dick. You'll see I do, because I'm going to put myself in your power. I'm going to tell you something I never told anybody. Not even Willie-Jay. About the time I fixed a guy." And Perry saw, as he went on, that Dick was interested; he was really listening. "It was a couple of summers ago. Out in Vegas. I was living in this old boarding house—it used to be a fancy cathouse. But all the fancy was gone. It was a place they should have torn down ten years back; anyway, it was sort of coming down by itself. The cheapest rooms were in the attic, and I lived up there. So did this nigger. His name was King; he was a transient. We were the only two up there—us and a million *cucarachas*. King, he wasn't too young, but he'd done roadwork and other outdoor stuff—he had a good build. He wore glasses, and he read a lot. He never shut his door. Every time I passed by, he was always lying back there buck-naked. He was out of work, and said he'd saved a few dollars from his last job, said he wanted to stay in bed awhile, read and fan himself and drink beer. The stuff he read, it was just junk—comic books and cowboy junk. He was O.K. Sometimes we'd have a beer together, and once he lent me ten dollars. I had no cause to hurt him. But one night we were sitting in the attic, it was so hot you couldn't sleep, so I said, 'Come on, King, let's go for a drive.' I had an old car I'd stripped and souped and painted silver—the Silver Ghost, I called it. We went for a long drive. Drove way out in the desert. Out there it was cool. We parked and drank a few more beers. King got out of the car, and I followed after him. He didn't see I'd picked up this chain. A bicycle chain I kept under the seat. Actually, I had no real idea to do it till I did it. I hit him across the face. Broke his glasses. I kept right on. Afterward, I didn't feel a thing. I left him there, and never heard a word about it. Maybe nobody ever found him. Just buzzards."

There was some truth in the story. Perry had known, under the circumstances stated, a Negro named King. But if the man was dead today it was none of Perry's doing; he'd never raised a hand against him. For all he knew, King might still be lying abed somewhere, fanning himself and sipping beer.

"Or did you? Kill him like you said?" Dick asked.

Perry was not a gifted liar, or a prolific one; however, once he told a fiction he usually stuck by it. "Sure I did. Only—a nigger. It's not the same." Presently, he said, "Know what it is that really bugs me? About that other thing? It's just I don't believe it—that anyone can get away with a thing like that." And he suspected that Dick didn't, either. For Dick was at least partly inhabited by Perry's mystical-moral apprehensions. Thus: "Now, just shut up!"

The car was moving. A hundred feet ahead, a dog trotted along the side of the road. Dick swerved toward it. It was an old half-dead mongrel, brittle-boned and mangy, and the impact, as it met the car, was little more than what a bird might make. But Dick was satisfied. "Boy!" he said—and it was what he always said after running down a dog, which was something he did whenever the opportunity arose. "Boy! We sure splattered him!"

Thanksgiving passed, and the pheasant season came to a halt, but not the beautiful Indian summer, with its flow of clear, pure days. The last of the out-of-town newsmen, convinced that the case was never going to be solved, left Garden City. But the case was by no means closed for the people of Finney County, and least of all for those who patronized Holcomb's favorite meeting place, Hartman's Café.

"Since the trouble started, we've been doing all the business we can handle," Mrs. Hartman said, gazing around her snug domain, every scrap of which was being sat or stood or leaned upon by tobacco-scented, coffee-drinking farmers, farm helpers, and ranch hands. "Just a bunch of old women," added Mrs. Hartman's cousin, Postmistress Clare, who happened to be on the premises. "If it was spring and work to be done, they wouldn't be here. But wheat's in, winter's on the way, they got nothing to do but sit around and scare each other. You know Bill Brown, down to the *Telegram?*

See the editorial he wrote? That one he called it 'Another Crime'? Said, 'It's time for everyone to stop wagging loose tongues.' Because that's a crime, too—telling plain-out lies. But what can you expect? Look around you. Rattlesnakes. Varmints. *Rumor*-mongers. See anything else? Ha! Like dash you do."

One rumor originating in Hartman's Café involved Taylor Jones, a rancher whose property adjoins River Valley Farm. In the opinion of a good part of the cafe's clientele, Mr. Jones and his family, not the Clutters, were the murderer's intended victims. "It makes harder sense," argued one of those who held this view. "Taylor Jones, he's a richer man than Herb Clutter ever was. Now, pretend the fellow who done it wasn't anyone from hereabouts. Pretend he'd been maybe hired to kill, and all he had was instructions on how to get to the house. Well, it would be mighty easy to make a mistake— take a wrong turn—and end up at Herb's place 'stead of Taylor's." The "Jones Theory" was much repeated—especially to the Joneses, a dignified and sensible family, who refused to be flustered.

A lunch counter, a few tables, an alcove harboring a hot grill and an ice-box and a radio—that's all there is to Hartman's Café. "But our customers like it," says the proprietress. "Got to. Nowhere else for them to go. 'Less they drive seven miles one direction or fifteen the other. Anyway, we run a friendly place, and the coffee's good since Mabel came to work"—Mabel being Mrs. Helm. "After the tragedy, I said, 'Mabel now that you're out of a job, why don't you come give me a hand at the cafe. Cook a little. Wait counter.' How it turned out—the only bad feature is, everybody comes in here, they pester her with questions. About the tragedy. But Mabel's not like Cousin Myrt. Or me. She's shy. Besides, she doesn't know anything special. No more than anybody else." But by and large the Hartman congregation continued to suspect that Mabel Helm knew a thing or two that she was holding back. And, of course, she did. Dewey had had several conversations with her and had requested that everything they said be kept secret. Particularly, she was not to mention the missing radio or the watch found in Nancy's shoe. Which is why she said to Mrs. Archibald William Warren-Browne, "Anybody reads the papers knows as much as I do. More. Because I don't read them."

Square, squat, in the earlier forties, an Englishwoman fitted out with an accent almost incoherently upper-class, Mrs. Archibald William Warren-Browne did not at all resemble the cafe's other frequenters, and seemed, within that setting, like a peacock trapped in a turkey pen. Once, explaining to an acquaintance why she and her husband had abandoned "family estates in the North of England," exchanging the hereditary home—"the jolliest, oh, the prettiest old priory"—for an old and highly unjolly farmhouse on the plains of western Kansas, Mrs. Warren-Browne said: "Taxes, my dear. Death duties. E*nor*mous, *crim*inal death duties. That's what drove us out of England. Yes, we left a year ago. Without regrets. None. We love it here. *Just* adore it. Though, of course, it's very *dif*ferent from our other life. The life we've always known. Paris and Rome. Monte. London. I do—oc*cas*ionally— think of London. Oh, I don't *really* miss it—the frenzy, and never a cab, and always worrying how one looks. Positively not. We love it here. I suppose some people—those aware of our past, the life we've led—wonder aren't we the tiniest bit *lonely*, out there in the wheat fields. Out West is where we meant to settle. Wyoming or Nevada—*la vraie chose.* We hoped when we got there some oil might stick to us. But on our way we stopped to visit friends in Garden City—friends *of* friends, *actually.* But they couldn't have been kinder. In*sisted* we linger on. And we thought, Well, why not? Why not hire a bit of land and start ranching? Or farming. Which is a decision we still haven't come to—whether to ranch or farm. Dr. Austin asked if we didn't find it perhaps too quiet. *Actually,* no. *Actually,* I've never known such bedlam. It's noisier than a bomb raid. *Train* whistles. Co*yotes.* Monsters *howl*ing the bloody night long. A horrid racket. And since the murders it seems to bother me more. So many things do. Our house—what an old creaker it is! Mark you, I'm not complaining. Really, it's quite a serviceable house—has all the mod. cons.—but, oh, how it coughs and grunts! And after dark, when the wind commences, that *hate*ful prairie wind, one hears the most ap*pall*ing moans. I mean, if one's a bit nervy, one can't help imagining—silly things. Dear God! That poor family! No, we never met them. I *saw* Mr. Clutter once. In the Federal Building."

Early in December, in the course of a single afternoon, two of the café's steadiest customers announced plans to pack up and leave not merely Finney County but the state. The first was a tenant farmer who worked for Lester McCoy, a well-known western-Kansas landowner and businessman. He said, "I had myself a talk with Mr. McCoy. Tried to let him know what's going on out here in Holcomb and hereabouts. How a body can't sleep. My wife can't sleep, and she won't allow me. So I told Mr. McCoy I like his place fine but he better hunt up another man. Count of we're movin' on. Down to East Colorado. Maybe then I'll get some rest."

The second announcement was made by Mrs. Hideo Ashida, who stopped by the café with three of her four red-cheeked children. She lined them up at the counter and told Mrs. Hartman, "Give Bruce a box of Cracker Jack. Bobby wants a Coke. Bonnie Jean? We know how you feel, Bonnie Jean, but come on, have a treat." Bonnie Jean shook her head, and Mrs. Ashida said, "Bonnie Jean's sort of blue. She don't want to leave here. The school here. And all her friends."

"Why, say," said Mrs. Hartman, smiling at Bonnie Jean. "That's nothing to be sad over. Transferring from Holcomb to Garden City High. Lots more boys—"

Bonnie Jean said, "You don't understand. Daddy's taking us away. To Nebraska."

Bess Hartman looked at the mother, as if expecting her to deny the daughter's allegation.

"It's true, Bess," Mrs. Ashida said.

"I don't know what to say," said Mrs. Hartman, her voice indignantly astonished, and also despairing. The Ashidas were a part of the Holcomb community everyone appreciated—a family likably high-spirited, yet hard-working and neighborly and generous, though they didn't have much to be generous with.

Mrs. Ashida said, "We've been talking on it a long time. Hideo, he thinks we can do better somewhere else."

"When you plan to go?"

"Soon as we sell up. But anyway not before Christmas. On account of a deal we've worked out with the dentist. About Hideo's Christmas present. Me and the kids, we're giving him three gold teeth. For Christmas."

Mrs. Hartman sighed. "I don't know what to say. Except I wish you wouldn't. Just up and leave us." She sighed again. "Seems like we're losing everybody. One way or another."

"Gosh, you think I want to leave?" Mrs. Ashida said. "Far as people go, this is the nicest place we ever lived. But Hideo, he's the man, and he says we can get a better farm in Nebraska. And I'll tell you something, Bess." Mrs. Ashida attempted a frown, but her plump, round, smooth face could not quite manage it. "We used to argue about it. Then one night I said, 'O.K., you're the boss, let's go.' After what happened to Herb and his family, I felt something around here had come to an end. I mean personally. For me. And so I quit arguing. I said O.K." She dipped a hand into Bruce's box of Cracker Jack. "Gosh, I can't get over it. I can't get it off my mind. I *liked* Herb. Did you know I was one of the last to see him alive? Uh-huh. Me and the kids. We been to the 4-H meeting in Garden City and he gave us a ride home. The last thing I said to Herb, I told him how I couldn't imagine his ever being afraid. That no matter what the situation was, he could talk his way out of it." Thoughtfully she nibbled a kernel of Cracker Jack, took a swig of Bobby's Coke, then said, "Funny, but you know, Bess, I'll bet he *wasn't* afraid. I mean, however it happened, I'll bet right up to the last he didn't believe it would. Because it couldn't. Not to him."

The sun was blazing. A small boat was riding at anchor in a mild sea: the *Estrellita*, with four persons aboard—Dick, Perry, a young Mexican, and Otto, a rich middle-aged German.

"Please. Again," said Otto, and Perry, strumming his guitar, sang in a husky sweet voice a Smoky Mountains song:

> "In this world today while we're living
> Some folks say the worst of us they can,
> But when we're dead and in our caskets,
> They always slip some lilies in our hand.
> Won't you give me flowers while I'm living . . ."

A week in Mexico City, and then he and Dick had driven south—Cuernavaca, Taxco, Acapulco. And it was in Acapulco, in a "jukebox honky-tonk," that they had met the hairy-legged and hearty Otto. Dick had "picked him up." But the gentleman, a vacationing Hamburg lawyer, "already had a friend"—a young native Acapulcan who called himself the Cowboy. "He proved to be a trustworthy person," Perry once said of the Cowboy. "Mean as Judas, some ways, but oh, man, a funny boy, a real fast jockey. Dick liked him, too. We got on great."

The Cowboy found for the tattooed drifters a room in the house of an uncle, undertook to improve Perry's Spanish, and shared the benefits of his liaison with the holidaymaker from Hamburg, in whose company and at whose expense they drank and ate and bought women. The host seemed to think his pesos well spent, if only because he relished Dick's jokes. Each day Otto hired the *Estrellita*, a deep-sea-fishing craft, and the four friends went trolling along the coast. The Cowboy skippered the boat; Otto sketched and fished; Perry baited hooks, daydreamed, sang, and sometimes fished; Dick did nothing—only moaned, complained of the motion, lay about sun-drugged and listless, like a lizard at siesta. But Perry said, "This is finally it. The way it ought to be." Still, he knew that it couldn't continue—that it was, in fact, destined to stop that very day. The next day Otto was returning to Germany, and Perry and Dick were driving back to Mexico City—at Dick's insistence. "Sure, baby," he'd said when they were debating the matter. "It's nice and all. With the sun on your back. But the dough's going-going-gone. And after we've sold the car, what have we got left?"

The answer was that they had very little, for they had by now mostly disposed of the stuff acquired the day of the Kansas City check-passing spree—the camera, the cuff links, the television sets. Also, they had sold, to a Mexico City policeman with whom Dick had got acquainted, a pair of binoculars and a gray Zenith portable radio. "What we'll do is, we'll go back to Mex, sell the car, and maybe I can get a garage job. Anyway, it's a better deal up there. Better opportunities. I sure could use some more of that Inez." Inez was a prostitute who had accosted Dick on the steps of the Palace of Fine Arts in Mexico City (the visit was part of a sightseeing tour taken to please Perry). She was eighteen, and Dick had promised to marry her. But he had also promised to marry Maria, a woman of fifty, who was the widow of a "very prominent Mexican banker." They had met in a bar, and the next morning she had paid him the equivalent of seven dollars. "So how about it?" Dick said to Perry. "We'll sell the wagon. Find a job. Save our dough. And see what happens." As though Perry couldn't predict precisely what would happen. Suppose they got two or three hundred for the old Chevrolet. Dick, if he knew Dick, and he did—*now* he did—would spend it right away on vodka and women.

While Perry sang, Otto sketched him in a sketchbook. It was a passable likeness, and the artist perceived one not very obvious aspect of the sitter's countenance—its mischief, an amused, babyish malice that suggested some unkind cupid aiming envenomed arrows. He was naked to the waist. (Perry was "ashamed" to take off his trousers, "ashamed" to wear swimming trunks, for he was afraid that the sight of his injured legs would "disgust people," and so, despite his underwater reveries, all the talk about skin-diving, he hadn't once gone into the water.) Otto reproduced a number of the tattoos ornamenting the subject's overmuscled chest, arms, and small and calloused but girlish hands. The sketchbook, which Otto gave Perry as a parting gift, contained several drawings of Dick—"nude studies."

Otto shut his sketchbook, Perry put down his guitar, and the Cowboy raised anchor, started the engine. It was time to go. They were ten miles out, and the water was darkening.

Perry urged Dick to fish. "We may never have another chance," he said. "Chance?"

"To catch a big one."

"I've got the bastard kind," Dick said. "I'm sick." Dick often had headaches of migraine intensity—"the bastard kind." He thought they were the result of his automobile accident. "Please, baby. Let's be very, very quiet."

Moments later Dick had forgotten his pain. He was on his feet, shouting with excitement. Otto and the Cowboy were shouting, too. Perry had hooked "a big one." Ten feet of soaring, plunging sailfish, it leaped, arched like a rainbow, dived, sank deep, tugged the line taut, rose, flew, fell, rose. An hour passed, and part of another, before the sweat-soaked sportsmen reeled it in.

There is an old man with an ancient wooden box camera who hangs around the harbor in Acapulco, and when the *Estrellita* docked, Otto commissioned him to do six portraits of Perry posed beside his catch. Technically, the old man's work turned out badly—brown and streaked. Still, they were remarkable photographs, and what made them so was Perry's expression, his look of unflawed fulfillment, of beatitude, as though at last, and as in one of his dreams, a tall yellow bird had hauled him to heaven.

Unit 8

In Cold Blood

- Comprehension Questions
- Psychological Aspects in Literature
- Discussion Guides
- Writing Exercise

COMPREHENSION QUESTIONS

For each of the following statements and questions, select the option containing the most complete or most accurate answer.

1. An idea that is constantly bothering Dick and Perry is best expressed in
(e) the quotation
   - □ a. "... there must be something wrong with us."
   - □ b. "Gosh, you think I want to leave?"
   - □ c. "This is finally it. The way it ought to be."
   - □ d. "We may never have another chance."

2. Dick liked to think of himself as
(j)
   - □ a. having "something wrong."
   - □ b. being shy with women.
   - □ c. being as sane as anyone.
   - □ d. having strong religious convictions.

3. By using the word "nigger" in reporting a conversation between Perry
(k) and Dick, the author, Truman Capote, was probably
   - □ a. demonstrating his racial prejudice.
   - □ b. using artistic license to mask his real feelings.
   - □ c. trying to arouse the readers' emotions.
   - □ d. accurately recording the language of two young toughs.

4. In the phrase, "... his *assessment* of Perry's character ...," the word
(l) *assessment* means
   - □ a. objection to.
   - □ b. evaluation of.
   - □ c. concern about.
   - □ d. error in judgment.

5. Dick and Perry had opposite attitudes in that
(c)
   - □ a. Perry was superstitious but Dick was not.
   - □ b. Dick was superstitious but Perry was not.
   - □ c. Perry pursued women but Dick did not.
   - □ d. Dick was shy with people but Perry was not.

6. Perry was worried deep down inside that they wouldn't get away with
(c) murder. From what we know of Dick, it seems that he
   - □ a. wasn't worried at all.
   - □ b. was worried about more important things.
   - □ c. was worried only about little things.
   - □ d. was worried about the same thing.

7. At the beginning of two of the chapters, the author uses the short
(i) sentences: "Mountains. Hawks wheeling in a white sky." He probably
does this to convey a feeling of
- ☐ a. happiness in a beautiful setting.
- ☐ b. loneliness in a vast, empty place.
- ☐ c. exhilaration at being in the great outdoors.
- ☐ d. fear of heights felt by Dick and Perry.

8. A week after the murders, Perry
(f) ☐ a. had no recollection of the details.
- ☐ b. could finally make the memories go away.
- ☐ c. had vivid memories that haunted him.
- ☐ d. would get a thrill thinking of the murders.

9. Perry's mother was
(b) ☐ a. an alcoholic.   ☐ c. an ex-convict.
- ☐ b. a drug addict.   ☐ d. a suicide.

10. Two things that Perry wanted badly from Dick were
(b) ☐ a. trust and admiration.   ☐ c. friendship and respect.
- ☐ b. love and kindness.   ☐ d. pity and sympathy.

11. Perry's story about killing a Black man was false. It seems likely that,
(h) before the Clutter murders, Perry had never
- ☐ a. met any Blacks.   ☐ c. committed a crime.
- ☐ b. been to Las Vegas.   ☐ d. killed anyone.

12. Dick seemed to enjoy killing
(b) ☐ a. people.   ☐ c. fish.
- ☐ b. dogs.   ☐ d. hawks.

13. After the murders, Hartman's Café in Holcomb was
(a) ☐ a. busy most of the time.
- ☐ b. headquarters for the investigation.
- ☐ c. where townspeople would quarrel.
- ☐ d. empty most of the time.

14. In the expression, "... a good part of the café's *clientele* ...," the
(l) word *clientele* means
- ☐ a. gossips.   ☐ c. managers.
- ☐ b. workers.   ☐ d. customers.

15. A rumor, started in Hartman's Café after the murders, said that
(a)   ☐ a. Herb Clutter had underworld connections.
      ☐ b. it was a revenge killing.
      ☐ c. a neighbor, Taylor Jones, was probably the killer.
      ☐ d. the Clutters were probably killed by mistake.

16. Mrs. Archibald William Warren-Browne delivers a long discourse in
(i)   many short sentences. The author shows with italics that she is over-emphasizing many short words and syllables. This gives the passage a tone of
      ☐ a. angry shouting.   ☐ c. nervous chatter.
      ☐ b. intellectual conversation.   ☐ d. comic monologue.

17. In one afternoon two residents of Holcomb announce they are leaving
(h)   town. This is an indication that
      ☐ a. there is a crime wave in Holcomb.
      ☐ b. people are fearful.
      ☐ c. there will be another murder.
      ☐ d. the police have failed in their job.

18. Dick and Perry crossed into Mexico at Laredo, Texas, and then
(d)   ☐ a. headed south to Mexico City.
      ☐ b. headed north to El Paso.
      ☐ c. went west to Baja California.
      ☐ d. went east to meet a friend.

19. On their fishing trips Otto sketched and fished; Perry daydreamed,
(d)   baited hooks, sang and sometimes fished; and Dick
      ☐ a. played the guitar or harmonica.
      ☐ b. did nothing but moan and complain.
      ☐ c. fished and made plans for the future.
      ☐ d. went skin-diving.

20. Dick says: "What we'll do is, we'll go back to Mex [Mexico City], sell
(g)   the car, and maybe I can get a garage job. Anyway, it's a better deal up there. Better opportunities . . . ." From this we can see that Dick and Perry
      ☐ a. have planned their future carefully.
      ☐ b. want to live within the law.
      ☐ c. are shrewd wheelers and dealers.
      ☐ d. live from day to day.

21. The author says that one of Otto's sketches showed in Perry's face "an
(k) amused, babyish malice that suggested some unkind cupid aiming
     envenomed arrows." What Otto saw may best be described as a
     ☐ a. hard appearance masking a loving personality.
     ☐ b. face like cupid but manly nevertheless.
     ☐ c. dangerously deceptive, sweet and innocent appearance.
     ☐ d. loving child who is filled with sadness.

22. Perry and Dick enjoyed fighting and catching a huge sailfish because it
(e) was
     ☐ a. a way of getting even with the world.
     ☐ b. a moment of fulfillment.
     ☐ c. their last day in Mexico.
     ☐ d. a re-enactment of the murders.

23. The author, Dick and Perry himself all lead us to the conclusion that
(f) Perry's personality problems
     ☐ a. relate to his childhood.
     ☐ b. began in prison.
     ☐ c. result from his sensitivity.
     ☐ d. stem from reading and dreaming.

24. Perry thought that Dick
(g) ☐ a. was "a normal."
     ☐ b. was closer to being normal than Perry was.
     ☐ c. was not entirely normal.
     ☐ d. was closer to being normal than most people.

25. From what Dick says about Perry, and from what Otto shows in his
(j) sketches, Perry seems to be
     ☐ a. angry, but calm inside.
     ☐ b. mean, but with a heart of gold.
     ☐ c. happy, but always in a rage.
     ☐ d. calm, but angry and mean inside.

Comprehension Skills: a—isolating details; b—recalling specific facts; c—retaining
concepts; d—organizing facts; e—understanding the main idea; f—drawing a
conclusion; g—making a judgment; h—making an inference; i—recognizing tone;
j—understanding characters; k—appreciation of literary forms; l—knowledge of
word meanings.

PSYCHOLOGICAL ASPECTS IN LITERATURE

Practice Exercise A

When Perry said, "I think there must be something wrong with us," he was making an admission he "hated to make." After all, it was "painful" to imagine that one might be "not just right"—particularly if whatever was wrong was not your own fault but "maybe a thing you were born with." Look at his own family! . . . His mother, an alcoholic, had strangled to death on her own vomit. Of her children . . . only the younger girl, Barbara, had entered ordinary life, married, begun raising a family. Fern, the other daughter, jumped out of a window of a San Francisco hotel. (Perry had ever since "tried to believe she slipped," for he'd loved Fern. She was "such a sweet person," so "artistic," a "terrific" dancer, and she could sing, too. "If she'd ever had any luck at all, with her looks and all, she could have got somewhere, been somebody." It was sad to think of her climbing over a window sill and falling fifteen floors.) And there was Jimmy, the older boy—Jimmy, who had one day driven his wife to suicide and killed himself the next.

1. Perry is painfully aware of the emotional problems that have plagued his family. The author seems to be hinting that Perry may be a victim of
   - ☐ a. alcoholism.
   - ☐ b. his family background.
   - ☐ c. suicidal tendencies.
   - ☐ d. social discrimination.

2. Perry seems to want to blame his sister Fern's suicide and his own problems on misfortune. On the lines provided, write a phrase from near the beginning of the passage and one from near the end that prove this.

   _____

   _____

Practice Exercise B

The car was moving. A hundred feet ahead, a dog trotted along the side of the road. Dick swerved toward it. It was an old half-dead mongrel, brittle-boned and mangy, and the impact, as it met the car, was little more than what a bird might make. But Dick was satisfied. "Boy!" he said—and it was what he always said after running down a dog, which was something he did whenever the opportunity arose. "Boy! We sure splattered him!"

1. In this episode, Dick may be trying to prove to himself or to Perry that he
   - ☐ a. is a fearless driver.
   - ☐ b. has "something wrong."
   - ☐ c. hates dogs.
   - ☐ d. is a cool killer.

2. In one sentence the author completely deflates the bravado or "macho" element of Dick's behavior. Circle the sentence in the passage above.

Practice Exercise C

[Mrs. Warren-Browne is explaining how she came to stay in Holcomb:]

And we thought . . . Why not hire a bit of land and start ranching? Or farming. Which is a decision we still haven't come to—whether to ranch or farm. Dr. Austin asked if we didn't find it perhaps too quiet . . . . *Actually*, I've never known such bedlam. It's noisier than a bomb raid. *Train* whistles. Co*yo*tes. Monsters *howl*ing the bloody night long. A horrid racket. And since the murders it seems to bother me more. So many things do. Our house— what an old creaker it is! Mark you, I'm not complaining. Really, it's quite a serviceable house—has all the mod. cons.—but, oh, how it coughs and grunts! And after dark, when the wind commences, that *hate*ful prairie wind, one hears the most ap*pall*ing moans. I mean, if one's a bit nervy, one can't help imagining—silly things. Dear God! That poor family! No, we never met them. I *saw* Mr. Clutter once. In the Federal Building."

1. By "listening" to the lady speak, you can tell she
   □ a. is frightened out of her wits. □ c. hates everything about Holcomb.
   □ b. is indecisive. □ d. just likes to complain.

2. In the passage, Mrs. Warren-Browne is mostly just chattering. Suddenly, toward the end of the passage, she reveals what is really on her mind. Write two short sentences which tell what is upsetting her most.

   _____

   _____

Practice Exercise D

While Perry sang, Otto sketched him in a sketchbook. It was a passable likeness, and the artist perceived one not very obvious aspect of the sitter's countenance—its mischief, an amused, babyish malice that suggested some unkind cupid aiming envenomed arrows. He was naked to the waist. (Perry was . . . "ashamed" to wear swimming trunks, for he was afraid that the sight of his injured legs would "disgust people," and so, despite his underwater reveries, all the talk about skindiving, he hadn't once gone into the water.)

1. The author tells us of *two* of Perry's character flaws—one that is obvious and the one that is hidden. Perry is
   □ a. cowardly and disgusting. □ c. self-conscious and mean.
   □ b. conceited and dishonest. □ d. arrogant and unfeeling.

2. Through Otto, the author helps us penetrate Perry's inner personality. Circle the sentence that contains Otto's revelation to the reader.

IN COLD BLOOD

DISCUSSION GUIDES

Analyzing Psychological Aspects in Literature

1. At the end of the selection you have read, the author says that Perry had a look of fulfillment as though at last a tall yellow bird had hauled him to heaven. The yellow bird hauling him to heaven is a recurring pleasant dream for Perry that the author mentions several times in the book. How does telling about recurring dreams help to get a reader "inside" a character's mind?

2. At one point the author includes a song that Perry sings. Find and re-read the words of the song. How does this song emphasize Perry's state of mind?

3. Dick liked to run over dogs. Perry made up a story about killing a Black man. Why do you think the author included this information? How does the use of these revelations about Dick and Perry help you to understand them?

Interpreting the Chapters

4. Perry seems to be more shy and more unsure of himself than Dick. Do you think this would make Perry more or less capable of committing murder? Explain the reasons for your opinion.

5. Do you think that both Dick and Perry participated in killing the four people in the Clutter family? Or did just one of them do all of the killing? Discuss the possibilities based on what you have learned about the two men. (Later in the book Dick and Perry provide the answer to this question in their confessions.)

6. Mrs Ashida emphasizes that she thinks Herb Clutter wasn't afraid when he was killed. Why does she dwell on this? What part does fear play in the lives of all the characters you have read about?

7. The postmistress of Holcomb says of the townspeople, ". . . they got nothing to do but sit around and scare each other." To what extent is this true? To what extent is this unfair to the people of Holcomb?

8. Whom do you like better, Dick or Perry? Give reasons for your opinion.

Analyzing the Author's Technique

9. Re-read the first few sentences of each chapter in the reading selection. In the chapters that tell about Dick and Perry, notice how the tone is stark and lonely. In contrast, the tone of the chapter that tells about the townspeople is warm and chatty. Why do you think the author uses a different tone in each case?

10. In most cases Truman Capote jumps in and out of conversations between characters and in and out of people's thoughts. Do you find this helps or hinders your enjoyment of the story? Explain why you think this technique makes you either a better or a worse reader-psychologist.

WRITING EXERCISE

Three years ago, Jim Baron left a successful law practice in Detroit and opened a small, one-pump gas station on the outskirts of Las Vegas, Nevada. During the day he spends most of his time reading, there are few customers. At night he travels into Las Vegas where he mugs and robs patrons as they leave the gambling casinos.

Instructions: Write a paragraph on one or more of the following themes that may shed some light on why Jim Baron is behaving as he does.

1. Write an account of events or childhood influences that may be affecting Jim Baron's present behavior.

2. Record a conversation between Jim Baron and a friend that may shed light on his thoughts and feelings.

3. Describe an action that reveals what kind of a man Jim Baron really is.

4. Record Jim Baron's train of thought after he has committed a robbery.

Unit 9
**Analyzing
Figurative and
Descriptive Language**

Babbitt

Introduction

> His name was George F. Babbitt. He was forty-six years old now, in April, 1920, and he made nothing in particular, neither butter nor shoes nor poetry, but he was nimble in the calling of selling houses for more than people could afford to pay.

With this concise description, Sinclair Lewis introduces his devastating caricature of the American businessman, George F. Babbitt. Earlier novelists had portrayed the American businessman as a ruthless tycoon, setting in motion vast sinister schemes. George Babbitt is strictly middle class, and his sins are limited to shady deals with municipal officials. But that is what is so disturbing about this novel—our sneaking suspicion that George Babbitt is more the rule in American society than the exception.

Babbitt is the very picture of conformity. He wears a three-piece suit with a Boosters' Club button pinned to his lapel and an Elk's Club tooth hanging from his watchchain. He wears rimless glasses and smokes fat cigars. While he is not fat, he looks extremely well-fed.

If you could see inside his head, even his thoughts would look like everyone else's. Like the mass-produced gadgets which he can't resist buying, Babbitt's ideas and beliefs are churned out in assembly-line fashion. Institutions such as the Chamber of Commerce, the Republican Party, the Presbyterian Church and the Elks Club dictate his every opinion. Their attitudes are his attitudes. If none of these institutions has spoken out concerning a particular issue of the day, Babbitt is at a loss as to how he feels about it.

The book, however, is not so much about Babbitt's conformity as about his dawning realization that he is little more than a puppet and about his futile attempt to break out of the mold. As the book opens, Babbitt is introduced as a prosperous man who buys the best of everything—from bathroom fixtures to the alarm clock that wakes him in the morning. But as the story develops, it becomes clear to the reader, and to George Babbitt, that he is not really happy. His wife bores him; a dinner party for their friends suddenly seems tiresome, and his closest friend shoots his wife during a quarrel and goes to prison. In the course of a few months, Babbitt turns into a "bloomin' liberal" and proceeds to alienate his friends, to take up with a Bohemian widow and her fast crowd of riff-raff, and to commit the unpardonable sin of seeing both sides of an issue. Babbitt is trying to "find himself," but he has no real idea of how to do this.

The tragedy of it all is the author's implication that, deep down, there really is nothing to find. Babbitt has been so brainwashed—by national advertising as well as by his beloved clubs—that it is too late for him to develop a personality of his own. In the end, his rebellion is thwarted when his wife takes sick. Their friends rally round in this time of trouble, he is "forgiven" for his recent mutiny, and he reluctantly returns to the fold.

Babbitt is a satire and, like most satires, there is not much plot. But reading this book is delicious fun because Babbitt is the kind of person you just love to hate! He is vain, smug and self-satisfied; he dreams of a fairy-child lover who calls him gay and valiant, but he is breathtakingly unromantic-looking. He is a pathetic figure, and yet he is not all that different from the rest of us. We, too, dress and think like our friends, only Babbitt does so more than most.

Sinclair Lewis was one of the most powerful social commentators of our century. His book *Main Street,* a satire of small-town America, appeared in 1920, followed by *Babbitt* in 1922. The impact of these two books on the American reading public was best described by historian Frederick Lewis Allen, who said:

> The effect of these two books was overwhelming. In two volumes of merciless literary photography and searing satire, Lewis revealed the ugliness of the American small town, the cultural poverty of its life, the tyranny of its mass prejudices, and the blatant vulgarity and insularity of the booster . . . . The intellectuals had only to read Lewis's books to realize that the qualities in American life which they most despised and feared were precisely the ones which he put under the microscope for cold-blooded examination. It was George F. Babbitt who was the archenemy of the enlightened, and it was the Main Street state of mind which stood in the way of American civilization.

Analyzing Figurative and Descriptive Language

The purpose of figurative and descriptive language is often misunderstood. Humorist James Thurber once recalled an old schoolteacher named Miss Groby who "was forever climbing up the margins of books and crawling between their lines, hunting for the little gold of phrase, making marks with a pencil. As Palamides hunted the Questing Beast, she hunted the Figure of Speech." Night after night, she sent her students searching for similes, metaphors, personifications, and all the rest. "It got so that figures of speech jumped out of the pages at you," complained Thurber, obscuring the meaning of whatever you were trying to read!

Figurative and descriptive language was never meant to distract the reader. In fact, just the opposite is intended. When skillfully used, figurative and descriptive language helps an author to get across the meaning of a passage more vividly—to highlight the one or two details that make an entire scene come alive or to make a startling comparison that unexpectedly penetrates and lays bare the real significance of a person or thing. Since description almost always uses figurative language, let's look first at some common figures of speech and then see how they work in a descriptive passage.

FIGURATIVE LANGUAGE

Figurative language allows a writer to endow words with meanings above and beyond their face value. There are many different forms of figurative language, generally referred to as *figures of speech*, but all of them serve to communicate both an idea *and* an attitude or feeling. The attitude or feeling conveyed in a figure of speech reveals the author's personal likes and dislikes, bias or prejudice, which he or she wants the reader to share, or at least appreciate. Some of the more common figures of speech include similes and metaphors, personification, onomatopoeia, alliteration, hyperbole and meiosis.

1. Similes. Similies, as well as metaphors, are figures of speech which use comparisons to reveal similarities between otherwise dissimilar things. A simile is a direct comparison introduced by the words *like* or *as.* For example, in the chapter from *Babbitt,* the author describes the tall office buildings in the city of Zenith as "sturdy as cliffs and delicate as steel rods." Ordinarily, one would not associate office buildings with either cliffs or steel rods. But the author has discovered likenesses between them; like cliffs of rock, they are sturdy, and like steel rods, they appear slender and delicate. The comparisons are good ones, and they enhance the reader's mental pictures of the towers of Zenith.

2. Metaphors. Like a simile, a metaphor also compares two unlike things. In this case, however, the comparison is implied, instead of being stated outright with the words *like* or *as.* For example, in the following passage George Babbitt goes into his bathroom one morning and is annoyed to find nothing but wet towels. Notice how the towels are called something else in the last line.

> "By golly, here they go and use up all the towels, every doggone one of 'em, and they use 'em and get 'em all wet and sopping, and never put out a dry one for me . . . ." He was pitching the chill abominations into the bath-tub . . . .

In the passage above, the phrase "chill abominations" is a metaphor used to describe the towels. It has been said that the best comparisons strike us with a sense of freshness—they may even startle or shock us—and yet we feel at the same time that they ring true. This is surely the case here. An "abomination" is something that is hateful and disgusting. A towel obviously is not something that arouses intense feelings in anyone, and certainly not hate or revulsion. But when it is wet and sopping and you want a dry, fluffy towel, the comparison suddenly seems appropriate. Here again, the author has conveyed a feeling or attitude toward the towels; in this case, it is an attitude of disgust. He also has conveyed an idea—that of chill and dampness.

In the following passage, George Babbitt is putting the finishing touches to his morning ritual of dressing for work. Where is the metaphor in this passage, and what does it compare?

> Last, he stuck in his lapel the Boosters' Club button. With the conciseness of great art the button displayed two words: "Boosters—Pep!" . . . It was his V.C., his Legion of Honor ribbon, his Phi Beta Kappa key.

The last sentence, "It was his V.C., his Legion of Honor ribbon, his Phi Beta Kappa key" is a metaphor comparing George Babbitt's Boosters' Club button with three distinguished awards. In any other context, a person would find it difficult to compare a Boosters' Club button with the Victoria Cross (Britain's highest military award), the Legion of Honor ribbon (an honored French award) and a Phi Beta Kappa Key (symbol of membership in a national college honor society). After all, a Boosters' Club button is not even an award; it is simply a badge of recognition used by a local civic group. Yet, Babbitt is as proud of this button as if it were one of these other awards, and therein lies the similarity that connects them. We can see Babbitt pinning his Boosters' Club button on his lapel with pride; but the feeling conveyed by the author is that it is a little bit pathetic, or at least ludicrous, for a grown man to feel this way about a tin button.

3. **Personification.** Personification is a figure of speech which gives the qualities of a person to an animal, an inanimate object, or an idea. For instance, Chapter 1 of *Babbitt* opens with a bird's-eye view of the city of Zenith in the early morning hours. Surveying the impressive new office buildings that rise high above the rest of the city, the author says: "The mist took pity on the fretted structures of earlier generations . . . ." This is an example of personification; the mist has been endowed with the human emotion pity. A mist cannot, of course, possess human feelings; yet, by saying that the mist took pity on the older, less elegant buildings in the city, the author conveys an attitude of kindly condescension towards these "poor cousins" of the new Zenith.

4. **Onomatopoeia.** The figure of speech in which words mimic sounds, such as the words "buzz" and "hiss," is called onomatopoeia. In the chapter you are about to read, George Babbitt is rudely awakened from his pleasant dreams by the rumble and bang of a milk truck, a barking dog, the thump of a rolled up newspaper hitting the front door, and this sound: "snap-ah-ah, snap-ah-ah, snap-ah-ah. Himself a pious motorist, Babbitt cranked with the unseen driver, with him waited through taut hours for the roar of the starting engine, with him agonized as the roar ceased and again began the infernal patient snap-ah-ah—a round, flat sound, a shivering cold-morning sound, a sound infuriating and inescapable."

The "snap-ah-ah" is an example of onomatopoeia because it is a word that imitates a sound. It is an effective literary device because it helps readers "hear" the sound for themselves and thus imagine its effect on a man trying to sleep in the morning.

5. **Alliteration.** The literary device in which the initial sounds of a group of two or more words are the same is called alliteration. For instance, in describing Babbitt's gray suit, the author writes, "White piping on the V of the vest added a flavor of law and learning." This sentence contains two examples of alliteration: "V of the vest" and "law and learning." Alliteration gives description a rhythmic flow and is often used in poetry.

In the following sentence, find the phrase containing three alliterative words. What effect do they contribute to the meaning of the sentence?

> Yet Babbitt was again dreaming of the fairy child, a dream more romantic than scarlet pagodas by a silver sea.

The alliterative phrase is "scarlet pagodas by a silver sea" with three words—scarlet, silver and sea—carrying the sound of "s." The meaning of the sentence concerns a wistful dream about an imaginary lover, "a dream more romantic than scarlet pagodas by a silver sea." A pagoda is a kind of temple seen in the Far East, and a silver sea brings to mind moonlight and fairy tales. It is an exotic image, and the lilting quality of the alliteration sounds as romantic as the imagery.

6. Hyperbole. Hyperbole, or exaggeration, is a common form of figurative language. When a writer or a speaker uses hyperbole, it is not intended as a deliberate lie. Rather, it is exaggeration used to emphasize a point. In the chapter from *Babbitt*, George Babbitt says of his son Ted, "And here I've told him a hundred times, if he'll go to college and law-school and make good, I'll set him up in business . . . ." Babbitt, of course, did not really say this a hundred times, but the effect of the exaggeration is to show how strongly Babbitt feels about the matter.

Sometimes hyperbole is used to achieve a sarcastic tone. For instance, when someone says, "Oh, big deal!" they imply by the tone of their voice that it's anything but a big deal. In the chapter you are about to read, George Babbitt's ritual of dressing in the morning involves lengthy discussions with his wife over trivial things such as whether a pair of pants needs pressing. The author comments on this by using hyperbole which means the opposite of what it says. What is the hyperbole in the following sentence, and what kind of tone does it create?

> He was able to get through the other crises of dressing with comparative resoluteness and calm.

Hyperbole is used in the phrase, "the other *crises* of dressing." A crisis is a crucial situation of the utmost importance. Obviously, it is a gross exaggeration to refer to the many small choices which we all make every morning in the process of getting dressed as "crises." What the author means is that these choices are anything but crises. Thus, the effect of the use of hyperbole in this instance is to give a derisive tone to the statement. It is a mildly sarcastic snipe at poor George Babbitt, who is always making mountains out of molehills.

7. Meiosis. Like hyperbole, or overstatement, *meiosis* or understatement, is also used to create a special tone. Meiosis is a figure of speech which says less than is really meant. In the first chapter of *Babbitt*, George Babbitt shaves in the morning and then reaches for a nice dry towel. He is extremely annoyed to find that the other members of his family have used all the towels and left them wet and sopping. In a fit of pique, he flings the wet towels into the bathtub. Just at that moment, his wife walks in and serenely remarks that he really needn't wash out the towels. The author notes that, "It is not recorded that [Babbitt] was able to answer." This is a classic example of meiosis because it understates Babbitt's feelings. Babbitt had no intention of washing out any towels, and he probably feels like exploding at his wife for thinking it. Thus, what the statement really means is that Babbitt was so choked up with indignation that he couldn't express the fury of his feelings. This technique of understatement is often used to achieve an ironic tone because it implies something very different, sometimes even the opposite, from what is actually said.

Descriptive writing is most effective when its details are carefully selected to achieve a certain feeling or attitude. For instance, an author writing a tale of terror and suspense set in an old castle is not going to mention the sunny nooks and cozy corners of the castle. The author is going to emphasize the winding stone staircase, the gloomy dungeon, the drafty halls and the turreted tower.

What impression does the author convey in the following description of the Babbitts' bathroom?

> Though the house was not large it had, like all houses on Floral Heights, an altogether royal bathroom of porcelain and glazed tile and metal sleek as silver. The towel-rack was a rod of clear glass set in nickel. The tub was long enough for a Prussian Guard, and above the set bowl was a sensational exhibit of tooth-brush holder, shaving-brush holder, soap-dish, sponge-dish, and medicine-cabinet, so glittering and so ingenious that they resembled an electrical instrument-board.

The entire passage is carefully calculated to give an impression of excessive luxury. It is a "royal bathroom" with accessories of silver, glass and nickel. The tub is long enough for a tall Prussian Guard! And the medicine cabinet is a "sensational exhibit" (notice the hyperbole) that resembles an electrical instrument board more than a cabinet for aspirin and bromides. Overall, it seems like a bathroom designed not for mere mortals like George Babbitt and family, but for a king. The effect of this description is one of showiness. And as it turns out, everything about George Babbitt and his life is more show than substance.

Descriptive language often relies on figures of speech to create a particular effect. The following descriptive passage from *Babbitt* employs several different figures of speech. How many can you spot? What effect do they create for the reader?

> . . . [Babbitt] could see the top of the Second National Tower, an Indiana limestone building of thirty-five stories.
> Its shining walls rose against April sky to a simple cornice like a streak of white fire. Integrity was in the tower, and decision. It bore its strength lightly as a tall soldier. As Babbitt stared, the nervousness was soothed from his face, his slack chin lifted in reverence. All he articulated was "That's one lovely sight!" but he was inspired by the rhythm of the city; his love of it renewed. He beheld the tower as a temple-spire of the religion of business, a faith passionate, exalted, surpassing common men . . . .

The description of the limestone walls of the Second National Tower rising up "like a streak of white fire" is a simile comparing the tall, white building with a flame. "Integrity was in the tower, and decision" is an example of personification which lends the human qualities of integrity and decision to the building. "It bore its strength [as] lightly as a tall soldier" is another simile, this time finding a likeness between the building and a tall soldier. And to Babbitt, the tower is "a temple-spire of the religion of business." This is a metaphor equating the building with a temple of worship or a church. The combined effect of the figures of speech used in this descriptive passage is to create a feeling of awe—until, that is, one remembers exactly what is being described. And what is the object of George Babbitt's reverence? A bank building! Surely it is inappropriate to use such elegant figures of speech to describe a bank. Thus, the author's skillful use of descriptive and figurative language leaves the reader with just the feeling which the author intended—one of disbelief at the lowly object of this man's highest feelings.

Without figurative language, an author would need a great many more words to get across the same idea that is expressed by a particularly apt figure of speech. Sinclair Lewis could have come right out and said that George Babbitt was a narrow-minded fuddy-duddy. But such bald statements could never equal the subtle shades of meaning conveyed by his skillful use of descriptive language.

As you read the chapter:

- Notice the description of the big, new factories in the city of Zenith.

- Watch for the passage describing George Babbitt's alarm clock.

- Pay particular attention to the paragraph describing Babbitt's eyeglasses.

- Be aware of how George Babbitt feels about the items in his suit pockets.

Babbitt
Sinclair Lewis

CHAPTER 1

The towers of Zenith aspired above the morning mist; austere towers of steel and cement and limestone, sturdy as cliffs and delicate as silver rods. They were neither citadels nor churches, but frankly and beautifully office-buildings.

The mist took pity on the fretted structures of earlier generations: the Post Office with its shingle-tortured mansard, the red brick minarets of hulking old houses, factories with stingy and sooted windows, wooden tenements colored like mud. The city was full of such grotesqueries, but the clean towers were thrusting them from the business center, and on the farther hills were shining new houses, homes—they seemed—for laughter and tranquillity.

Over a concrete bridge fled a limousine of long sleek hood and noiseless engine. These people in evening clothes were returning from an all-night rehearsal of a Little Theater play, an artistic adventure considerably illuminated by champagne. Below the bridge curved a railroad, a maze of green and crimson lights. The New York Flyer boomed past, and twenty lines of polished steel leaped into the glare.

In one of the skyscrapers the wires of the Associated Press were closing down. The telegraph operators wearily raised their celluloid eye-shades after a night of talking with Paris and Peking. Through the building crawled the scrubwomen, yawning, their old shoes slapping. The dawn mist spun away. Cues of men with lunch-boxes clumped toward the immensity of new factories, sheets of glass and hollow tile, glittering shops where five thousand men worked beneath one roof, pouring out the honest wares that would be sold up the Euphrates and across the veldt. The whistles rolled out in greeting a chorus cheerful as the April dawn; the song of labor in a city built—it seemed—for giants.

There was nothing of the giant in the aspect of the man who was beginning to awaken on the sleeping-porch of a Dutch Colonial house in that residential district of Zenith known as Floral Heights.

His name was George F. Babbitt. He was forty-six years old now, in April, 1920, and he made nothing in particular, neither butter nor shoes nor poetry, but he was nimble in the calling of selling houses for more than people could afford to pay.

His large head was pink, his brown hair thin and dry. His face was babyish in slumber, despite his wrinkles and the red spectacle-dents on the slopes of his nose. He was not fat but he was exceedingly well fed; his cheeks were pads, and the unroughened hand which lay helpless upon the khaki-colored blanket was slightly puffy. He seemed prosperous, extremely married and unromantic; and altogether unromantic appeared this sleeping-porch, which looked on one sizable elm, two respectable grass-plots, a cement driveway, and a corrugated iron garage. Yet Babbitt was again dreaming of the fairy child, a dream more romantic than scarlet pagodas by a silver sea.

For years the fairy child had come to him. Where others saw but Georgie Babbitt, she discerned gallant youth. She waited for him, in the darkness beyond mysterious groves. When at last he could slip away from the crowded house he darted to her. His wife, his clamoring friends, sought to follow, but he escaped, the girl fleet beside him, and they crouched together on a shadowy hillside. She was so slim, so white, so eager! She cried that he was gay and valiant, that she would wait for him, that they would sail—

Rumble and bang of the milk-truck.

Babbitt moaned, turned over, struggled back toward his dream. He could see only her face now, beyond misty waters. The furnace-man slammed the basement door. A dog barked in the next yard. As Babbitt sank blissfully into a dim warm tide, the paper-carrier went by whistling, and the rolled-up *Advocate* thumped the front door. Babbitt roused, his stomach constricted with alarm. As he relaxed, he was pierced by the familiar and irritating rattle of some one cranking a Ford: snap-ah-ah, snap-ah-ah, snap-ah-ah. Himself a pious motorist, Babbitt cranked with the unseen driver, with him waited through taut hours for the roar of the starting engine, with him agonized as the roar ceased and again began the infernal patient snap-ah-ah—a round, flat sound, a shivering cold-morning sound, a sound infuriating and inescapable. Not till the rising voice of the motor told him that the Ford was moving was he released from the panting tension. He glanced once at his favorite tree, elm twigs against the gold patina of sky, and fumbled for sleep as for a drug. He who had been a boy very credulous of life was no longer greatly interested in the possible and improbable adventures of each new day.

He escaped from reality till the alarm-clock rang, at seven-twenty.

It was the best of nationally advertised and quantitatively produced alarm-clocks, with all modern attachments, including cathedral chime, intermittent alarm, and a phosphorescent dial. Babbitt was proud of being awakened by such a rich device. Socially it was almost as creditable as buying expensive cord tires.

He sulkily admitted now that there was no more escape, but he lay and detested the grind of the real-estate business, and disliked his family, and disliked himself for disliking them. The evening before, he had played poker at Vergil Gunch's till midnight, and after such holidays he was irritable before breakfast. It may have been the tremendous home-brewed beer of the prohibition-era and the cigars to which that beer enticed him; it may have been resentment of return from this fine bold man-world to a restricted region of wives and stenographers, and of suggestions not to smoke so much.

From the bedroom beside the sleeping-porch, his wife's detestably cheerful "Time to get up, Georgie boy," and the itchy sound, the brisk and scratchy sound, of combing hairs out of a stiff brush.

He grunted; he dragged his thick legs, in faded baby-blue pajamas, from under the khaki blanket; he sat on the edge of the cot, running his fingers through his wild hair, while his plump feet mechanically felt for his slippers. He looked regretfully at the blanket—forever a suggestion to him of freedom and heroism. He had bought it for a camping trip which had never come off. It symbolized gorgeous loafing, gorgeous cursing, virile flannel shirts.

He creaked to his feet, groaning at the waves of pain which passed behind his eyeballs. Though he waited for their scorching recurrence, he looked blurrily out at the yard. It delighted him, as always; it was the neat yard of a successful business man of Zenith, that is, it was perfection, and made him also perfect. He regarded the corrugated iron garage. For the three-hundred-and-sixty-fifth time in a year he reflected, "No class to that tin shack. Have to build me a frame garage. But by golly it's the only thing on the place that isn't up-to-date!" While he stared he thought of a community garage for his acreage development, Glen Oriole. He stopped puffing and jiggling. His arms were akimbo. His petulant, sleep-swollen face was set in harder lines. He suddenly seemed capable, an official, a man to contrive, to direct, to get things done.

On the vigor of his idea he was carried down the hard, clean, unused-looking hall into the bathroom.

Though the house was not large it had, like all houses on Floral Heights, an altogether royal bathroom of porcelain and glazed tile and metal sleek as silver. The towel-rack was a rod of clear glass set in nickel. The tub was long enough for a Prussian Guard, and above the set bowl was a sensational exhibit of tooth-brush holder, shaving-brush holder, soap-dish, sponge-dish, and medicine-cabinet, so glittering and so ingenious that they resembled an electrical instrument-board. But the Babbitt whose god was Modern Appliances was not pleased. The air of the bathroom was thick with the smell of a heathen toothpaste. "Verona been at it again! 'Stead of sticking to Lilidol, like I've re-peat-ed-ly asked her, she's gone and gotten some confounded stinkum stuff that makes you sick!"

The bath-mat was wrinkled and the floor was wet. (His daughter Verona eccentrically took baths in the morning, now and then.) He slipped on the mat, and slid against the tub. He said "Damn!" Furiously he snatched up his tube of shaving-cream, furiously he lathered, with a belligerent slapping of the unctuous brush, furiously he raked his plump cheeks with a safety-razor. It pulled. The blade was dull. He said, "Damn—oh—oh—damn it!"

He hunted through the medicine-cabinet for a packet of new razor-blades (reflecting, as invariably, "Be cheaper to buy one of these dinguses and strop your own blades,") and when he discovered the packet, behind the round box of bicarbonate of soda, he thought ill of his wife for putting it there and very well of himself for not saying "Damn." But he did say it, immediately afterward, when with wet and soap-slippery fingers he tried to remove the horrible little envelope and crisp clinging oiled paper from the new blade.

Then there was the problem, oft-pondered, never solved, of what to do with the old blade, which might imperil the fingers of his young. As usual, he tossed it on top of the medicine-cabinet, with a mental note that some day he must remove the fifty or sixty other blades that were also temporarily, piled up there. He finished his shaving in a growing testiness increased by his spinning headache and by the emptiness in his stomach. When he was done, his round face smooth and streamy and his eyes stinging from soapy water, he reached for a towel. The family towels were wet, wet and clammy and vile, all of them wet, he found, as he blindly snatched them—his own face-towel, his wife's, Verona's, Ted's, Tinka's, and the lone bath-towel with the huge welt of initial. Then George F. Babbitt did a dismaying thing. He wiped his face on the guest-towel! It was a pansy-embroidered trifle which always hung there to indicate that the Babbitts were in the best Floral Heights society. No one had ever used it. No guest had ever dared to. Guests secretively took a corner of the nearest regular towel.

He was raging, "By golly, here they go and use up all the towels, every doggone one of 'em, and they use 'em and get 'em all wet and sopping, and never put out a dry one for me—of course, I'm the goat!—and then I want one and—I'm the only person in the doggone house that's got the slightest doggone bit of consideration for other people and thoughtfulness and consider there may be others that may want to use the doggone bathroom after me and consider—"

He was pitching the chill abominations into the bath-tub, pleased by the vindictiveness of that desolate flapping sound; and in the midst his wife serenely trotted in, observed serenely, "Why Georgie dear, what are you doing? Are you going to wash out the towels? Why, you needn't wash out the towels. Oh, Georgie, you didn't go and use the guest-towel, did you?"

It is not recorded that he was able to answer.

For the first time in weeks he was sufficiently roused by his wife to look at her.

Myra Babbitt—Mrs. George F. Babbitt—was definitely mature. She had creases from the corners of her mouth to the bottom of her chin, and her plump neck bagged. But the thing that marked her as having passed the line was that she no longer had reticences before her husband, and no longer worried about not having reticences. She was in a petticoat now, and corsets which bulged, and unaware of being seen in bulgy corsets. She had become so dully habituated to married life that in her full matronliness she was as sexless as an anemic nun. She was a good woman, a kind woman, a dilligent woman, but no one, save perhaps Tinka her ten-year-old, was at all interested in her or entirely aware that she was alive.

After a rather thorough discussion of all the domestic and social aspects of towels she apologized to Babbitt for his having an alcoholic headache; and he recovered enough to endure the search for a B.V.D. undershirt which had, he pointed out, malevolently been concealed among his clean pajamas.

He was fairly amiable in the conference on the brown suit.

"What do you think, Myra?" He pawed at the clothes hunched on a chair in their bedroom, while she moved about mysteriously adjusting and patting her petticoat and, to his jaundiced eye, never seeming to get on with her dressing. "How about it? Shall I wear the brown suit another day?"

"Well, it looks awfully nice on you."

"I know, but gosh, it needs pressing."

"That's so. Perhaps it does."

"It certainly could stand being pressed, all right."

"Yes, perhaps it wouldn't hurt it to be pressed."

"But gee, the coat doesn't need pressing. No sense in having the whole darn suit pressed, when the coat doesn't need it."

"That's so."

"But the pants certainly need it, all right. Look at them—look at those wrinkles—the pants certainly do need pressing."

"That's so. Oh, Georgie, why couldn't you wear the brown coat with the blue trousers we were wondering what we'd do with them?"

"Good Lord! Did you ever in all my life know me to wear the coat of one suit and the pants of another? What do you think I am? A busted bookkeeper?"

"Well, why don't you put on the dark gray suit today, and stop in at the tailor and leave the brown trousers?"

"Well, they certainly need— Now where the devil is that gray suit? Oh, yes, here we are."

He was able to get through the other crises of dressing with comparative resoluteness and calm.

His first adornment was the sleeveless dimity B.V.D. undershirt, in which he resembled a small boy humorlessly wearing a cheesecloth tabard at a civic pageant. He never put on B.V.D.'s without thanking the God of Progress that he didn't wear tight, long, old-fashioned undergarments, like his father-in-law and partner, Henry Thompson. His second embellishment was combing and slicking back his hair. It gave him a tremendous forehead, arching up two inches beyond the former hair-line. But most wonder-working of all was the donning of his spectacles.

There is character in spectacles—the pretentious tortoise-shell, the meek pince-nez of the school teacher, the twisted silver-framed glass of the old villager. Babbitt's spectacles had huge, circular, frameless lenses of the very best glass; the ear-pieces were thin bars of gold. In them he was the modern business man; one who gave orders to clerks and drove a car and played occasional golf and was scholarly in regard to Salesmanship. His head suddenly appeared not babyish but weighty, and you noted his heavy, blunt nose, his straight mouth and thick, long upper lip, his chin overfleshy but strong; with respect you beheld him put on the rest of his uniform as a Solid Citizen.

The gray suit was well cut, well made, and completely undistinguished. It was a standard suit. White piping on the V of the vest added a flavor of law and learning. His shoes were black laced boots, good boots, honest boots, standard boots, extraordinarily uninteresting boots. The only frivolity was in his purple knitted scarf. With considerable comment on the matter to Mrs. Babbitt (who, acrobatically fastening the back of her blouse to her skirt with a safety-pin, did not hear a word he said), he chose between the purple scarf and a tapestry effect with stringless brown harps among blown palms, and into it he thrust a snake-head pin with opal eyes.

A sensational event was changing from the brown suit to the gray the contents of his pockets. He was earnest about these objects. They were of eternal importance, like baseball or the Republican Party. They included a fountain pen and a silver pencil (always lacking a supply of new leads) which belonged in the righthand upper vest pocket. Without them he would have felt naked. On his watch-chain were a gold penknife, silver cigar-cutter, seven keys (the use of two of which he had forgotten), and incidentally a good watch. Depending from the chain was a large, yellowish elk's-tooth—proclamation of his membership in the Brotherly and Protective Order of Elks. Most significant of all was his loose-leaf pocket note-book, that modern and efficient note-book which contained the addresses of people whom he had forgotten, prudent memoranda of postal money-orders which had reached their destinations months ago, stamps which had lost their mucilage, clippings of verses by T. Cholmondeley Frink and of the newspaper editorials from which Babbitt got his opinions and his polysyllables, notes to be sure and do things which he did not intend to do, and one curious inscription—D.S.S.D.M.Y.P.D.F.

But he had no cigarette-case. No one had ever happened to give him one, so he hadn't the habit, and people who carried cigarette-cases he regarded as effeminate.

Last, he stuck in his lapel the Boosters' Club button. With the conciseness of great art the button displayed two words: "Boosters—Pep!" It made Babbitt feel loyal and important. It associated him with Good Fellows, with men who were nice and human, and important in business circles. It was his V.C., his Legion of Honor ribbon, his Phi Beta Kappa key.

With the subtleties of dressing ran other complex worries. "I feel kind of punk this morning," he said. "I think I had too much dinner last evening. You oughtn't to serve those heavy banana fritters."

"But you asked me to have some."

"I know, but— I tell you, when a fellow gets past forty he has to look after his digestion. There's a lot of fellows that don't take proper care of themselves. I tell you at forty a man's a fool or his doctor— I mean, his own doctor. Folks don't give enough attention to this matter of dieting. Now I think— Course a man ought to have a good meal after the day's work, but it would be a good thing for both of us if we took lighter lunches."

"But Georgie, here at home I always do have a light lunch."

"Mean to imply I make a hog of myself, eating down-town? Yes, sure! You'd have a swell time if you had to eat the truck that new steward hands out to us at the Athletic Club! But I certainly do feel out of sorts, this morning. Funny, got a pain down here on the left side—but no, that wouldn't be appendicitis, would it? Last night, when I was driving over to Verg Gunch's, I felt a pain in my stomach, too. Right here it was—kind of a sharp shooting pain. I— Where'd that dime go to? Why don't you serve more prunes at breakfast? Of course I eat an apple every evening—an apple a day keeps the doctor away—but still, you ought to have more prunes, and not all these fancy doodads."

"The last time I had prunes you didn't eat them."

"Well, I didn't feel like eating 'em, I suppose. Matter of fact, I think I did eat some of 'em. Anyway—I tell you it's mighty important to— I was saying to Verg Gunch, just last evening, most people don't take sufficient care of their diges—"

"Shall we have the Gunches for our dinner, next week?"

"Why sure; you bet."

"Now see here, George: I want you to put on your nice dinner-jacket that evening."

"Rats! The rest of 'em won't want to dress."

"Of course they will. You remember when you didn't dress for the Littlefields' supper-party, and all the rest did, and how embarrassed you were."

"Embarrassed, hell! I wasn't embarrassed. Everybody knows I can put on as expensive a Tux. as anybody else, and I should worry if I don't happen to have it on sometimes. All a darn nuisance, anyway. All right for a woman, that stays around the house all the time, but when a fellow's worked like the dickens all day, he doesn't want to go and hustle his head off getting into the soup-and-fish for a lot of folks that he's seen in just reg'lar ordinary clothes that same day."

"You know you enjoy being seen in one. The other evening you admitted you were glad I'd insisted on your dressing. You said you felt a lot better for it. And oh, Georgie, I do wish you wouldn't say 'Tux.' It's 'dinner-jacket.' "

"Rats, what's the odds?"

"Well, it's what all the nice folks say. Suppose Lucile McKelvey heard you calling it a 'Tux.' "

"Well, that's all right now! Lucile McKelvey can't pull anything on me! Her folks are common as mud, even if her husband and her dad are million-aires! I suppose you're trying to rub in *your* exalted social position! Well, let me tell you that your revered paternal ancestor, Henry T., doesn't even call it a 'Tux.'! He calls it a 'bobtail jacket for a ringtail monkey,' and you couldn't get him into one unless you chloroformed him!"

"Now don't be horrid, George."

"Well, I don't want to be horrid, but Lord! you're getting as fussy as Verona. Ever since she got out of college she's been too rambunctious to live with—doesn't know what she wants—well, I know what she wants!— all she wants is to marry a millionaire, and live in Europe, and hold some preacher's hand, and simultaneously at the same time stay right here in Zenith and be some blooming kind of a socialist agitator or boss charity-worker or some damn thing! Lord, and Ted is just as bad! He wants to go to college, and he doesn't want to go to college. Only one of the three that knows her own mind is Tinka. Simply can't understand how I ever came to have a pair of shillyshallying children like Rone and Ted. I may not be any Rockefeller or James J. Shakespeare, but I certainly do know my own mind, and I do keep right on plugging along in the office and— Do you know the latest? Far as I can figure out, Ted's new bee is he'd like to be a movie actor and— And here I've told him a hundred times, if he'll go to college and law-school and make good, I'll set him up in business and— Verona just exactly as bad. Doesn't know what she wants. Well, well, come on! Aren't you ready yet? The girl rang the bell three minutes ago."

Before he followed his wife, Babbitt stood at the western-most window of their room. This residential settlement, Floral Heights, was on a rise; and though the center of the city was three miles away—Zenith had between three and four hundred thousand inhabitants now—he could see the top of the Second National Tower, an Indiana limestone building of thirty-five stories.

Its shining walls rose against April sky to a simple cornice like a streak of white fire. Integrity was in the tower, and decision. It bore its strength lightly as a tall soldier. As Babbitt stared, the nervousness was soothed from his face, his slack chin lifted in reverence. All he articulated was "That's one lovely sight!" but he was inspired by the rhythm of the city; his love of it renewed. He beheld the tower as a temple-spire of the religion of business, a faith passionate, exalted, surpassing common men; and as he clumped down to breakfast he whistled the ballad "Oh, by gee, by gosh, by jingo" as though it were a hymn melancholy and noble.

Unit 9

Babbitt

- Comprehension Questions

- Analyzing Figurative and Descriptive Language

- Discussion Guides

- Writing Exercise

COMPREHENSION QUESTIONS

For each of the following statements and questions, select the option containing the most complete or most accurate answer.

1. George Babbitt is a
(b) □ a. teacher.   □ c. mechanic.
     □ b. salesman.   □ d. lawyer.

2. The city of Zenith might best be described as
(c) □ a. prosperous and thriving.
     □ b. decaying.
     □ c. provincial.
     □ d. raw and untamed.

3. The towers of Zenith which George Babbitt admired so much were
(a) □ a. church spires.   □ c. colleges.
     □ b. historical monuments.   □ d. office buildings.

4. The "song of labor" heard in the city of Zenith every morning is sung by
(a) □ a. church bells.   □ c. factory whistles.
     □ b. humming telegraph wires.   □ d. birds.

5. The one thing which George Babbitt's life lacks is
(c) □ a. respectability.   □ c. glamour.
     □ b. love.   □ d. money.

6. One hint that George Babbitt's life is not entirely satisfying is his
(h) □ a. recurring dream of the fairy child.
     □ b. corrugated iron garage.
     □ c. concern for his digestive system.
     □ d. habit of being late for work.

7. The tone of George Babbitt's dream about the fairy child is
(i) □ a. frightening and disturbing.
     □ b. wild and exciting.
     □ c. passionate.
     □ d. wistful and yearning.

8. The alarm clock, the bathroom cabinet, the pansy-embroidered guest
(d) towel, and their address in the Floral Heights residential community
are all symbols of
□ a. George Babbitt's inner dissatisfaction.
□ b. a corrupt and decadent society.
□ c. the family's affluence.
□ d. the Babbitts' appreciation of the finer things in life.

9. George Babbitt's idea of a real man is one who
(j) □ a. carries a cigarette case and a leather briefcase.
□ b. plays poker, smokes cigars and goes on camping trips.
□ c. obeys the laws of the land.
□ d. has high moral principles.

10. Which of the following best defines *testiness* as used in, "He finished
(l) his shaving in a growing *testiness* increased by his spinning headache and
by the emptiness in his stomach"?
□ a. Irritability □ c. Depression
□ b. Anxiety □ d. Anticipation

11. The author states that George Babbitt's god was Modern Appliances and
(e) that he worshipped the God of Progress. This is his way of saying that
Babbitt
□ a. had no religious values.
□ b. valued the material products of an industrial society.
□ c. valued modern and up-to-date ideas and theories.
□ d. valued religion in his own way.

12. The author says that for the first time in weeks George Babbitt was
(f) sufficiently roused by his wife to look at her. From the description of
Myra Babbitt in the chapter, the reader might conclude that what he
saw left George
□ a. impressed. □ c. mystified.
□ b. satisfied. □ d. disillusioned.

13. The item of apparel which did the most to transform Babbitt from a
(g) grumpy family man into a respected member of the community was his
□ a. spectacles. □ c. silver pencil.
□ b. gray suit. □ d. Boosters' Club button.

14. The elk's-tooth proclaiming his membership in the Order of Elks and his
(j) Booster Club button are evidence that George Babbitt is a
□ a. loner. □ c. joiner.
□ b. nonconformist. □ d. social reformer.

15. When Babbitt dressed, he "put on the rest of his uniform as a Solid
(k) Citizen." This figure of speech is used to point out that Babbitt
    ☐ a. knows how to dress in style.
    ☐ b. dresses and acts like everyone else in his social class.
    ☐ c. possesses colorless clothing and has a colorless character.
    ☐ d. is not interested in what he wears.

16. Which of the following best defines *effeminate* as used in, ". . . people
(l) who carried cigarette cases he regarded as *effeminate*"?
    ☐ a. Old-fashioned   ☐ c. Antisocial
    ☐ b. Unmanly   ☐ d. Impractical

17. Politically, one might expect George Babbitt to be
(h) ☐ a. reactionary.   ☐ c. liberal.
    ☐ b. conservative.   ☐ d. radical.

18. Babbitt's strong convictions about the importance of dieting and eating
(g) right are probably
    ☐ a. the words of a health-food nut.
    ☐ b. an insight into Babbitt's austere lifestyle.
    ☐ c. proof of Babbitt's great will power.
    ☐ d. more talk than anything else.

19. Mrs. Babbitt refers to Lucile McKelvey as "nice folks" presumably
(f) because
    ☐ a. she has nice manners and a pleasant way about her.
    ☐ b. she knows enough not to call a "dinner-jacket" a "Tux."
    ☐ c. her husband and father are both millionaires.
    ☐ d. she has an aristocratic background.

20. Similes and metaphors are most effective when the comparisons are
(k) fresh and startling, as well as appropriate. George Babbitt says that
    Lucile McKelvey's folks "are common as mud." The simile "common
    as mud" is
    ☐ a. unimaginative.   ☐ c. meaningless.
    ☐ b. forceful.   ☐ d. thought-provoking.

21. Babbitt's objection to his son Ted and his daughter Verona is that they
(b) ☐ a. have no interest in joining their father's business.
    ☐ b. don't seem to know what they want out of life.
    ☐ c. have no respect for their elders.
    ☐ d. run around with a "fast crowd."

22. To George Babbitt, anything that is old-fashioned is
(g) ☐ a. useless and inferior.
     ☐ b. charming and quaint.
     ☐ c. trustworthy and respectable.
     ☐ d. inherently superior to modern items.

23. George Babbit's mood in Chapter 1 progresses from
(d) ☐ a. resentful to cranky to cheerful.
     ☐ b. optimistic to cross to pessimistic.
     ☐ c. enthusiastic to cautious to unenthusiastic.
     ☐ d. sulky to cross to ill-mannered.

24. George Babbitt, who represents middle-class Americans in the early
(e) 1920s, is primarily interested in
     ☐ a. government reform.   ☐ c. making and spending money.
     ☐ b. religion.   ☐ d. creating great works of art.

25. The mood of the closing scene of Chapter 1, in which Babbitt looks out
(i) over the towers of Zenith, is one of
     ☐ a. nostalgia.   ☐ c. indifference.
     ☐ b. despair.   ☐ d. reverence.

Comprehension Skills: a—isolating details; b—recalling specific facts; c—retaining concepts; d—organizing facts; e—understanding the main idea; f—drawing a conclusion; g—making a judgment; h—making an inference; i—recognizing tone; j—understanding characters; k—appreciation of literary forms; l—knowledge of word meanings.

ANALYZING FIGURATIVE AND DESCRIPTIVE LANGUAGE

Practice Exercise A

The dawn mist spun away. Cues of men with lunch boxes clumped toward the immensity of new factories, sheets of glass and hollow tile, glittering shops where five thousand men worked beneath one roof, pouring out the honest wares that would be sold up the Euphrates and across the veldt. The whistles rolled out in greeting a chorus cheerful as the April dawn; the song of labor in a city built—it seemed—for giants.

1. This description of the big, new factories in Zenith gives the reader a better feeling for
   ☐ a. the workers of Zenith.
   ☐ b. assembly-production methods.
   ☐ c. international trade.
   ☐ d. the city of Zenith.

2. On the line provided, write the simile used in the above passage.

   _____

Practice Exercise B

It was the best of nationally advertised and quantitatively produced alarm-clocks, with all modern attachments, including cathedral chime, intermittent alarm, and a phosphorescent dial. Babbitt was proud of being awakened by such a rich device. Socially it was almost as creditable as buying expensive cord tires.

1. The attitude conveyed in this description suggests that George Babbitt regarded his alarm clock as
   ☐ a. old fashioned.   ☐ c. a commonplace household device.
   ☐ b. a status symbol.   ☐ d. an annoyance.

2. On the lines provided, write the sentence which compares the alarm clock with another product of similar social significance.

   _____

   _____

Practice Exercise C

There is character in spectacles—the pretentious tortoise-shell, the meek pince-nez of the school teacher, the twisted silver-framed glass of the old villager. Babbitt's spectacles had huge, circular, frameless lenses of the very best glass; the ear-pieces were thin bars of gold. In them he was the modern business man; one who gave orders to clerks and drove a car and played occasional golf and was scholarly in regard to Salesmanship. His head suddenly appeared not babyish but weighty, and you noted his heavy, blunt nose, his straight mouth and thick, long upper lip, his chin overfleshy but strong; with respect you beheld him put on the rest of his uniform as a Solid Citizen.

1. This description of a pair of spectacles is intended to emphasize how they affect Babbitt's
   - ☐ a. appearance.
   - ☐ b. intelligence.
   - ☐ c. character.
   - ☐ d. eyesight.

2. On the lines provided, write two phrases that "personify" eyeglass frames by associating them with human qualities.

   _____

   _____

Practice Exercise D

A sensational event was changing from the brown suit to the gray the contents of his pockets. He was earnest about these objects. They were of eternal importance, like baseball or the Republican Party.

1. Saying that the objects in his suit pockets were "of eternal importance" is an example of
   - ☐ a. meiosis.
   - ☐ b. a metaphor.
   - ☐ c. hyperbole.
   - ☐ d. alliteration.

2. On the line provided, write a two-word example of hyperbole which is used to describe the act of transferring the contents of Babbitt's pockets.

   _____

DISCUSSION GUIDES

Analyzing Figurative and Descriptive Language

1. Some people assume that figurative language is always flowery and ornate. Based on the figurative language used in Chapter 1 of *Babbitt*, do you think this is an accurate assumption? Give examples to support your opinion.

2. Sinclair Lewis described Babbitt's alarm clock as "nationally advertised and quantitatively produced." How do Sinclair Lewis's descriptions of Babbitt lead to the conclusion that he is a "nationally advertised and quantitatively produced" man?

Interpreting the Chapter

3. What do you think the fairy child in his dream represents to George Babbitt?

4. Myra Babbitt sometimes calls her husband "Georgie boy," and she no longer minds being seen by him in bulging corsets or girdles. What does this suggest to you about the nature of their relationship?

5. We think of ourselves today as a nation of consumers. What evidences of a consumer society can you point to in this chapter from *Babbitt?*

6. In what ways is George Babbitt an "Everyman" character—that is, someone who represents the average person?

7. Does Sinclair Lewis want the reader to despise or sympathize with George Babbitt? Cite an example in the chapter which supports your opinion.

Analyzing the Author's Technique

8. The word "zenith" means the high point of something, the very best— the epitome. What do you think was Sinclair Lewis's purpose in naming George Babbitt's city Zenith?

9. Why do you suppose the author begins *Babbitt* with a description, not of George Babbitt, but of the city of Zenith?

10. Why do you think Sinclair Lewis chose to present to the reader the private side of George Babbitt—getting out of bed in the morning, dressing and shaving—before presenting George Babbitt as the outside world sees him?

WRITING EXERCISE

> To George F. Babbitt, as to most prosperous citizens of Zenith, his motor car was poetry and tragedy, love and heroism. The office was his pirate ship but the car his perilous excursion ashore.

Imagine that you have just won a brand new sports car. Using figurative language, write a paragraph describing your car. Use as many types of figurative language as you can—simile, metaphor, personification, onomatopoeia, alliteration, hyperbole (exaggeration) and meiosis (understatement). Include the answers to the following questions in your description:

a. What does the car look like on the outside? on the inside?

b. How does it handle on the road?

c. What is its "character" or "personality"?

d. How does it make you feel?

Unit 10
The Use of Allegory

Watership Down

Introduction

A *down* is an expanse of open, high, grassy land. Specifically, the *downs* refer to the rolling chalk uplands in the southeast of England. The trees that dot the lower slopes are scrawny and stunted, and vegetation is sparse. But from the grassy top of the downs, one can enjoy a scenic view of the surrounding countryside. What is more important, if you are a rabbit, is that you can also spot the approach of a man, a fox or other *elil* (a rabbit word for enemies). In short, a down is the perfect location for a rabbit warren.

Watership Down is the story of a small band of rabbits who leave the apparent security of the large, well-established Sandleford rabbit warren because one of them—a clairvoyant rabbit named Fiver—has had a vision. He sees their field covered with blood and senses a terrible danger in the offing. He warns the Chief Rabbit of the dangers, but the Chief Rabbit doesn't believe him and neither do most of the others. They are fat and sleek, and it is no happy prospect to range across the open land, at the mercy of elil of all kinds, in search of a new home. Even Hazel, Fiver's brother, is reluctant to believe in the vision. But Fiver had also foretold the flood that came last autumn and could tell where wire snares had been set. So he convinces a few of the others—the timid rabbits who are easily swayed, a few who were in disfavor with the Chief Rabbit, and some of the outskirters who lived on the edge of the warren—and the unlikely band sets off. A few days later, the men came. They sent gas down the tunnels and burrows, shot the rabbits as they frantically escaped out of their holes, and then ravaged the field with a bulldozer. The Sandleford warren was to be replaced by a housing development.

The chapter in this unit is titled "General Woundwort." At this point in the book, the survivors of the Sandleford warren have founded a new community on Watership Down. Despite many hardships and setbacks, the outlook for the new warren is promising in all respects except one—there are no females among them. So they resolve to liberate some does from a larger warren. They settle upon the distant warren of Efrafa as a likely candidate for their raid, but a more unfortunate choice could hardly have been found. Efrafa is run like a police state by a fierce rabbit named General Woundwort, who has no intention of letting does—or anyone else, for that matter—undermine his power by leaving the warren. So a plan is devised and Thlayli, one of the largest and strongest members of Watership Down, infiltrates Efrafa as a spy. After installing himself as a member of the Efrafan Owsla (police force), Thlayli hopes to start a revolt among the does and lead some back to Watership Down.

Watership Down is more than a story about rabbits; it is a tense drama, and it is impossible not to become all on edge to see how each new danger or problem is resolved. Because of this, it is one of those books that, once picked up, cannot be put down until all comes out right in the end. It is about the kinds of decisions people have to make, the way people treat each other, and the rules they live by. *Watership Down* is an allegory—that is, a story that can be enjoyed on its most obvious or surface level and also studied for its significance in our own lives. As is the case with all expertly-done allegories, readers quickly lose sight of the fine line between the story and their own world.

The author, Richard Adams, has been compared to other such famous makers of fables and allegories as Lewis Carroll, who wrote *Alice in Wonderland,* and J.R.R. Tolkien, who created *The Hobbitt* and *The Lord of the Rings* trilogy. Very few authors can succeed in capturing the attention of adults with characters that are generally thought of as best suited for children's books. But those few who have succeeded are famous and their works are classic and timeless.

A Glossary of Rabbit Language

Efrafa: the name of the warren founded by General Woundwort

elil: enemies of rabbits

hlessi (plural, hlessil): a wandering rabbit, living in the open

mark: a division within Efrafa, such as the Near Hind Mark, the Right Flank Mark, the Neck Mark, the Near Fore Mark, and the Right Fore Mark (Members of each "mark" are identified by a scar in the appropriate place on their bodies.)

ni-frith: noon

Owsla: the police force in Efrafa (An Owsla is made up of the biggest and strongest rabbits in the warren.)

silfay: to go above ground to feed

The Use of Allegory

It's hard to swallow a bitter pill, but if you coat it with sugar, it goes down easier. Similarly, nobody likes to be told that they're silly or hypocritical or conceited. But if you sugarcoat such a message by disguising it within another more agreeable story, it is easier to take.

This, essentially, is how allegory works. An allegory is a story that can be appreciated on two levels. The first or surface level is the story itself, which has characters, a setting and a plot just like any other story. On another level, however, the author gives the fictional story a meaning or significance that speaks directly to the reader about a certain situation.

For example, on the surface, an allegory might be a story about little green Martians who refuse to let their offspring go to school with little *blue* Martians. On another level, however, the planet Mars might represent the planet Earth, with the green Martians representing white Americans and the blue Martians, Black Americans. Just as the green Martians don't want their offspring to go to school with blue Martians, neither do some white Americans want their children to attend the same school as Black children. The meaning behind the story, of course, is that the color of one's skin has nothing to do with the kind of person you are.

The children's story of "The Emperor and His New Clothes" is also written in the form of an allegory. On one level, it is the story of a vain emperor who lets some shady tailors talk him into walking through the streets of the city stark naked. But on another level, this story is about anyone, including the reader, who allows flatterers and phonies to overcome his own common sense.

These two examples have certain things in common which make them allegories: 1) the surface story is complete in itself; 2) the story can be interpreted on another level; 3) the story contains a meaning or significance independent of the action described.

1. The Surface Story. Something that is on the surface is in plain sight and is immediately apparent. Thus, when we speak of the *surface story* of an allegory, we are talking about the story on its most obvious level.

The surface story of an allegory is always complete in itself. Like any other story, it has a setting, characters and a plot which, together, form a tale that is enjoyable in its own right. Often this surface story has a fanciful quality to it. The characters may be animals—like Mollie the mare, Moses the raven, and the pigs Major, Napoleon and Snowball, who figure in George Orwell's *Animal Farm.* The setting might be some imaginary place like the planet Mars, the distant future, or the make-believe provinces of Lilliput and Brobdingnag in *Gulliver's Travels.* These fabulous elements may make the surface story of an allegory appear to be a simple child's tale, or something that is not meant to be taken seriously. But nothing could be further from the truth.

The following passage taken from *Watership Down* describes a rabbit warren called Efrafa which is presided over by a large rabbit named General Woundwort. In what ways does this account of a rabbit community conform to our definition of the surface story in an allegory?

> Efrafa grew up round the crossing point of two green bridle paths, one of which (the east-to-west) was tunnel-like, bordered on both sides by a thick growth of trees and bushes. The immigrants, under Woundwort's direction, dug their holes between the roots of the trees, in the undergrowth and along the ditches. From the first the warren prospered. Woundwort watched over them with a tireless zeal that won their loyalty even while they feared him. When the does stopped digging, Woundwort himself went on with their work while they slept. If a man was coming, Woundwort spotted him half a mile away. He fought rats, magpies, gray squirrels and, once, a crow. When litters were kindled, he kept an eye on their growth, picked out the strongest youngsters for the Owsla [police force] and trained them himself. He would allow no rabbit to leave the warren. Quite early on, three who tried to do so were hunted down and forced to return.

The above passage presents a complete account of the founding of a community—from the whimsical point of view of a rabbit hole. The setting is Efrafa, a rabbit warren located at the crossing point of two bridle paths. The characters are a colony of rabbits led by a rabbit called Woundwort, who is regarded by the others with a mixture of respect, fear and loyalty. Woundwort rules with an iron hand, and a conflict is in the offing between Woundwort and any rabbits who try to leave the warren. A mere child's tale? Perhaps. But these rabbits promise to be quite different from that pleasant species of bunny immortalized by the likes of Flopsy, Mopsy, Cottontail and Peter.

2. **The Allegorical Level.** In an allegory, every element of the surface story represents a corresponding element in real life. Together, they form another level of meaning.

The characters, for example, are usually personifications of human ideas, values or qualities. They might represent such things as good or evil, ambition or laziness. Scrooge is the personification of greed, and Satan is the personification of evil. The characters in an allegory are usually personifications of this kind.

The following passage from the chapter in this unit describes the character of General Woundwort. What human quality or character trait do you think this rabbit is intended to represent?

> After a few days' wandering, [Woundwort] came upon a small warren and, snarling and clawing, forced them to accept him. Soon he had become Chief Rabbit, having killed both the previous Chief and a rival named Fiorin. In combat he was terrifying, fighting entirely to kill, indifferent to any wounds he received himself and closing with his adversaries until his weight overbore and exhausted them . . . . When he had explored the limits of his own strength, he set to work to satisfy his longing for still more power in the only possible way—by increasing the power of the rabbits about him. He needed a bigger kingdom.

The outstanding characteristic of General Woundwort is his ruthless ambition. He is a fierce fighter who believes in eliminating his opponents, not just besting them. His belligerence, however, is not the common garden variety that is all brawn and no brains. Woundwort uses his superior fighting abilities to become the Chief Rabbit of the warren. But even this triumph does not satisfy him. The taste of power leaves him hungry for more, so he sets about increasing his power by increasing the size of his kingdom. Woundwort, then, is a personification of the kind of leader who will stop at nothing in his single-minded pursuit of power.

As we mentioned earlier, the characters are not the only elements of an allegory that have a double identity. The setting, plot and surrounding details are also intended to represent something else, with each element relating to the others to form an integrated structure of its own.

The following passage describes the organization of Efrafa under General Woundwort's direction. How many details in this account can you interpret with reference to the real world?

> As the warren grew, so Woundwort developed his system to keep it under control. Crowds of rabbits feeding at morning and evening were likely to attract attention. He devised the Marks, each controlled by its own officers and sentries, with feeding times changed regularly to give all a share of early morning and sunset—the favorite hours for silflay [feeding] . . . . The Owsla [police] had privileges in regard to feeding, mating and freedom of movement . . . .
>
> When it was no longer possible for Woundwort to be everywhere, the Council was set up. Some of the members came from the Owsla, but others were selected solely for their loyalty or their cunning as advisers. Old Snowdrop was growing deaf, but no one knew more than he about organizing a warren for safety. On his advice, the runs and burrows of the various Marks were not connected underground, so that disease or poison, if they came, would spread less readily. Conspiracy would also spread less readily.

On an allegorical level, the warren of Efrafa is intended to represent a police state where the rights of individuals are restricted by the government. Daily routines such as feeding have been regimented so that the rabbits eat not when they want to, but when they have been assigned to. This particular rule was instituted for a good reason—the safety of the entire warren. But this reason soon becomes an excuse for any and all restrictions.

The Owsla, or police force, has been exalted into an elite organization with special privileges which emphasize their prestige and glorify such traits as physical strength and blind loyalty. A Council has been set up to further extend the long arm of the law. In police states everywhere, specialists like Snowdrop are employed for their expertise in protecting not so much the people as the government in power. Unconnected burrows provide protection against the spread of disease or poison; but, more important, they restrict mingling among the citizens and thereby hinder the organization of a revolt. Police states usually have an ulterior motive for their actions, and the warren of Efrafa is a good example of how individual rights are increasingly restricted in the guise of the common good.

3. The Underlying Meaning. When an author writes a story in the form of an allegory, it's usually to make a point about something. As we noted at the beginning of the lesson, a sugar coating makes a bitter pill easier to swallow. An allegory is a kind of sugar coating too because it couches an unpleasant or unflattering truth within a seemingly innocent story.

Such a message might be religious, moral or political. For instance, the imaginary country of Lilliput in *Gulliver's Travels* represents the world of British politics in the eighteenth century. The allegorical intention of the author was to point up the treacherous interests in power in his day. Often an allegory is prompted by a particular situation in the public eye at the time, such as racial discrimination or political corruption. A good allegory, however, does not become dated by the passage of years. Circumstances may change, but human nature remains the same, and what happened once can happen again.

We just saw how General Woundwort establishes a large warren and goes to great lengths to protect it against attacks from both within and without. We saw how, on another level, the rabbit warren represents a police state with its repressive security measures. What does the following passage suggest to you about the point which the author of this allegory might have wished to get across?

> To feel that rabbits were competing to risk their lives at his orders gratified Woundwort, although he believed—and so did his Council and his Owsla—that he was giving the warren peace and security at a price which was modest enough.

Clearly, the author hopes that the reader will consider whether the price of peace in Woundwort's warren was, indeed, reasonable. Do we want to sacrifice personal freedoms in the interests of national security? And how do we know whether such sacrifices are truly necessary? How much of it is required in the interests of the country and how much is required simply to feed the ego of a power-hungry leader? As we saw earlier, the encroachments on personal freedoms in Efrafa developed gradually, but the sum total was dictatorship and repression. Thus, the author might also wish to open the reader's eyes to those small invasions on our personal lives that, by themselves, may seem for the public good but, together, may reveal an ominous pattern of government influence that should be checked by the citizens.

An allegory, then, is a story with an ulterior motive. On one level it entertains, and on another level it carries a message. And although the message may be disturbing, an allegory brings the matter to our attention in a less painful way. As you read the chapter about General Woundwort and Efrafa, keep in mind the dual intention of an allegory, and consider how the characters and their situation apply to our own world.

As you read the chapter:

- Pay special attention to the account of the Wide Patrols. Notice what the patrols, Woundwort and Efrafa come to represent.

- Be aware of the passage that tells about several problems in Efrafa which are on Woundwort's mind.

- Notice General Woundwort's conversation with Captain Chervil in which they discuss candidates for Owsla officers.

- Pay attention to Woundwort's private views on Efrafa when he meets Thlayli, the big rabbit who plans to infiltrate the warren.

Watership Down
Richard Adams

CHAPTER 34

Like an obelisk towards which the principal streets of a town converge, the strong will of a proud spirit stands prominent and commanding in the middle of the art of war.

Clausewitz, *On War*

Dusk was falling on Efrafa. In the failing light, General Woundwort was watching the Near Hind Mark at silflay along the edge of the great pasture field that lay between the warren and the iron road. Most of the rabbits were feeding near the Mark holes, which were close beside the field, concealed among the trees and undergrowth bordering a lonely bridle path. A few, however, had ventured out into the field, to browse and play in the last of the sun. Further out still were the sentries of the Owsla, on the alert for the approach of men or elil and also for any rabbit who might stray too far to be able to get underground quickly if there should be an alarm.

Captain Chervil, one of the two officers of the Mark, had just returned from a round of his sentries and was talking to some of the does near the center of the Mark ground when he saw the General approaching. He looked quickly about to see whether anything was at fault. Since all seemed to be well, he began nibbling at a patch of sweet vernal with the best air of indifference that he could manage.

General Woundwort was a singular rabbit. Some three years before, he had been born—the strongest of a litter of five—in a burrow outside a cottage garden near Cole Henley. His father, a happy-go-lucky and reckless buck, had thought nothing of living close to human beings except that he would be able to forage in their garden in the early morning. He had paid dearly for his rashness. After two or three weeks of spoiled lettuces and nibbled cabbage plants, the cottager had lain in wait and shot him as he came through the potato patch at dawn. The same morning the man set to work to dig out the doe and her growing litter. Woundwort's mother escaped, racing across the kale field toward the downs, her kittens doing their best to follow her. None but Woundwort succeeded. His mother, bleeding from a shotgun pellet, made her way along the hedges in broad daylight, with Woundwort limping beside her.

It was not long before a weasel picked up the scent of the blood and followed it. The little rabbit cowered in the grass while his mother was killed before his eyes. He made no attempt to run, but the weasel, its hunger satisfied, left him alone and made off through the bushes. Several hours later a kind old schoolmaster from Overton, walking through the fields, came upon Woundwort nuzzling the cold, still body and crying. He carried him home to his own kitchen and saved his life, feeding him with milk from a nasal dropper until he was old enough to eat bran and greenstuff. But Woundwort grew up very wild and, like Cowper's hare, would bite when he could. In a month he was big and strong and had become savage. He nearly killed the schoolmaster's cat, which had found him at liberty in the kitchen and tried to torment him. One night, a week later, he tore the wire from the front of his hutch and escaped to the open country.

Most rabbits in his situation, lacking almost all experience of wild life, would have fallen victim at once to the elil: but not Woundwort. After a few days' wandering, he came upon a small warren and, snarling and clawing, forced them to accept him. Soon he had become Chief Rabbit, having killed both the previous Chief and a rival named Fiorin. In combat he was terrifying, fighting entirely to kill, indifferent to any wounds he received himself and closing with his adversaries until his weight overbore and exhausted them. Those who had no heart to oppose him were not long in feeling that here was a leader indeed.

Woundwort was ready to fight anything except a fox. One evening he attacked and drove off a foraging Aberdeen puppy. He was impervious to the fascination of the mustelidae, and hoped someday to kill a weasel, if not a stoat. When he had explored the limits of his own strength, he set to work to satisfy his longing for still more power in the only possible way—by increasing the power of the rabbits about him. He needed a bigger kingdom. Men were the great danger, but this could be circumvented by cunning and discipline. He left the small warren, taking his followers with him, and set out to look for a place suited to his purpose, where the very existence of rabbits could be concealed and extermination made very difficult.

Efrafa grew up round the crossing point of two green bridle paths, one of which (the east-to-west) was tunnel-like, bordered on both sides by a thick growth of trees and bushes. The immigrants, under Woundwort's direction, dug their holes between the roots of the trees, in the undergrowth and along the ditches. From the first the warren prospered. Woundwort watched over them with a tireless zeal that won their loyalty even while they feared him. When the does stopped digging, Woundwort himself went on with their work while they slept. If a man was coming, Woundwort spotted him half a mile away. He fought rats, magpies, gray squirrels and, once, a crow. When litters were kindled, he kept an eye on their growth, picked out the strongest youngsters for the Owsla and trained them himself. He would allow no rabbit to leave the warren. Quite early on, three who tried to do so were hunted down and forced to return.

As the warren grew, so Woundwort developed his system to keep it under control. Crowds of rabbits feeding at morning and evening were likely to attract attention. He devised the Marks, each controlled by its own officers and sentries, with feeding times changed regularly to give all a share of early morning and sunset—the favorite hours for silflay. All signs of rabbit life were concealed as closely as possible. The Owsla had privileges in regard to feeding, mating and freedom of movement. Any failure of duty on their part was liable to be punished by demotion and loss of privileges. For ordinary rabbits, the punishments were more severe.

When it was no longer possible for Woundwort to be everywhere, the Council was set up. Some of the members came from the Owsla, but others were selected solely for their loyalty or their cunning as advisers. Old Snowdrop was growing deaf, but no one knew more than he about organizing a warren for safety. On his advice, the runs and burrows of the various Marks were not connected underground, so that disease or poison, if they came, would spread less readily. Conspiracy would also spread less readily. To visit the burrows of another Mark was not allowed without an officer's permission. It was on Snowdrop's advice, too, that Woundwort at length ordered that the warren was not to extend further, on account of the risk of detection and the weakening of central control. He was persuaded only with difficulty, for the new policy frustrated his restless desire of power after power. This now needed another outlet, and soon after the warren had been stopped from growing he introduced the Wide Patrols.

The Wide Patrols began as mere forays or raids, led by Woundwort, into the surrounding country. He would simply pick four or five of the Owsla and take them out to look for trouble. On the first occasion they were lucky enough to find and kill a sick owl that had eaten a mouse that had eaten poison-dressed seed corn. On the next, they came upon two hlessil whom they compelled to return with them to join the warren. Woundwort was no mere bully. He knew how to encourage other rabbits and to fill them with a spirit of emulation. It was not long before his officers were asking to be allowed to lead patrols. Woundwort would give them tasks—to search for hlessil in a certain direction or to find out whether a particular ditch or barn contained rats which could later be attacked in force and driven out. Only from farms and gardens were they ordered to keep clear. One of these patrols, led by a certain Captain Orchis, discovered a small warren two miles to the east, beyond the Kingsclere-Overton road, on the outskirts of Nutley Copse. The General led an expedition against it and broke it up, the prisoners being brought back to Efrafa, where a few of them later rose to be Owsla members themselves.

As the months went on, the Wide Patrols became systematic; during summer and early autumn there were usually two or three out at a time. There came to be no other rabbits for a long way round Efrafa and any who might wander into the neighborhood by chance were quickly picked up. Casualties in the Wide Patrols were high, for the elil got to know that they went out. Often it would take all a leader's courage and skill to complete his task and bring his rabbits—or some of his rabbits—back to the warren. But the Owsla were proud of the risks they ran: and, besides, Woundwort was in the habit of going out himself to see how they were getting on. A patrol leader, more than a mile from Efrafa, limping up a hedgerow in the rain, would come upon the General squatting like a hare under a tussock of darnel, and find himself required then and there to report what he had been doing or why he was off his route. The patrols were the training grounds of cunning trackers, swift runners and fierce fighters, and the casualties— although there might be as many as five or six in a bad month—suited Woundwort's purpose, for numbers needed keeping down and there were always fresh vacancies in the Owsla, which the younger bucks did their best to be good enough to fill. To feel that rabbits were competing to risk their lives at his orders gratified Woundwort, although he believed—and so did his Council and his Owsla—that he was giving the warren peace and security at a price which was modest enough.

Nevertheless, this evening, as he came out from among the ash trees to talk to Captain Chervil, the General was feeling seriously concerned about several things. It was less and less easy to keep the size of the warren under control. Overcrowding was becoming a grave problem, and this despite the fact that many of the does were re-absorbing their litters before birth. While their doing so was all to the good in itself, some of them were growing restive and hard to manage. Not long ago a group of does had come before the Council and asked to leave the warren. They had been peaceable at first, offering to go as far away as the Council wished: but when it had become plain that their request was not going to be granted on any terms, they had become first petulant and then aggressive and the Council had had to take strong measures. There was still a good deal of bad feeling over the business. Then, in the third place, the Owsla had lately lost a certain amount of respect among the rank and file.

Four wandering rabbits—giving themselves out to be some kind of embassy from another warren—had been held and impressed into the Right Flank Mark. He had intended, later, to find out where they had come from. But they had succeeded in playing a very simple trick, bamboozling the Mark commander, attacking his sentries and escaping by night. Captain Bugloss, the officer responsible, had, of course, been demoted and expelled from the Owsla, but his disgrace, though very proper, only added to the General's difficulties. The truth was that Efrafa had become, for the moment, short of good officers. Ordinary Owsla—sentries—were not too hard to find, but officers were another matter and he had lost three in less than a month. Bugloss was as good as a casualty: he would never hold rank again. But, worse, Captain Charlock—a brave and resourceful rabbit—while leading the pursuit of the fugitives, had been run down on the iron road by a train: a further proof, if any were needed, of the wicked malice of men. Worst of all, only two nights ago a patrol which had been out to the north had returned with the shocking news that its leader, Captain Mallow, an officer of exceptional prestige and experience, had been killed by a fox. It was an odd business. The patrol had picked up the scent of a fairly large party of rabbits evidently coming toward Efrafa from the north. They had been following it but had not yet sighted their quarry when suddenly a strange rabbit had burst in upon them as they were nearing the edge of some woodland. They had, of course, tried to stop him and at that moment the fox, which had apparently been following him closely, had come from the open combe beyond and killed poor Mallow in an instant. All things considered, the patrol had come away in good order and Groundsel, the second in command, had done well. But nothing more had been seen of the strange rabbit; and the loss of Mallow, with nothing to show for it, had upset and demoralized the Owsla a good deal.

Other patrols had been sent out at once, but all that they had established was that the rabbits from the north had crossed the iron road and disappeared southward. It was intolerable that they should have passed so close to Efrafa and gone their way without being apprehended. Even now they might possibly be caught, if only there were a really enterprising officer to put in charge of the search. It would certainly need an enterprising officer—Captain Campion perhaps—for patrols seldom crossed the iron road, and the wet country beyond—the country near the river—was only partly known. He would have gone himself, but with the recent disciplinary troubles in the warren he could not take the risk; and Campion could hardly be spared just now. No—infuriating as it was, the strangers were best forgotten for the moment. The first thing was to replace the Owsla losses—and preferably with rabbits who knew how to deal ruthlessly with any further signs of dissension. They would simply have to promote the best they had got, draw their horns in for a time and concentrate on training until things got back to normal.

Woundwort greeted Captain Chervil rather abstractedly and went on turning the problem over in his mind.

"What are your sentries like, Chervil?" he asked at length. "Do I know any of them?"

"They're a good lot, sir," replied Chervil. "You know Marjoram: he's been on patrol with you as a runner. And I think you know Moneywort."

"Yes, I know them," said Woundwort, "but they wouldn't make officers. We need to replace Charlock and Mallow: that's what I'm getting at."

"That's difficult, sir," said Chervil. "That sort of rabbit doesn't hop out of the grass."

"Well, they've got to hop from somewhere," said Woundwort. "You'd better think about it and tell me any ideas that occur to you. Anyway, I want to go round your sentries now. Come with me, will you?"

They were about to set off when a third rabbit approached—none other than Captain Campion himself. It was Campion's principal duty to search the outskirts of Efrafa at morning and evening and to report anything new—the tire marks of a tractor in mud, the droppings of a sparrow hawk or the spreading of fertilizer on a field. An expert tracker, he missed little or nothing and was one of the very few rabbits for whom Woundwort felt a genuine respect.

"Do you want me?" said Woundwort, pausing.

"Well, I think so, sir," replied Campion. "We've picked up a hlessi and brought him in."

"Where was he?"

"Down by the arch, sir. Just this side of it."

"What was he doing?"

"Well, sir, he says he's come a long way on purpose to join Efrafa. That's why I thought you might like to see him."

"*Wants* to join Efrafa?" asked Woundwort, puzzled.

"That's what he says, sir."

"Why can't the Council see him tomorrow?"

"Just as you like, sir, of course. But he strikes me as being a bit out of the ordinary. I'd say, a distinctly useful rabbit."

"H'm," said Woundwort, considering. "Well, all right. I haven't got long, though. Where is he now?"

"At the Crixa, sir." Campion meant the crossing point of the two bridle paths, which was about fifty yards away, among the trees. "Two of my patrol are with him."

Woundwort made his way back to the Crixa. Chervil, being on duty with his Mark, remained where he was. Campion accompanied the General.

At this hour the Crixa was all green shade, with red gleams of sun that winked through the leaves. The damp grass along the edges of the paths was dotted with spikes of mauve bugle, and the sanicles and yellow archangels flowered thickly. Under an elder bush, on the far side of the track, two Owslafa, or Council police, were waiting; and with them was the stranger.

Woundwort saw at once what Campion had meant. The stranger was a big rabbit, heavy but alert, with a rugged, seasoned appearance and the look of a fighter. He had a curious thick growth of fur—a kind of topknot—on the crown of his head. He stared at Woundwort with a detached, appraising air which the General had not encountered for a very long time.

"Who are you?" said Woundwort.

"My name is Thlayli," replied the Stranger.

"Thlayli, *sir*," prompted Campion.

The stranger said nothing.

"The patrol brought you in, I'm told. What were you doing?"

"I've come to join Efrafa."

"Why?"

"I'm surprised you ask. It's your warren, isn't it? Is there anything odd about someone wanting to join?"

Woundwort was nonplused. He was no fool and it was, he could not help feeling, extremely odd that any right-minded rabbit should choose to walk into Efrafa of his own accord. But he could hardly say so.

"What can you do?"

"I can run and fight and spoil a story telling it. I've been an officer in an Owsla."

"Fight, can you? Could you fight him?" said Woundwort, looking at Campion.

"Certainly, if you wish." The stranger reared up and aimed a heavy cuff at Campion, who leaped back just in time.

"Don't be a fool," said Woundwort. "Sit down. Where were you in an Owsla?"

"Far off. The warren was destroyed by men, but I escaped. I've been wandering some time. It won't surprise you that I heard of Efrafa. I've come a long way to join it. I thought you might have some use for me."

"Are you alone?"

"I am now."

Woundwort considered again. It was likely enough that this rabbit had been an officer in an Owsla. Any Owsla would want him. If he was speaking the truth, he had had wits enough to escape the destruction of his warren and survive a long journey through open country. It must have been a very long journey, for there was no warren within the normal range of the Efrafan patrols.

"Well," he said at length, "I dare say we might be able to find some use for you, as you put it. Campion here will look after you tonight, and tomorrow morning you'll come before the Council. Meanwhile, don't start fighting, do you see? We can give you plenty to do without that."

"Very well."

The following morning, after the Council had discussed the predicament of the warren due to the recent losses, General Woundwort proposed that, for a start, they might do worse than try the big newcomer as an officer in the Near Hind Mark, under the instruction of Captain Chervil. The Council, having seen him, agreed. By ni-Firth Thlayli, still bleeding from the Mark gash inflicted in his left haunch, had taken up his duties.

Unit 10

Watership Down

- Comprehension Questions
- The Use of Allegory
- Discussion Guides
- Writing Exercise

COMPREHENSION QUESTIONS

For each of the following statements and questions, select the option containing the most complete or most accurate answer.

1. The story of Efrafa is an allegory in which General Woundwort repre-
(k) sents a
   - ☐ a. rebel.
   - ☐ b. dictator.
   - ☐ c. capitalist.
   - ☐ d. democratic leader.

2. Which of the following best defines *impervious* as used in, "He was
(l) *impervious* to the fascination of the mustelidae (weasel-like animals),
   and hoped someday to kill a weasel, if not a stoat"?
   - ☐ a. Ignorant
   - ☐ b. Unaware of
   - ☐ c. Unaffected by
   - ☐ d. Intrigued by

3. General Woundwort led his followers away from the first, smaller
(c) warren in order to
   - ☐ a. test their loyalty.
   - ☐ b. find a more abundant food supply.
   - ☐ c. locate the warren next to a garden.
   - ☐ d. increase his power by expanding the warren.

4. The system of government instituted by General Woundwort proved
(f) to be
   - ☐ a. efficient.
   - ☐ b. disastrous.
   - ☐ c. unsuitable for rabbits.
   - ☐ d. too idealistic.

5. The majority of the members of Efrafa seem to be
(h) ☐ a. waiting for a chance to escape.
   - ☐ b. plotting to overthrow General Woundwort.
   - ☐ c. concerned about the future.
   - ☐ d. satisfied with their warren.

6. The successful management of a large warren like Efrafa requires that
(f) its members be highly
   - ☐ a. creative.
   - ☐ b. disciplined.
   - ☐ c. ambitious.
   - ☐ d. educated.

7. The responsibilities of Chief Rabbit in a warren are
(h) □ a. largely ceremonial in nature.
     □ b. of little consequence.
     □ c. limited to military strategy.
     □ d. the security and well-being of the entire warren.

8. The Council was created in order to
(c) □ a. give the other rabbits some say in major policy-making decisions.
     □ b. extend General Woundwort's authority.
     □ c. act as a forum for complaints and suggestions.
     □ d. choose General Woundwort's successor.

9. In his own eyes, General Woundwort sees himself as a
(j) □ a. benevolent protector.
     □ b. harsh dictator.
     □ c. sympathetic leader.
     □ d. victim of circumstances.

10. The two qualities which were of primary importance in furthering
(j) General Woundwort's career are his
     □ a. good nature and willingness to work.
     □ b. large size and good health.
     □ c. courage and wits.
     □ d. sense of humor and ability to get along with others.

11. The runs and burrows of the various Marks or sections of Efrafa were
(a) not connected underground in order to prevent
     □ a. further growth of the warren.
     □ b. cave-ins.
     □ c. detection from above.
     □ d. the spread of disease or poison.

12. The decision of the Council to limit the growth of the warren was
(b) based on
     □ a. food shortages.
     □ b. space limitations.
     □ c. the risks of detection and internal dissent.
     □ d. a general consensus of the group.

13. The mood among the does of Efrafa was one of
(i) □ a. discontent.   □ c. fear.
     □ b. satisfaction.   □ d. hostility.

WATERSHIP DOWN   313

14. The decision of the Council against allowing a group of does to leave
(g) Efrafa was probably
    □ a. in the best interests of the warren.
    □ b. in the best interests of the does.
    □ c. unwise in the long run.
    □ d. wise in the long run.

15. The first Wide Patrols were sent out by General Woundwort shortly
(d) after the
    □ a. training of the Owsla.
    □ b. decision to limit Efrafa's growth.
    □ c. division of Efrafa into Marks.
    □ d. death of Captain Mallow.

16. General Woundwort is concerned because the Owsla has
(b) □ a. turned against him.
    □ b. failed to attract new members.
    □ c. asked to leave the warren.
    □ d. lost both officers and prestige.

17. Which of the following best defines *impressed* as used in, "Four wander-
(l) ing rabbits—giving themselves out to be some kind of embassy from
    another warren—had been held and *impressed* into the Right Flank
    Mark"?
    □ a. Drafted   □ c. Tricked
    □ b. Invited   □ d. Admitted

18. Captain Bugloss, who was the officer on duty when the four captured
(a) rabbits escaped from Efrafa, was punished by
    □ a. imprisonment.   □ c. death.
    □ b. expulsion from the Owsla. □ d. expulsion from the warren.

19. The embassy of rabbits which escaped from Efrafa, the subsequent
(d) sighting of a large party of strange rabbits, and the unlucky death of
    Captain Mallow caused
    □ a. an increase in security measures.
    □ b. a decline in Owsla recruits.
    □ c. a loss of face for the Owsla.
    □ d. an uprising against General Woundwort.

20. The price the rabbits of Efrafa paid for security under General
(g) Woundwort was a loss of
    □ a. prestige.   □ c. pride.
    □ b. freedom.   □ d. hope.

21. Which of the following best defines *nonplused* as used in, "Woundwort
(l) was *nonplused*. He was no fool and it was, he could not help feeling,
extremely odd that any right-minded rabbit should choose to walk into
Efrafa of his own accord"?
   □ a. Completely puzzled   □ c. Unexpectedly sympathetic
   □ b. Very disappointed   □ d. Quite indignant

22. Thlayli, the newcomer who wants to join Efrafa, replies to General
(i) Woundwort's questions in a tone that is
   □ a. submissive.   □ c. arrogant.
   □ b. respectful.   □ d. friendly.

23. A main idea behind this chapter is to help the reader better under-
(e) stand the
   □ a. organization of a rabbit warren.
   □ b. creation of a police state.
   □ c. concept of survival of the fittest.
   □ d. conflict between man and animal.

24. The history of Efrafa shows that the development of a dictatorship
(e) is often
   □ a. decided upon by a majority of the population.
   □ b. forced upon an unwilling population.
   □ c. evidenced by a sudden shift in governing policy.
   □ d. a gradual, almost imperceptible process.

25. The following sentence illustrates the *physical* point of view of this
(k) story: "The damp grass along the edges of the paths was dotted with
spikes of mauve bugle, and the sanicles and yellow archangels flowered
thickly." From the preceding description, it is clear that this story is
told from the *physical* point of view of a
   □ a. person.   □ c. bird.
   □ b. small animal.   □ d. very large animal.

Comprehension Skills: a—isolating details; b—recalling specific facts; c—retaining
concepts; d—organizing facts; e—understanding the main idea; f—drawing a
conclusion; g—making a judgment; h—making an inference; i—recognizing tone;
j—understanding characters; k—appreciation of literary forms; l—knowledge of
word meanings.

THE USE OF ALLEGORY

Practice Exercise A

The Wide Patrols began as mere forays or raids, led by Woundwort, into the surrounding country. He would simply pick four or five of the Owsla and take them out to look for trouble. On the first occasion they were lucky enough to find and kill a sick owl that had eaten a mouse that had eaten poison-dressed seed corn. On the next, they came upon two hlessil whom they compelled to return with them to join the warren. Woundwort was no mere bully. He knew how to encourage other rabbits and to fill them with a spirit of emulation. It was not long before his officers were asking to be allowed to lead patrols. Woundwort would give them tasks—to search for hlessil in a certain direction or to find out whether a particular ditch or barn contained rats which could later be attacked in force and driven out. Only from farms and gardens were they ordered to keep clear. One of these patrols, led by a certain Captain Orchis, discovered a small warren two miles to the east, beyond the Kingsclere-Overton road, on the outskirts of Nutley Copse. The General led an expedition against it and broke it up, the prisoners being brought back to Efrafa, where a few of them later rose to be Owsla members themselves.

1. In this passage Efrafa, under General Woundwort's leadership, has come to represent
   ☐ a. the epitome of evil in the world.
   ☐ b. a typical police department.
   ☐ c. an aggressor nation.
   ☐ d. a mindless horde.

2. We are told that Woundwort is no mere bully. He knew how to make others work for him. Underline two sentences that tell of incidents in which the rabbits were anxious to carry out Woundwort's ideas and plans.

Practice Exercise B

Nevertheless, this evening, as he came out from among the ash trees to talk to Captain Chervil, the General was feeling seriously concerned about several things. It was less and less easy to keep the size of the warren under control. Overcrowding was becoming a grave problem, and this despite the fact that many of the does were re-absorbing their litters before birth. While their doing so was all to the good in itself, some of them were growing restive and hard to manage. Not long ago a group of does had come before the Council and asked to leave the warren. They had been peaceable at first, offering to go as far away as the Council wished: but when it had become plain that their request was not going to be granted on any terms, they had become first petulant and then aggressive and the Council had had to take strong measures. There was still a good deal of bad feeling over the business. Then, in the third place, the Owsla had lately lost a certain amount of respect among the rank and file.

1. A social problem represented in this passage creates several political problems. That social problem is
   - ☐ a. lack of communication.
   - ☐ b. overpopulation.
   - ☐ c. racial conflict.
   - ☐ d. class conflict.

2. Several allegorical ideas are suggested in the passage. On the lines provided, write a word or phrase from the box which corresponds to each quotation.

political repression	emigration	birth control
political unrest	loss of respect for law and order	

a. Owsla had lately lost a certain amount of respect among the rank and file

_____

b. re-absorbing their litters

_____

c. some of them were growing restive and hard to manage

_____

d. offering to go as far away as the Council wished

_____

e. the Council had had to take strong measures

_____

Practice Exercise C

No—infuriating as it was, the strangers were best forgotten for the moment. The first thing was to replace the Owsla losses—and preferably with rabbits who knew how to deal ruthlessly with any further signs of dissention. They would simply have to promote the best they had got, draw their horns in for a time and concentrate on training until things got back to normal.

Woundwort greeted Captain Chervil rather abstractedly and went on turning the problem over in his mind.

"What are your sentries like, Chervil?" he asked at length. "Do I know any of them?"

"They're a good lot, sir," replied Chervil. "You know Marjoram: he's been on patrol with you as a runner. And I think you know Moneywort."

"Yes, I know them," said Woundwort, "but they wouldn't make officers. We need to replace Charlock and Mallow: that's what I'm getting at."

"That's difficult, sir," said Chervil. "That sort of rabbit doesn't hop out of the grass."

"Well, they've got to hop from somewhere," said Woundwort. "You'd better think about it and tell me any ideas that occur to you. Anyway, I want to go round your sentries now. Come with me, will you?"

1. General Woundwort faces a problem of government that might be typical in a dictatorship. The problem is that
   - ☐ a. the army is about to mutiny because General Woundwort is losing his authority.
   - ☐ b. dictators often find it hard to recruit men for the army.
   - ☐ c. where there is no freedom, the army is never very good.
   - ☐ d. the military must deal with enemies both within and without the country.

2. The names of General Woundwort and his soldiers all have something in common. Look up these names in a good dictionary and, on the lines provided, tell what it is they have in common.

_____

_____

Practice Exercise D

The stranger was a big rabbit, heavy but alert, with a rugged, seasoned appearance and the look of a fighter. He had a curious thick growth of fur—a kind of topknot—on the crown of his head. He stared at Woundwort with a detached, appraising air which the General had not encountered for a very long time.

"Who are you?" said Woundwort.

"My name is Thlayli," replied the Stranger.

"Thlayli, *sir,*" prompted Campion.

The stranger said nothing.

"The patrol brought you in, I'm told. What were you doing?"

"I've come to join Efrafa."

"Why?"

"I'm surprised you ask. It's your warren, isn't it? Is there anything odd about someone wanting to join?"

Woundwort was nonplused. He was no fool and it was, he could not help feeling, extremely odd that any right-minded rabbit should choose to walk into Efrafa of his own accord. But he could hardly say so.

1. In the passage above, Thlayli wants to infiltrate Efrafa as a spy. The method he uses with General Woundwort is
   - ☐ a. bluff and insolence.
   - ☐ c. modesty and reserve.
   - ☐ b. lies and trickery.
   - ☐ d. brawn and muscle.

2. Thlayli uses Woundwort's private views about Efrafa against him. On the lines provided, write two sentences which reveal that Woundwort is aware that the strictly organized society which he has imposed on the rabbits is not necessarily a desirable way of life.

_____

_____

_____

_____

_____

DISCUSSION GUIDES

Analyzing the Use of Allegory

1. Sometimes an allegory is written to draw attention to a disturbing situation in the public eye at the time. Do you think the author had a real-life situation in mind when he was writing about General Woundwort and Efrafa? Explain.

2. In your opinion, is the allegorical message contained in this chapter likely to become outdated in the future? Give a reason for your answer.

3. Suppose you are assigned to write an allegory based on current events throughout the world—religious, social, political, racial or economic. What situation would you choose to be the basis of your allegory?

Interpreting the Chapter

4. How would you rate the quality of General Woundwort's leadership? Be prepared to justify your rating.

5. There are sometimes circumstances in the real world that seem to require, and even cry out for, a leader like General Woundwort. Give an example of such circumstances.

6. Why, in spite of an overpopulation problem, does General Woundwort refuse to let anyone leave Efrafa? Where in the real world are people forbidden to leave their country?

7. Are the intelligence-gathering activities of the Owsla comparable to any organization in our own government? If so, what? What point might the author have wished to make concerning our own intelligence-gathering operations?

8. The Owsla in Efrafa are very concerned with their public image. Why was this so important to them? Can you think of any instances when our own government has gone to great lengths to save face? Explain.

Analyzing the Author's Technique

9. The author uses a special "rabbit" vocabulary with words like *elil*, *silflay*, *hlessil* and *Owsla*. What effect does this technique have on the story as a whole?

10. While reading *Watership Down*, the reader gets the dual impression of being in both a rabbit warren and in the real world. How does the author use setting and characterization to convey this feeling?

WRITING EXERCISE

Fables are regarded as a kind of allegory. Aesop, a Greek slave who lived about 550 or 600 B.C., is probably the best known fabulist. You may know some of his stories from your childhood reading, although his fables were not written just for children, but for adults as well. Each fable teaches a moral lesson.

On this page and the next, you will find short summaries of four of Aesop's fables. Following each summary there is a quotation from the fable from which the ending has been omitted. Using your own ideas, complete each quotation with any words you think would make an interesting or amusing conclusion. Then, in a short sentence or two, explain the allegorical lesson to be learned from the fable.

You are *not* expected to guess Aesop's exact words. After you have completed each exercise, however, you may enjoy seeing how Aesop finished each quotation. The exact quotations from Aesop's fables are located in the answer key at the back of the book.

1. The Shepherd's Boy

A young boy became lonely tending sheep day after day, and he craved company. To create a little excitement and attract people to his lonely hillside, he raised the cry of "Wolf!" After the boy had done this several times, the villagers grew tired with the boy and his tricks:

The boy called out "Wolf! Wolf!" and the villagers came out to help him. A few days afterward he tried the same trick, and again they came to help. Shortly after this a wolf actually came, but

_____

_____

_____

_____

_____

_____

_____

2. The Town Mouse and the Country Mouse

A mouse who lives a very simple, spartan life in the country comes to visit his cousin who lives a very luxurious life in the city. The food is excellent and the accomodations are the best. But, as in all big cities, there are dangers: cats, traps and mouse-hating people. After many close escapes, the country mouse returns to his poor country home saying:

Better beans and bacon in peace than

_____

_____

_____

_____

_____

_____

3. The Eagle and the Arrow

A large eagle generously gives some of his feathers to a hunter for use in making arrows. One day, while the eagle is sitting and watching for rabbits, he is shot in the breast with an arrow. He sees that:

The shaft of the arrow had been feathered with one of his own plumes. We often give our enemies

_____

_____

_____

_____

_____

_____

Unit 11
The Use of Symbols

Lord of
the Flies

Introduction

As *Lord of the Flies* begins, a group of English boys, whose ages range from 6 to 12, are being evacuated by air from some future war. The plane is shot down, but the passenger compartment containing the boys is ejected and lands them safely on a deserted island. The boys soon shed their civilized veneer to become savages of the worst sort.

All the boys are well-educated children, brought up by their parents to be good Englishmen. We meet Ralph and "Piggy" first. Ralph is a good-looking boy, likeable and a natural leader. Piggy is fat, nearsighted and nervous. He constantly polishes his glasses and gives good advice which no one wants to listen to. The two boys find a conch shell, the kind you can blow into and use like a trumpet for signaling. Ralph learns to blow it and attracts the other boys who have been wandering about the island since the crash.

An odd-looking group of boys appears in the black cloaks and caps of a boy's choir. They arrive marching two-by-two led by Jack who is acting much like a drill sergeant. Back home he was their prefect, or leader. Jack, who is very much the dictator, wants to be chief on the island—"I can sing C sharp," he announces. But he is not as attractive a boy as Ralph, and Ralph is elected chief. A rivalry develops immediately between the two.

Ralph, with his conch shell to call assemblies and with Piggy to give unheeded advice, becomes the legislative head of government. Jack decides that he and his choir will be "hunters"—the military arm of the society.

At first everything is fun—a whole island to themselves and no adults. The weather is beautiful and there is plenty of fruit to eat. It is truly a Garden of Eden. It is decided that the first task must be to build a signal fire on a mountaintop to attract rescuers. But "acting like a bunch of kids," in Piggy's words, they manage to set the forest on fire. Nothing is as easy as it should be, and the only thing that turns out to be "fun" is hunting the pigs that live on the island.

The first pig is killed and eaten with great delight. Jack paints his face with clay, and there is dancing and chanting, *"Kill the pig. Cut her throat. Spill her blood."* The choirboys are well on their way to becoming full-fledged savages.

The little boys, referred to as "littluns," tell of beasts they think they have seen. They have been dreaming or imagining things, but their insistence is enough to make the older boys apprehensive. Fear begins to stalk them.

One night, while all are asleep, there is an air battle high over the island. A plane is shot down and the pilot descends on the island in a parachute, but he is dead. He lands on the mountain where the signal fire was built, tangled in his parachute in such a way that when the wind blows his body bobs up and down in the harness. Discovering the dead parachutist in darkness, the boys are convinced it is "the beast" they have been worrying about, and they flee in terror. Tension over fear of the beast drives the final wedge between Jack and Ralph. Jack goes off, followed by some of his hunters, to form a separate tribe that will hunt and have fun.

There is no question now that Jack has become a bloodthirsty savage. Ralph and Piggy are trying to hold together the last shreds of an orderly society but are having little success at it. "The fire's the most important thing," Ralph says. "Without the fire we can't be rescued." It is the last feeble link with the world they came from and they can't keep it alive. Jack and his hunters go off and kill a large pig for a "feast." They disembowel it and place its head on a sharpened stick as a peace offering to "the beast."

William Golding, author of *Lord of the Flies*, was a schoolteacher in England for fifteen years from 1945 to 1960. Before that, he was a lieutenant in the Royal Navy in charge of a rocket warship. From his experience as a schoolteacher, he learned firsthand how schoolboys act and how close they are to being young savages when left to their own devices. As a naval officer, he learned firsthand of the savage nature of adults engaged in war. The two ideas merge in *Lord of the Flies* where he shows that the evil lurking just below the surface of the boys on the island is the same evil that is a threat to humankind in an age of atomic weapons. Unleashed from the restraints of civilization, he says, people quickly return to savagery and chaos. And the governing evil that brings this about is "the lord of the flies," the evil that is within us all.

The Use of Symbols

Beginners at the study of literature sometimes object that teachers read too much into a story. "Why," they ask, "can't we just read the story and enjoy it without tearing it apart?" This is a legitimate question; one that should be answered.

The attitude usually arises from "a remembrance of things past" when we could read or listen to a story, become engrossed in the surface action and enjoy it for that alone. It was enough to feel the delicious sense of relief when Red Riding Hood was saved from the Wolf without worrying about a deeper significance to the story. It didn't matter a bit that the author may have intended Red Riding Hood to be a symbol of innocence in the world or the Wolf to be something more than a talking canine.

If we do see Red Riding Hood as a symbol of innocence, however, and then see the Wolf as a symbol of evil, we suddenly take a small plunge beneath the surface of the story to find a conflict between good and evil. By adding this little bit of understanding to the story, we come to enjoy it more.

Just so, in more mature reading, we can enjoy a story more if we penetrate the surface to deal with the deeper meanings that the author conveys to us through symbols. Two of the best known symbols in literature are the raft and the river in Mark Twain's *Huckleberry Finn*. Huck Finn and his friend Jim are traveling down the Mississippi River on a raft. Jim, a slave, is trying to make his way to freedom. Huck is escaping from the complexities and corruption of the adult world. Every time they find themselves in trouble, they flee to the raft and the river. Sooner or later every reader must come to feel that for Huck and Jim the raft and the river mean freedom and safety. This is their symbolism.

Once you accept the fact that most stories are loaded with symbolism, the symbols are not at all hard to spot. Then, as you become a more experienced reader, symbols have more meaning for you, you understand more about the stories you read, and consequently you enjoy your reading more.

Generally speaking, there are three kinds of symbols that appear in literature: *things* may be symbols, *characters* may be symbols, and *actions* or *events* may be symbols. On a higher level, even the story itself may be a symbol, as is the case with *Watership Down* where a rabbit world is a symbol of our own world. When the entire story is a symbol, the story is called an allegory.

Many people feel that William Golding's *Lord of the Flies* is also an allegory. As you watch a group of boys try to establish a civilized way of living only to fall into chaos and savagery, you are tempted to say, "How like our own world where people fall into chaos and savagery through wars, just like the boys do on the island." Once you have made this discovery, you have hit on the major symbolism of the book. But beyond this, the book is rich in other symbols. Let's look at some of them.

1. **Things as Symbols.** Three objects play extremely important roles in *Lord of the Flies:* a conch shell, a signal fire, and the gruesome severed head of a pig which has been impaled on a stick.

When the boys arrive on the island, Ralph, who becomes their leader, finds the shell. He blows on it to call meetings, and anyone who wants to speak must hold the shell. Thus, the shell comes to be a symbol of parliamentary rule of order. Watch how the conch shell works as a symbol in the following passage:

> The sound of the inexpertly blown conch interrupted them. As though he were serenading the rising sun, Jack went on blowing till the shelters were astir and the hunters crept to the platform and the littluns whimpered as now they so frequently did. Ralph rose obediently, and Piggy, and they went to the platform.
> "Talk," said Ralph bitterly, "talk, talk, talk."
> He took the conch from Jack.
> "This meeting—"
> Jack interrupted him.
> "I called it."
> "If you hadn't called it I should have. You just blew the conch."
> "Well, isn't that calling it?"
> "Oh, take it! Go on—talk!"
> Ralph thrust the conch into Jack's arms and sat down on the trunk.

The first thing the boys had done when they arrived on the island was build a signal fire to attract the attention of rescuers from the outside world. As long as they could keep the signal fire going, there was hope of rescue and return to civilization. Keeping the fire burning required a cooperative, constructive and creative community effort. The fire, when controlled and maintained, is a civilizing force in their society. Thus, the struggle to keep the signal fire going becomes a symbol for maintaining civilization.

Having seen what they thought was a "beast" at the site of their first signal fire, they have abandoned it. Things have been going from bad to worse, but Jack and Piggy think of something sensible to do. In the following passage a sense of community order has returned as a result of working to build a fire.

> Piggy lifted the conch as though to add power to his next words.
> "We got no fire on the mountain. But what's wrong with a fire down here? A fire could be built on them rocks. On the sand, even. We'd make smoke just the same."
> "That's right!"
> "Smoke!"
> "By the bathing pool!"
> The boys began to babble. Only Piggy could have the intellectual daring to suggest moving the fire from the mountain . . . .
> The greatest ideas are the simplest. Now there was something to be done they worked with passion. Piggy was so full of delight and expanding liberty in Jack's departure, so full of pride in his contribution to the good of society, that he helped to fetch wood.

By contrast, the group of boys led by Jack, who has formed his own "tribe," creates a rather disturbing symbol. They kill a pig, disembowel it and cut off its head which they set on a sharpened stick as a sacrifice offering to the "beast" that they imagine is roaming the island. The pile of guts and the head are soon covered with flies. Simon—a strange, quiet boy— has been in hiding, watching. Left alone with the head, Simon confronts it. The author uses the head as something very ancient and very dreadful, the main symbol of his story from which the novel gets its name.

> Even the butterflies deserted the open space where the obscene thing grinned and dripped. Simon lowered his head, carefully keeping his eyes shut, then sheltered them with his hand. There were no shadows under the trees but everywhere a pearly stillness, so that what was real seemed illusive and without definition. The pile of guts was a black blob of flies that buzzed like a saw. After a while these flies found Simon. Gorged, they alighted by his runnels of sweat and drank. They tickled under his nostrils and played leap-frog on his thighs. They were black and iridescent green and without number; and in front of Simon, the Lord of the Flies hung on his stick and grinned. At last Simon gave up and looked back; saw the white teeth and dim eyes, the blood—and his gaze was held by that ancient, inescapable recognition.

The author clearly identifies the head as "Lord of the Flies," making it as horrible and repulsive as he possibly can. This thing is a symbol of evil—no question about it. But what is the "ancient, inescapable recognition" that holds Simon?

Many times an author will use symbolism that is not obvious to the general reading audience. But once the reader knows the author's intentions—perhaps from reading a review or notes in the book itself—the story takes on new and important meanings and new interest. This is where serious study of good literature pays off. One of the Biblical names for the devil is Beelzebub, which is a Greek translation of the Hebrew name *Ba'alzevuv* meaning "lord of the flies." So it's no wonder that Simon experiences an "ancient, inescapable recognition." He is facing an evil as old as man—the devil himself.

2. **Characters as Symbols.** On a very elementary level, we saw Red Riding Hood as a symbol of sweet innocence and the Wolf as a symbol of evil. Characters that stand for good or evil are very common throughout literature. Another common character symbol is "Everyman." This is the character that symbolizes you and me, all the ordinary people in the world. In *An American Tragedy*, Clyde Griffiths is "Everyman." In *Watership Down*, the rabbit Hazel represents a wise and democratic leader while General Woundwort is a symbol of dictatorship and oppression.

In *Lord of the Flies* there are four major characters, each of whom represents a special influence in society. Ralph is a traditional politician-leader type, the kind we always elect to office because he is attractive and likeable.

"Piggy" is a thinker, an intellectual. He represents science, technology and practical intelligence. We don't like this kind of person too much, and we certainly don't want to listen to his boring conversation and strange ideas.

Jack is a soldier, a hunter, an oppressive dictator. We need his type to do our hunting for us and wage wars. We are in serious trouble, however, if he gets the upper hand in our society.

Simon is a mystic or a prophet. We never listen to his kind even though he is the only one to see things clearly. In fact, we tend to persecute and kill our prophets, which is exactly what happens to Simon in the story.

Jack has been a leader of choirboys back in England. Their voices, as well as their appearance, were angelic before coming to the island. Now Jack has become a savage and leader of a savage tribe. This change represents the savage that lurks just below the surface in each of us no matter how good and civilized we seem. Here is a view of Jack as he becomes a savage chieftain:

> Far off along the beach, Jack was standing before a small group of boys. He was looking brilliantly happy.
>
> "Hunting," he said. He sized them up. Each of them wore the remains of a black cap and ages ago they had stood in two demure rows and their voices had been the song of angels.
>
> "We'll hunt. I'm going to be chief."
>
> They nodded, and the crisis passed easily.
>
> "And then—about the beast."
>
> They moved, looked at the forest.
>
> "I say this. We aren't going to bother about the beast . . . . Now listen. We might go later to the castle rock. But now I'm going to get more of the biguns [older boys] away from the conch and all that. We'll kill a pig and give a feast." He paused and went on more slowly. "And about the beast. When we kill we'll leave some of the kill for it. Then it won't bother us, maybe."
>
> He stood up abruptly.
>
> "We'll go into the forest now and hunt."

Jack has become the picture of a savage, hunting in the forest with his "tribe," prepared to offer a meat sacrifice to some unknown evil spirit—the "beast."

3. **Actions as Symbols.** The action in many stories—the shootout in a cowboy movie, for example—may represent the conflict between good and evil in the world. If the good guys win, we see a symbolic triumph of good over evil. A different kind of symbol appears in *Gulliver's Travels*. The countries of Lilliput and Blefuscu have been at war for thirty-six years over the issue of which end of a soft-boiled egg you should break when you eat it. This is, of course, a symbolic satire of the poor excuses nations use for going to war against one another.

After killing their pig, Jack and some of his hunters raid Ralph's camp to obtain fire for cooking. Ralph has been trying desperately to keep some semblance of a civilized society alive. During the raid, Piggy has stood clutching the conch. In the aftermath of the raid, the following scene occurs. How do you read the symbolism of this action?

> Presently Ralph rose to his feet, looking at the place where the savages had vanished. Samneric came, talking in an awed whisper.
> "I thought it was—"
> "—and I was—"
> "—scared."
> Piggy stood above them on the platform, still holding the conch . . . .
> "When I saw Jack I was sure he'd go for the conch. Can't think why."
> The group of boys looked at the white shell with affectionate respect. Piggy placed it in Ralph's hands and the littluns, seeing the familiar symbol, started to come back.
> "Not here."
> He turned toward the platform, feeling the need for ritual. First went Ralph, the white conch cradled, then Piggy very grave, then the twins, then the littluns and the others.

A very similar scene might have taken place in England during World War II when savage Nazi air raids were threatening to destroy a thousand years of civilized culture and parliamentary rule. The Prime Minister with his symbols of office solemnly enters the halls of Parliament and mounts the podium to try to reassure the people that civilization will survive against the forces of darkness.

Shaken by the attack, Ralph and his followers solemnly turn for comfort and reassurance to their symbols of order, the conch and their parliamentary type of assembly.

Once an author has established the major symbols in a story, they are used consistently as a unifying force to hold the narrative together and give it direction. And out of these symbols grow major ideas—the controlling themes—that the author wants to get across to the reading audience.

In *Lord of the Flies* William Golding shows how defects of human nature can move a society from order into chaos. First he gives us symbols of order and civilization: the conch shell and the signal fire; Ralph, Piggy and Simon. On the side of descent into chaos and savagery, he gives us Jack and his choirboy hunters and the devil himself—the lord of the flies. The action swirls about these symbols so that we come to understand not just the surface conflict among a group of boys, but the larger story of a whole world struggling to save itself from darkness.

As you read the chapter:

- Notice how Piggy is always polishing his eyeglasses. Think about the symbolism of Piggy's glasses in the passage where Ralph suggests having a smaller signal fire.

- Notice the significance of Jack's appearance when he and his followers raid the other boys for fire.

- Be aware of what is happening to Ralph is his capacity as leader after the raid.

- Consider carefully what the pig's head—the lord of the flies—is saying to Simon about the "Beast."

Lord of the Flies
William Golding

CHAPTER 8
GIFT FOR THE DARKNESS

Piggy looked up miserably from the dawn-pale beach to the dark mountain.

"Are you sure? Really sure, I mean?"

"I told you a dozen times now," said Raph, "we saw it."

"D'you think we're safe down here?"

"How the hell should I know?"

Ralph jerked away from him and walked a few paces along the beach. Jack was kneeling and drawing a circular pattern in the sand with his forefinger. Piggy's voice came to them, hushed.

"Are you sure? Really?"

"Go up and see," said Jack contemptuously, "and good riddance."

"No fear."

"The beast had teeth," said Ralph, "and big black eyes."

He shuddered violently. Piggy took off his one round of glass and polished the surface.

"What we going to do?"

Ralph turned toward the platform. The conch glimmered among the trees, a white blob against the place where the sun would rise. He pushed back his mop.

"I don't know."

He remembered the panic flight down the mountainside.

"I don't think we'd ever fight a thing that size, honestly, you know. We'd talk but we wouldn't fight a tiger. We'd hide. Even Jack 'ud hide."

Jack still looked at the sand.

"What about my hunters?"

Simon came stealing out of the shadows by the shelters. Ralph ignored Jack's question. He pointed to the touch of yellow above the sea.

"As long as there's light we're brave enough. But then? And now that thing squats by the fire as though it didn't want us to be rescued—"

He was twisting his hands now, unconsciously. His voice rose.

"So we can't have a signal fire. . . . We're beaten."

A point of gold appeared above the sea and at once all the sky lightened.

"What about my hunters?"

"Boys armed with sticks."

Jack got to his feet. His face was red as he marched away. Piggy put on his one glass and looked at Ralph.

"Now you done it. You been rude about his hunters."

"Oh shut up!"

The sound of the inexpertly blown conch interrupted them. As though he were serenading the rising sun, Jack went on blowing till the shelters were astir and the hunters crept to the platform and the littluns whimpered as now they so frequently did. Ralph rose obediently, and Piggy, and they went to the platform.

"Talk," said Ralph bitterly, "talk, talk, talk."

He took the conch from Jack.

"This meeting—"

Jack interrupted him.

"I called it."

"If you hadn't called it I should have. You just blew the conch."

"Well, isn't that calling it?"

"Oh, take it! Go on—talk!"

Ralph thrust the conch into Jack's arms and sat down on the trunk.

"I've called an assembly," said Jack, "because of a lot of things. First, you know now, we've seen the beast. We crawled up. We were only a few feet away. The beast sat up and looked at us. I don't know what it does. We don't even know what it is—"

"The beast comes out of the sea—"

"Out of the dark—"

"Trees—"

"Quiet!" shouted Jack. "You, listen. The beast is sitting up there, whatever it is—"

"Perhaps it's waiting—"

"Hunting—"

"Yes, hunting."

"Hunting," said Jack. He remembered his age-old tremors in the forest. "Yes. The beast is a hunter. Only—shut up! The next thing is that we couldn't kill it. And the next thing is that Ralph said my hunters are no good."

"I never said that!"

"I've got the conch. Ralph thinks you're cowards, running away from the boar and the beast. And that's not all."

There was a kind of sigh on the platform as if everyone knew what was coming. Jack's voice went on, tremulous yet determined, pushing against the uncooperative silence.

"He's like Piggy. He says things like Piggy. He isn't a proper chief."

Jack clutched the conch to him.

"He's a coward himself."

For a moment he paused and then went on.

"On top, when Roger and me went on—he stayed back."

"I went too!"

"After."

The two boys glared at each other through screens of hair.

"I went on too," said Ralph, "then I ran away. So did you."

"Call me a coward then."

Jack turned to the hunters.

"He's not a hunter. He'd never have got us meat. He isn't a prefect and we don't know anything about him. He just gives orders and expects people to obey for nothing. All this talk—"

"All this talk!" shouted Ralph. "Talk, talk! Who wanted it? Who called the meeting?"

Jack turned, red in the face, his chin sunk back. He glowered up under his eyebrows.

"All right then," he said in tones of deep meaning, and menace, "all right."

He held the conch against his chest with one hand and stabbed the air with his index finger.

"Who thinks Ralph oughtn't to be chief?"

He looked expectantly at the boys ranged round, who had frozen. Under the palms there was deadly silence.

"Hands up," said Jack strongly, "whoever wants Ralph not to be chief?"

The silence continued, breathless and heavy and full of shame. Slowly the red drained from Jack's cheeks, then came back with a painful rush. He licked his lips and turned his head at an angle, so that his gaze avoided the embarrassment of linking with another's eye.

"How many think—"

His voice tailed off. The hands that held the conch shook. He cleared his throat, and spoke loudly.

"All right then."

He laid the conch with great care in the grass at his feet. The humiliating tears were running from the corner of each eye.

"I'm not going to play any longer. Not with you."

Most of the boys were looking down now, at the grass or their feet. Jack cleared his throat again.

"I'm not going to be part of Ralph's lot—"

He looked along the right-hand logs, numbering the hunters that had been a choir.

"I'm going off by myself. He can catch his own pigs. Anyone who wants to hunt when I do can come too."

He blundered out of the triangle toward the drop to the white sand.

"Jack!"

Jack turned and looked back at Ralph. For a moment he paused and then cried out, high-pitched, enraged.

"—No!"

He leapt down from the platform and ran along the beach, paying no heed to the steady fall of his tears; and until he dived into the forest Ralph watched him.

Piggy was indignant.

"I been talking, Ralph, and you just stood there like—"

Softly, looking at Piggy and not seeing him, Ralph spoke to himself.

"He'll come back. When the sun goes down he'll come." He looked at the conch in Piggy's hand.

"What?"

"Well there!"

Piggy gave up the attempt to rebuke Ralph. He polished his glass again and went back to his subject.

"We can do without Jack Merridew. There's others besides him on this island. But now we really got a beast, though I can't hardly believe it, we'll need to stay close to the platform; there'll be less need of him and his hunting. So now we can really decide on what's what."

"There's no help, Piggy. Nothing to be done."

For a while they sat in depressed silence. Then Simon stood up and took the conch from Piggy, who was so astonished that he remained on his feet. Ralph looked up at Simon.

"Simon? What is it this time?"

A half-sound of jeering ran round the circle and Simon shrank from it.

"I thought there might be something to do. Something we—"

Again the pressure of the assembly took his voice away. He sought for help and sympathy and chose Piggy. He turned half toward him, clutching the conch to his brown chest.

"I think we ought to climb the mountain."

The circle shivered with dread. Simon broke off and turned to Piggy who was looking at him with an expression of derisive incomprehension.

"What's the good of climbing up to this here beast when Ralph and the other two couldn't do nothing?"

Simon whispered his answer.

"What else is there to do?"

His speech made, he allowed Piggy to lift the conch out of his hands. Then he retired and sat as far away from the others as possible.

Piggy was speaking now with more assurance and with what, if the circumstances had not been so serious, the others would have recognized as pleasure.

"I said we could all do without a certain person. Now I say we got to decide on what can be done. And I think I could tell you what Ralph's going to say next. The most important thing on the island is the smoke and you can't have no smoke without a fire."

Ralph made a restless movement.

"No go, Piggy. We've got no fire. That thing sits up there—we'll have to stay here."

Piggy lifted the conch as though to add power to his next words.

"We got no fire on the mountain. But what's wrong with a fire down here? A fire could be built on them rocks. On the sand, even. We'd make smoke just the same."

"That's right!"

"Smoke!"

"By the bathing pool!"

The boys began to babble. Only Piggy could have the intellectual daring to suggest moving the fire from the mountain.

"So we'll have the fire down here," said Ralph. He looked about him. "We can build it just here between the bathing pool and the platform. Of course—"

He broke off, frowning, thinking the thing out, unconsciously tugging at the stub of a nail with his teeth.

"Of course the smoke won't show so much, not be seen so far away. But we needn't go near, near the—"

The others nodded in perfect comprehension. There would be no need to go near.

"We'll build the fire now."

The greatest ideas are the simplest. Now there was something to be done they worked with passion. Piggy was so full of delight and expanding liberty in Jack's departure, so full of pride in his contribution to the good of society, that he helped to fetch wood. The wood he fetched was close at hand, a fallen tree on the platform that they did not need for the assembly, yet to the others the sanctity of the platform had protected even what was useless there. Then the twins realized they would have a fire near them as a comfort in the night and this set a few littluns dancing and clapping hands.

The wood was not so dry as the fuel they had used on the mountain. Much of it was damply rotten and full of insects that scurried; logs had to be lifted from the soil with care or they crumbled into sodden powder. More than this, in order to avoid going deep into the forest the boys worked near at hand on any fallen wood no matter how tangled with new growth. The skirts of the forest and the scar were familiar, near the conch and the shelters and sufficiently friendly in daylight. What they might become in darkness nobody cared to think. They worked therefore with great energy and cheerfulness, though as time crept by there was a suggestion of panic in the energy and hysteria in the cheerfulness. They built a pyramid of leaves and twigs, branches and logs, on the bare sand by the platform. For the first time on the island, Piggy himself removed his one glass, knelt down and focused the sun on tinder. Soon there was a ceiling of smoke and a bush of yellow flame.

The littluns who had seen few fires since the first catastrophe became wildly excited. They danced and sang and there was a partyish air about the gathering.

At last Ralph stopped work and stood up, smudging the sweat from his face with a dirty forearm.

"We'll have to have a small fire. This one's too big to keep up."

Piggy sat down carefully on the sand and began to polish his glass.

"We could experiment. We could find out how to make a small hot fire and then put green branches on to make smoke. Some of them leaves must be better for that than the others."

As the fire died down so did the excitement. The littluns stopped singing and dancing and drifted away toward the sea or the fruit trees or the shelters.

Ralph flopped down in the sand.

"We'll have to make a new list of who's to look after the fire."

"If you can find 'em."

He looked round. Then for the first time he saw how few biguns there were and understood why the work had been so hard.

"Where's Maurice?"

Piggy wiped his glass again.

"I expect . . . no, he wouldn't go into the forest by himself, would he?"

Ralph jumped up, ran swiftly round the fire and stood by Piggy, holding up his hair.

"But we've got to have a list! There's you and me and Samneric and—"

He would not look at Piggy but spoke casually.

"Where's Bill and Roger?"

Piggy leaned forward and put a fragment of wood on the fire.

"I expect they've gone. I expect they won't play either."

Ralph sat down and began to poke little holes in the sand. He was surprised to see that one had a drop of blood by it. He examined his bitten nail closely and watched the little globe of blood that gathered where the quick was gnawed away.

Piggy went on speaking.

"I seen them stealing off when we was gathering wood. They went that way. The same way as he went himself."

Ralph finished his inspection and looked up into the air. The sky, as if in sympathy with the great changes among them, was different today and so misty that in some places the hot air seemed white. The disc of the sun was dull silver as though it were nearer and not so hot, yet the air stifled.

"They always been making trouble, haven't they?"

The voice came near his shoulder and sounded anxious.

"We can do without 'em. We'll be happier now, won't we?"

Ralph sat. The twins came, dragging a great log and grinning in their triumph. They dumped the log among the embers so that sparks flew.

"We can do all right on our own, can't we?"

For a long time while the log dried, caught fire and turned red hot, Ralph sat in the sand and said nothing. He did not see Piggy go to the twins and whisper with them, nor how the three boys went together into the forest.

"Here you are."

He came to himself with a jolt. Piggy and the other two were by him. They were laden with fruit.

"I thought perhaps," said Piggy, "we ought to have a feast, kind of."

The three boys sat down. They had a great mass of the fruit with them and all of it properly ripe. They grinned at Ralph as he took some and began to eat.

"Thanks," he said. Then with an accent of pleased surprise—"Thanks!"

"Do all right on our own," said Piggy. "It's them that haven't no common sense that make trouble on this island. We'll make a little hot fire—"

Ralph remembered what had been worrying him.

"Where's Simon?"

"I don't know."

"You don't think he's climbing the mountain?"

Piggy broke into noisy laughter and took more fruit.

"He might be." He gulped his mouthful. "He's cracked."

Simon had passed through the area of fruit trees but today the littluns had been too busy with the fire on the beach and they had not pursued him there. He went on among the creepers until he reached the great mat that was woven by the open space and crawled inside. Beyond the screen of leaves the sunlight pelted down and the butterflies danced in the middle their unending dance. He knelt down and the arrow of the sun fell on him. That other time the air had seemed to vibrate with heat; but now it threatened. Soon the sweat was running from his long coarse hair. He shifted restlessly but there was no avoiding the sun. Presently he was thirsty, and then very thirsty.

He continued to sit.

Far off along the beach, Jack was standing before a small group of boys. He was looking brilliantly happy.

"Hunting," he said. He sized them up. Each of them wore the remains of a black cap and ages ago they had stood in two demure rows and their voices had been the song of angels.

"We'll hunt. I'm going to be chief."

They nodded, and the crisis passed easily.

"And then—about the beast."

They moved, looked at the forest.

"I say this. We aren't going to bother about the beast."

He nodded at them.

"We're going to forget the beast."

"That's right!"

"Yes!"

"Forget the beast!"

If Jack was astonished by their fervor he did not show it.

"And another thing. We shan't dream so much down here. This is near the end of the island."

They agreed passionately out of the depths of their tormented private lives.

"Now listen. We might go later to the castle rock. But now I'm going to get more of the biguns away from the conch and all that. We'll kill a pig and give a feast." He paused and went on more slowly. "And about the beast. When we kill we'll leave some of the kill for it. Then it won't bother us, maybe."

He stood up abruptly.

"We'll go into the forest now and hunt."

He turned and trotted away and after a moment they followed him obediently.

They spread out, nervously, in the forest. Almost at once Jack found the dung and scattered roots that told of pig and soon the track was fresh. Jack signaled the rest of the hunt to be quiet and went forward by himself. He was happy and wore the damp darkness of the forest like his old clothes. He crept down a slope to rocks and scattered trees by the sea.

The pigs lay, bloated bags of fat, sensuously enjoying the shadows under the trees. There was no wind and they were unsuspicious; and practice had made Jack silent as the shadows. He stole away again and instructed his hidden hunters. Presently they all began to inch forward sweating in the silence and heat. Under the trees an ear flapped idly. A little apart from the rest, sunk in deep maternal bliss, lay the largest sow of the lot. She was black and pink; and the great bladder of her belly was fringed with a row of piglets that slept or burrowed and squeaked.

Fifteen yards from the drove Jack stopped, and his arm, straightening, pointed at the sow. He looked round in inquiry to make sure that everyone understood and the other boys nodded at him. The row of right arms slid back.

"Now!"

The drove of pigs started up; and at a range of only ten yards the wooden spears with fire-hardened points flew toward the chosen pig. One piglet, with a demented shriek, rushed into the sea trailing Roger's spear behind it. The sow gave a gasping squeal and staggered up, with two spears sticking in her fat flank. The boys shouted and rushed forward, the piglets scattered and the sow burst the advancing line and went crashing away through the forest.

"After her!"

They raced along the pig-track, but the forest was too dark and tangled so that Jack, cursing, stopped them and cast among the trees. Then he said nothing for a time but breathed fiercely so that they were awed by him and looked at each other in uneasy admiration. Presently he stabbed down at the ground with his finger.

"There—"

Before the others could examine the drop of blood, Jack had swerved off, judging a trace, touching a bough that gave. So he followed, mysteriously right and assured, and the hunters trod behind him.

He stopped before a covert.

"In there."

They surrounded the covert but the sow got away with the sting of another spear in her flank. The trailing butts hindered her and the sharp, cross-cut points were a torment. She blundered into a tree, forcing a spear still deeper; and after that any of the hunters could follow her easily by the drops of vivid blood. The afternoon wore on, hazy and dreadful with damp heat; the sow staggered her way ahead of them, bleeding and mad, and the hunters followed, wedded to her in lust, excited by the long chase and the dropped blood. They could see her now, nearly got up with her, but she spurted with her last strength and held ahead of them again. They were just behind her when she staggered into an open space where bright flowers grew and butterflies danced round each other and the air was hot and still.

Here, struck down by the heat, the sow fell and the hunters hurled themselves at her. This dreadful eruption from an unknown world made her frantic; she squealed and bucked and the air was full of sweat and noise and blood and terror. Roger ran round the heap, prodding with his spear whenever pigflesh appeared. Jack was on top of the sow, stabbing downward with his knife. Roger found a lodgment for his point and began to push till he was leaning with his whole weight. The spear moved forward inch by inch and the terrified squealing became a high-pitched scream. Then Jack found the throat and the hot blood spouted over his hands. The sow collapsed under them and they were heavy and fulfilled upon her. The butterflies still danced, preoccupied in the center of the clearing.

At last the immediacy of the kill subsided. The boys drew back, and Jack stood up, holding out his hands.

"Look."

He giggled and flicked them while the boys laughed at his reeking palms. Then Jack grabbed Maurice and rubbed the stuff over his cheeks.

This time Robert and Maurice acted the two parts; and Maurice's acting of the pig's efforts to avoid the advancing spear was so funny that the boys cried with laughter.

At length even this palled. Jack began to clean his bloody hands on the rock. Then he started work on the sow and paunched her, lugging out the hot bags of colored guts, pushing them into a pile on the rock while the others watched him. He talked as he worked.

"We'll take the meat along the beach. I'll go back to the platform and invite them to a feast. That should give us time."

Roger spoke.

"Chief—"

"Uh—?"

"How can we make a fire?"

Jack squatted back and frowned at the pig.

"We'll raid them and take fire. There must be four of you; Henry and you, Bill and Maurice. We'll put on paint and sneak up; Roger can snatch a branch while I say what I want. The rest of you can get this back to where we were. We'll build the fire there. And after that—"

He paused and stood up, looking at the shadows under the trees. His voice was lower when he spoke again.

"But we'll leave part of the kill for . . ."

He knelt down again and was busy with his knife. The boys crowded round him. He spoke over his shoulder to Roger.

"Sharpen a stick at both ends."

Presently he stood up, holding the dripping sow's head in his hands.

"Where's that stick?"

"Here."

"Ram one end in the earth. Oh—it's rock. Jam it in that crack. There."

Jack held up the head and jammed the soft throat down on the pointed end of the stick which pierced through into the mouth. He stood back and the head hung there, a little blood dribbling down the stick.

Instinctively the boys drew back too; and the forest was very still. They listened, and the loudest noise was the buzzing of flies over the spilled guts.

Jack spoke in a whisper.

"Pick up the pig."

Maurice and Robert skewered the carcass, lifted the dead weight, and stood ready. In the silence, and standing over the dry blood, they looked suddenly furtive.

Jack spoke loudly.

"This head is for the beast. It's a gift."

The silence accepted the gift and awed them. The head remained there, dim-eyed, grinning faintly, blood blackening between the teeth. All at once they were running away, as fast as they could, through the forest toward the open beach.

Simon stayed where he was, a small brown image, concealed by the leaves. Even if he shut his eyes the sow's head still remained like an after-image. The half-shut eyes were dim with the infinite cynicism of adult life. They assured Simon that everything was a bad business.

"I know that."

Simon discovered that he had spoken aloud. He opened his eyes quickly and there was the head grinning amusedly in the strange daylight, ignoring the flies, the spilled guts, even ignoring the indignity of being spiked on a stick.

He looked away, licking his dry lips.

A gift for the beast. Might not the beast come for it? The head, he thought, appeared to agree with him. Run away, said the head silently, go back to the others. It was a joke really—why should you bother? You were just wrong, that's all. A little headache, something you ate, perhaps. Go back, child, said the head silently.

Simon looked up, feeling the weight of his wet hair, and gazed at the sky. Up there, for once, were clouds, great bulging towers that sprouted away over the island, grey and cream and copper-colored. The clouds were sitting on the land; they squeezed, produced moment by moment this close, tormenting heat. Even the butterflies deserted the open space where the obscene thing grinned and dripped. Simon lowered his head, carefully keeping his eyes shut, then sheltered them with his hand. There were no shadows under the trees but everywhere a pearly stillness, so that what was real seemed illusive and without definition. The pile of guts was a black blob of flies that buzzed like a saw. After a while these flies found Simon. Gorged, they alighted by his runnels of sweat and drank. They tickled under his nostrils and played leap-frog on his thighs. They were black and iridescent green and without number; and in front of Simon, the Lord of the Flies hung on his stick and grinned. At last Simon gave up and looked back; saw the white teeth and dim eyes, the blood—and his gaze was held by that ancient, inescapable recognition. In Simon's right temple, a pulse began to beat on the brain.

Ralph and Piggy lay in the sand, gazing at the fire and idly flicking pebbles into its smokeless heart.

"That branch is gone."

"Where's Samneric?"

"We ought to get some more wood. We're out of green branches."

Ralph sighed and stood up. There were no shadows under the palms on the platform; only this strange light that seemed to come from everywhere at once. High up among the bulging clouds thunder went off like a gun.

"We're going to get buckets of rain."

"What about the fire?"

Ralph trotted into the forest and returned with a wide spray of green which he dumped on the fire. The branch crackled, the leaves curled and the yellow smoke expanded.

Piggy made an aimless little pattern in the sand with his fingers.

"Trouble is, we haven't got enough people for a fire. You got to treat Samneric as one turn. They do everything together—"

"Of course."

"Well, that isn't fair. Don't you see? They ought to do two turns."

Ralph considered this and understood. He was vexed to find how little he thought like a grownup and sighed again. The island was getting worse and worse.

Piggy looked at the fire.

"You'll want another green branch soon."

Ralph rolled over.

"Piggy. What are we going to do?"

"Just have to get on without 'em."

"But—the fire."

He frowned at the black and white mess in which lay the unburnt ends of branches. He tried to formulate.

"I'm scared."

He saw Piggy look up; and blundered on.

"Not of the beast. I mean I'm scared of that too. But nobody else understands about the fire. If someone threw you a rope when you were drowning. If a doctor said take this because if you don't take it you'll die—you would, wouldn't you? I mean?"

" 'Course I would."

"Can't they see? Can't they understand? Without the smoke signal we'll die here? Look at that!"

A wave of heated air trembled above the ashes but without a trace of smoke.

"We can't keep one fire going. And they don't care. And what's more—" He looked intensely into Piggy's streaming face.

"What's more, *I* don't sometimes. Supposing I got like the others—not caring. What 'ud become of us?"

Piggy took off his glasses, deeply troubled.

"I dunno, Ralph. We just got to go on, that's all. That's what grownups would do."

Ralph, having begun the business of unburdening himself, continued.

"Piggy, what's wrong?"

Piggy looked at him in astonishment.

"Do you mean the—?"

"No, not it . . . I mean . . . what makes things break up like they do?"

Piggy rubbed his glasses slowly and thought. When he understood how far Ralph had gone toward accepting him he flushed pinkly with pride.

"I dunno, Ralph. I expect it's him."

"Jack?"

"Jack." A taboo was evolving round that word too.

Ralph nodded solemnly.

"Yes," he said, "I suppose it must be."

The forest near them burst into uproar. Demoniac figures with faces of white and red and green rushed out howling, so that the littluns fled screaming. Out of the corner of his eye, Ralph saw Piggy running. Two figures rushed at the fire and he prepared to defend himself but they grabbed half-burnt branches and raced away along the beach. The three others stood still, watching Ralph; and he saw that the tallest of them, stark naked save for paint and a belt, was Jack.

Ralph had his breath back and spoke.

"Well?"

Jack ignored him, lifted his spear and began to shout.

"Listen all of you. Me and my hunters, we're living along the beach by a flat rock. We hunt and feast and have fun. If you want to join my tribe come and see us. Perhaps I'll let you join. Perhaps not."

He paused and looked round. He was safe from shame or self-consciousness behind the mask of his paint and could look at each of them in turn. Ralph was kneeling by the remains of the fire like a sprinter at his mark and his face was half-hidden by hair and smut. Samneric peered together round a palm tree at the edge of the forest. A littlun howled, creased and crimson, by the bathing pool and Piggy stood on the platform, the white conch gripped in his hands.

"Tonight we're having a feast. We've killed a pig and we've got meat. You can come and eat with us if you like."

Up in the cloud canyons the thunder boomed again. Jack and the two anonymous savages with him swayed, looking up, and then recovered. The littlun went on howling. Jack was waiting for something. He whispered urgently to the others.

"Go on—now!"

The two savages murmured. Jack spoke sharply.

"Go on!"

The two savages looked at each other, raised their spears together and spoke in time.

"The Chief has spoken."

Then the three of them turned and trotted away.

Presently Ralph rose to his feet, looking at the place where the savages had vanished. Samneric came, talking in an awed whisper.

"I thought it was—"

"—and I was—"

"—scared."

Piggy stood above them on the platform, still holding the conch.

"That was Jack and Maurice and Robert," said Ralph. "Aren't they having fun?"

"I thought I was going to have asthma."

"Sucks to your ass-mar."

"When I saw Jack I was sure he'd go for the conch. Can't think why."

The group of boys looked at the white shell with affectionate respect. Piggy placed it in Ralph's hands and the littluns, seeing the familiar symbol, started to come back.

"Not here."

He turned toward the platform, feeling the need for ritual. First went Ralph, the white conch cradled, then Piggy very grave, then the twins, then the littluns and the others.

"Sit down all of you. They raided us for fire. They're having fun. But the—"

Ralph was puzzled by the shutter that flickered in his brain. There was something he wanted to say; then the shutter had come down.

"But the—"

They were regarding him gravely, not yet troubled by any doubts about his sufficiency. Ralph pushed the idiot hair out of his eyes and looked at Piggy.

"But the . . . oh . . . the fire! Of course, the fire!"

He started to laugh, then stopped and became fluent instead.

"The fire's the most important thing. Without the fire we can't be rescued. I'd like to put on war-paint and be a savage. But we must keep the fire burning. The fire's the most important thing on the island, because, because—"

He paused again and the silence became full of doubt and wonder.

Piggy whispered urgently. "Rescue."

"Oh yes. Without the fire we can't be rescued. So we must stay by the fire and make smoke."

When he stopped no one said anything. After the many brilliant speeches that had been made on this very spot Ralph's remarks seemed lame, even to the littluns.

At last Bill held out his hands for the conch.

"Now we can't have the fire up there—because we can't have the fire up there—we need more people to keep it going. Let's go to this feast and tell them the fire's hard on the rest of us. And the hunting and all that, being savages I mean—it must be jolly good fun."

Samneric took the conch.

"That must be fun like Bill says—and as he's invited us—"

"—to a feast—"

"—meat—"

"—crackling—"

"—I could do with some meat—"

Ralph held up his hand.

"Why shouldn't we get our own meat?"

The twins looked at each other. Bill answered.

"We don't want to go in the jungle."

Ralph grimaced.

"He—you know—goes."

"He's a hunter. They're all hunters. That's different."

No one spoke for a moment, then Piggy muttered to the sand.

"Meat—"

The littluns sat, solemnly thinking of meat, and dribbling. Overhead the cannon boomed again and the dry palm fronds clattered in a sudden gust of hot wind.

"You are a silly little boy," said the Lord of the Flies, "just an ignorant, silly little boy."

Simon moved his swollen tongue but said nothing.

"Don't you agree?" said the Lord of the Flies. "Aren't you just a silly little boy?"

Simon answered him in the same silent voice.

"Well then," said the Lord of the Flies, "you'd better run off and play with the others. They think you're batty. You don't want Ralph to think you're batty, do you? You like Ralph a lot, don't you? And Piggy, and Jack?"

Simon's head was tilted slightly up. His eyes could not break away and the Lord of the Flies hung in space before him.

"What are you doing out here all alone? Aren't you afraid of me?"

Simon shook.

"There isn't anyone to help you. Only me. And I'm the Beast."

Simon's mouth labored, brought forth audible words.

"Pig's head on a stick."

"Fancy thinking the Beast was something you could hunt and kill!" said the head. For a moment or two the forest and all the other dimly appreciated places echoed with the parody of laughter. "You knew, didn't you? I'm part of you? Close, close, close! I'm the reason why it's no go? Why things are what they are?"

The laughter shivered again.

"Come now," said the Lord of the Flies. "Get back to the others and we'll forget the whole thing."

Simon's head wobbled. His eyes were half closed as though he were imitating the obscene thing on the stick. He knew that one of his times was coming on. The Lord of the Flies was expanding like a balloon.

"This is ridiculous. You know perfectly well you'll only meet me down there—so don't try to escape!"

Simon's body was arched and stiff. The Lord of the Flies spoke in the voice of a schoolmaster.

"This has gone quite far enough. My poor, misguided child, do you think you know better than I do?"

There was a pause.

"I'm warning you. I'm going to get angry. D'you see? You're not wanted. Understand? We are going to have fun on this island. Understand? We are going to have fun on this island! So don't try it on, my poor misguided boy, or else—"

Simon found he was looking into a vast mouth. There was blackness within, a blackness that spread.

"—Or else," said the Lord of the Flies, "we shall do you. See? Jack and Roger and Maurice and Robert and Bill and Piggy and Ralph. Do you. See?"

Simon was inside the mouth. He fell down and lost consciousness.

Unit 11

Lord of
the Flies

- Comprehension
  Questions
- The Use of Symbols
- Discussion Guides
- Writing Exercise

COMPREHENSION QUESTIONS

For each of the following statements and questions, select the option containing the most complete or most accurate answer.

1. Certain facts show that the action in this chapter goes from
(d) ☐ a. one day to the next.   ☐ c. late morning until late at night.
    ☐ b. dawn to late afternoon.   ☐ d. night until the next morning.

2. Piggy's eyeglasses
(b) ☐ a. looked like sunglasses.
    ☐ b. were too large for him.
    ☐ c. were useless because both lenses were broken.
    ☐ d. had only one lens.

3. The color of the conch shell was
(b) ☐ a. white.   ☐ c. pink and yellow.
    ☐ b. pink.   ☐ d. blue.

4. After discussing the beast, the boys decided
(a) ☐ a. to fight it.   ☐ c. to hunt it.
    ☐ b. to leave it alone.   ☐ d. to trick it.

5. From the way Ralph acted when Jack blew the conch, you can assume
(h) he felt that
    ☐ a. meetings were not being held often enough.
    ☐ b. only Piggy should blow the conch.
    ☐ c. there was too much talk and not enough action.
    ☐ d. the beast was about to make an appearance.

6. From the arguments between Jack and Ralph about the beast, you can
(f) conclude that when they saw it,
    ☐ a. Jack stayed to face it and Ralph ran away.
    ☐ b. Ralph stayed to face it and Jack ran away.
    ☐ c. Jack summoned his hunters but they ran away.
    ☐ d. Jack and Ralph ran away together.

7. Jack called a meeting with the conch in order to
(c) ☐ a. have Ralph ousted as chief.
☐ b. give Ralph one last chance.
☐ c. have Simon made chief.
☐ d. give Simon a chance to speak.

8. The boys would not elect Jack chief, but that did not keep them from
(g) ☐ a. listening to Piggy.   ☐ c. hunting the beast.
☐ b. following his example.   ☐ d. fighting with Ralph.

9. Piggy suggested building a signal fire on the beach instead of on the
(h) mountain because
☐ a. the boys were afraid to go to the mountain.
☐ b. there was no more firewood on the mountain.
☐ c. they wouldn't have to carry logs so far.
☐ d. Jack had ordered them to stay away from the mountain.

10. At one point Jack said to Ralph: "I'm not going to play any longer. Not
(i) with you." Most of the boys were looking down now, at the grass or
their feet. Jack cleared his throat again. "I'm not going to be part of
Ralph's lot . . . ." This speech sounds like a
☐ a. savage attack.
☐ b. political speech in Parliament.
☐ c. childish tantrum.
☐ d. diplomatic maneuver.

11. In the expression "I'm not going to be part of *Ralph's lot,*" *Ralph's lot*
(l) means
☐ a. Ralph and his group.   ☐ c. Ralph's territory.
☐ b. the kind of luck Ralph has.   ☐ d. Ralph's ideas for getting rescued.

12. The boys always meet to talk on a natural platform near the beach. This
(k) could be symbolic of a
☐ a. schoolyard or playground.
☐ b. reviewing stand for military parades.
☐ c. stage in a theater or auditorium.
☐ d. meeting house of government.

13. When Jack left Ralph and his group of boys, Piggy
(g) ☐ a. was sorry to see him go.
☐ b. felt relieved to see him go.
☐ c. didn't care one way or the other.
☐ d. would have liked Jack to come back.

14. Because Simon acted differently from the other boys, there was a
(j) feeling among them that he was
   □ a. somewhat smarter than the rest.
   □ b. probably dull and ignorant.
   □ c. perhaps a little "batty."
   □ d. someone worth listening to.

15. At one point Ralph says, "No go, Piggy. We've got no fire." The lord of
(e) the flies says, "I'm the reason it's no go." The idea is that
   □ a. Ralph's orderly society isn't working.
   □ b. there is not enough food to go around.
   □ c. there is no chance of rescue.
   □ d. things are so bad that they are bound to get better.

16. There was only one trouble with building a signal fire on the beach
(d) instead of the mountain, and that was that
   □ a. it would not stay lit there.
   □ b. it would burn the littluns.
   □ c. Ralph did not want it there.
   □ d. it couldn't be seen as far.

17. Ralph had a nervous habit; it was
(a) □ a. scratching his nose.   □ c. pulling his ear.
   □ b. biting his nails.   □ d. chewing his fist.

18. The boys would not vote for Jack as leader, but they
(c) □ a. refused to help Ralph.   □ c. sneaked off to join Jack.
   □ b. wanted to replace Ralph.   □ d. decided to make Jack a general.

19. After Jack left, Ralph became frantic about making a new list of people
(e) to tend the fire because
   □ a. he wanted desperately to maintain a sense of order.
   □ b. he was afraid the littluns would catch cold.
   □ c. Jack had known where to find the best firewood.
   □ d. he wanted everyone to do his share of work.

20. After Jack and the other boys had left, Piggy asked, "We can do all right
(f) on our own, can't we?" Ralph doesn't answer. From what has been
   happening, the reader must conclude that the answer is
   □ a. maybe.   □ c. yes and no.
   □ b. yes.   □ d. no.

21. Speaking about the choirboys turned hunters, the author says, ". . . ages
(l) ago they had stood in two *demure* rows and their voices had been the
song of angels." The word *demure* means
    □ a. unruly and disorganized.   □ c. quiet and shy.
    □ b. straight and stiff.   □ d. loud and strong.

22. According to the story, Jack "wore the damp darkness of the forest like
(k) his old clothes." This is a way of saying that Jack
    □ a. felt damp and dirty in the forest.
    □ b. was comfortable hunting in the forest.
    □ c. now used damp leaves in place of his old clothing.
    □ d. is damp and dark inside.

23. The author gives a gruesome description of the boys killing a pig. Then
(i) he describes giggling and laughing. This change of tone is probably used
to provide
    □ a. humor.   □ c. drama.
    □ b. tension.   □ d. relief.

24. Personification is a figure of speech that gives human form to animals,
(k) objects or ideas. Which of the following is the best example of
personification?
    □ a. They looked suddenly furtive.
    □ b. This head is for the beast. It's a gift.
    □ c. The silence accepted the gift.
    □ d. The head remained there, dim-eyed.

25. When the head speaks to Simon, it becomes a character in the story. The
(j) way it speaks is like a
    □ a. schoolteacher talking to a little boy.
    □ b. sergeant talking to a soldier.
    □ c. god talking to a man.
    □ d. company president talking to a worker.

Comprehension Skills: a—isolating details; b—recalling specific facts; c—retaining
concepts; d—organizing facts; e—understanding the main idea; f—drawing a
conclusion; g—making a judgment; h—making an inference; i—recognizing tone;
j—understanding characters; k—appreciation of literary forms; l—knowledge of
word meanings.

THE USE OF SYMBOLS

Practice Exercise A

At last Ralph stopped work and stood up, smudging the sweat from his face with a dirty forearm.

"We'll have to have a small fire. This one's too big to keep up."

Piggy sat down carefully on the sand and began to polish his glass.

"We could experiment. We could find out how to make a small hot fire and then put green branches on to make smoke. Some of them leaves must be better for that than the others."

1. Symbolically speaking, Piggy seems to be polishing his glass because
   ☐ a. he is nervous and has nothing to do with his hands.
   ☐ b. he is thinking and wants to see things more clearly.
   ☐ c. they keep getting dirty as he works.
   ☐ d. it is a tradition in civilized society.

2. Piggy seems to represent science and technology in the island society. Which sentence in the passage seems to bear this out? Write the sentence on the lines provided.

   _____

   _____

Practice Exercise B

The forest near them burst into uproar. Demoniac figures with faces of white and red and green rushed out howling, so that the littluns fled screaming. Out of the corner of his eye, Ralph saw Piggy running. Two figures rushed at the fire and he prepared to defend himself but they grabbed half-burnt branches and raced away along the beach. The three others stood still, watching Ralph; and he saw that the tallest of them, stark naked save for paint and a belt, was Jack.

Ralph had his breath back and spoke.

"Well?"

Jack ignored him, lifted his spear and began to shout.

"Listen all of you. Me and my hunters, we're living along the beach by a flat rock. We hunt and feast and have fun. If you want to join my tribe come and see us. Perhaps I'll let you join. Perhaps not."

He paused and looked around. He was safe from shame or self-consciousness behind the mask of his paint and could look at each of them in turn. Ralph was kneeling by the remains of the fire like a sprinter at his mark and his face was half-hidden by hair and smut . . . .

"Tonight we're going to have a feast. We've killed a pig and we've got meat. You can come and eat with us if you like."

1. Jack has pulled off a raid. But it is hinted at here that
   □ a. Jack is losing his enthusiasm for hunting.
   □ b. Ralph may not be as brave as Jack.
   □ c. Jack may need a mask to hide behind.
   □ d. Ralph will probably win out in the end.

2. Circle the paragraph above that makes Jack sound more like the little boy he is than the savage chief he pretends to be.

Practice Exercise C

Ralph was puzzled by the shutter that flickered in his brain. There was something he wanted to say; then the shutter had come down.

"But the—"

They were regarding him gravely, not yet troubled by any doubts about his sufficiency. Ralph pushed the idiot hair out of his eyes and looked at Piggy.

"But the . . . oh . . . the fire! Of course, the fire!"

He started to laugh, then stopped and became fluent instead.

"The fire's the most important thing. Without the fire we can't be rescued. I'd like to put on war-paint and be a savage. But we must keep the fire burning. The fire's the most important thing on the island, because, because—"

He paused again and the silence became full of doubt and wonder.

Piggy whispered urgently. "Rescue."

"Oh yes. Without the fire we can't be rescued. So we must stay by the fire and make smoke."

When he stopped no one said anything. After the many brilliant speeches that had been made on this very spot Ralph's remarks seemed lame, even to the littluns.

1. We noted in the lesson that the fire is a symbol of a link with civilization. In this passage
   ☐ a. Ralph seems to be losing his hold on this symbol.
   ☐ b. the fire seems to mean more to the littluns now.
   ☐ c. Ralph is more determined than ever to maintain the fire.
   ☐ d. Ralph is deliberately lying to the boys.

2. On the lines provided, write the sentence that sums up the effectiveness of Ralph's speech.

   _____

   _____

   _____

   _____

Practice Exercise D

"What are you doing out here all alone? Aren't you afraid of me?"
Simon shook.
"There isn't anyone to help you. Only me. And I'm the Beast."
Simon's mouth labored, brought forth audible words.
"Pig's head on a stick."
"Fancy thinking the Beast was something you could hunt and kill!" said the head. For a moment or two the forest and all the other dimly appreciated places echoed with the parody of laughter. "You knew, didn't you? I'm part of you? Close, close, close! I'm the reason why it's no go? Why things are what they are?"

1. We read that the boys are afraid of a "Beast." The pig's head says, "I'm the Beast." This means that
   ☐ a. the boys have been hunting Beasts all along—pigs.
   ☐ b. since the head is a dead Beast there is nothing to be afraid of.
   ☐ c. the boys have created their own Beast.
   ☐ d. it is the flies that the boys should be afraid of.

2. It was pointed out in the lesson that the lord of the flies is evil or the devil. In this passage the lord of the flies says he knows that Simon has figured out where the devil lives. ("You knew, didn't you?") On the lines provided, write a sentence that tells where evil can be found.

_____

_____

DISCUSSION GUIDES

Analyzing the Use of Symbols

1. When Jack comes raiding for fire, Piggy says, "When I saw Jack I was sure he'd go for the conch. Can't think why." In terms of symbolism, why would you expect Jack to "go for the conch"? In what way do real dictators "go for the conch" when they assume power?

2. It was pointed out in the lesson that Simon represents a mystic or prophet who can see things clearly. The boys are afraid of "the beast" on the mountain, but Simon, who is very timid, says, "I think we ought to climb the mountain. What else is there to do?" How is this in keeping with Simon's role as a prophet?

3. During the struggle for civil rights, Martin Luther King said, "I have been to the mountaintop." In what ways are Dr. King's mountain and Simon's mountain the same? How was Martin Luther King a prophet symbol?

Interpreting the Chapter

4. The lesson spoke of "Everyman" characters—characters who represent the common people such as you and me. In what ways is Ralph an "Everyman" character?

5. The boys hope that adults will see their fire and come to save them. In the end, a naval officer from a British cruiser does come to rescue the boys. Then he goes back to fighting his war. Some critics have said that this raises the question: "Now, who will save the adults?" What is meant by this question?

6. Some critics feel that *Lord of the Flies* is similar to the story of Adam and Eve in the Garden of Eden. How are the stories similar?

7. William Golding said that he would have liked Ralph "to make it," but that the "nice guy" frequently loses. How does this apply to what you have read?

Analyzing the Author's Technique

8. The author uses children to portray problems of the adult world. Why may this be a better way of getting his message across than using adults?

9. William Golding seems to go out of his way to create the most disgusting images possible of the death of the pig and the flies afterward. Was this necessary? How would it change the meaning of the story if he just said, "The boys killed the pig and placed its head on a pole as an offering to the beast"?

10. The pig's head speaks to Simon in a tone you would not expect from a devil. Why do you suppose William Golding chose to use the tone he did? (Review the last six or seven paragraphs of the chapter where you are told whom the head sounds like.)

WRITING EXERCISE

Choose a favorite comic strip and in two short paragraphs describe what you consider to be a *character symbol* and an *action symbol*.

Example: In the comic strip "Blondie," Dagwood is a character symbol. He stands for all of the well-meaning but ineffectual pushovers in the world who never quite manage to assert themselves with anyone.

Dagwood frequently races out the door in the morning on his way to work. This is an action symbol which, in a comic vein, represents the difficulty we all have of getting started in the morning.

Unit 12
**Identifying Themes
in Literature**

Huckleberry Finn

Introduction

What can be more satisfying than life on a raft? It's hard to believe that a body could ever grow weary of a lazy excursion down the Mississippi River where the air is so mild you can go without clothes, and the most taxing question of the moment is whether to slide into the water for another dip or put out the fishing lines first. Such is the life of Huckleberry Finn, who is surely the most appealing hero in American folklore.

Huckleberry Finn is a fourteen-year-old boy who instinctively rebels against being "sivilized." In a small Southern town of the 1840s, being civilized means wearing clothes that make you feel all cramped up and living "so dismal regular and decent" that a boy couldn't stand it. The civilizing influence in Huck's life is the Widow Douglas, who has unofficially adopted Huck to provide him with a Christian home.

Unfortunately, just as Huck is getting sort of used to the widow's ways, his drunken father returns from an extended binge and kidnaps him. The two of them live in a crude cabin in a thickly wooded area on the Illinois side of the Mississippi River. Except for the beatings, Huck enjoys this vacation away from civilization. But when his father goes off for days at a time and leaves him locked up in the cabin, or chases him around the room brandishing a clasp knife in a drunken hallucination, Huck decides he has had enough. With an elaborate plan designed to make it look as though he's been murdered, Huck makes his escape downriver.

Huck's first stop is Jackson's Island, where he is startled and shocked to meet Jim, a slave belonging to the Widow Douglas's sister, Miss Watson. Jim has run off after overhearing Miss Watson's plans to sell him to a New Orleans slave dealer.

Huck swears not to turn Jim in, and this creates a moral dilemma for him throughout the story. In the mid-1800s, when this story takes place, slavery was backed by the laws of property and was generally supported by society—especially in the southern slave states. According to what he has been taught all his life, Huck's conscience dictates that he must return Jim to his owner.

But their shared experiences on the river create a feeling of brotherhood between them. After much soul-searching, Huck decides not to betray Jim. This is an important step in his rebellion against social pressures that result in injustice.

Huck and Jim fix up the raft with a wigwam of sorts and a firebox, and head for Cairo, Illinois, where the Mississippi and the Ohio Rivers meet. At this point, they plan to buy passage on a steamboat up the Ohio River to deliver Huck and, more importantly, Jim, to the Free States. Their plan is thwarted, however, when a thick fog and a swift current conspire to carry them past Cairo in the night. Since their raft cannot be paddled upstream, against the current, they must continue downriver, proceeding deeper and deeper into slave country.

The chapter in this unit begins with a glimpse at Huck's and Jim's lazy progress down the Mississippi River. Navigating at night and lying low by day, they pass the time swimming, fishing, or just lying on their backs, speculating whether the stars in the night sky "was made or only just happened." It is this mood of carefree tranquility that most people associate with *Huckleberry Finn*. Their serene existence is disrupted, however, by the intrusion of two shady characters—the duke and the king—whom Huck rescues from an angry mob. They board the raft and promptly set about making themselves at home. Sizing up Huck and Jim as a couple of country bumpkins, the two frauds pass themselves off as the descendants of royalty and "allow" Huck and Jim to treat them as such. Huck has seen their type before, but his philosophy toward such characters reveals a maturity far beyond his years. This chapter is a good example of how the author expresses serious themes and social criticism within a comic framework.

The author, Samuel Langhorne Clemens—or Mark Twain, as he chose to call himself—was born in 1835 and grew up in Hannibal, Missouri, a small town on the Mississippi River. As a young man, he worked as a riverboat pilot—one of the most glamorous occupations of the time. Migrating out West during the Civil War, he worked as a printer and established a reputation as a humorist with short newspaper pieces inspired by the folk stories of the western frontier. *Huckleberry Finn*, which has been called a central document of American culture, was written in fits and starts over a period of eight years. It was finished only after a long summer visit to the scenes of his boyhood—a visit which apparently refueled Twain's creative energy.

A Glossary of River Language and Other Expressions

   camp meeting: a religious revival meeting, usually held in a tent

   chute: a narrow channel to the mainland with swift-flowing water

   Dauphin: a French word referring to the eldest son of a king, who is the heir to the throne

   galluses: suspenders

galoot: an awkward, ungainly person

jour printer: short for journeyman printer; one who works by the day and is not yet a master printer

mesmerism: hypnotism

nation as in, "I'm *nation* sorry": a euphemism for "damnation"

phrenology: character analysis based on a study of the subject's skull

scow: a large, flat-bottomed boat with square ends used for carrying freight

sweep: a long oar mounted in a bracket and used to propel or steer a boat

towhead: a small island or obstruction in a river

Identifying Themes
in Literature

A theme is, simply, a central idea in a piece of writing. It's easy to find the theme in nonfiction because it's stated in black and white right in the title or the first paragraph. For instance, if the theme of an essay is a defense of capital punishment, the article may be titled "In Defense of Capital Punishment." Similarly, the theme of a report on the evils of cigarette smoking will be clearly expressed in a topic sentence such as, "Scientific evidence has proved that cigarette smoking is a major cause of lung cancer."

Identifying themes in fiction, however, is not quite as straightforward. This is because fictional themes deal not so much with bald statements of fact as with feelings, attitudes and values about life. Furthermore, literary themes are not stated directly, but, rather, are implied by the story. It is for this reason that many students mistakenly conclude that themes in literature are something an English teacher pulls out of a hat, and which only serve to make the study of literature exasperating.

This is, of course, not the case at all. As a matter of fact, identifying the themes, which means understanding what the story is really about, adds tremendously to the enjoyment of fiction. You have probably recognized certain themes yourself without even being aware of it. If you've read *Romeo and Juliet*, or have seen the play or movie, you probably deplored the senseless feuding that led to the deaths of the young lovers; this is one of the major themes of the story. A favorite moment in *The Wizard of Oz* is the scene in which the wizard gives courage to the lion, a heart to the tinman, and a brain to the scarecrow. Of course the wizard, who turns out to be a humbug, cannot really give such things away; people must find these things within themselves. This is the theme of the story and this is what makes the movie so meaningful that people watch it over and over again.

It is important to be able to recognize themes in literature because they give an added dimension to our enjoyment of a story. For instance, it is *entertaining* to read about a boy who travels down the Mississippi River on a raft; but the story becomes *meaningful* to us on a more intimate level when viewed in the light of its theme—an escape from civilization. None of us is likely to travel by raft down the Mississippi, but it's a good bet that all of us, at one time or another, will want to run away from the hypocrisy and corruptness of civilization. A theme, then, is an abstract concept made concrete by a story. Or, putting it another way, a story is about imaginary characters, but a theme is an idea in the story that can be applied in some way to you and me.

The more you read, the easier it is to identify themes in literature. But it helps to be aware of some universal themes and some of the accepted conventions (that is, ways of doing things) that help reveal the underlying themes of a story. We will talk about three of the ways in which an author expresses a theme: 1) through character; 2) through actions and events, and 3) through symbols and imagery.

1. **Themes Expressed through Characters.** The characters in a story, especially the main characters, are almost always used to help develop theme. One of the most common themes that is presented through character is a young person's transformation from child to adult. This is a story of lost innocence and the dawning realization that other people and things are not always what they seem to be. A child assumes that the world is a just place; an adult knows that it is not. This kind of theme follows the character's disillusionment upon discovering that the world is not what it should be, and that character's coming to terms with some new knowledge. In *Great Expectations* by Charles Dickens, this transformation takes place in the young boy Pip.

Another common theme represented by the characters in a story is inhumanity. It is an appalling but true fact that for as long as anyone can remember, people have treated one another cruelly. We have all seen instances of this even in our own limited experiences, and probably every one of us has felt, if only fleetingly, the urge to mistreat another person. Because this unenviable impulse is common to us all, it is a favorite theme in literature; like growing up, it is something we all recognize. Alex Haley's book *Roots*, which relates the horrors of life on a slave ship, is a good example of the theme of inhumanity.

The character of Huck Finn illustrates another popular theme in literature—escape. In order to escape from his father, who is the town drunkard, and a respectable widow who is determined to "civilize" him, Huck travels down the Mississippi River on a raft with an escaped slave named Jim. The theme here has to do with Huck's escape from civilization, or society, which he finds too confining. In the following passage, how is the character of Huck used to suggest this theme?

> . . . we lit the pipes, and dangled our legs in the water, and talked about all kinds of things—we was always naked, day and night, whenever the mosquitoes would let us—the new clothes Buck's folks made for me was too good to be comfortable, and besides I didn't go much on clothes, nohow.
>
> Sometimes we'd have that whole river all to ourselves for the longest time. Yonder was the banks and the islands, across the

water; and maybe a spark—which was a candle in a cabin window; and sometimes on the water you could see a spark or two—on a raft or a scow, you know; and maybe you could hear a fiddle or a song coming over from one of them crafts. It's lovely to live on a raft.

The fact that Huck and Jim try to avoid wearing clothes while they're on the raft indicates that they are at odds with the trappings of civilization. Huck says he doesn't feel comfortable in clothes at any time, suggesting that deep down he prefers the natural to the civilized state. Notice, too, how the lonesomeness of the river appeals to Huck. "It's lovely to live on a raft," he says, after describing to the reader how secluded they are, with the whole river all to themselves. Obviously, Huck is the kind of person who likes to be left alone, and it is not hard to visualize him as a hermit.

Should you find other references to an escape from civilization in your reading, as you do throughout *Huckleberry Finn*, you would have good reason to believe that this is a theme of the story. And if you find that this theme is being reinforced by other symbols and allusions that enlarge upon the same idea, you can be certain that you are dealing with a major theme.

2. Themes Expressed through Actions and Events. Certain actions and events are so appropriate for expressing a particular theme that, when you come across them in your reading, you can almost always count on their being thematically significant.

One of the most common of these is a natural disaster, such as a flood or a hurricane, or even just a raging thunderstorm. An event like this is frequently used by authors to develop the theme of human frailty in the face of nature, or nature's total indifference to human preferences.

Wars and revolutions are often used to bring out the theme of social change. Wars bring changes—most notably, the breakdown of established customs and ways of thinking. No matter who wins, a country is never quite the same after a war as before it. The Civil War in the United States brought an end to the gracious lifestyle of the big Southern plantations. World War I marked the end of the Victorian Age in England, an era marked by sharply defined social classes and excessive prudery, and the beginning of a more liberated, egalitarian society. The theme of social change is especially significant in the historical novel. Historical novels are traditionally set in an era of conflict involving the breakdown of one society and the building of another. When a war or revolution figures in a story, try to decide how this event changes the social order. This idea may be emphasized by radical changes in the characters' lifestyles, values, and even fashions. If you find this to be so, then social change is undoubtedly a major theme of the story.

Another action that is often a good clue to identifying themes in literature is the journey. When a journey makes up a significant portion of a book, you can be sure it is important in developing a theme.

A journey can take many forms—in *Moby Dick*, it takes the form of a voyage on a whaling ship. In a story by Nathaniel Hawthorne called "Young Goodman Brown," the journey consists only of a midnight walk from the town into the forest. *Huckleberry Finn* also contains an important journey. In the following passage, what form does this journey take?

Two or three days and nights went by; I reckon I might say they swum by, they slid along so quiet and smooth and lovely. Here is the way we put in the time. It was a monstrous big river down there—sometimes a mile and a half wide; we run nights, and laid up and hid daytimes; soon as night was most gone we stopped navigating and tied up—nearly always in the dead water under a towhead; and then cut young cottonwoods and willows, and hid the raft with them.

This journey takes the form of a raft trip down a river. A journey can be an escape *from* something as well as a quest *for* something. In *Huckleberry Finn* it is an escape, with Huck trying to escape from civilization and Jim, the runaway slave, trying to escape to freedom. The river journey adds to the escape theme which we have just seen expressed in Huck's character.

In deciding how this raft trip develops theme, the reader should be alert for symbols and imagery that help explain what is driving Huck away from civilization.

3. **Themes Expressed through Symbols and Imagery.** Themes in a story are frequently suggested and developed through the author's use of symbolism and imagery. The elements of a story are often symbolic of something else—that is, they have added meanings above and beyond their literal meaning. Imagery develops tone and mood in a passage, thus suggesting feelings and attitudes toward the material. When certain symbols and images are repeated in the same story, they probably contribute to the development of a common theme.

In *Huckleberry Finn,* the author uses symbols and imagery to contrast the goodness of nature with the corruptness of civilization. He does this by establishing a special tone and mood for the river, and another for civilization. What impression do you get of nature, represented here by the river, from the following passage?

> . . . we slid into the river and had a swim, so as to freshen up and cool off; then we set down on the sandy bottom where the water was about knee deep, and watched the daylight come. Not a sound anywheres—perfectly still—just like the whole world was asleep, only sometimes the bullfrogs a-cluttering, maybe.

The mood of this passage is soothing and quiet, and the tone is almost reverent. The river is like a sanctuary for Huck, a place of repose and safety. Compare this with his references to civilization, found further on in the same descriptive passage:

> . . . and you make out a log cabin in the edge of the woods, away on the bank on t'other side of the river, being a woodyard, likely, and piled by them cheats so you can throw a dog through it any-wheres; then the nice breeze springs up, and comes fanning you from over there, so cool and fresh and sweet to smell on account of the woods and the flowers; but sometimes not that way, because

they've left dead fish laying around, gars and such, and they do get pretty rank; and next you've got the full day, and everything smiling in the sun, and the songbirds just going it!

Wherever civilization has left its mark, life is rank and corrupt. The wood-yard on the other side of the river is piled by "cheats" who stack wood so loosely "you can throw a dog through it"—in other words, a customer buying lumber stacked this way will get less than he thinks he's getting. On the banks of the river, men have thrown away gars—a kind of fish often regarded as junk-fish—leaving them to rot in the sun. Their stench over-whelms the sweet smells of the woods and flowers.

The contrasting images which the author uses to depict nature and civili-zation contribute to the theme of the story, which is Huck's escape from civilization. We are beginning to understand what it is about society—besides wearing clothes—that so repels Huck.

Symbolism is also at work developing the theme of *Huckleberry Finn*. The raft and the river symbolize freedom and safety for Huck and Jim. Huck encounters danger, trouble and duplicity whenever he steps ashore; his only escape from this kind of world is offered by the raft and the river—hence their thematic meanings.

Considered as a whole, the characters, actions and events, and imagery and symbolism in *Huckleberry Finn* all work together to develop the same theme—that of Huck's attempt to escape civilized society. The different attitudes toward nature and civilization are established in the first paragraph of the chapter you are about to read. And as you continue the chapter, it becomes even clearer that nothing but trouble comes from shore. This idea is made concrete in the persons of two unsavory characters, the "Duke" and the "King," who board the raft and upset the peace and tranquility of Huck and Jim's idyllic life on the river.

As you read the chapter:

- Identify the theme of the passage in which Huck describes what he and Jim do after breakfast.

- Notice what theme the duke represents in the passage in which he explains why he was running away.

- Be aware of the passage in which Huck explains why it's impor-tant that everyone on a raft be friends.

- Pay special attention to the last paragraph of the chapter in which Huck lets on to the reader that he is not taken in by the "Duke" and the "King."

Huckleberry Finn
Mark Twain

CHAPTER 19

Two or three days and nights went by; I reckon I might say they swum by, they slid along so quiet and smooth and lovely. Here is the way we put in the time. It was a monstrous big river down there—sometimes a mile and a half wide; we run nights, and laid up and hid daytimes; soon as night was most gone we stopped navigating and tied up—nearly always in the dead water under a towhead; and then cut young cottonwoods and willows, and hid the raft with them. Then we set out the lines. Next we slid into the river and had a swim, so as to freshen up and cool off; then we set down on the sandy bottom where the water was about knee deep, and watched the daylight come. Not a sound anywheres—perfectly still—just like the whole world was asleep, only sometimes the bullfrogs a-cluttering, maybe. The first thing to see, looking away over the water, was a kind of dull line—that was the woods on t'other side; you couldn't make nothing else out; then a pale place in the sky; then more paleness spreading around; then the river softened up away off, and warn't black any more, but gray; you could see little dark spots drifting along ever so far away—trading scows, and such things; and long black streaks—rafts: sometimes you could hear a sweep screaking; or jumbled-up voices, it was so still, and sounds come so far; and by and by you could see a streak on the water which you know by the look of the streak that there's a snag there in a swift current which breaks on it and makes that streak look that way; and you see the mist curl up off of the water, and the east reddens up, and the river, and you make out a log cabin in the edge of the woods, away on the bank on t'other side of the river, being a woodyard, likely, and piled by them cheats so you can throw a dog through it anywheres; then the nice breeze springs up, and comes fanning you from over there, so cool and fresh and sweet to smell on account of the woods and the flowers; but sometimes not that way, because they've left dead fish laying around, gars and such, and they do get pretty rank; and next you've got the full day, and everything smiling in the sun, and the songbirds just going it!

A little smoke couldn't be noticed now, so we would take some fish off of the lines and cook up a hot breakfast. And afterwards we would watch the lonesomeness of the river, and kind of lazy along, and by and by lazy off to sleep. Wake up by and by, and look to see what done it, and maybe see a steamboat coughing along upstream, so far off towards the other side you couldn't tell nothing about her only whether she was a stern-wheel or side-wheel; then for about an hour there wouldn't be nothing to hear nor nothing to see—just solid lonesomeness. Next you'd see a raft sliding by, away off yonder, and maybe a galoot on it chopping, because they're most always doing it on a raft; you'd see the ax flash and come down—you don't hear nothing; you see that ax go up again, and by the time it's above the man's head then you hear the *k'chunk!*—it had took all that time to come over the water. So we would put in the day, lazying around, listening to the stillness. Once there was a thick fog, and the rafts and things that went by was beating tin pans so the steamboats wouldn't run over them. A scow or a raft went by so close we could hear them talking and cussing and laughing—heard them plain; but we couldn't see no sign of them; it made you feel crawly; it was like spirits carrying on that way in the air. Jim said he believed it was spirits; but I says:

"No; spirits wouldn't say, 'Dern the dern fog.' "

Soon as it was night out we shoved; when we got her out to about the middle we let her alone, and let her float wherever the current wanted her to; then we lit the pipes, and dangled our legs in the water, and talked about all kinds of things—we was always naked, day and night, whenever the mosquitoes would let us—the new clothes Buck's folks made for me was too good to be comfortable, and besides I didn't go much on clothes, nohow.

Sometimes we'd have that whole river all to ourselves for the longest time. Yonder was the banks and the islands, across the water; and maybe a spark—which was a candle in a cabin window; and sometimes on the water you could see a spark or two—on a raft or a scow, you know; and maybe you could hear a fiddle or a song coming over from one of them crafts. It's lovely to live on a raft. We had the sky up there, all speckled with stars, and we used to lay on our backs and look up at them, and discuss about whether they was made or only just happened. Jim he allowed they was made, but I allowed they happened; I judged it would have took too long to *make* so many. Jim said the moon could 'a' *laid* them; well, that looked kind of reasonable, so I didn't say nothing against it, because I've seen a frog lay most as many, so of course it could be done. We used to watch the stars that fell, too, and see them streak down. Jim allowed they'd got spoiled and was hove out of the nest.

Once or twice of a night we would see a steamboat slipping along in the dark, and now and then she would belch a whole world of sparks up out of her chimbleys, and they would rain down in the river and look awful pretty; then she would turn a corner and her lights would wink out and her pow-wow shut off and leave the river still again; and by and by her waves would get to us, a long time after she was gone, and joggle the raft a bit, and after that you wouldn't hear nothing for you couldn't tell how long, except maybe frogs or something.

After midnight the people on shore went to bed, and then for two or three hours the shores was black—no more sparks in the cabin windows. These sparks was our clock—the first one that showed again meant morning was coming, so we hunted a place to hide and tie up right away.

One morning about daybreak I found a canoe and crossed over a chute to the main shore—it was only two hundred yards—and paddled about a mile up a crick amongst the cypress woods, to see if I couldn't get some berries. Just as I was passing a place where a kind of a cowpath crossed the crick, here comes a couple of men tearing up the path as tight as they could foot it. I thought I was a goner, for whenever anybody was after anybody I judged it was *me*—or maybe Jim. I was about to dig out from there in a hurry, but they was pretty close to me then, and sung out and begged me to save their lives—said they hadn't been doing nothing, and was being chased for it— said there was men and dogs a-coming. They wanted to jump right in, but I says:

"Don't you do it. I don't hear the dogs and horses yet; you've got time to crowd through the brush and get up the crick a little ways; then you take to the water and wade down to me and get in—that'll throw the dogs off the scent."

They done it, and soon as they was aboard I lit out for our towhead, and in about five or ten minutes we heard the dogs and the men away off, shouting. We heard them come along towards the crick, but couldn't see them; they seemed to stop and fool around awhile; then, as we got further and further away all the time, we couldn't hardly hear them at all; by the time we had left a mile of woods behind us and struck the river, everything was quiet, and we paddled over to the towhead and hid in the cottonwoods and was safe.

One of these fellows was about seventy or upwards, and had a bald head and very gray whiskers. He had an old battered-up slouch hat on, and a greasy blue woolen shirt, and ragged old blue jeans britches stuffed into his boot tops, and home-knit galluses—no, he only had one. He had an old long-tailed blue jeans coat with slick brass buttons flung over his arm, and both of them had big, fat, ratty-looking carpetbags.

The other fellow was about thirty, and dressed about as ornery. After breakfast we all laid off and talked, and the first thing that come out was that these chaps didn't know one another.

"What got you into trouble?" says the baldhead to t'other chap.

"Well, I'd been selling an article to take the tartar off the teeth—and it does take it off, too, and generly the enamel along with it—but I stayed about one night longer than I ought to, and was just in the act of sliding out when I ran across you on the trail this side of town, and you told me they were coming, and begged me to help you to get off. So I told you I was expecting trouble myself, and would scatter out *with* you. That's the whole yarn—what's yourn?"

"Well, I'd ben a-runnin' a little temperance revival thar 'bout a week, and was the pet of the women folks, big and little, for I was makin' it mighty warm for the rummies, I *tell* you, and takin' as much as five or six dollars a night—ten cents a head, children free—and business a-growin' all the time, when somehow or another a little report got around last night that I had a way of puttin' in my time with a private jug on the sly. Somebody rousted me out this mornin', and told me the people was getherin' on the quiet with their dogs and horses, and they'd be along pretty soon and give me 'bout half an hour's start, and then run me down if they could; and if they got me they'd tar and feather me and ride me on a rail, sure. I didn't wait for no breakfast—I warn't hungry."

"Old man," said the young one, "I reckon we might double-team it together; what do you think?"

"I ain't undisposed. What's your line—mainly?"

"Jour printer by trade; do a little in patent medicines; theater actor—tragedy, you know; take a turn to mesmerism and phrenology when there's a chance; teach singing-geography school for a change; sling a lecture some-times—oh, I do lots of things—most anything that comes handy, so it ain't work. What's your lay?"

"I've done considerble in the doctoring way in my time. Layin' on o' hands is my best holt—for cancer and paralysis, and sich things; and I k'n tell a fortune pretty good when I've got somebody along to find out the facts for me. Preachin's my line, too, and workin' camp meetin's, and missionaryin' around."

Nobody never said anything for a while; then the young man hove a sigh and says:

"Alas!"

"What're you alassin' about?" says the baldhead.

"To think I should have lived to be leading such a life, and be degraded down into such company." And he begun to wipe the corner of his eye with a rag.

"Dern your skin, ain't the company good enough for you?" says the baldhead, pretty pert and uppish.

"Yes, it *is* good enough for me; it's as good as I deserve; for who fetched me so low when I was so high? *I* did myself. I don't blame *you*, gentlemen—far from it; I don't blame anybody. I deserve it all. Let the cold world do its worst; one thing I know—there's a grave somewhere for me. The world may go on just as it's always done, and take everything from me—loved ones, property, everything; but it can't take that. Some day I'll lie down in it and forget it all, and my poor broken heart will be at rest." He went on a-wiping.

"Drot your pore broken heart," says the baldhead; "what are you heaving your pore broken heart at *us* f'r? *We* hain't done nothing."

"No, I know you haven't. I ain't blaming you, gentlemen. I brought myself down—yes, I did it myself. It's right I should suffer—perfectly right—I don't make any moan."

"Brought you down from whar? Whar was you brought down from?"

"Ah, you would not believe me; the world never believes—let it pass—'tis no matter. The secret of my birth—"

"The secret of your birth! Do you mean to say—"

"Gentlemen," says the young man, very solemn, "I will reveal it to you, for I feel I may have confidence in you. By rights I am a duke!"

Jim's eyes bugged out when he heard that; and I reckon mine did, too. Then the baldhead says: "No! you can't mean it?"

"Yes. My great-grandfather, eldest son of the Duke of Bridgewater, fled to this country about the end of the last century, to breathe the pure air of freedom; married here, and died, leaving a son, his own father dying about the same time. The second son of the late duke seized the titles and estates—the infant real duke was ignored. I am the lineal descendant of that infant—I am the rightful Duke of Bridgewater; and here am I, forlorn, torn from my high estate, hunted of men, despised by the cold world, ragged, worn, heartbroken, and degraded to the companionship of felons on a raft!"

Jim pitied him ever so much, and so did I. We tried to comfort him, but he said it warn't much use, he couldn't be much comforted; said if we was a mind to acknowledge him, that would do him more good than most anything else; so we said we would, if he would tell us how. He said we ought to bow when we spoke to him, and say "Your Grace," or "My Lord," or "Your Lordship"—and he wouldn't mind it if we called him plain "Bridgewater," which, he said, was a title anyway, and not a name; and one of us ought to wait on him at dinner, and do any little thing for him he wanted done.

Well, that was all easy, so we done it. All through dinner Jim stood around and waited on him, and says, "Will yo' Grace have some o' dis or some o' dat?" and so on, and a body could see it was mighty pleasing to him.

But the old man got pretty silent by and by—didn't have much to say, and didn't look pretty comfortable over all that petting that was going on around that duke. He seemed to have something on his mind. So, along in the afternoon, he says:

"Looky here, Bilgewater," he says, "I'm nation sorry for you, but you ain't the only person that's had troubles like that."

"No?"

"No, you ain't. You ain't the only person that's ben snaked down wrongfully out'n a high place."

"Alas!"

"No, you ain't the only person that's had a secret of his birth." And, by jings, *he* begins to cry.

"Hold! What do you mean?"

"Bilgewater, kin I trust you?" says the old man, still sort of sobbing.

"To the bitter death!" He took the old man by the hand and squeezed it, and says, "That secret of your being: speak!"

"Bilgewater, I am the late Dauphin!"

You bet you, Jim and me stared this time. Then the duke says:

"You are what?"

"Yes, my friend, it is too true—your eyes is lookin' at this very moment on the pore disappeared Dauphin, Looy the Seventeen, son of Looy the Sixteen and Marry Antonette."

"You! At your age! No! You mean you're the late Charlemagne; you must be six or seven hundred years old, at the very least."

"Trouble has done it, Bilgewater, trouble has done it; trouble has brung these gray hairs and this premature balditude. Yes, gentlemen, you see before you, in blue jeans and misery, the wanderin', exiled, trampled-on, and sufferin' rightful King of France."

Well, he cried and took on so that me and Jim didn't know hardly what to do, we was so sorry—and so glad and proud we'd got him with us, too. So we set in, like we done before with the duke, and tried to comfort *him*. But he said it warn't no use, nothing but to be dead and done with it all could do him any good; though he said it often made him feel easier and better for a while if people treated him according to his rights, and got down on one knee to speak to him, and always called him "Your Majesty," and waited on him first at meals, and didn't set down in his presence till he asked them. So Jim and me set to majestying him, and doing this and that and t'other for him, and standing up till he told us we might set down. This done him heaps of good, and so he got cheerful and comfortable. But the duke kind of soured on him, and didn't look a bit satisfied with the way things was going; still, the king acted real friendly towards him, and said the duke's great-grandfather and all the other Dukes of Bilgewater was a good deal thought of by *his* father, and was allowed to come to the palace considerable; but the duke stayed huffy a good while, till by and by the king says:

"Like as not we got to be together a blamed long time on this h-yer raft, Bilgewater, and so what's the use o' your bein' sour? It'll only make things oncomfortable. It ain't my fault I warn't born a duke, it ain't your fault you warn't born a king—so what's the use to worry? Make the best o' things the way you find 'em, says I—that's my motto. This ain't no bad thing that we've struck here—plenty grub and an easy life—come, give us your hand, duke, and le's all be friends."

The duke done it, and Jim and me was pretty glad to see it. It took away all the uncomfortableness and we felt mighty good over it, because it would 'a' been a miserable business to have any unfriendliness on the raft; for what you want, above all things, on a raft, is for everybody to be satisfied, and feel right and kind towards the others.

It didn't take me long to make up my mind that these liars warn't no kings nor dukes at all, but just low-down humbugs and frauds. But I never said nothing, never let on; kept it to myself; it's the best way; then you don't have no quarrels, and don't get into no trouble. If they wanted us to call them kings and dukes, I hadn't no objections, 'long as it would keep peace in the family; and it warn't no use to tell Jim, so I didn't tell him. If I never learnt nothing else out of pap, I learnt that the best way to get along with his kind of people is to let them have their own way.

Unit 12

Huckleberry Finn

- Comprehension Questions
- Identifying Themes in Literature
- Discussion Guides
- Writing Exercise

COMPREHENSION QUESTIONS

For each of the following statements and questions, select the option containing the most complete or most accurate answer.

1. Huck and Jim's method of traveling was
(d) ☐ a. travel by day, hide at night.
    ☐ b. keep to midstream, out of view of the shore.
    ☐ c. run an hour, rest an hour.
    ☐ d. travel at night, hide by day.

2. At this point in their journey, the river was
(b) ☐ a. very wide.   ☐ c. filled with rapids.
    ☐ b. very narrow.   ☐ d. winding and twisted.

3. Huck and Jim would hide the raft by
(a) ☐ a. submerging it slightly.
    ☐ b. covering it with cottonwood trees.
    ☐ c. covering it with a camouflage net.
    ☐ d. pulling it up on the bank.

4. From Huck's description of life on the river, a reader must conclude
(f) that he
    ☐ a. found it tiring.   ☐ c. enjoyed it.
    ☐ b. was bored by it.   ☐ d. was in constant fear.

5. During the day, the river was
(c) ☐ a. deserted most of the time.
    ☐ b. full of traffic.
    ☐ c. completely without sound.
    ☐ d. haunted by spirits.

6. At the beginning of the chapter the author establishes a tone that can
(i) best be described as
    ☐ a. violent.   ☐ c. peaceful.
    ☐ b. tense with anticipation.   ☐ d. feverishly active.

7. Huck describes life on the river as
(e) ☐ a. lazy.   ☐ c. dangerous.
    ☐ b. uneventful.   ☐ d. suspenseful.

8. The expression "listening to the stillness" is an example of a figure of
(k) speech called
    ☐ a. hyperbole (an exaggeration).
    ☐ b. simile (a comparison).
    ☐ c. meiosis (understatement).
    ☐ d. oxymoron (seems to contradict itself).

9. Speaking of stars, Huck says, "Jim he allowed they was made" and later,
(k) "I didn't say nothing against it." These are examples of the author's
    use of
    ☐ a. allegory.   ☐ c. understatement.
    ☐ b. dialect.   ☐ d. exaggeration.

10. Huck and Jim watched "sparks" on the river—candles in cabin windows.
(d) They used these "sparks" as a kind of
    ☐ a. clock.   ☐ c. danger signal.
    ☐ b. weather forecaster.   ☐ d. guidepost.

11. The fact that Huck, without questions, helped two fugitives shows
(j) that he
    ☐ a. is foolish.
    ☐ b. is a schemer.
    ☐ c. has too much self-confidence.
    ☐ d. has a generous nature.

12. Huck tells the two men being chased how to throw the dogs off their
(h) scent. This shows Huck to be
    ☐ a. an experienced escapee.   ☐ c. a shrewd schemer.
    ☐ b. trail wise.   ☐ d. overly cautious.

13. The ages of the two men who came aboard the raft were about
(b) ☐ a. 70 and 30.   ☐ c. 40 or 50 for both.
    ☐ b. 50 and 20.   ☐ d. 25 or 30 for both.

14. Both men who came on board the raft were
(j) ☐ a. honest men down on their luck.
    ☐ b. poor hoboes.
    ☐ c. reformed con men.
    ☐ d. swindlers.

15. " 'Dern your skin, ain't the company good enough for you?' says the
(l) baldhead, pretty *pert and uppish.*" *Pert and uppish* means
    ☐ a. angry and tearful.   ☐ c. bold and arrogant.
    ☐ b. head high and smiling.   ☐ d. bright and cheerful.

16. The younger man says he is the Duke of Bridgewater. The other man
(k) calls him "Bilgewater." This is an example of
    ☐ a. comedy.   ☐ c. drama.
    ☐ b. irony.   ☐ d. poetic justice.

17. The two men conspired
(a) ☐ a. to get rid of Huck and Jim.
    ☐ b. to use the raft in their schemes.
    ☐ c. to get Huck and Jim to wait on them.
    ☐ d. to turn Jim in as a runaway slave.

18. Because of the way each man played up to the other's lies, you might
(h) infer that
    ☐ a. both were a bit foolish.
    ☐ b. they understood one another.
    ☐ c. each was afraid of the other.
    ☐ d. they were being polite.

19. Jim pitied the Duke of Bridgewater. From this reaction you would
(g) take Jim to be
    ☐ a. naive and goodhearted.
    ☐ b. a schemer himself.
    ☐ c. not quite honest.
    ☐ d. devoted and subservient.

20. Both the duke and the Dauphin could cry at will. This shows that they
(g) were
    ☐ a. mentally retarded.   ☐ c. good actors.
    ☐ b. soft-hearted.   ☐ d. under great stress.

21. The older man announced that he was the King of France because
(f) ☐ a. he liked the sound of it.
    ☐ b. there was some truth to it.
    ☐ c. he wanted to outrank the duke.
    ☐ d. he was insane.

22. The older man says, ". . . your eyes is lookin' at this very moment on
(i) the pore disappeared Dauphin, Looy the Seventeen, son of Looy the
Sixteen and Marry Antonette." For a "king," this language is
   ☐ a. plainly offensive.
   ☐ b. comically ludicrous.
   ☐ c. high-handed and autocratic.
   ☐ d. modest and cloying.

23. When the older man says that trouble has caused his "*premature* baldi-
(l) tude," *premature* means
   ☐ a. before graying.   ☐ c. complete hair loss.
   ☐ b. before maturing.   ☐ d. coming too soon.

24. Huck was concerned about
(e) ☐ a. keeping peace on the raft.
     ☐ b. getting rid of the men.
     ☐ c. the raft's sinking with four on board.
     ☐ d. where they were all going.

25. Huck figured that letting the two men have their own way would
(c) ☐ a. make the men leave sooner.
     ☐ b. keep him and Jim out of trouble.
     ☐ c. keep them from crying again.
     ☐ d. make him and Jim happier.

Comprehension Skills: a—isolating details; b—recalling specific facts; c—retaining
concepts; d—organizing facts; e—understanding the main idea; f—drawing a
conclusion; g—making a judgment; h—making an inference; i—recognizing tone;
j—understanding characters; k—appreciation of literary forms; l—knowledge of
word meanings.

IDENTIFYING THEMES IN LITERATURE

Practice Exercise A

... we would watch the lonesomeness of the river, and kind of lazy along, and by and by lazy off to sleep. Wake up by and by, and look to see what done it, and maybe see a steamboat coughing along upstream, so far off towards the other side you couldn't tell nothing about her only whether she was a stern-wheel or side-wheel; then for about an hour there wouldn't be nothing to hear nor nothing to see—just solid lonesomeness. Next you'd see a raft sliding by, away off yonder, and maybe a galoot on it chopping, because they're most always doing it on a raft; you'd see the ax flash and come down—you don't hear nothing; you see that ax go up again, and by the time it's above the man's head then you hear the *k'chunk!*—it had took all that time to come over the water. So we would put in the day, lazying around, listening to the stillness.

1. The author establishes a mood in this passage which also expresses a theme. What is this theme?
   - ☐ a. The river prohibits close companionship.
   - ☐ b. There is tranquility in being alone with nature.
   - ☐ c. A river is an active force in civilization.
   - ☐ d. The calm of nature hides many dangers.

2. Two words beginning with *l* are repeated in the passage to help emphasize both the mood and the theme. Find these words and circle them.

Practice Exercise B

"What got you into trouble?" says the baldhead to [the duke].

"Well, I'd been selling an article to take the tartar off the teeth—and it does take it off, too, and generly the enamel along with it—but I stayed about one night longer than I ought to, and was just in the act of sliding out when I ran across you on the trail this side of town, and you told me they were coming, and begged me to help you to get off. So I told you I was expecting trouble myself, and would scatter out *with* you. That's the whole yarn—what's yourn?"

1. What theme is represented by the character of the duke in this passage?
   - ☐ a. Humanity's desperate struggle for survival
   - ☐ b. The loss of innocence in adulthood
   - ☐ c. The process of mental and moral growth
   - ☐ d. The deceitful nature of humankind

2. We noted in the lesson that escape is a major theme in *Huckleberry Finn.* Find at least two colloquial (slang) expressions in this passage that refer to escape and circle them.

Practice Exercise C

[the king] ". . . give us your hand, duke, and le's all be friends."

The duke done it, and Jim and me was pretty glad to see it. It took away all the uncomfortableness and we felt mighty good over it, because it would 'a' been a miserable business to have any unfriendliness on the raft; for what you want, above all things, on a raft, is for everybody to be satisfied, and feel right and kind towards the others.

1. In developing his theme, Twain uses the raft as a symbol of
   - ☐ a. great plans and ambitions.
   - ☐ b. laughter and gaiety.
   - ☐ c. peace and harmony.
   - ☐ d. disillusionment and despair.

2. On the lines provided, copy that part of the passage in which Huck describes the proper atmosphere on a raft.

   _____

   _____

   _____

Practice Exercise D

It didn't take me long to make up my mind that these liars warn't no kings nor dukes at all, but just low-down humbugs and frauds. But I never said nothing, never let on; kept it to myself; it's the best way; then you don't have no quarrels, and don't get into no trouble. If they wanted us to call them kings and dukes, I hadn't no objections, 'long as it would keep peace in the family; and it warn't no use to tell Jim, so I didn't tell him. If I never learnt nothing else out of pap, I learnt that the best way to get along with his kind of people is to let them have their own way.

1. The main idea, or theme, of the above passage might be expressed as
   - ☐ a. "honesty is the best policy."
   - ☐ b. "it doesn't pay to stir up trouble."
   - ☐ c. "if you look for the best in people, you're bound to find it."
   - ☐ d. "each of us is beautiful in our own way."

2. On the lines provided, write the sentence that states Huck's philosophy regarding people like the duke and the king and explains how Huck learned this lesson.

   _____

   _____

DISCUSSION GUIDES

Analyzing Theme

1. The form of *Huckleberry Finn* is based on the "picaresque" novel, or novel of the road. This type of novel consists of a series of episodes, or adventures, that befall the hero on his journey. In what ways is this format particularly appropriate for expressing the theme of escape?

2. Mark Twain prefaces *Huckleberry Finn* with a notice that warns, "Persons attempting to find a motive in this narrative will be prosecuted; persons attempting to find a moral in it will be banished; persons attempting to find a plot in it will be shot." What do you think Twain *did* want his reader to find in *Huckleberry Finn?*

Interpreting the Chapter

3. Do you think that Huck is mature for his age (fourteen)? Support your opinion with specific references to things that Huck does or says.

4. Try to imagine Huck Finn as an adult. Describe him—his occupation, lifestyle, and so on—at about age thirty. Explain why some of his characteristics and values may remain the same and why some may change.

5. Do you think that Mark Twain is guilty of stereotyping in his characterization of Jim? Point to passages in the chapter to support your opinion.

6. *Huckleberry Finn* was once banned by certain libraries and schools for being "coarse," "inelegant" and "trash." Based on the chapter you have read, what exactly do you think these authorities objected to?

7. One critic said of *Huckleberry Finn* that, "One can read it at ten and then annually ever after, and each year find that it is as fresh as the year before, that it has changed only in becoming somewhat larger." How might a reader's appreciation of *Huckleberry Finn* grow over the years?

Analyzing the Author's Technique

8. Why do you suppose Mark Twain chose a raft trip down the Mississippi River as an appropriate vehicle for Huck's escape? If you were writing an up-dated version of *Huckleberry Finn*, what would you choose as the modern-day counterparts to Huck's raft and the Mississippi River?

9. In an explanatory note to *Huckleberry Finn*, the author comments on his use of dialect in the book saying, "The shadings have not been done in a haphazard fashion, or by guesswork; but painstakingly, and with these several forms of speech." How does Twain's use of dialect enhance characterization in *Huckleberry Finn?* What does it contribute to the "flavor" of the story?

10. During his lifetime Mark Twain was revered as "America's funny man" and he is still remembered, first and last, as a humorist. How does his technique in the chapter which you read support this claim to fame?

WRITING EXERCISE

Here is a list of eight popular themes that authors use in their writing:

1. Inhumanity	5. Growing Up
2. War and Social Change	6. Growing Old
3. The Power of Money	7. Confronting the Forces of Nature
4. Escape	8. Searching for a New Life

Pick a theme you would like to use in a story and complete the following steps. Before you begin to write, look at the two examples given below.

Step One: Write a summary paragraph that tells what your story will be about.

Step Two: Choose at least one device to point out the theme to readers—a character, an action or event, an image or a thing. Explain how you will use the device in the story. (Review the lesson, if necessary, to see how this works.)

Step Three: Write a title for your story that points to the theme you have chosen.

Example 1

Theme   Escape from Oppression

Summary Paragraph   The director of security forces in San Arebrabo realizes that the newly elected president is going to use the army to launch a reign of terror in order to establish himself as dictator. He resigns and flees for his life with his wife and children.

Theme Devices	The family is led in their escape by an old ranch hand named Bolivar (Simon Bolivar was the great South American liberator). There is a sea to cross in order to get to safety, reminiscent of the Red Sea in the Bible.
Title	Flight from San Arebrabo

Example 2

Theme	Searching for a New Life
Summary Paragraph	Kat Smith (alias Krazy Kat), a city gang leader, sees his younger brother killed in intergang warfare. He feels there must be a better way to live and sets out to find it.
Theme Devices	Kat, having no real home, finds that as he travels he can spend the night in museums and historical monuments by hiding in them until they close. In these places he discovers the good and bad values from which he can choose to shape a new life.
Title	Krazy Kat Reforms

Unit 13
Analyzing Satire

Breakfast of
Champions

Introduction

In the opening paragraphs of the first chapter of *Breakfast of Champions*, Kurt Vonnegut tells what the story is about:

> This is a tale of a meeting of two lonesome, skinny, fairly old white men on a planet which was dying fast.
>
> One of them was a science-fiction writer named Kilgore Trout. He was a nobody at the time, and he supposed his life was over. He was mistaken. As a consequence of the meeting, he became one of the most beloved and respected human beings in history.
>
> The man he met was an automobile dealer, a *Pontiac* dealer named Dwayne Hoover. Dwayne Hoover was on the brink of going insane.

The book ends before Kilgore Trout becomes beloved and respected, but Vonnegut tells us along the way that Kilgore will one day be recognized by the American Academy of Arts and Science as a pioneer in the field of mental health. Right now he is an unrecognized genius whose philosophy is disguised in science fiction novels that sell only in pornography shops. Kilgore Trout has never been paid for his books.

He has exactly one fan, an eccentric millionaire named Eliot Rosewater who sees to it that Kilgore is invited to the dedication of a new arts center in Midland City. Kilgore brings with him a copy of one of his books, *Now It Can Be Told*, which will have a devastating effect on the other major character in the book, Dwayne Hoover.

Dwayne Hoover is a well-to-do car dealer in Midland City. He owns several Burger Chefs, Holiday Inns and a radio station in addition to "Dwayne Hoover's Exit Eleven Pontiac Village," just off the Interstate. Dwayne is a widower—his wife drank some Drano a few years back—and he has no one in the world except Sparky, a dog that cannot wag its tail, and his mistress, Francine Pefko, who works at the Pontiac Agency. As Vonnegut states, Dwayne Hoover is on the brink of going insane.

Dwayne is the American economic success model, but he confesses to Francine Pefko that he has "lost his way." He tells her, "I need somebody to take me by the hand and lead me out of the woods." Francine suggests that he might be able to get help from the artists who are coming to the opening of the Mildred Barry Memorial Center for the Arts in Midland City. This sets the scene for the fateful meeting between Dwayne and Kilgore Trout.

The chapter in this unit focuses on Dwayne Hoover and his growing madness. Dwayne has recently developed a new symptom, "echolalia," which makes him repeat whatever he hears. It is explained earlier in the book that Dwayne's illness is the result of "bad chemicals" that his body is producing, and we are told of two other classes of people who have suffered from bad chemicals—German Nazis during World War II and presidential assassins.

Only two other characters appear in the chapter. One is Wayne Hoobler, a Black ex-convict recently paroled, whose dream is to work for Dwayne Hoover. He had seen and believed Dwayne's advertisements, "ASK ANYBODY—YOU CAN TRUST DWAYNE." Dwayne has rejected Wayne's plea for a job and, broken-hearted, Wayne hangs around the used car lot talking to himself. Through Wayne Hoobler, Vonnegut reduces stereotyping to the absurd. The image of this character is so preposterous that the reader is forced to reject stereotyping altogether—and this is exactly the author's purpose.

The other character is Patty Keene, a waitress in a Burger Chef where Dwayne has gone for lunch. In the midst of his illness, Dwayne doesn't take much more notice of Patty than he does of Wayne Hoobler. Both characters are in the story simply to enable Vonnegut to get his message across.

Of all the serious themes that Vonnegut throws at his readers, one seems to control the telling of the tale. It is that America has lost its way in its rush into economic and technological success. We have left ruin and violence in our wake, and we have become machines ourselves, robots devoid of free will, programmed to do the things we do. We are loving machines, hating machines, typing and filing machines. It is this revelation contained in Kilgore Trout's novel, that finally drives Dwayne Hoover beserk.

In his preface to *Breakfast of Champions*, Kurt Vonnegut says that he learned his writing trade from Phoebe Hurty. "She was funny," he says. "She was liberating. She taught us to be impolite in conversation not only about sexual matters, but about American history and famous heroes, about the distribution of wealth, about school, about everything." These are the earmarks of every satirist who ever lived—being funny and impolite about important issues that need correcting.

Like most of Vonnegut's work, *Breakfast of Champions* is completely outrageous. It is funny and it is sad. It is insulting and compassionate. It is outstanding modern satire.

Analyzing Satire

Let's assume that you share a room with someone whose favorite decor is "comfortably sloppy." Let's assume further that you are fed up with the mess. There are several ways that you can call attention to the situation; you can use anger, criticism or satire.

>**Anger:** "I can't stand this mess! Either clean it up or get out!"

Since anger usually provokes anger in return, this approach is likely to result in an angry response as the target of your outburst storms out to sulk for the rest of the day.

>**Criticism:** "Honestly, you are the sloppiest person I've ever known."

Because no one likes to be criticized, you can expect your roommate to respond in kind. "Well, you're not so perfect either." Stalemate. But then there is satire.

>**Satire:** "Terry, dear, I can't find the cat. I think she may have gotten lost in the piles of clothes and old magazines you use to decorate our room. Would you please help me look?"

In this case, the use of satire to get your point across makes it harder for someone to take offense. It would be difficult not to smile at your remark, but your point would have hit home just the same. This is the way satire works in literature, too. Satire exposes human follies, pretensions, vices and evils in such a way that one must smile in spite of oneself. It is the only way that most of us can stand to read unpleasant truths about ourselves and our society.

Satire is very old. There is evidence which suggests that the Roman Emperor Augustus passed a law against satire 2,000 years ago—dictators hate satire. Geoffrey Chaucer's *Canterbury Tales*, written in the fourteenth century, is heavy with devastating satire. One of the most famous satires of all time is Jonathan Swift's *Gulliver's Travels* which was written early in the eighteenth century. Nearer to our own time, there are such great satirists as Mark Twain, George Bernard Shaw, Sinclair Lewis and George Orwell.

Not all satirists are novelists; satire can take many forms. You will find much satire in your newspaper. Cartoonists, such as Herblock, Oliphant and Mauldin, are superb satirists. Al Capp's "Lil Abner," G. E. Trudeau's "Doonesbury," and even Charles Schulz's "Peanuts" are loaded with satire. Columnists, such as Art Buchwald, have attained national reputations as satirists. Popular standup comedians have also pelted us with memorable satire—Will Rogers, Lenny Bruce, Mort Sahl, Bill Cosby and Dick Gregory, for example.

It is important to note, however, that humor is only a part of satire. In order for humor to be satire, there must be serious criticism mixed in with the laughter. There must be a sneer or a snarl, or a thinly veiled expression of contempt for something that the satirist clearly despises. Bob Hope, Carol Burnett and the late Jack Benny, for instance, are not satirists. While their humor is often directed at our human foibles, it is always in good fun and never seriously critical of people or society. Satire must be humor with a sharp bite to it, like this caustic gibe at Congress from Mark Twain:

> It could probably be shown by facts and figures that there is no distinctly native American criminal class except Congress.

Besides its biting quality, satire has other distinguishing characteristics.

1. Satire Deals with Serious Themes. Good satire is usually so funny that casual readers lose sight of the gravity of the subjects that are being discussed. In *Breakfast of Champions*, Kurt Vonnegut deals with such serious human problems as loneliness, fear, greed, racial discrimination, and the self-destructive nature of our plasticized, mechanized society. The tone of his narrative, however, is wry humor. What serious themes can you find in the following passage about Dwayne Hoover's "echolalia"?

> Though his mental health had improved remarkably since break-fast, a new symptom of illness made itself known. It was incipient echolalia. Dwayne found himself wanting to repeat out loud whatever had just been said.
>
> So when the radio told him, "You can always trust Dwayne," [a line from his own used-car commercial] he echoed the last word. "Dwayne," he said.
>
> When the radio said there had been a tornado in Texas, Dwayne said this out loud: "Texas."
>
> Then he heard that husbands of women who had been raped during the war between India and Pakistan wouldn't have anything to do with their wives anymore. The women, in the eyes of their husbands, had become *unclean,* said the radio.
>
> "Unclean," said Dwayne.

Dwayne Hoover, the symbol of American economic success, is on the verge of a mental breakdown—a very serious situation. Still, his new symptom, "echolalia," is funny. But what has happened to Dwayne, and to many others among us, is not at all funny. We have become insensitive to radio and TV commercials, to tornadoes in Texas, and to the plight of thousands of abused and deserted women in some other part of the world. Perhaps on the next Fourth of July when you hear that "the highway death toll this weekend is expected to hit 575," you will cluck your tongue and say, "575," and you will do nothing. That will be a classic case of echolalia, and the satirist will have made his point.

2. Satire Uses Very Little Plot or Character Development. Plots in satiric novels are either very thin or nonexistent. This is because the satirist is not as interested in telling a story as in getting a message across to the reader. Sometimes a satiric novel is just a series of vaguely related episodes. Frequently, some sort of journey made by one of the characters is used as a device to tie things together.

Breakfast of Champions uses two devices to tie twenty-four chapters and many short comments and episodes together. First, there is Kilgore Trout's journey from New York to the Arts Festival in Midland City. The other device is Dwayne Hoover's aimless meandering on his way to insanity. There is no plot, no suspense and no climax except for the meeting between Dwayne and Kilgore which ends in Dwayne Hoover's going berserk.

Characters pop in and out of satire, but they contribute nothing to moving the story along as they do in other kinds of fiction. Characters in satire are static, or flat. That is, they don't change or develop as the story moves along; they just bumble about until the author is through using them and then they disappear.

Satire is actually quite chaotic. However, the satirist will say, "Life is chaotic, so I am closer to the truth than you think." In the chapter from *Breakfast of Champions* which you will read, you are told about Dwayne Hoover's echolalia, a bit about a Black ex-convict who hopes Dwayne will give him a job, a bit about the John Kennedy assassination, a little about Germany, a lot about a Burger Chef waitress, something about a boy who was killed playing football, and some information about recent discoveries in geology.

None of this contributes to plot development or characterization, but all of it contributes to the ideas that the author is trying to convey to his readers.

In the following paragraph, Dwayne Hoover does nothing more earth-shaking than go for a hamburger. Yet notice how the author uses the paragraph to comment on a particular facet of American society.

> Dwayne had a hamburger and French fries and a Coke at his newest Burger Chef, which was out on Crestview Avenue, across the street from where the new John F. Kennedy High School was going up. John F. Kennedy had never been in Midland City, but he was a President of the United States who was shot to death. Presidents of the country were often shot to death. The assassins were confused by some of the same bad chemicals which troubled Dwayne.

Vonnegut uses the passage to remind us that Americans have a pretty bad record when it comes to killing Presidents. It comes, he says, from the same insanity—the same bad chemicals—that afflicts Dwayne Hoover. (Incidentally, it has been shown in recent years that many kinds of mental illness are caused by certain shortages and surpluses of crucial body chemicals. So on this point Vonnegut is serious.)

3. **Satire Distorts the World It Describes.** Literary satirists frequently distort the world in the same way that cartoonists do, in order to make their messages strike home. In the cartoonist's world, battleships can be tiny and their mock admirals huge; Congressmen can sit atop the capitol dome; little businessmen swing from huge dollar signs; animals or inanimate objects are given human forms and voices. Well-known people are caricatured rather than drawn true-to-life, and they are made to look fierce or wise or silly as suits the cartoonist's purpose.

In the world that Kurt Vonnegut creates for *Breakfast of Champions*, America is spoken of as a place that *was*, history is oversimplified to a tale of white men's greed and violence; earth is a wrecked planet and the continents are pictured as thick slabs drifting on molten glurp. Each of these descriptions carries a grain of truth. It can be argued, for example, that the United States is no longer as it *was* or as it was conceived by the founding fathers. But to imply that the country no longer exists is satiric distortion. It is a device used to impress the reader that things are not as they should be.

The characters, too, are something less than real people. Kilgore Trout is an oldish writer, a philosopher who writes in the science fiction mode but whose work only sells in pornography shops. Dwayne Hoover is not much more than a symbol moving in a half-real world. Subordinate characters drop into the story as they are needed to make a point and then drop out again. How is Patty Keene caricatured or distorted in the following passage, and what purpose does she serve in the satire?

> Dwayne's waitress at the Burger Chef was a seventeen-year-old white girl named Patty Keene. Her hair was yellow. Her eyes were blue. She was very old for a mammal. Most mammals were senile or dead by the time they were seventeen. But Patty was a sort of mammal which developed very slowly, so the body she rode around in was only now mature.
>
> She was a brand-new adult, who was working in order to pay off the tremendous doctors' and hospital bills her father had run up in the process of dying of cancer of the colon and then cancer of the everything.
>
> This was in a country where everybody was expected to pay his own bills for everything, and one of the most expensive things a person could do was get sick.

Patty is a waitress. She is seventeen, her hair is yellow and her eyes are blue. We get to know Patty's problems, but we never get to know her as a real person. Vonnegut describes her as a mammal, not a woman, and she is a "brand-new adult," not a young lady. Vonnegut uses Patty and a few short paragraphs to point with devastating accuracy at the dehumanizing effects of overpriced health care in our society.

4. Satire Often Uses Understatement and Shock Imagery. Much of Kurt Vonnegut's satire arises from a deadpan, tongue-in-cheek style that is marked by deliberate understatement and oversimplification. This is a technique that is frequently found in satiric works. Notice how he reduces the horrible actions of the Germans in World War II, and their subsequent spectacular recovery, to a few lines that are made more shocking by their understatement.

> . . . the people in a country called Germany were so full of bad chemicals for a while that they actually built factories whose only purpose was to kill people by the millions. The people were delivered by railroad trains . . . .
>
> After they got well again, they manufactured a cheap and durable automobile which became popular all over the world, especially among young people . . . .
>
> People called it "the beetle."

This is all illustrated with little drawings of German flags, a Volkswagon and a bug. "Good heavens!" you want to say, "How can you speak so casually and flippantly about killing millions of people? This is nothing to make fun of!" And that is exactly the reaction that Vonnegut as a satirist hopes to evoke from his readers. This is *not* a subject to be spoken of lightly, and he wants to move readers to sit up and take notice of that fact by forcing them to reject his flippant attitude.

Shock is another tool of satire. A satirist will deliberately use obscenities, violence and frightening imagery to rivet your attention to the page. Vonnegut could have simply said that Patty Keene's father died of cancer. Instead he offers the shocking image of a man riddled with disease, amassing a huge debt as he dies:

> . . . the tremendous doctors' and hospital bills her father had run up in the process of dying of cancer of the colon and then cancer of the everything.

You squirm in discomfort under the impact of this imagery. You will notice, too, that the speech is deliberately colloquial, which is another mark of satire. The expressions "run up" and "cancer of the everything" are used in place of the more precise speech you have become accustomed to in other kinds of reading.

As you read the following chapter from *Breakfast of Champions*, notice what Vonnegut is satirizing and how he goes about it. Does the chapter change the ways in which you view the world and other people?

As you read the chapter:

- Try to determine the real target of Vonnegut's satire in the passage where he describes Patty Keene as being "stupid on purpose."

- Notice how the author satirizes the way English is taught in schools, and try to decide what method he would prefer.

- Pay special attention to the passage in which the author describes football and Thanksgiving satirically.

- Notice the passage in which Vonnegut claims that people don't usually pay attention to what others are saying to them.

Breakfast of Champions
Kurt Vonnegut, Jr.

CHAPTER 15

◆

Dwayne Hoover got through lunch all right that day. He remembered now about Hawaiian Week. The ukuleles and so on were no longer mysterious. The pavement between his automobile agency and the new Holiday Inn was no longer a trampoline.

He drove to lunch alone in an air-conditioned demonstrator, a blue Pontiac *Le Mans* with a cream interior, with his radio on. He heard several of his own radio commercials, which drove home the point: "You can always trust Dwayne."

Though his mental health had improved remarkably since breakfast, a new symptom of illness made itself known. It was incipient echolalia. Dwayne found himself wanting to repeat out loud whatever had just been said.

So when the radio told him, "You can always trust Dwayne," he echoed the last word. "Dwayne," he said.

When the radio said there had been a tornado in Texas, Dwayne said this out loud: "Texas."

Then he heard that husbands of women who had been raped during the war between India and Pakistan wouldn't have anything to do with their wives anymore. The women, in the eyes of their husbands, had become *unclean*, said the radio.

"Unclean," said Dwayne.

◆ As for Wayne Hoobler, the black ex-convict whose only dream was to work for Dwayne Hoover: he had learned to play hide-and-seek with Dwayne's employees. He did not wish to be ordered off the property for hanging around the used cars. So, when an employee came near, Wayne would wander off to the garbage and trash area behind the Holiday Inn, and gravely study the remains of club sandwiches and empty packs of Salem cigarettes and so on in the cans back there, as though he were a health inspector or some such thing.

When the employee went away, Wayne would drift back to the used cars, keeping the boiled eggs of his eyes peeled for the real Dwayne Hoover.

The real Dwayne Hoover, of course, had in effect denied that he was Dwayne. So, when the real Dwayne came out at lunch time, Wayne, who had nobody to talk to but himself, said this to himself: "That ain't Mr. Hoover. Sure *look* like Mr. Hoover, though. Maybe Mr. Hoover sick today." And so on.

Dwayne had a hamburger and French fries and a Coke at his newest Burger Chef, which was out on Crestview Avenue, across the street from where the new John F. Kennedy High School was going up. John F. Kennedy had never been in Midland City, but he was a President of the United States who was shot to death. Presidents of the country were often shot to death. The assassins were confused by some of the same bad chemicals which troubled Dwayne.

▶Dwayne certainly wasn't alone, as far as having bad chemicals inside of him was concerned. He had plenty of company throughout all history. In his own lifetime, for instance, the people in a country called Germany were so full of bad chemicals for a while that they actually built factories whose only purpose was to kill people by the millions. The people were delivered by railroad trains.

When the Germans were full of bad chemicals, their flag looked like this:

Here is what their flag looked like after they got well again:

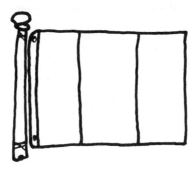

BEST-SELLING CHAPTERS

After they got well again, they manufactured a cheap and durable automobile which became popular all over the world, especially among young people. It looked like this:

People called it "the beetle." A real beetle looked like this:

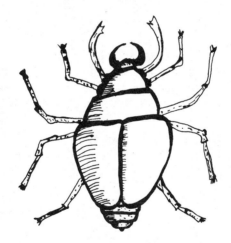

The mechanical beetle was made by Germans. The real beetle was made by the Creator of the Universe.

◗ Dwayne's waitress at the Burger Chef was a seventeen-year-old white girl named Patty Keene. Her hair was yellow. Her eyes were blue. She was very old for a mammal. Most mammals were senile or dead by the time they were seventeen. But Patty was a sort of mammal which developed very slowly, so the body she rode around in was only now mature.

She was a brand-new adult, who was working in order to pay off the tremendous doctors' and hospital bills her father had run up in the process of dying of cancer of the colon and then cancer of the everything.

This was in a country where everybody was expected to pay his own bills for everything, and one of the most expensive things a person could do was get sick. Patty Keene's father's sickness cost ten times as much as all the trips to Hawaii which Dwayne was going to give away at the end of Hawaiian Week.

♦ Dwayne appreciated Patty Keene's brand-newness, even though he was not sexually attracted to women that young. She was like a new automobile, which hadn't even had its radio turned on yet, and Dwayne was reminded of a ditty his father would sing sometimes when his father was drunk. It went like this:

> *Roses are red,*
> *And ready for plucking.*
> *You're sixteen,*
> *And ready for high school.*

♦ Patty Keene was stupid on purpose, which was the case with most women in Midland City. The women all had big minds because they were big animals, but they did not use them much for this reason: unusual ideas could make enemies, and the women, if they were going to achieve any sort of comfort and safety, needed all the friends they could get.

So, in the interests of survival, they trained themselves to be agreeing machines instead of thinking machines. All their minds had to do was to discover what other people were thinking, and then they thought that, too.

♦ Patty knew who Dwayne was. Dwayne didn't know who Patty was. Patty's heart beat faster when she waited on him—because Dwayne could solve so many of her problems with the money and power he had. He could give her a fine house and new automobiles and nice clothes and a life of leisure, and he could pay all the medical bills—as easily as she had given him his hamburger and his French fries and his Coke.

Dwayne could do for her what the Fairy Godmother did for Cinderella, if he wanted to, and Patty had never been so close to such a magical person before. She was in the presence of the supernatural. And she knew enough about Midland City and herself to understand that she might never be this close to the supernatural ever again.

Patty Keene actually imagined Dwayne's waving a magic wand at her troubles and dreams. It looked like this:

She spoke up bravely, to learn if supernatural assistance was possible in her case. She was willing to do without it, expected to do without it—to work hard all her life, to get not much in return, and to associate with other men and women who were poor and powerless, and in debt. She said this to Dwayne:

"Excuse me for calling you by name, Mr. Hoover, but I can't help knowing who you are, with your picture in all your ads and everything. Besides—everybody else who works here told me who you were. When you came in, they just buzzed and buzzed."

"Buzzed," said Dwayne. This was his echolalia again.

♦ "I guess that isn't the right word," she said. She was used to apologizing for her use of language. She had been encouraged to do a lot of that in school. Most white people in Midland City were insecure when they spoke, so they kept their sentences short and their words simple, in order to keep embarrassing mistakes to a minimum. Dwayne certainly did that. Patty certainly did that.

This was because their English teachers would wince and cover their ears and give them flunking grades and so on whenever they failed to speak like English aristocrats before the First World War. Also: they were told that they were unworthy to speak or write their language if they couldn't love or understand novels and poems and plays about people long ago and far away, such as *Ivanhoe*.

♦ Patty Keene flunked English during the semester when she had to read and appreciate *Ivanhoe*, which was about men in iron suits and the women who loved them. And she was put in a remedial reading class, where they made her read *The Good Earth*, which was about Chinamen.

It was during this same semester that she lost her virginity. She was raped by a white gas-conversion unit installer named Don Breedlove in the parking lot outside the Bannister Memorial Fieldhouse at the County Fairgrounds after the Regional High School Basketball Play-offs. She never reported it to the police. She never reported it to anybody, since her father was dying at the time.

There was enough trouble already.

♦ The Bannister Memorial Fieldhouse was named in honor of George Hickman Bannister, a seventeen-year-old boy who was killed while playing high school football in 1924. George Hickman Bannister had the largest tombstone in Calvary Cemetery, a sixty-two-foot obelisk with a marble football on top.

The marble football looked like this:

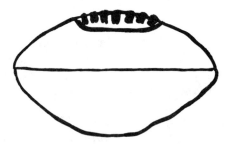

Football was a war game. Two opposing teams fought over the ball while wearing armor made out of leather and cloth and plastic.

George Hickman Bannister was killed while trying to get a hold of the ball on Thanksgiving Day. Thanksgiving Day was a holiday when everybody in the country was expected to express gratitude to the Creator of the Universe, mainly for food.

♦ George Hickman Bannister's obelisk was paid for by public subscription, with the Chamber of Commerce matching every two dollars raised with a dollar of its own. It was for many years the tallest structure in Midland City. A city ordinance was passed which made it illegal to erect anything taller than that, and it was called *The George Hickman Bannister Law*.

The ordinance was junked later on to allow radio towers to go up.

♦ The two largest monuments in town, until the new Mildred Barry Memorial Arts Center went up in Sugar Creek, were constructed supposedly so that George Hickman Bannister would never be forgotten. But nobody ever thought about him anymore by the time Dwayne Hoover met Kilgore Trout. There wasn't much to think about him, actually, even at the time of his death, except that he was young.

And he didn't have any relatives in town anymore. There weren't any Bannisters in the phone book, except for *The Bannister*, which was a motion picture theater. Actually, there wouldn't even be a *Bannister Theater* in there after the new phonebooks came out. The Bannister had been turned into a cut-rate furniture store.

George Hickman Bannister's father and mother and sister, Lucy, moved away from town before either the tombstone or the fieldhouse was completed, and they couldn't be located for the dedication ceremonies.

▶ It was a very restless country, with people tearing around all the time. Every so often, somebody would stop to put up a monument.

There were monuments all over the country. But it was certainly unusual for somebody from the common people to have not one but *two* monuments in his honor, as was the case with George Hickman Bannister.

Technically, though, only the tombstone had been erected specifically for him. The fieldhouse would have gone up anyway. The money was appropriated for the fieldhouse two years before George Hickman Bannister was cut down in his prime. It didn't cost anything extra to name it after him.

▶ Calvary Cemetery, where George Hickman Bannister was at rest, was named in honor of a hill in Jerusalem, thousands of miles away. Many people believed that the son of the Creator of the Universe had been killed on that hill thousands of years ago.

Dwayne Hoover didn't know whether to believe that or not. Neither did Patty Keene.

▶ And they certainly weren't worrying about it now. They had other fish to fry. Dwayne was wondering how long his attack of echolalia was likely to last, and Patty Keene had to find out if her brand-newness and prettiness and outgoing personality were worth a lot to a sweet, sort of sexy, middle-aged old Pontiac dealer like Dwayne.

"Anyway," she said, "it certainly is an honor to have you visit us, and those aren't the right words, either, but I hope you know what I mean."

"Mean," said Dwayne.

"Is the food all right?" she said.

"All right," said Dwayne.

"It's what everybody else gets," she said. "We didn't do anything special for you."

"You," said Dwayne.

▶ It didn't matter much what Dwayne said. It hadn't mattered much for years. It didn't matter much what most people in Midland City said out loud, except when they were talking about money or structures or travel or machinery—or other measurable things. Every person had a clearly defined part to play—as a black person, a female high school drop-out, a Pontiac dealer, a gynecologist, a gas-conversion burner installer. If a person stopped living up to expectations, because of bad chemicals or one thing or another, everybody went on imagining that the person was living up to expectations anyway.

That was the main reason the people in Midland City were so slow to detect insanity in their associates. Their imaginations insisted that nobody changed much from day to day. Their imaginations were flywheels on the ramshackle machinery of the awful truth.

♦ When Dwayne left Patty Keene and his Burger Chef, when he got into his demonstrator and drove away, Patty Keene was persuaded that she could make him happy with her young body, with her bravery and cheerfulness. She wanted to cry about the lines in his face, and the fact that his wife had eaten Drano, and that his dog had to fight all the time because it couldn't wag its tail, about the fact that his son was a homosexual. She knew all those things about Dwayne. Everybody knew those things about Dwayne.

She gazed at the tower of radio station WMCY, which Dwayne Hoover owned. It was the tallest structure in Midland City. It was eight times as tall as the tombstone of George Hickman Bannister. It had a red light on top of it—to keep airplanes away.

She thought about all the new and used cars Dwayne owned.

♦ Earth scientists had just discovered something fascinating about the continent Patty Keene was standing on, incidentally. It was riding on a slab about forty miles thick, and the slab was drifting around on molten glurp. And all the other continents had slabs of their own. When one slab crashed into another one, mountains were made.

♦ The mountains of West Virginia, for instance, were heaved up when a huge chunk of Africa crashed into North America. And the coal in the state was formed from forests which were buried by the crash.

Patty Keene hadn't heard the big news yet. Neither had Dwayne. Neither had Kilgore Trout. I only found out about it day before yesterday. I was reading a magazine, and I also had the television on. A group of scientists was on television, saying that the theory of floating, crashing, grinding slabs was more than a theory. They could prove it was true now, and that Japan and San Francisco, for instance, were in hideous danger, because that was where some of the most violent crashing and grinding was going on.

They said, too, that ice ages would continue to occur. Mile-thick glaciers would, geologically speaking, continue to go down and up like window blinds.

Unit 13

Breakfast of Champions

- Comprehension Questions
- Analyzing Satire
- Discussion Guides
- Writing Exercise

COMPREHENSION QUESTIONS

For each of the following statements and questions, select the option containing the most complete or most accurate answer.

1. Dwayne Hoover was afflicted with
(b) □ a. an old football injury.
   □ b. a childhood disease.
   □ c. chronic arthritis.
   □ d. mental illness.

2. As he listened to his car radio, Dwayne Hoover found he had
(a) □ a. incipient radiola.   □ c. syncopation.
   □ b. echolalia.   □ d. estralita.

3. Wayne Hoobler was
(a) □ a. an ex-convict who wanted to work for Dwayne Hoover.
   □ b. Dwayne Hoover's cousin who owned the Burger Chef.
   □ c. a salesman who worked for Dwayne Hoover.
   □ d. the man who washed and waxed new cars.

4. According to Kurt Vonnegut, the thing that Presidential assassins, Nazis
(d) and Dwayne Hoover had in common was
   □ a. bad luck.   □ c. bad chemicals.
   □ b. bad intentions.   □ d. bad spirits.

5. The satiric humor of Kurt Vonnegut's illustrations arises from one of
(k) the same satiric devices used in his writing. This is
   □ a. complexity and exaggeration.
   □ b. shock and revulsion.
   □ c. accuracy and directness.
   □ d. understatement and oversimplification.

6. In describing Patty Keene, Vonnegut spoke of "the body she rode
(k) around in." This can be thought of as
   □ a. a psychological analysis.
   □ b. exaggeration.
   □ c. a distortion of reality.
   □ d. hyperbole.

7. The author points out that "Patty Keene was stupid on purpose"
(j) □ a. in order to impress Dwayne Hoover.
   □ b. as a means of survival.
   □ c. in order to get fired.
   □ d. because it was her nature.

8. Vonnegut suggests that in our society women are forced to be
(e) □ a. dress-up machines.   □ c. thinking machines.
   □ b. talking machines.   □ d. agreeing machines.

9. It is said that Dwayne Hoover could pay Patty Keene's bills as easily as
(h) she had served him a hamburger. This implies
   □ a. criticism of economic inequality.
   □ b. mockery of male chauvinism.
   □ c. an indictment of impure meat.
   □ d. criticism of fast-food chains.

10. Dwayne Hoover seemed supernatural to Patty Keene because of his
(f) □ a. echolalia.   □ c. personality.
   □ b. wealth.   □ d. eyes.

11. Patty Keene tried to speak to Dwayne Hoover because she
(c) □ a. loved him.   □ c. needed help.
   □ b. feared him as a boss. □ d. knew about his son.

12. According to Kurt Vonnegut—Patty, Dwayne and most other white
(j) people use short sentences and simple words because when they speak
   they feel
   □ a. aggressive.   □ c. outgoing.
   □ b. insecure.   □ d. sophisticated.

13. In the expression ". . . their English teachers would *wince* and cover
(l) their ears . . . ," the word *wince* means
   □ a. smile as though happy.   □ c. shiver as if excited.
   □ b. frown as though unhappy. □ d. flinch as if in pain.

14. From his remarks about English teachers, you may infer that Vonnegut
(h) feels that reading old novels such as *Ivanhoe* is
   □ a. not essential in English education.
   □ b. helpful in developing good speech habits.
   □ c. unjustly kept from poor people.
   □ d. essential for a well-rounded education.

15. In the expression "a *remedial* reading class," the word *remedial* means
    (l) □ a. advanced.   □ c. corrective.
        □ b. classical.   □ d. foreign.

16. George Hickman Bannister was
    (b) □ a. a war hero.
        □ b. a boy killed playing football.
        □ c. an artist killed in World War II.
        □ d. a friend of Patty Keene.

17. George Bannister's tombstone was the tallest structure in Midland City
    (d) until
        □ a. a radio tower was built.
        □ b. it was torn down.
        □ c. a new hero was found.
        □ d. a water tower was built.

18. Which of the following expressions might Vonnegut have used in his
    (g) satirical discussion of George Bannister?
        □ a. Once a hero, always a hero.
        □ b. Old soldiers never die.
        □ c. Here today, gone tomorrow.
        □ d. You can't get something for nothing.

19. Vonnegut describes Thanksgiving Day as a holiday when everybody
    (i) expresses gratitude to the Creator, mainly for food. The tone of this
        remark can best be called
        □ a. sarcastic.   □ c. ominous.
        □ b. angry.   □ d. reverent.

20. From what you can gather from the chapter, Patty Keene's efforts to
    (f) get help from Dwayne Hoover were
        □ a. successful.   □ c. partly successful.
        □ b. unsuccessful.   □ d. conditional.

21. Patty Keene thought she could make Dwayne Hoover happy. She gazed
    (g) at the tower of the radio station he owned and thought about all his
        new and used cars. She was probably also thinking about his
        □ a. money.   □ c. problems.
        □ b. sad life.   □ d. kindness and generosity.

22. Dwayne Hoover's dog had to fight all the time because it
(a)   □ a. was mean.   □ c. had bad chemicals.
      □ b. couldn't wag its tail.   □ d. hated life.

23. The WMCY radio tower "was eight times as tall as the tombstone of
(e) George Bannister." What point is Vonnegut making?
      □ a. Science had come a long way since Bannister's death.
      □ b. The tower should have been named after Bannister.
      □ c. George Bannister has been forgotten.
      □ d. There was no need to make the tower so tall.

24. Vonnegut speaks of continents as crashing, grinding slabs. Japan and
(i) San Francisco, he says, "were in hideous danger." To produce the
    proper effect, the author creates a tone which is
      □ a. mysterious.   □ c. serious.
      □ b. humorous.   □ d. ironic.

25. According to information in the story, the mountains of West Virginia
(c) were formed by
      □ a. an earthquake.   □ c. a volcano.
      □ b. a collision of continents.   □ d. a receding glacier.

Comprehension Skills: a—isolating details; b—recalling specific facts; c—retaining concepts; d—organizing facts; e—understanding the main idea; f—drawing a conclusion; g—making a judgment; h—making an inference; i—recognizing tone; j—understanding characters; k—appreciation of literary forms; l—knowledge of word meanings.

ANALYZING SATIRE

Practice Exercise A

Patty Keene was stupid on purpose, which was the case with most women in Midland City. The women all had big minds because they were big animals, but they did not use them much for this reason: unusual ideas could make enemies, and the women, if they were going to achieve any sort of comfort and safety, needed all the friends they could get.

So, in the interests of survival, they trained themselves to be agreeing machines instead of thinking machines. All their minds had to do was to discover what other people were thinking, and then they thought that, too.

1. In the above passage Kurt Vonnegut's satire is directed at a society
    □ a. in which women are stupid.
    □ b. that forces women to act stupid.
    □ c. that doesn't provide education for women.
    □ d. that regards women as big animals.

2. Circle the two sentences that imply that the women in Midland City are robots without free will.

Practice Exercise B

"I guess that isn't the right word," she said. She was used to apologizing for her use of language. She had been encouraged to do a lot of that in school. Most white people in Midland City were insecure when they spoke, so they kept their sentences short and their words simple, in order to keep embarrassing mistakes to a minimum. Dwayne certainly did that. Patty certainly did that.

This was because their English teachers would wince and cover their ears and give them flunking grades and so on whenever they failed to speak like English aristocrats before the First World War.

1. Kurt Vonnegut probably would prefer that English teachers
    □ a. drill students more to overcome their insecurity.
    □ b. have students practice overcoming their embarrassment.
    □ c. accept fluent, colloquial English from students.
    □ d. not correct students at all.

2. Circle the sentence in which the author uses exaggeration to satirize the way English is taught in school.

Practice Exercise C

Football was a war game. Two opposing teams fought over the ball while wearing armor made out of leather and cloth and plastic.

George Hickman Bannister was killed while trying to get a hold of the ball on Thanksgiving Day. Thanksgiving Day was a holiday when everybody in the country was expected to express gratitude to the Creator of the Universe, mainly for food.

1. The effect of the satire in this passage gives the impression that George Bannister died
   □ a. for a good cause.   □ c. by mistake.
   □ b. without pain.   □ d. for nothing.

2. Satire often uses contrast to make a point. On the line provided, write two words that the author uses to create satire through contrast.

_____

Practice Exercise D

It didn't matter much what Dwayne said. It hadn't mattered much for years. It didn't matter much what most people in Midland City said out loud, except when they were talking about money or structures or travel or machinery—or other measurable things. Every person had a clearly defined part to play—as a black person, a female high school drop-out, a Pontiac dealer, a gynecologist, a gas-conversion burner installer. If a person stopped living up to expectations, because of bad chemicals or one thing or another, everybody went on imagining that the person was living up to expectations anyway.

That was the main reason the people in Midland City were so slow to detect insanity in their associates. Their imaginations insisted that nobody changed much from day to day.

1. The author suggests that if you speak about problems or ideas that do not deal with money or other material things,
   □ a. it is not important.
   □ b. it is not worth listening to.
   □ c. no one pays attention.
   □ d. people think you have bad chemicals.

2. Throughout *Breakfast of Champions* Vonnegut suggests that people have become specialized machines that are programmed to do what they do. Underline the sentence that presents the idea of people as programmed machines.

BREAKFAST OF CHAMPIONS   411

DISCUSSION GUIDES

Analyzing Satire

1. One definition of satire is "telling the truth laughing." Tell why you think *Breakfast of Champions* does or does not fit this definition.

2. One definition of a satirist says, "Satirists are clear-eyed, sharp-tongued, hot tempered, outwardly disillusioned and secretly idealistic." From what you have read of Kurt Vonnegut, how may you apply these characteristics to him?

3. It is generally agreed that there are two kinds of satire—bitter satire and gentle satire. The difference is as the names imply: one is harsh, angry and biting; the other is more like a fond slap on the wrist. Explain which kind you think Vonnegut writes. (Consider the possibility that he may write both kinds.) Use examples from the chapter to prove your point.

4. Satirists often pretend to be simple-minded and naive. This is a trick to make you think harder. Try to explain why the trick works. Show how it works in the chapter.

Interpreting the Chapter

5. Why do you think Vonnegut uses "echolalia" as one of the symptoms of Dwayne Hoover's growing insanity? How does this symptom tie in with Vonnegut's satire as a whole?

6. Vonnegut says that lots of people throughout history have had "bad chemicals" like Dwayne Hoover. The Germans of World War II are given as examples. Make your own list of people with "bad chemicals."

7. Speaking about most of the people of Midland City, Vonnegut says: "Their imaginations were flywheels on the ramshackle machinery of the awful truth." What does he mean by this? (A flywheel is a heavy disk or wheel that allows an engine and its machinery to operate smoothly without being torn apart by its own inertia. In a sense, a flywheel holds things in check.)

8. Two characters have similar-sounding names—Dwayne Hoover, Vonnegut's symbol of American economic success, and Wayne Hoobler, the ex-convict who hangs around Dwayne's used-car lot hoping for a job. Why do you think Vonnegut did this?

9. Kurt Vonnegut illustrated this book himself. Do you think the illustrations add to the story or detract from it?

10. In the preface to *Breakfast of Champions*, Kurt Vonnegut said that during the Great Depression a lady named Phoebe Hurty taught him to be impolite:

> She was funny. She was liberating. She taught us to be impolite in conversation not only about sexual matters, but about American history and famous heroes, about the distribution of wealth, about school, about everything.

    a. How is Vonnegut "impolite" in *Breakfast of Champions?*

    b. What does he accomplish by being impolite?

WRITING EXERCISE

Below you will find six of Mark Twain's sharpest satiric barbs aimed at schools, doctors, preachers and the world in general. A crucial word or two has been omitted from each quotation. Complete each quotation by circling the word or phrase which creates the most effective satire. Correct your answers using the answer key at the back of the book. Then, on the lines provided, write a sentence that states the target of Twain's satire and his point of view.

1. I have never let my schooling interfere with my _____.

    lunch   education   hobbies

_____

_____

2. All you need in this life is ignorance and confidence, and then _____ is sure.

    stupidity   disappointment   success

_____

_____

3. Fleas can be taught nearly anything that a _____ can.

    congressman   dog   fly

_____

_____

4. He charged nothing for his preaching and it was _____ .

    awe inspiring   worth it   in vain

_____

_____

5. He has been a doctor a year now and has had two patients—no, three, I think—yes, it was three; I attended their _____.

    funerals   weddings   operations

_____

_____

6. Most writers regard truth as their most valuable possession and therefore are most _____ in its use.

    generous   indifferent   economical

_____

_____

My Life
and
Hard Times

Introduction

The "chapters" in *My Life and Hard Times* are really short episodes, recollections of things that were supposed to have happened during James Thurber's boyhood in Columbus, Ohio. With tongue in cheek, Thurber calls the book an "autobiography" although it was written before he was forty and it is so full of comic exaggeration that it is impossible to tell where the grain of truth leaves off and the leg pulling begins.

The reminiscences date from the turn of the century until Thurber left Ohio State University in 1918. The only clues to their age, however, are allusions to such things as rumble seats, which used to be open-air features of old cars; iceboxes and icemen, the precursors of electric refrigerators; and peppery grandfathers and great uncles who had fought in the Civil War and who were still alive then. As humor the stories are as fresh as if they were written yesterday.

The two episodes in this unit are "The Dog That Bit People" and "University Days."

Thurber loved animals, especially dogs, and so his stories and the cartoons that he drew to illuminate his stories are full of them. But of all Thurber's dogs, Muggs, the dog that bit people, is most famous. While most of Thurber's dogs look like worried bassets, or bloodhounds who carry the weight of the world on their shoulders, the dog that bit people is clearly an Airedale, which Thurber describes as a "big, burly, choleric dog." He resembles, in a most remarkable way, Little Orphan Annie's dog, Sandy, except that where Sandy is often seen smiling, Muggs always frowns. He hates people.

Nevertheless, Thurber's mother insists on defending Muggs—he isn't well, she says—and she keeps peace of a sort in the neighborhood by sending boxes of candy at Christmas to people Muggs has bitten. When Muggs expires at the ripe old age of eleven, Mrs. Thurber has forty names on her candy list. During his long life, Muggs has been cursed at, shot at and poisoned, but in the end it is his own meanness which carries him away. Mrs. Thurber would like to put "Flights of angels sing thee to thy rest" on his tombstone, but the other family members, who have been bitten innumerable times, insist on the dignified Latin inscription *cave canem*, which means "beware of the dog."

Thurber attended Ohio State University where he was a good English student, as might be expected, but he was never able to conquer required courses in science, physical education and military drill. These and one other course, Principles of Economics, which he did manage to pass, are the subject of "University Days." The author tells about his own troubles with the first three courses, but it is the star tackle of the football team, a lovable ox named Bolenciecwcz, who is immortalized as a student of economics. There has never been a funnier oral quiz than the one that was designed especially to keep Bolenciecwcz scholastically eligible to play in a crucial game against Illinois. It might be considered the first Polish joke of the century except for the fact that the professors, and Thurber himself, come off as badly in school as does Bolenciecwcz, and it's all good fun.

The author began his writing career as a journalist and during his early years is best remembered for his role as an editor, writer and cartoonist for *The New Yorker* magazine. He liked to think of his work as serious social commentary, and in a way it was. However, even the most pointed of his pieces don't have the satiric sting of Kurt Vonnegut, Sinclair Lewis or Jonathan Swift. Thurber is a humorist and one of the best who ever lived. He is able to nudge us in our weak spots and make us laugh at our most secret fears, foibles and frustrations without making us feel guilty about them.

As you read the lesson and the two episodes from *My Life and Hard Times*, try to see the difference between satire, which is tough, and humor, which is more gentle. Notice, especially, that there is no bitter aftertaste left when you are finished laughing at Thurber's humor as you must have felt when reading Vonnegut. Also notice Thurber's polish and technical excellence. He was an expert at his craft and took pride in the fact that his short pieces were done as well as any longer, more serious works of literature.

Understanding
Humor

Everyone loves to laugh. We enjoy coming across things that give us pleasure, amuse us, make us smile and feel good. Without times of joy, life could become quite intolerable.

Literature without laughter quickly becomes intolerable, too. Even serious literature that deals with deep, somber themes must have its lighter moments, or it simply becomes too oppressive to continue reading. Just as you can't long tolerate a friend who constantly moans and groans, it is very difficult to stay with a story that doesn't provide an occasional opportunity to laugh or smile. William Shakespeare was well aware of this, and so in the midst of his most moving tragedies you will find relief in the form of comic scenes and funny lines. No matter how dire the circumstances in a Dickens novel, there will always be two or three comic characters whose job it is to relieve the tension. There is also a whole body of literature, satire, that uses laughter to preach and teach about serious subjects.

Books written purely for the sake of making you laugh, that do not deal in serious themes or burden the reader with a sense of guilt, however, are few and far between. But they are precious for their rarity, and when they appear they hold their place well on the best-seller lists. Their authors are never recognized as giants of literature, but they are always well loved— such delightful people as P. G. Wodehouse, Jean Kerr, Erma Bombeck and James Thurber.

But what is humor? Why do we laugh at some things and not at others? Actually, it is very difficult to explain *why* something is funny. In the first place, not everyone finds the same things funny, and in the second place, as soon as you start to explain why something is funny, it isn't funny anymore. Nevertheless, in your study of literature you may find it helpful to know some of the basic tenets of humor that have come to be recognized by writers and comedians as sound guides to the art of being funny.

1. **The Humorous Condition.** It is almost dismaying to think that there are *rules* for being funny, but there are, and here are some of them:

Humor must give pleasure and it must not be serious or threatening. This seems obvious, but no doubt you know of occasions where people have made jokes that were inappropriate for the place, the audience and the situation. There are times when humor, instead of being enjoyable, is actually painful. Humor doesn't work well at a funeral, and you wouldn't tell a bawdy joke at a church tea. Biting sarcasm is rarely funny because it hurts, especially if you are its object.

Humor must arouse interest and feeling—but not intense interest or intense feeling. If you don't know or care anything about the science of genetics, the many jokes going around about cloning will neither interest nor amuse you. Stories about drunks usually arouse both interest and feelings, but the interest and feeling will be too intense for someone who is suffering with an alcoholic in the family.

Humor must be spontaneous and fresh. Old jokes are not funny, although an old subject with a fresh twist often works well. If the humor is obvious and stale, it makes you wince rather than laugh. That's why puns don't work as humor unless they are exceptionally imaginative and original. A reader or listener must respond instantly and spontaneously to a joke, or it is not funny. There is nothing that falls so flat as a joke that has to be explained.

Does the opening passage from James Thurber's "The Dog That Bit People" fulfill these three requirements?

> Probably no man should have as many dogs in his life as I have had, but there was more pleasure than distress in them for me except in the case of an Airedale named Muggs. He gave me more trouble than all the other fifty-four or -five put together, although my moment of keenest embarrassment was the time a Scotch terrier named Jeannie, who had just had six puppies in the clothes closet of a fourth floor apartment in New York, had the unexpected seventh and last at the corner of Eleventh Street and Fifth Avenue during a walk she had insisted on taking. Then, too, there was the prize winning French poodle, a great big black poodle—none of your little, untroublesome white miniatures—who got sick riding in the rumble seat of a car with me on her way to the Greenwich Dog Show. She had a red rubber bib tucked around her throat and, since a rain storm came up when we were half way through the Bronx, I had to hold over her a small green umbrella, really more of a parasol.

The subject is dogs—always a good topic for a nation of dog and cat lovers. Even people who do not like dogs rarely feel threatened by them and will probably be interested in the embarrassment that dog lovers experience with their pets. It is an old subject, but Thurber's images of a bibbed and parsoled poodle and a Scotch terrier having a pup on Fifth Avenue give an unusual twist to dog stories that have gone before.

2. **The Element of Surprise.** Surprise is one of the oldest, most popular and most dependable ways of getting people to laugh. Shout "SURPRISE!" at a birthday party and everyone bursts out laughing. Hide from a baby and

suddenly reappear, and the child will giggle till it's out of breath. It must be a pleasant, non-threatening surprise, of course. It is not funny to surprise someone with the news that their cat has been killed.

In written humor we may be surprised when a comic character, a poor failure by nature, suddenly appears as wealthy Lord Bullmarket. In the movie M.A.S.H. humor is created when the pompous Major Burns is suddenly brought low by Radar, the meek company clerk. Shock, coincidence and sudden reversals (the pleasant kind, when you expect a small piece of pie and get a large one) can all be used to generate smiles and laughter.

Muggs, who was a mean-tempered dog, was full of surprises. What else happens in this passage that is unexpected?

> He [Muggs] was never in a very good humor, even after a meal. Nobody knew exactly what was the matter with him, but whatever it was it made him irascible, especially in the mornings. Roy [Thurber's brother] never felt very well in the morning, either, especially before breakfast, and once when he came downstairs and found that Muggs had moodily chewed up the morning paper he hit him in the face with a grapefruit and then jumped up on the dining room table, scattering dishes and silverware and spilling the coffee. Muggs' first free leap carried him all the way across the table and into a brass fire screen in front of the gas grate but he was back on his feet in a moment and in the end he got Roy and gave him a pretty vicious bite in the leg.

Thurber tells us that both Muggs and Roy are grouchy in the morning. What is truly surprising in this passage is not Muggs's behavior, but Roy's outrageous reaction when he discovers that Muggs has destroyed his morning paper.

3. Humor in the Absurd, Illogical and Ludicrous. Clowns are funny because they are absurd; they do illogical and ludicrous things. No matter how many times they've seen it, people always laugh at the huge circus clown who gets out of a tiny car and is soon followed by his Saint Bernard dog. The whole thing makes no sense at all, but it is very funny.

An author may achieve the absurd through exaggeration or overstatement, such as Sinclair Lewis did in *Babbitt* when he thanked "the God of Progress" for the invention of George Babbitt's B.V.D.'s. An author may create incongruous situations that are funny because they are ludicrous. Snoopy of "Peanuts" is ridiculous and impossible as the Red Baron, but he is funny as well. An example of logical illogic that resulted in absurdity appeared in James Michener's *Hawaii* to demonstrate the "civilizing" effect of clothing on the newly christianized Hawaiian men. Two of them, having only one suit between them, logically decided to share it. So one came to church wearing only the pants while the other wore the coat and nothing else.

A good deal of Thurber's humor is based on the ludicrous and the absurd. In "The Dog That Bit People," Thurber tells us that his mother was the only one who ever defended Muggs. As he tells it, her defense was not always logical, as in this episode:

One time my mother went to the Chittenden Hotel to call on a woman mental healer who was lecturing in Columbus on the subject of "Harmonious Vibrations." She wanted to find out if it was possible to get harmonious vibrations into a dog. "He's a large tan-colored Airedale," mother explained. The woman said that she had never treated a dog but she advised my mother to hold the thought that he did not bite and would not bite. Mother was holding the thought the very next morning when Muggs got the iceman but she blamed that slip-up on the iceman. "If you didn't think he would bite you, he wouldn't," mother told him. He stomped out of the house in a terrible jangle of vibrations.

4. Humor Through Identification. Just as we are able to identify with fictional characters we can also identify with humorous situations. This is because we have many likes and dislikes, habits and impulses, fears and frustrations that we share in common. We get hungry and thirsty and sometimes carry eating and drinking to excess; we worry about not being sufficiently attractive; we are ambitious but are suspicious of too much ambition; we are greedy but don't like other people to be greedy; we follow fads and usually deny that we do. We fear authority, approach vending machines with the suspicion that they will cheat us, and even the most intrepid flyer worries deep down about an airplane crashing.

When these things are paraded in public, and perhaps colored with comic exaggeration, we find them funny because we instantly identify with the situation. Thus, jokes about vending machines that don't work, passes at members of the opposite sex which fail miserably, airplanes with maniacs for pilots, and clothes that are too extreme rarely fail to rouse an audience to laughter. In such cases we are laughing at ourselves; it is a form of relief for our own frustrations.

James Thurber's characters are famous for being very run-of-the mill humans with all the fears and frustrations that plague the best of us. Can you identify with the poor Fuller Brush man in the following scene?

A few months before Muggs died, he got to "seeing things." He would rise slowly from the floor, growling low, and stalk stiff-legged and menacing toward nothing at all. Sometimes the Thing would be just a little to the right or left of a visitor. Once a Fuller Brush salesman got hysterics. Muggs came wandering into the room like Hamlet following his father's ghost. His eyes were fixed on a spot just to the left of the Fuller Brush man, who stood it until Muggs was about three slow, creeping paces from him. Then he shouted. Muggs wavered on past him into the hallway grumbling to himself but the Fuller Brush man went on shouting. I think mother had to throw a pan of cold water on him before he stopped.

We all have a latent fear of growling menacing dogs, and if you know Airedales you know they are good-sized heavy dogs that look as if they could do some damage when riled. So we can easily picture—even feel—the fear of the Fuller Brush man as Muggs came toward him stiff-legged and growling. But it's not a real situation, all comes right in the end, and so we can laugh at the joke and at our own relief.

5. **Humor in Feeling Superior.** You may recall that the first rule of humor is that it must give pleasure. Nothing gives more pleasure than feeling that you are superior to someone else. Part of the fun in watching clowns is that they give us an opportunity to feel superior. They act so dumb that we *know* we are smarter than they are. Children, especially, who live in an inferior world, love to watch the antics of someone more put upon than they themselves are.

One of the funniest scenes from Thurber's "University Days" is the one in the economics classroom when both professor and students are trying to get a correct answer from the star tackle of the football team in order to save him for a crucial game against Illinois. He was not dumber than an ox, we are told, but he was not any smarter. So no matter how inept you have been in class, you can't help but feel superior to poor Bolenciecwcz as he faces his greatest challenge.

> One day when we were on the subject of transportation and distribution, it came Bolenciecwcz's turn to answer a question. "Name one means of transportation," the professor said to him. No light came into the big tackle's eyes. "Just any means of transportation," said the professor. Bolenciecwcz sat staring at him . . . ." You may choose among steam, horse-drawn, or electrically propelled vehicles," said the instructor. "I might suggest the one which we commonly take in making long journeys across land." There was a profound silence in which everybody stirred uneasily, including Bolenciecwcz and Mr. Bassum. Mr. Bassum abruptly broke this silence in an amazing manner. "Choo-choo-choo," he said, in a low voice, and turned instantly scarlet . . . . "Toot, toot, too-tooooooot!" Some student with a deep voice moaned, and we all looked encouragingly at Bolenciecwcz. Somebody else gave a fine imitation of a locomotive letting off steam. Mr. Bassum himself rounded off the little show. "Ding, dong, ding, dong," he said, hopefully. Bolenciecwcz was staring at the floor now, trying to think, his great brow furrowed, his huge hands rubbing together, his face red.

The fine line between humor and satire is very clear here. In satire, Bolenciecwcz would be a subject of ridicule or sarcasm; he would be used to show the failure of colleges to teach, for example. But here, while we feel superior to poor Bolenciecwcz, we also sympathize with him because we have been this same route ourselves; maybe not over something as elementary as a choo-choo train, but in just such a situation where we blushed painfully in our ignorance.

MY LIFE AND HARD TIMES

You may have noticed as you read each example of Thurber's humor that a joke is a combination of things. The scene in the classroom not only makes you feel superior to Bolenciecwcz, but there is a sharp element of surprise when the professor breaks down and goes "choo-choo-choo." The situation is completely absurd, but you can still identify with the big tackle in his embarrassment. Thus, the scene combines all of the tried and true elements of humor. Humor is never one thing; it is an emotional *process* that joins the technique of the writer and the mood of the reader to create laughter, a chuckle, or a smile. You find it everywhere you go, especially in your reading. So look for it, be aware of it, and enjoy it.

As you read the selections:

- In "The Dog That Bit People," notice what technique Thurber uses to create humor during the scene with the mice in the pantry.

- In "The Dog That Bit People," notice which element of humor is at work in the passage where Muggs gets picked up by his tail.

- In "University Days," try to identify the technique for achieving humor in the passage where Thurber finally sees something through his microscope.

- In "University Days," be aware of the way in which Thurber makes General Littlefield a humorous figure.

My Life and Hard Times
James Thurber

THE DOG THAT BIT PEOPLE

Probably no one man should have as many dogs in his life as I have had, but there was more pleasure than distress in them for me except in the case of an Airedale named Muggs. He gave me more trouble than all the other fifty-four or -five put together, although my moment of keenest embarrassment was the time a Scotch terrier named Jeannie, who had just had six puppies in the clothes closet of a fourth floor apartment in New York, had the unexpected seventh and last at the corner of Eleventh Street and Fifth Avenue during a walk she had insisted on taking. Then, too, there was the prize winning French poodle, a great big black poodle—none of your little, untroublesome white miniatures—who got sick riding in the rumble seat of a car with me on her way to the Greenwich Dog Show. She had a red rubber bib tucked around her throat and, since a rain storm came up when we were half way through the Bronx, I had to hold over her a small green umbrella, really more of a parasol. The rain beat down fearfully and suddenly the driver of the car drove into a big garage, filled with mechanics. It happened so quickly that I forgot to put the umbrella down and I will always remember, with sickening distress, the look of incredulity mixed with hatred that came over the face of the particular hardened garage man that came over to see what we wanted, when he took a look at me and the poodle. All garage men, and people of that intolerant stripe, hate poodles with their curious haircut, especially the pom-poms that you got to leave on their hips if you expect the dogs to win a prize.

But the Airedale, as I have said, was the worst of all my dogs. He really wasn't my dog, as a matter of fact: I came home from a vacation one summer to find that my brother Roy had bought him while I was away. A big, burly, choleric dog, he always acted as if he thought I wasn't one of the family. There was a slight advantage in being one of the family, for he didn't bite the family as often as he bit strangers. Still, in the years that we had him he bit everybody but mother, and he made a pass at her once but missed. That was during the month when we suddenly had mice, and Muggs refused to do anything about them. Nobody ever had mice exactly like the mice we had that month. They acted like pet mice, almost like mice somebody had trained. They were so friendly that one night when mother entertained at dinner the Friraliras, a club she and my father had belonged to for twenty years, she put down a lot of little dishes with food in them on the pantry floor so that the mice would be satisfied with that and wouldn't come into the dining room. Muggs stayed out in the pantry with the mice, lying on the floor, growling to himself—not at the mice, but about all the people in the next room that he would have liked to get at. Mother slipped out into the pantry once to see how everything was going. Everything was going fine. It made her so mad to see Muggs lying there, oblivious of the mice—they came running up to her—that she slapped him and he slashed at her, but didn't make it. He was sorry immediately, mother said. He was always sorry, she said, after he bit someone, but we could not understand how she figured this out. He didn't act sorry.

Mother used to send a box of candy every Christmas to the people the Airedale bit. The list finally contained forty or more names. Nobody could understand why we didn't get rid of the dog. I didn't understand it very well myself, but we didn't get rid of him. I think that one or two people tried to poison Muggs—he acted poisoned once in a while—and old Major Moberly fired at him once with his service revolver near the Seneca Hotel in East Broad Street—but Muggs lived to be almost eleven years old and even when he could hardly get around he bit a Congressman who had called to see my father on business. My mother had never liked the Congressman—she said the signs of his horoscope showed he couldn't be trusted (he was Saturn with the moon in Virgo)—but she sent him a box of candy that Christmas. He sent it right back, probably because he suspected it was trick candy. Mother persuaded herself it was all for the best that the dog had bitten him, even though father lost an important business association because of it. "I wouldn't be associated with such a man," mother said. "Muggs could read him like a book."

Nobody Knew Exactly What Was the Matter with Him

BEST-SELLING CHAPTERS

We used to take turns feeding Muggs to be on his good side, but that didn't always work. He was never in a very good humor, even after a meal. Nobody knew exactly what was the matter with him, but whatever it was it made him irascible, especially in the mornings. Roy never felt very well in the morning, either, especially before breakfast, and once when he came downstairs and found that Muggs had moodily chewed up the morning paper he hit him in the face with a grapefruit and then jumped up on the dining room table, scattering dishes and silverware and spilling the coffee. Muggs' first free leap carried him all the way across the table and into a brass fire screen in front of the gas grate but he was back on his feet in a moment and in the end he got Roy and gave him a pretty vicious bite in the leg. Then he was all over it; he never bit anyone more than once at a time. Mother always mentioned that as an argument in his favor; she said he had a quick temper but that he didn't hold a grudge. She was forever defending him. I think she liked him because he wasn't well. "He's not strong," she would say, pityingly, but that was inaccurate; he may not have been well but he was terribly strong.

One time my mother went to the Chittenden Hotel to call on a woman mental healer who was lecturing in Columbus on the subject of "Harmonious Vibrations." She wanted to find out if it was possible to get harmonious vibrations into a dog. "He's a large tan-colored Airedale," mother explained. The woman said that she had never treated a dog but she advised my mother to hold the thought that he did not bite and would not bite. Mother was holding the thought the very next morning when Muggs got the iceman but she blamed that slip-up on the iceman. "If you didn't think he would bite you, he wouldn't," mother told him. He stomped out of the house in a terrible jangle of vibrations.

Lots of People Reported Our Dog to the Police

One morning when Muggs bit me slightly, more or less in passing, I reached down and grabbed his short stumpy tail and hoisted him into the air. It was a foolhardy thing to do and the last time I saw my mother, about six months ago, she said she didn't know what possessed me. I don't either, except that I was pretty mad. As long as I held the dog off the floor by his tail he couldn't get at me, but he twisted and jerked so, snarling all the time, that I realized I couldn't hold him that way very long. I carried him to the kitchen and flung him onto the floor and shut the door on him just as he crashed against it. But I forgot about the backstairs. Muggs went up the backstairs and down the frontstairs and had me cornered in the living room. I managed to get up onto the mantelpiece above the fireplace, but it gave way and came down with a tremendous crash throwing a large marble clock, several vases, and myself heavily to the floor. Muggs was so alarmed by the racket that when I picked myself up he had disappeared. We couldn't find him anywhere, although we whistled and shouted, until old Mrs. Detweiler called after dinner that night. Muggs had bitten her once, in the leg, and she came into the living room only after we assured her that Muggs had run away. She had just seated herself when, with a great growling and scratching of claws, Muggs emerged from under a davenport where he had been quietly hiding all the time, and bit her again. Mother examined the bite and put arnica on it and told Mrs. Detweiler that it was only a bruise. "He just bumped you," she said. But Mrs. Detweiler left the house in a nasty state of mind.

Lots of people reported our Airedale to the police but my father held a municipal office at the time and was on friendly terms with the police. Even so, the cops had been out a couple times—once when Muggs bit Mrs. Rufus Sturtevant and again when he bit Lieutenant-Governor Malloy—but mother told them that it hadn't been Muggs' fault but the fault of the people who were bitten. "When he starts for them, they scream," she explained, "and that excites him." The cops suggested that it might be a good idea to tie the dog up, but mother said that it mortified him to be tied up and that he wouldn't eat when he was tied up.

Muggs at his meals was an unusual sight. Because of the fact that if you reached toward the floor he would bite you, we usually put his food plate on top of an old kitchen table with a bench alongside the table. Muggs would stand on the bench and eat. I remember that my mother's Uncle Horatio, who boasted that he was the third man up Missionary Ridge, was splutteringly indignant when he found out that we fed the dog on a table because we were afraid to put his plate on the floor. He said he wasn't afraid of any dog that ever lived and that he would put the dog's plate on the floor if we would give it to him. Roy said that if Uncle Horatio had fed Muggs on the ground just before the battle he would have been the first man up Missionary Ridge. Uncle Horatio was furious. "Bring him in! Bring him in now!" he shouted. "I'll feed the —— on the floor!" Roy was all for giving him a chance, but my father wouldn't hear of it. He said that Muggs had already been fed. "I'll feed him again!" bawled Uncle Horatio. We had quite a time quieting him.

BEST-SELLING CHAPTERS

Muggs at His Meals Was an Unusual Sight

In his last year Muggs used to spend practically all of his time outdoors. He didn't like to stay in the house for some reason or other—perhaps it held too many unpleasant memories for him. Anyway, it was hard to get him to come in and as result the garbage man, the iceman, and the laundryman wouldn't come near the house. We had to haul the garbage down to the corner, take the laundry out and bring it back, and meet the iceman a block from home. After this had gone on for some time we hit on an ingenious arrangement for getting the dog in the house so that we could lock him up while the gas meter was read, and so on. Muggs was afraid of only one thing, an electrical storm. Thunder and lightning frightened him out of his senses (I think he thought a storm had broken the day the mantelpiece fell). He would rush into the house and hide under a bed or in a clothes closet. So we fixed up a thunder machine out of a long narrow piece of sheet iron with a wooden handle on one end. Mother would shake this vigorously when she wanted to get Muggs into the house. It made an excellent imitation of thunder, but I suppose it was the most roundabout system for running a household that was ever devised. It took a lot out of mother.

A few months before Muggs died, he got to "seeing things." He would rise slowly from the floor, growling low, and stalk stiff-legged and menacing toward nothing at all. Sometimes the Thing would be just a little to the right or left of a visitor. Once a Fuller Brush salesman got hysterics. Muggs came wandering into the room like Hamlet following his father's ghost. His eyes were fixed on a spot just to the left of the Fuller Brush man, who stood it until Muggs was about three slow, creeping paces from him. Then he shouted. Muggs wavered on past him into the hallway grumbling to himself but the Fuller man went on shouting. I think mother had to throw a pan of cold water on him before he stopped. That was the way she used to stop us boys when we got into fights.

Muggs died quite suddenly one night. Mother wanted to bury him in the family lot under a marble stone with some such inscription as "Flights of angels sing thee to thy rest" but we persuaded her it was against the law. In the end we just put up a smooth board above his grave along a lonely road. On the board I wrote with an indelible pencil "Cave Canem." Mother was quite pleased with the simple classic dignity of the old Latin epitaph.

UNIVERSITY DAYS

I passed all the other courses that I took at my University, but I could never pass botany. This was because all botany students had to spend several hours a week in a laboratory looking through a microscope at plant cells, and I could never see through a microscope. I never once saw a cell through a microscope. This used to enrage my instructor. He would wander around the laboratory pleased with the progress all the students were making in drawing the involved and, so I am told, interesting structure of flower cells, until he came to me. I would just be standing there. "I can't see anything," I would say. He would begin patiently enough, explaining how anybody can see through a microscope, but he would always end up in a fury, claiming that I could *too* see through a microscope but just pretended that I couldn't. "It takes away from the beauty of flowers anyway," I used to tell him. "We are not concerned with beauty in this course," he would say. "We are concerned solely with what I may call the *mechanics* of flars." "Well," I'd say, "I can't see anything." "Try it just once again," he'd say, and I would put my eye to the microscope and see nothing at all, except now and again a nebulous milky substance—a phenomenon of maladjustment. You were supposed to see a vivid, restless clockwork of sharply defined plant cells. "I see what looks like a lot of milk," I would tell him. This, he claimed, was the result of my not having adjusted the microscope properly, so he would readjust it for me, or rather, for himself. And I would look again and see milk.

I finally took a deferred pass, as they called it, and waited a year and tried again. (You had to pass one of the biological sciences or you couldn't graduate.) The professor had come back from vacation brown as a berry, bright-eyed, and eager to explain cell-structure again to his classes. "Well," he said to me, cheerily, when we met in the first laboratory hour of the semester, "we're going to see cells this time, aren't we?" "Yes, sir," I said. Students to right of me and to left of me and in front of me were seeing cells; what's more, they were quietly drawing pictures of them in their notebooks. Of course, I didn't see anything.

"We'll try it," the professor said to me, grimly, "with every adjustment of the microscope known to man. As God is my witness, I'll arrange this glass so that you see cells through it or I'll give up teaching. In twenty-two years of botany, I—" He cut off abruptly for he was beginning to quiver all over, like Lionel Barrymore, and he genuinely wished to hold onto his temper; his scenes with me had taken a great deal out of him.

So we tried it with every adjustment of the microscope known to man. With only one of them did I see anything but blackness or the familiar lacteal opacity, and that time I saw, to my pleasure and amazement, a variegated constellation of flecks, specks, and dots. These I hastily drew. The instructor, noting my activity, came back from an adjoining desk, a smile on his lips and his eyebrows high in hope. He looked at my cell drawing. "What's that?" he demanded, with a hint of a squeal in his voice. "That's what I saw," I said. "You didn't, you didn't, you *did*n't!" he screamed, losing control of his temper instantly, and he bent over and squinted into the microscope. His head snapped up. "That's your eye!" he shouted. "You've fixed the lens so that it reflects! You've drawn your eye!"

He Was Beginning to Quiver All Over Like Lionel Barrymore

Another course that I didn't like, but somehow managed to pass, was economics. I went to that class straight from the botany class, which didn't help me any in understanding either subject. I used to get them mixed up. But not as mixed up as another student in my economics class who came there direct from a physics laboratory. He was a tackle on the football team, named Bolenciecwcz. At that time Ohio State University had one of the best football teams in the country, and Bolenciecwcz was one of its outstanding stars. In order to be eligible to play it was necessary for him to keep up in his studies, a very difficult matter, for while he was not dumber than an ox he was not any smarter. Most of his professors were lenient and helped him along. None gave him more hints, in answering questions, or asked him simpler ones than the economics professor, a thin, timid man named Bassum. One day when we were on the subject of transportation and distribution, it came Bolenciecwcz's turn to answer a question. "Name one means of transportation," the professor said to him. No light came into the big tackle's eyes. "Just any means of transportation," said the professor. Bolenciecwcz sat staring at him. "That is," pursued the professor, "any medium, agency, or method of going from one place to another."

Bolenciecwcz Was Trying to Think

BEST-SELLING CHAPTERS

Bolenciecwcz had the look of a man who is being led into a trap. "You may choose among steam, horse-drawn, or electrically propelled vehicles," said the instructor. "I might suggest the one which we commonly take in making long journeys across land." There was a profound silence in which everybody stirred uneasily, including Bolenciecwcz and Mr. Bassum. Mr. Bassum abruptly broke this silence in an amazing manner. "Choo-choo-choo," he said, in a low voice, and turned instantly scarlet. He glanced appealingly around the room. All of us, of course, shared Mr. Bassum's desire that Bolenciecwcz should stay abreast of the class in economics, for the Illinois game, one of the hardest and most important of the season, was only a week off. "Toot, toot, too-toooooot!" some student with a deep voice moaned, and we all looked encouragingly at Bolenciecwcz. Somebody else gave a fine imitation of a locomotive letting off steam. Mr. Bassum himself rounded off the little show. "Ding, dong, ding, dong," he said, hopefully. Bolenciecwcz was staring at the floor now, trying to think, his great brow furrowed, his huge hands rubbing together, his face red.

"How did you come to college this year, Mr. Bolenciecwcz?" asked the professor. "Chuffa chuffa, chuffa chuffa."

"M'father sent me," said the football player.

"What on?" asked Bassum.

"I git an 'lowance," said the tackle, in a low, husky voice, obviously embarrassed.

"No, no," said Bassum. "Name a means of transportation. What did you ride here on?"

"Train," said Bolenciecwcz.

"Quite right," said the professor. "Now, Mr. Nugent, will you tell us——"

If I went through anguish in botany and economics—for different reasons—gymnasium work was even worse. I don't even like to think about it. They wouldn't let you play games or join in the exercises with your glasses on and I couldn't see with mine off. I bumped into professors, horizontal bars, agricultural students, and swinging iron rings. Not being able to see, I could take it but I couldn't dish it out. Also, in order to pass gymnasium (and you had to pass it to graduate) you had to learn to swim if you didn't know how. I didn't like the swimming pool, I didn't like swimming, and I didn't like the swimming instructor, and after all these years I still don't. I never swam but I passed my gym work anyway, by having another student give my gymnasium number (978) and swim across the pool in my place. He was a quiet, amiable blonde youth, number 473, and he would have seen through a microscope for me if we could have got away with it, but we couldn't get away with it. Another thing I didn't like about gymnasium work was that they made you strip the day you registered. It is impossible for me to be happy when I am stripped and being asked a lot of questions. Still, I did better than a lanky agricultural student who was cross-examined just before I was. They asked each student what college he was in—that is, whether Arts, Engineering, Commerce, or Agriculture. "What college are you in?" the instructor snapped at the youth in front of me. "Ohio State University," he said promptly.

It wasn't that agricultural student but it was another a whole lot like him who decided to take up journalism, possibly on the ground that when farming went to hell he could fall back on newspaper work. He didn't realize, of course, that that would be very much like falling back full-length on a kit of carpenter's tools. Haskins didn't seem cut out for journalism, being too embarrassed to talk to anybody and unable to use a typewriter, but the editor of the college paper assigned him to the cow barns, the sheep house, the horse pavilion, and the animal husbandry department generally. This was a genuinely big "beat," for it took up five times as much ground and got ten times as great a legislative appropriation as the College of Liberal Arts. The agricultural student knew animals, but nevertheless his stories were dull and colorlessly written. He took all afternoon on each of them, on account of having to hunt for each letter on the typewriter. Once in a while he had to ask somebody to help him hunt. "C" and "L," in particular, were hard letters for him to find. His editor finally got pretty much annoyed at the farmer-journalist because his pieces were so uninteresting. "See here, Haskins," he snapped at him one day, "why is it we never have anything hot from you on the horse pavilion? Here we have two hundred head of horses on this campus—more than any other university in the Western Conference except Purdue—and yet you never get any real low down on them. Now shoot over to the horse barns and dig up something lively." Haskins shambled out and came back in about an hour; he said he had something. "Well, start it off snappily," said the editor. "Something people will read." Haskins set to work and in a couple of hours brought a sheet of typewritten paper to the desk; it was a two-hundred word story about some disease that had broken out among the horses. Its opening sentence was simple but arresting. It read: "Who has noticed the sores on the tops of the horses in the animal husbandry building?"

Ohio State was a land grant university and therefore two years of military drill was compulsory. We drilled with old Springfield rifles and studied the tactics of the Civil War even though the World War was going on at the time. At 11 o'clock each morning thousands of freshmen and sophomores used to deploy over the campus, moodily creeping up on the old chemistry building. It was good training for the kind of warfare that was waged at Shiloh but it had no connection with what was going on in Europe. Some people used to think there was German money behind it, but they didn't dare say so or they would have been thrown in jail as German spies. It was a period of muddy thought and marked, I believe, the decline of higher education in the Middle West.

As a soldier I was never any good at all. Most of the cadets were glumly indifferent soldiers, but I was no good at all. Once General Littlefield, who was commandant of the cadet corps, popped up in front of me during regimental drill and snapped, "You are the main trouble with this university!" I think he meant that my type was the main trouble with the university but he may have meant me individually. I was mediocre at drill, certainly—that is, until my senior year. By that time I had drilled longer than anybody else in the Western Conference, having failed at military at the end of each preceding year so that I had to do it all over again. I was the only senior still in uniform. The uniform which, when new, had made me look like an interurban railway conductor, now that it had become faded and too tight made me look like Bert Williams in his bellboy act. This had a definitely bad effect on my morale. Even so, I had become by sheer practise little short of wonderful at squad maneuvers.

One day General Littlefield picked our company out of the whole regiment and tried to get it mixed up by putting it through one movement after another as fast as we could execute them: squads right, squads left, squads on right into line, squads right about, squads left front into line etc. In about three minutes one hundred and nine men were marching in one direction and I was marching away from them at an angle of forty degrees, all alone. "Company, halt!" shouted General Littlefield, "That man is the only man who has it right!" I was made a corporal for my achievement.

The next day General Littlefield summoned me to his office. He was swatting flies when I went in. I was silent and he was silent too, for a long time. I don't think he remembered me or why he had sent for me, but he didn't want to admit it. He swatted some more flies, keeping his eyes on them narrowly before he let go with the swatter. "Button up your coat!" he snapped. Looking back on it now I can see that he meant me although he was looking at a fly, but I just stood there. Another fly came to rest on a paper in front of the general and began rubbing its hind legs together. The general lifted the swatter cautiously. I moved restlessly and the fly flew away. "You startled him!" barked General Littlefield, looking at me severely. I said I was sorry. "That won't help the situation!" snapped the General, with cold military logic. I didn't see what I could do except offer to chase some more flies toward his desk, but I didn't say anything. He stared out the window at the faraway figures of co-eds crossing the campus toward the library. Finally, he told me I could go. So I went. He either didn't know which cadet I was or else he forgot what he wanted to see me about. It may have been that he wished to apologize for having called me the main trouble with the university; or maybe he had decided to compliment me on my brilliant drilling of the day before and then at the last minute decided not to. I don't know. I don't think about it much any more.

Unit 14

My Life
and Hard Times

- Comprehension Questions
- Understanding Humor
- Discussion Guides
- Writing Exercise

COMPREHENSION QUESTIONS

For each of the following statements and questions, select the option containing the most complete or most accurate answer.

1. According to Thurber, garage men
   (b) ☐ a. hate poodles.   ☐ c. hated Muggs.
       ☐ b. love poodles.   ☐ d. hate Airedales.

2. Muggs bit everyone
   (d) ☐ a. without exception.   ☐ c. except James Thurber.
       ☐ b. except mother.   ☐ d. except Roy.

3. In the expression, "a big, burly, *choleric* dog," *choleric* means
   (l) ☐ a. lazy.   ☐ c. crazy.
       ☐ b. sickly.   ☐ d. angry.

4. From the way mother acted, it would seem she was
   (j) ☐ a. a very logical person.   ☐ c. an illogical person.
       ☐ b. a rather mean person.   ☐ d. a practical person.

5. Every Christmas mother would
   (a) ☐ a. put out food for the mice.
       ☐ b. plan to get rid of Muggs.
       ☐ c. prepare for Muggs' tantrums.
       ☐ d. send candy to people Muggs had bitten.

6. It is probably fair to say that
   (g) ☐ a. no one could change Muggs' behavior.
       ☐ b. Muggs' behavior was changeable.
       ☐ c. deep down Muggs was soft-hearted.
       ☐ d. strict punishment would have changed Muggs.

7. Mother was determined
   (e) ☐ a. to treat Muggs' disorder.
       ☐ b. to dispose of Muggs.
       ☐ c. to defend Muggs.
       ☐ d. to train Muggs as a mouser.

8. From Mother's actions, one might infer that she considered Muggs
(h) ☐ a. a human being.   ☐ c. an attack dog.
    ☐ b. a nuisance to everyone.   ☐ d. one of the family.

9. A reader should infer that feeding Muggs
(h) ☐ a. made him more vicious.
    ☐ b. made no difference in his attitude.
    ☐ c. made him sleepy.
    ☐ d. made him more docile.

10. Muggs seemed to be in an especially bad mood
(c) ☐ a. in the morning.   ☐ c. on hot days.
    ☐ b. after supper.   ☐ d. when it rained.

11. The scene where Thurber picked Muggs up by the tail may best be
(k) described as
    ☐ a. drama.   ☐ c. slapstick.
    ☐ b. parlor humor.   ☐ d. satire.

12. The police were probably
(f) ☐ a. strict about leash laws.
    ☐ b. too lenient with Muggs.
    ☐ c. being bribed by mother.
    ☐ d. fond of Muggs.

13. The description of Muggs eating from a table may best be termed
(i) ☐ a. ludicrous.   ☐ c. frightening.
    ☐ b. tense.   ☐ d. moving.

14. Muggs
(b) ☐ a. died by poisoning.
    ☐ b. died of heartbreak.
    ☐ c. was killed by Major Moberly.
    ☐ d. died suddenly of old age.

15. One of Thurber's problems in school was that he couldn't pass
(a) ☐ a. physics.   ☐ c. botany.
    ☐ b. anatomy.   ☐ d. chemistry.

16. In "University Days," the professor's exclamation "Well . . . we're going
(k) to see cells this time, aren't we?" can best be described as
    ☐ a. an expression of comic exaggeration.
    ☐ b. a buildup to a comic letdown.
    ☐ c. a comic surprise.
    ☐ d. a comic absurdity.

17. When it came to Thurber and microscopes, the mild professor was
(g) ☐ a. extremely patient.
    ☐ b. not willing to make an effort.
    ☐ c. a model teacher.
    ☐ d. not able to keep his temper.

18. Everyone wanted to help Bolenceicwcz because
(e) ☐ a. they wanted to save him from the professor's anger.
    ☐ b. he was a favorite among fraternity members.
    ☐ c. they wanted to save him for the game with Illinois.
    ☐ d. he was related to the college dean.

19. Underlying the comic questioning of Bolenciecwcz was a tone of
(i) ☐ a. anger.   ☐ c. annoyance.
    ☐ b. embarrassment.   ☐ d. irony.

20. In the expression "his professors were *lenient* and helped him always,"
(l) *lenient* means
    ☐ a. gently tolerant.
    ☐ b. sorry.
    ☐ c. disgusted.
    ☐ d. well trained.

21. From his description of his experience in gym, it must be inferred that
(h) Thurber
    ☐ a. had poor eyesight.   ☐ c. had no one to help him.
    ☐ b. was sickly.   ☐ d. was good only at swimming.

22. Because his articles for the newspaper had been dull, the agricultural
(d) student wrote about
    ☐ a. the Illinois game.   ☐ c. a new farming implement.
    ☐ b. sores on the horses.   ☐ d. horse racing.

23. From Thurber's description of military drill at Ohio State, you must
    (f) conclude that
         □ a. the leader kept abreast of new tactics.
         □ b. no one took the course.
         □ c. it was outdated.
         □ d. it was one of the most popular courses on campus.

24. A good description of General Littlefield would be
    (j) □ a. astute tactician.   □ c. cruel disciplinarian.
         □ b. pompous dolt.   □ d. military engineer.

25. During Thurber's visit to General Littlefield's office, the general
    (c) □ a. couldn't remember what he wanted to say.
         □ b. reprimanded Thurber for his misconduct.
         □ c. complimented Thurber on his performance during drill.
         □ d. apologized to Thurber for having insulted him.

Comprehension Skills: a—isolating details; b—recalling specific facts; c—retaining
concepts; d—organizing facts; e—understanding the main idea; f—drawing a
conclusion; g—making a judgment; h—making an inference; i—recognizing tone;
j—understanding characters; k—appreciation of literary forms; l—knowledge of
word meanings.

UNDERSTANDING HUMOR

Practice Exercise A

[The mice] were so friendly that one night when mother entertained at dinner ... she put down a lot of little dishes with food in them on the pantry floor so that the mice would be satisfied with that and wouldn't come into the dining room. Muggs stayed out in the pantry with the mice, lying on the floor, growling to himself—not at the mice, but about all the people in the next room that he would have liked to get at. Mother slipped out into the pantry once to see how everything was going. Everything was going fine. It made her so mad to see Muggs lying there, oblivious of the mice—they came running up to her—that she slapped him and he slashed at her, but didn't make it. He was sorry immediately, mother said. He was always sorry, she said, after he bit someone, but we could not understand how she figured this out. He didn't act sorry.

1. The humor in this passage stems from a situation which
   - ☐ a. allows you to feel superior.
   - ☐ b. is absurd and illogical.
   - ☐ c. arouses intense feeling.
   - ☐ d. makes a cute animal story.

2. Mrs. Thurber liked to make excuses for Muggs' behavior. Circle the sentences that describe the human characteristic that she attributed to Muggs.

Practice Exercise B

One morning when Muggs bit me slightly, more or less in passing, I reached down and grabbed his short stumpy tail and hoisted him into the air. It was a foolhardy thing to do and the last time I saw my mother, about six months ago, she said she didn't know what possessed me. I don't either, except that I was pretty mad. As long as I held the dog off the floor by his tail he couldn't get at me, but he twisted and jerked so, snarling all the time, that I realized I couldn't hold him that way very long. I carried him to the kitchen and flung him onto the floor and shut the door on him just as he crashed against it. But I forgot about the backstairs. Muggs went up the backstairs and down the frontstairs and had me cornered in the living room. I managed to get up onto the mantelpiece above the fireplace, but it gave way and came down with a tremendous crash throwing a large marble clock, several vases, and myself heavily to the floor.

1. The humor in this passage arises primarily from
   - ☐ a. lack of logic.
   - ☐ b. violence.
   - ☐ c. sympathy.
   - ☐ d. surprise.

2. Part of what makes Thurber funny is the fact that his stories are supposedly autobiographical. Circle two sentences which Thurber uses to make the story sound more convincingly true than it probably is.

Practice Exercise C

So we tried it with every adjustment of the microscope known to man. With only one of them did I see anything but blackness or the familiar lacteal opacity, and that time I saw, to my pleasure and amazement, a variegated constellation of flecks, specks, and dots. These I hastily drew. The instructor, noting my activity, came back from an adjoining desk, a smile on his lips and his eyebrows high in hope. He looked at my cell drawing. "What's that?" he demanded, with a hint of a squeal in his voice. "That's what I saw," I said. "You didn't, you didn't, you *didn*'t!" he screamed, losing control of his temper instantly, and he bent over and squinted into the microscope. His head snapped up. "That's your eye!" he shouted. "You've fixed the lens so that it reflects! You've drawn your eye!"

1. Several elements of humor are at work here, but the most obvious are
   - ☐ a. aggravation and reversal.
   - ☐ b. lack of logic and clowning.
   - ☐ c. identification and surprise.
   - ☐ d. hostility and superiority.

2. To heighten tension and increase the comic effect, the author uses a sentence that is an obvious exaggeration (hyperbole). Circle that sentence.

Practice Exercise D

The next day General Littlefield summoned me to his office. He was swatting flies when I went in. I was silent and he was silent too, for a long time. I don't think he remembered me or why he had sent for me, but he didn't want to admit it. He swatted some more flies, keeping his eyes on them narrowly before he let go with the swatter. "Button up your coat!" he snapped. Looking back on it now I can see that he meant me although he was looking at a fly, but I just stood there. Another fly came to rest on a paper in front of the general and began rubbing its hind legs together. The general lifted the swatter cautiously. I moved restlessly and the fly flew away. "You startled him!" barked General Littlefield, looking at me severely. I said I was sorry. "That won't help the situation!" snapped the general, with cold military logic.

1. General Littlefield is a funny character because
   - ☐ a. you develop an instant dislike for him.
   - ☐ b. it is easy to feel sympathetic towards him.
   - ☐ c. generals are always comic.
   - ☐ d. he is a person in authority who looks silly.

2. General Littlefield issues one order and two expressions of reproach that seem trivial for a general. Circle these in the passage above.

DISCUSSION GUIDES

Analyzing Humor

1. Many humorists use stereotypes to get laughs—absentminded professors, corrupt politicians, loud-mouthed tourists in Bermuda shorts, and so on. Why do we find stereotypes humorous?

2. It is apparently funny when people get hurt—witness slapstick comedy. How does Thurber use this device? When is getting hurt *not* funny?

3. Compare *Mad* magazine humor with Thurber's humor, which may be called *The New Yorker* magazine humor.

Interpreting the Selections

4. To what extent can you believe in Muggs as a dog that really existed as described?

5. Why would a dog lover find the story of Muggs funny? Why would a dog hater find it funny? Why may either a dog lover or dog hater find the story *not* funny?

6. Do you find that teachers or professors sometimes show undue or unfair leniency to one sort of student or another, such as happened in the case of Bolenciecwcz?

7. *My Life and Hard Times* is an "autobiography." How would you describe James Thurber based on what you have read? (If you want to check your opinion, a good biography of Thurber is *The Clocks of Columbus* by Charles S. Holmes.)

Analyzing the Author's Technique

8. Thurber's people are notably ordinary. Why do you think this has enhanced his popularity?

9. Thurber's technique and Charles Schulz's (author of "Peanuts") are similar in many ways. How are they similar?

10. You have learned that Thurber was a humorist rather than a satirist. How would "The Dog That Bit People" have been different if Thurber had intended it to be a satire?

WRITING EXERCISE

All of us, at one time or another, have had something funny happen to us. These episodes make good stories—ones we enjoy telling our friends and acquaintances.

Instructions: Think of something funny that has happened to you recently. It may be something to do with a pet, something that happened to you in school, or a topic of your own choosing. Pretend you are writing a letter to a friend, describing the funny situation. Feel free to stretch the truth a little by exaggerating the details or the reactions of the people involved. Answering the following questions in your own mind may help you choose the best topic to write about:

1. Was the situation light and non-threatening?

2. Was there an element of surprise?

3. Did anything happen that was absurd or illogical?

4. Was it a situation that others can identify with?

Unit 15
Experiencing Fiction

The Godfather

Introduction

To the old world Italians, the role of godfather in the religious life of a family is a sacred relationship. "Italians have a little joke," explains a character in *The Godfather*, "that the world is so hard a man must have two fathers to look after him, and that's why they have godfathers." A child's godfather gives presents on birthdays and at Christmas, and looks after the child if something happens to the parents.

The Italian underworld is organized into "Families;" the *don*, or leader, of each Family is also called "the godfather" because he, too, takes care of others. People come to him for help—to reason with a greedy landlord, to get a young boy a job, to borrow a desperately needed sum of money—above all, to obtain a kind of rough justice in a society that does not always protect the rights of its weaker members. In return for such favors, the don asks for that man's friendship and respect, and the performance of some small service should it ever be necessary.

The Godfather, by Mario Puzo, follows the ebb and flow of the Corleone Family fortunes in the New York underworld of the 1940s. As the book opens, Don Vito Corleone is hosting an extravagant wedding reception for his daughter, Connie. By tradition, no Sicilian can refuse a request on his daughter's wedding day. Thus the Don spends part of the day hearing the many requests for favors from men who respectfully call him "Godfather." At the Don's side are Tom Hagen and Sonny Corleone. As *consigliore*, or legal advisor, for the Corleone family, Tom Hagen advises the Don and sees that his orders are carried out. Sonny Corleone, the Don's eldest son, is being groomed for the time when he will run the Family business. Also present at the wedding party are Michael Corleone and his girl friend, Kay Adams, the product of an old New England family. Michael, who is the Don's youngest son, rejected the Family business and enlisted in the Marines where he soon rose to the rank of captain and was decorated for bravery. Upon his discharge as a war hero, he entered Dartmouth College.

With his daughter's wedding behind him, the Don attends to an item of business which could become very nasty. Virgil Sollozzo, an important underworld figure, wants the Corleone Family to join him in a vast narcotics operation. Don Corleone has reservations about this new venture and, in a meeting with Sollozzo, politely refuses his proposition. Sonny, however, makes an inexcusable mistake. Without thinking, he shoots off his mouth and reveals to Sollozzo that he is in favor of the drug deal. Sollozzo now knows that Family opinion concerning the deal is divided.

Three months later, Sollozzo makes his move and has the Don gunned down in the street. Incredibly, in spite of the five bullets that have been pumped into him, the Don is still alive. A second attempt is made on the Godfather's life while he is in the hospital, but it is foiled by Michael Corleone, who has returned home temporarily in this time of crisis.

At this point, Sollozzo contacts Sonny, who is now the acting head of the Corleone Family, and requests another meeting. He wants Michael to listen to his deal and relay his terms to Sonny. As a "civilian," Michael is not expected to make trouble. But just in case, Sollozzo is being escorted to the secret meeting by a corrupt police captain named McCluskey. There is an un-written rule in the underworld against killing a policeman; it creates too much heat for everyone.

Sollozzo is in for a surprise, though. Michael, the "straight" Corleone, realizes that his father's life is in jeopardy as long as Sollozzo lives. He is the only one who can get close to Sollozzo, and therefore he must be the one to kill him.

In the chapter you are about to read, Michael Corleone "makes his bones" (a rite of initiation in the underworld) with the double murder of Sollozzo and McCluskey. It is a daring scheme, and Michael is a rank amateur in a deadly game. The element of planning is critical and the tension mounts as the moment of truth approaches when Michael must make his move into the world of crime.

The author, Mario Puzo, is the son of a railroad worker and grew up in Hell's Kitchen, an aptly named neighborhood on New York City's west side. "At a very early age," recalls Puzo, "I discovered libraries. In the summer-time I was one of the great Tenth Avenue athletes, but in the wintertime I became a sissy. I read books."

Puzo's first two novels, *The Dark Arena* and *The Fortunate Pilgrim*, were warmly praised by critics. But it was *The Godfather*, published in 1969, that made his name and fortune. Its depiction of the Italian underworld is so realistic that many readers assume he must have been writing from first-hand experience. Even members of the Mafia were impressed by its authenticity. "After the book became famous," comments Puzo, "I was introduced to a few gentlemen related to the material . . . They refused to believe that I had never had the confidence of a don." But the book was written entirely from research and from the stories told by his Italian immigrant mother when he was growing up.

Experiencing Fiction

Each best-selling chapter in this book has been selected because it illustrates a particular literary element or genre. The lessons that accompany these chapters examine each of these elements and show how and why an author uses them in a carefully controlled way to tell a story. But there is one thing the author cannot control, and that is the effect the book has on the reader. So you, in fact, are the last and most important element needed to make a book successful. You must participate actively in making real an experience that the author has attempted to create for you.

If an author has done a good job with the various literary elements, you will be drawn into the story. The story then becomes an experience for you just as a movie, a play, a concert, going for a hike in the woods, or falling in love are experiences. As you read, you apply your mind to what is going on and your feelings are aroused, just as in any other experience you may have. In the end, either you enjoy the experience or you don't, and it either adds to your store of knowledge or it doesn't, depending on how well you and the author have got along together.

The experience of reading is a very complicated psychological process which neither doctors nor philosophers have yet explained to everyone's satisfaction. We know for sure, however, that readers do have an experience when they read and that this experience is very important in determining whether a book is good or bad, whether it is a success or a failure. For our purposes, let's just look at four aspects of a reader's experience with a book.

First, you must help in creating the experience. You are not dealing with real life, after all, but with words on paper. So you must imagine the situation that the author is describing. If the author has done a good job, you will imagine so intensely that you will, in a way, participate in what is going on.

Second, you react to the situation. Having become a participant in the story, you react to what is going on as you would when undergoing any other experience. There are people to like or dislike, ideas to accept or reject, and events to play on the full range of your emotions.

Third, if the book is well done and you truly have had an experience reading it, you are bound to have broadened your background, learned from the experience and perhaps you will have changed your perspective of life because of it, just as you do after an experience you have had in real life.

Fourth, either you like the book or you don't. It's either an enjoyable and entertaining experience or it's not. You know this intuitively, just as you know whether or not you are enjoying a movie while you are watching it. People read to be entertained, to escape from the humdrum and problems of life. If the book has engaged you in an imaginative experience, chances are good that it will have entertained you and you will decide that you like it.

Let's examine these four aspects of a reader's experience in more detail and see how each applies to the chapter from *The Godfather*.

1. Imagination. We have shown in earlier lessons how the author builds a plot, fills the story with characters and places them in a setting. No effort is spared in making the situation and the people of the story real for you. But most of the time the situation, the setting and the characters are like nothing and no one you have ever experienced before. You were certainly not in Hawaii in 1830 with the characters of James Michener's book *Hawaii*. You never lived in a rabbit warren or talked with rabbits of the kind you meet in *Watership Down*, nor did you come to America in a slave ship with Kunta Kinte of *Roots*. And it's not likely that you have been associated with organized crime, or with characters like those in *The Godfather*. How, then, can you understand and enjoy a story told from the viewpoint of strange characters in a setting that is totally foreign to anything you have ever experienced?

Using bits and pieces of information you have garnered from your real-life experiences, you apply your mind to the new situation and, with the author's help, you begin to create the experience within your imagination. The key elements you need are characters and incidents. Where there are people and there is something happening, you will at least participate in the experience to the extent of observing what is going on. If the author has done a good job, and if you have a strong, active imagination, you become emotionally embroiled in the situation, you take sides, and before you know it you are involved in something that is very close to a real-life experience. How might your imagination go to work on this opening passage from the reading selection?

> It was Tom Hagen who had to make all the arrangements for Michael's leaving the country, his false passport, his seaman's card, his berth on an Italian freighter that would dock in a Sicilian port. Emissaries were sent that very day by plane to Sicily to prepare a hiding place with the Mafia chief in the hill country.
>
> Sonny arranged for a car and an absolutely trustworthy driver to be waiting for Michael when he stepped out of the restaurant where the meeting would be held with Sollozzo. The driver would be Tessio himself, who had volunteered for the job. It would be a

beat-up-looking car but with a fine motor. It would have phony license plates and the car itself would be untraceable. It had been saved for a special job requiring the best.

In this passage many people are doing many things to assure the success of Michael's mission, and somehow you are there watching and maybe worrying. The mission is murder, not a situation you are likely to become involved in in real life, but if you have become interested in the story you at least want to see how these things are arranged in the underworld. If you have an active imagination you may wonder whether Tessio is as trustworthy as Sonny thinks he is. Has he checked the tires and remembered to put gas in the tank? You are imaginatively involved. Without your involvement all of the author's efforts will have been for naught. If you are not somehow sharing the experience that the author has painstakingly prepared, the story will fall flat on its face.

2. Reaction. How you react to the missionary invasion of Hawaii in 1830 when you read Michener's historical novel *Hawaii* depends a great deal on how you feel about missionaries before you read the book. If you believe in evangelical Christianity, you will admire the generous motives and personal sacrifice of such men as Abner Hale. If you are of a different turn of mind, you may abhor the missionaries' meddling with the culture of the islands. Readers of Italian origin are bound to approach *The Godfather* differently from the way readers with Irish, Polish or Jewish roots would. Native New Yorkers will step more easily into the settings than readers in Idaho or Nebraska. If Mario Puzo had not had an old-country Italian mother to tell him stories, *The Godfather* may have been told from the perspective of a police blotter rather than from inside an Italian family; and the reader's reaction would be quite different. All of these things are important to the way a story is created and the way it is read. Both author and reader bring themselves, their backgrounds and life values and attitudes, into the creation of the experience in a work of fiction.

In the following passage, Mario Puzo, a veteran of World War II, has his characters use an analogy from the World War II era to justify murder and gang warfare. Why will different readers react differently to Clemenza's philosophy in this passage?

"How bad will it be?" Michael asked.

"Very bad," Clemenza said. "It means an all-out war with the Tattaglia Family against the Corleone Family. Most of the others will line up with the Tattaglias. The Sanitation Department will be sweeping up a lot of dead bodies this winter." He shrugged. "These things have to happen once every ten years or so. It gets rid of the bad blood. And then if we let them push us around on the little things they wanta take over everything. You gotta stop them at the beginning. Like they shoulda stopped Hitler at Munich, they should never let him get away with that, they were just asking for big trouble when they let him get away with that."

Michael had heard his father say this same thing before, only in 1939 before the war actually started. If the Families had been running the State Department there would never have been World War II, he thought with a grin.

England and France knuckled under to Adolf Hitler at Munich, and millions of people lived to regret letting him "push us around on the little things." People from the World War II era and students of history will respond at once to the aptness of Clemenza's analogy and will see a wry humor in the notion of letting the Families run the State Department. If you have never heard of Munich you cannot react strongly to what Clemenza is saying. If you have been horrified by recent news of a CIA-organized crime conspiracy to assassinate Fidel Castro in 1960, you may experience a small shiver to think how close the Families have come to the State Department in real life. If you have strong feelings about the sacredness of human life you will probably be appalled by the image of bodies being loaded on garbage trucks. Others who are more callous and have strong feelings about gangsters may smile and accept the impending warfare as a distinct social benefit.

3. **Enlargement of Experience.** Every experience in life provides a slightly different view of the world; sometimes it's a larger, more panoramic view, while other times it's just a small peek at another side of a question. These views result in learning more about the world and its people, and perhaps more about yourself. As a result of the learning that comes through experience, people change. From school experiences you grow in knowledge and ability to the point where you can hold a job and plan a career. As the result of social experiences you change from a bashful, naive youngster to a self-possessed and experienced adult.

Reading is an enlargement of experience, too, and from your experiences with reading you learn and your perspectives may change just as they do when you have a real-life experience. What might you learn and how can your perspectives change as a result of reading the following passage? Michael wants to know how long he will have to remain in hiding after he has killed Sollozzo and McCluskey.

> "OK," Mike said. "How long do you think before I can come back?"
>
> "At least a year," Sonny said.
>
> Tom Hagen put in, "The Don might be able to work faster than that, Mike, but don't count on it. The time element hinges on a lot of factors. How well we can plant stories with the newsmen. How much the Police Department wants to cover up. How violently the other Families react. There's going to be a hell of a lot of heat and trouble. That's the only thing we can be sure of."

Most people grow up believing that policemen enforce the law impartially for everyone and that newspapers print only what they know to be true. As we grow older we hear about police scandals and we find that sometimes rumor, gossip and bias pass for impartial news coverage. The result is that our younger, more naive image of these venerable institutions becomes tarnished. In this passage, Tom Hagen tells Michael (and he tells us, too, since we are observing the action) that the time of Michael's return from hiding in Sicily after the murders will depend in part on how well he can plant stories with the newspapers and how much the Police Department wants to cover up the association of policemen like Captain McCluskey with the crime Families. You have learned a sad lesson which may change your perspective of the world you live in.

A word of caution, however: What you read in fiction is not always gospel truth; it is certainly biased—that is, it is colored by the author to suit his or her purposes. So you must keep in mind that the experience you are dealing with must be considered and evaluated carefully. There is no need to believe everything an author says any more than you believe everything you hear elsewhere in the world.

4. Entertainment. We read non-fiction—history, mathematics, science, newspapers, essays, and all the rest—in order to gather information and in order to learn. While we also learn from reading fiction, our primary reason for picking up a good novel is not to learn but to be entertained. Most of what we call entertainment in our lives is diversion, a pleasant change from the dull routine of everyday life. In a way, entertainment is excitement, an escape from the ordinary.

A story is an escape, too, but it is a different kind of escape than some other forms of amusement because when you read a story you escape not just *away* from something but *into* the life of the story. When someone says, "I just can't get into this book," they mean it quite literally. They don't like the book, can't get interested in it, because they haven't succeeded in escaping into the experience of the story. This may be the author's fault, the reader's fault, or a combination of the two.

One of the most entertaining aspects of reading fiction is that it affords an opportunity to participate in all sorts of wild, wicked and bizarre experiences from which we can emerge safe, unscathed and scot-free of punishment for our misdeeds simply by shutting the book. It is like a ride on a roller coaster. You may scream as the roller coaster takes you into a make-believe brush with death and danger, but you know you are really quite safe and there will be laughter and delicious relief at the end.

How does the following scene, one of the most dramatic and horrifying of the book, provide a reader with entertainment?

> Sollozzo was leaning toward him. Michael, his belly covered by the table, unbuttoned his jacket and listened intently. He could not understand a word the man was saying. It was literally gibberish to him. His mind was so filled with pounding blood that no word registered. Underneath the table his right hand moved to the gun tucked into his waistband and he drew it free. At that moment the waiter came to take their order and Sollozzo turned his head to speak to the waiter. Michael thrust the table away from him with his left hand and his right hand shoved the gun

almost against Sollozzo's head. The man's coordination was so acute that he had already begun to fling himself away at Michael's motion. But Michael, younger, his reflexes sharper, pulled the trigger. The bullet caught Sollozzo squarely between his eye and his ear and when it exited on the other side blasted out a huge gout of blood and skull fragments onto the petrified waiter's jacket. Instinctively Michael knew that one bullet was enough. Sollozzo had turned his head in that last moment and he had seen the light of life die in the man's eyes as clearly as a candle goes out.

If you have become as intensely involved in the story as most people do who read the book, your pulse beats faster and your spine tingles in the minutes preceding the shooting. The shooting itself is the moment of unbearable excitement—the plunge down the roller coaster—and finally, there you are at the end, safe and sound. You were never in any real danger from flying bullets and there are no skull fragments on your jacket. The danger, excitement and horror were all part of an imaginative experience that you entered into with the author, and that's entertainment. It is the most potent reason why so many people have read and enjoyed *The Godfather.*

As you read the chapter:

- Pay close attention to Clemenza's lesson on how to murder someone in a restaurant.

- Notice the passage in which Michael explains what makes his father, the Don, great.

- Try to imagine how you would react if you were in the restaurant when the murders occurred.

- Notice how you feel after Michael escapes from New York on board the Italian freighter.

The Godfather
Mario Puzo

CHAPTER 11

It was Tom Hagen who had to make all the arrangements for Michael's leaving the country, his false passport, his seaman's card, his berth on an Italian freighter that would dock in a Sicilian port. Emissaries were sent that very day by plane to Sicily to prepare a hiding place with the Mafia chief in the hill country.

Sonny arranged for a car and an absolutely trustworthy driver to be waiting for Michael when he stepped out of the restaurant where the meeting would be held with Sollozzo. The driver would be Tessio himself, who had volunteered for the job. It would be a beat-up-looking car but with a fine motor. It would have phony license plates and the car itself would be untraceable. It had been saved for a special job requiring the best.

Michael spent the day with Clemenza, practicing with the small gun that would be gotten to him. It was a .22 filled with soft-nosed bullets that made pinpricks going in and left insulting gaping holes when they exited from the human body. He found that it was accurate up to five of his steps away from a target. After that the bullets might go anywhere. The trigger was tight but Clemenza worked on this with some tools so that it pulled easier. They decided to leave it noisy. They didn't want an innocent bystander misunderstanding the situation and interfering out of ignorant courage. The report of the gun would keep them away from Michael.

Clemenza kept instructing him during the training session. "Drop the gun as soon as you've finished using it. Just let your hand drop to your side and the gun slip out. Nobody will notice. Everybody will think you're still armed. They'll be staring at your face. Walk out of the place very quickly but don't run. Don't look anybody directly in the eye but don't look away from them either. Remember, they'll be scared of you, believe me, they'll be scared of you. Nobody will interfere. As soon as you're outside Tessio will be in the car waiting for you. Get in and leave the rest to him. Don't be worried about accidents. You'd be surprised how well these affairs go. Now put this hat on and let's see how you look." He clapped a gray fedora on

Michael's head. Michael, who never wore a hat, grimaced. Clemenza reassured him. "It helps against identification, just in case. Mostly it gives witnesses an excuse to change their identification when we make them see the light. Remember, Mike, don't worry about prints. The butt and trigger are fixed with special tape. Don't touch any other part of the gun, remember that."

Michael said, "Has Sonny found out where Sollozzo is taking me?"

Clemenza shrugged. "Not yet. Sollozzo is being very careful. But don't worry about him harming you. The negotiator stays in our hands until you come back safe. If anything happens to you, the negotiator pays."

"Why the hell should he stick his neck out?" Michael asked.

"He gets a big fee," Clemenza said. "A small fortune. Also he is an important man in the Families. He knows Sollozzo can't let anything happen to him. Your life is not worth the negotiator's life to Sollozzo. Very simple. You'll be safe all right. We're the ones who catch hell afterwards."

"How bad will it be?" Michael asked.

"Very bad," Clemenza said. "It means an all-out war with the Tattaglia Family against the Corleone Family. Most of the others will line up with the Tattaglias. The Sanitation Department will be sweeping up a lot of dead bodies this winter." He shrugged. "These things have to happen once every ten years or so. It gets rid of the bad blood. And then if we let them push us around on the little things they wanta take over everything. You gotta stop them at the beginning. Like they shoulda stopped Hitler at Munich, they should never let him get away with that, they were just asking for big trouble when they let him get away with that."

Michael had heard his father say this same thing before, only in 1939 before the war actually started. If the Families had been running the State Department there would never have been World War II, he thought with a grin.

They drove back to the mall and to the Don's house, where Sonny still made his headquarters. Michael wondered how long Sonny could stay cooped up in the safe territory of the mall. Eventually he would have to venture out. They found Sonny taking a nap on the couch. On the coffee table was the remains of his late lunch, scraps of steak and bread crumbs and a half-empty bottle of whiskey.

His father's usually neat office was taking on the look of a badly kept furnished room. Michael shook his brother awake and said, "Why don't you stop living like a bum and get this place cleaned up?"

Sonny yawned. "What the hell are you, inspecting the barracks? Mike, we haven't got the word yet where Sollozzo and McCluskey plan to take you. If we don't find that out, how the hell are we going to get the gun to you?"

"Can't I carry it on me?" Michael asked. "Maybe they won't frisk me and even if they do maybe they'll miss it if we're smart enough. And even if they find it—so what. They'll just take it off me and no harm done."

Sonny shook his head. "Nah," he said. "We have to make this a sure hit on Sollozzo. Remember, get him first if you possibly can. McCluskey is slower and dumber. You should have plenty of time to take him. Did Clemenza tell you to be sure to drop the gun?"

"A million times," Michael said.

Sonny got up from the sofa and stretched. "How does your jaw feel, kid?"

"Lousy," Michael said. The left side of his face ached except those parts that felt numb because of the drugged wire holding it together. He took the bottle of whiskey from the table and swigged directly from it. The pain eased.

Sonny said, "Easy, Mike, now is no time to get slowed up by booze."

Michael said, "Oh, Sonny, stop playing the big brother. I've been in combat against tougher guys than Sollozzo and under worse conditions. Where the hell are his mortars? Has he got air cover? Heavy artillery? Land mines? He's just a wise guy with a big-wheel cop sidekick. Once anybody makes up their mind to kill them there's no other problem. That's the hard part, making up your mind. They'll never know what hit them."

Tom Hagen came into the room. He greeted them with a nod and went directly to the falsely listed telephone. He called a few times and then shook his head at Sonny. "Not a whisper," he said. "Sollozzo is keeping it to himself as long as he can."

The phone rang. Sonny answered it and he held up a hand as if to signal for quiet though no one had spoken. He jotted some notes down on a pad, then said, "OK, he'll be there," and hung up the phone.

Sonny was laughing. "That Sollozzo, he really is something. Here's the deal. At eight tonight he and Captain McCluskey pick up Mike in front of Jack Dempsey's bar on Broadway. They go someplace to talk, and get this. Mike and Sollozzo talk in Italian so that the Irish cop don't know what the hell they are talking about. He even tells me, don't worry, he knows McCluskey doesn't know one word in Italian unless it's 'soldi' and he's checked you out, Mike, and knows you can understand Sicilian dialect."

Michael said dryly, "I'm pretty rusty but we won't talk long."

Tom Hagen said, "We don't let Mike go until we have the negotiator. Is that arranged?"

Clemenza nodded. "The negotiator is at my house playing pinochle with three of my men. They wait for a call from me before they let him go."

Sonny sank back in the leather armchair. "Now how the hell do we find out the meeting place? Tom, we've got informers with the Tattaglia Family, how come they haven't given us the word?"

Hagen shrugged. "Sollozzo is really damn smart. He's playing this close to the vest, so close that he's not using any men as a cover. He figures the captain will be enough and that security is more important than guns. He's right too. We'll have to put a tail on Mike and hope for the best."

Sonny shook his head. "Nah, anybody can lose a tail when they really want to. That's the first thing they'll check out."

By this time it was five in the afternoon. Sonny, with a worried look on his face, said, "Maybe we should just let Mike blast whoever is in the car when it tries to pick him up."

Hagen shook his head. "What if Sollozzo is not in the car? We've tipped our hand for nothing. Damn it, we have to find out where Sollozzo is taking him."

Clemenza put in, "Maybe we should start trying to figure why he's making it such a big secret."

Michael said impatiently, "Because it's the percentage. Why should he let us know anything if he can prevent it? Besides, he smells danger. He must be leery as hell even with that police captain for his shadow."

Hagen snapped his fingers. "That detective, that guy Phillips. Why don't you give him a ring, Sonny? Maybe he can find out where the hell the captain can be reached. It's worth a try. McCluskey won't give a damn who knows where he's going."

Sonny picked up the phone and dialed a number. He spoke softly into the phone, then hung up. "He'll call us back," Sonny said.

They waited for nearly another thirty minutes and then the phone rang. It was Phillips. Sonny jotted something down on his pad and then hung up. His face was taut. "I think we've got it," he said. "Captain McCluskey always has to leave word on where he can be reached. From eight to ten tonight he'll be at the Luna Azure up in the Bronx. Anybody know it?"

Tessio spoke confidently. "I do. It's perfect for us. A small family place with big booths where people can talk in private. Good food. Everybody minds their own business. Perfect." He leaned over Sonny's desk and arranged stubbed-out cigarettes into map figures. "This is the entrance. Mike, when you finish just walk out and turn left, then turn the corner. I'll spot you and put on my headlights and catch you on the fly. If you have any trouble, yell and I'll try to come in and get you out. Clemenza, you gotta work fast. Send somebody up there to plant the gun. They got an old-fashioned toilet with a space between the water container and the wall. Have your man tape the gun behind there. Mike, after they frisk you in the car and find you're clean, they won't be too worried about you. In the restaurant, wait a bit before you excuse yourself. No, better still, ask permission to go. Act a little in trouble first, very natural. They can't figure anything. But when you come out again, don't waste any time. Don't sit down again at the table, start blasting. And don't take chances. In the head, two shots apiece, and out as fast as your legs can travel."

Sonny had been listening judiciously. "I want somebody very good, very safe, to plant that gun," he told Clemenza.

Clemenza said emphatically, "The gun will be there."

"OK," Sonny said. "Everybody get rolling."

Tessio and Clemenza left. Tom Hagen said, "Sonny, should I drive Mike down to New York?"

"No," Sonny said. "I want you here. When Mike finishes, then our work begins and I'll need you. Have you got those newspaper guys lined up?"

Hagen nodded. "I'll be feeding them info as soon as things break."

Sonny got up and came to stand in front of Michael. He shook his hand. "OK, kid," he said, "you're on. I'll square it with Mom your not seeing her before you left. And I'll get a message to your girl friend when I think the time is right. OK?"

"OK," Mike said. "How long do you think before I can come back?"

"At least a year," Sonny said.

Tom Hagen put in, "The Don might be able to work faster than that, Mike, but don't count on it. The time element hinges on a lot of factors. How well we can plant stories with the newsmen. How much the Police

Department wants to cover up. How violently the other Families react. There's going to be a hell of a lot of heat and trouble. That's the only thing we can be sure of."

Michael shook Hagen's hand. "Do your best," he said. "I don't want to do another three-year stretch away from home."

Hagen said gently, "It's not too late to back out, Mike, we can get somebody else, we can go back over our alternatives. Maybe it's not necessary to get rid of Sollozzo."

Michael laughed. "We can talk ourselves into any viewpoint," he said. "But we figured it right the first time. I've been riding the gravy train all my life, it's about time I paid my dues."

"You shouldn't let that broken jaw influence you," Hagen said. "McCluskey is a stupid man and it was business, not personal."

For the second time he saw Michael Corleone's face freeze into a mask that resembled uncannily the Don's. "Tom, don't let anybody kid you. It's all personal, every bit of business. They call it business. OK. But it's personal as hell. You know where I learned that from? The Don. My old man. The Godfather. If a bolt of lightning hit a friend of his the old man would take it personal. He took my going into the Marines personal. That's what makes him great. The Great Don. He takes everything personal. Like God. He knows every feather that falls from the tail of a sparrow or however the hell it goes. Right? And you know something? Accidents don't happen to people who take accidents as a personal insult. So I came late, OK, but I'm coming all the way. Damn right, I take that broken jaw personal; damn right, I take Sollozzo trying to kill my father personal." He laughed. "Tell the old man I learned it all from him and that I'm glad I had this chance to pay him back for all he did for me. He was a good father." He paused and then he said thoughtfully to Hagen, "You know, I can never remember him hitting me. Or Sonny. Or Freddie. And of course Connie, he wouldn't even yell at her. And tell me the truth, Tom, how many men do you figure the Don killed or had killed?"

Tom Hagen turned away. "I'll tell you one thing you didn't learn from him: talking the way you're talking now. There are things that have to be done and you do them and you never talk about them. You don't try to justify them. They can't be justified. You just do them. Then you forget it."

Michael Corleone frowned. He said quietly, "As the *Consigliori*, you agree that it's dangerous to the Don and our Family to let Sollozzo live?"

"Yes," Hagen said.

"OK," Michael said. "Then I have to kill him."

Michael Corleone stood in front of Jack Dempsey's restaurant on Broadway and waited for his pickup. He looked at his watch. It said five minutes to eight. Sollozzo was going to be punctual. Michael had made sure he was there in plenty of time. He had been waiting fifteen minutes.

All during the ride from Long Beach into the city he had been trying to forget what he had said to Hagen. For if he believed what he said, then his life was set on an irrevocable course. And yet, could it be otherwise after tonight? He might be dead after tonight if he didn't stop all this crap, Michael thought grimly. He had to keep his mind on the business at hand.

Sollozzo was no dummy and McCluskey was a very tough egg. He felt the ache in his wired jaw and welcomed the pain, it would keep him alert.

Broadway wasn't that crowded on this cold winter night, even though it was near theater time. Michael flinched as a long black car pulled up to the curb and the driver, leaning over, opened the front door and said, "Get in, Mike." He didn't know the driver, a young punk with slick black hair and an open shirt, but he got in. In the back seat were Captain McCluskey and Sollozzo.

Sollozzo reached a hand over the back of the seat and Michael shook it. The hand was firm, warm and dry. Sollozzo said, "I'm glad you came, Mike. I hope we can straighten everything out. All this is terrible, it's not the way I wanted things to happen at all. It should never have happened."

Michael Corleone said quietly, "I hope we can settle things tonight, I don't want my father bothered any more."

"He won't be," Sollozzo said sincerely. "I swear to you by my children he won't be. Just keep an open mind when we talk. I hope you're not a hot-head like your brother Sonny. It's impossible to talk business with him."

Captain McCluskey grunted. "He's a good kid, he's all right." He leaned over to give Michael an affectionate pat on the shoulder. "I'm sorry about the other night, Mike. I'm getting too old for my job, too grouchy. I guess I'll have to retire pretty soon. Can't stand the aggravation, all day I get aggravation. You know how it is." Then with a doleful sigh, he gave Michael a thorough frisk for a weapon.

Michael saw a slight smile on the driver's lips. The car was going west with no apparent attempt to elude any trailers. It went up on to the West Side Highway, speeding in and out of traffic. Anyone following would have had to do the same. Then to Michael's dismay it took the exit for the George Washington Bridge, they were going over to New Jersey. Whoever had given Sonny the info on where the meeting was to be held had given him the wrong dope.

The car threaded through the bridge approaches and then was on it, leaving the blazing city behind. Michael kept his face impassive. Were they going to dump him into the swamps or was it just a last-minute change in meeting place by the wily Sollozzo? But when they were nearly all the way across, the driver gave the wheel a violent twist. The heavy automobile jumped into the air when it hit the divider and bounced over into the lanes going back to New York City. Both McCluskey and Sollozzo were looking back to see if anyone had tried doing the same thing. The driver was really hitting it back to New York and then they were off the bridge and going toward the East Bronx. They went through the side streets with no cars behind them. By this time it was nearly nine o'clock. They had made sure there was no one on their tail. Sollozzo lit up a cigarette after offering his pack to McCluskey and Michael, both of whom refused. Sollozzo said to the driver, "Nice work. I'll remember it."

Ten minutes later the car pulled up in front of a restaurant in a small Italian neighborhood. There was no one on the streets and because of the lateness of the hour only a few people were still at dinner. Michael had been worried that the driver would come in with them, but he stayed outside with his car. The negotiator had not mentioned a driver, nobody had. Technically Sollozzo had broken the agreement by bringing him along. But Michael decided not to mention it, knowing they would think he would be afraid to mention it, afraid of ruining the chances for the success of the parley.

The three of them sat at the only round table, Sollozzo refusing a booth. There were only two other people in the restaurant. Michael wondered whether they were Sollozzo plants. But it didn't matter. Before they could interfere it would be all over.

McCluskey asked with real interest, "Is the Italian food good here?"

Sollozzo reassured him. "Try the veal, it's the finest in New York." The solitary waiter had brought a bottle of wine to the table and uncorked it. He poured three glasses full. Surprisingly McCluskey did not drink. "I must be the only Irishman who don't take the booze," he said. "I seen too many good people get in trouble because of the booze."

Sollozzo said placatingly to the captain, "I am going to talk Italian to Mike, not because I don't trust you but because I can't explain myself properly in English and I want to convince Mike that I mean well, that it's to everybody's advantage for us to come to an agreement tonight. Don't be insulted by this, it's not that I don't trust you."

Captain McCluskey gave them both an ironic grin. "Sure, you two go right ahead," he said. "I'll concentrate on my veal and spaghetti."

Sollozzo began speaking to Michael in rapid Sicilian. He said, "You must understand that what happened between me and your father was strictly a business matter. I have a great respect for Don Corleone and would beg for the opportunity to enter his service. But you must understand that your father is an old-fashioned man. He stands in the way of progress. The business I am in is the coming thing, the wave of the future, there are untold millions of dollars for everyone to make. But your father stands in the way because of certain unrealistic scruples. By doing this he imposes his will on men like myself. Yes, yes, I know, he says to me, 'Go ahead, it's your business,' but we both know that is unrealistic. We must tread on each other's corns. What he is really telling me is that I cannot operate my business. I am a man who respects himself and cannot let another man impose his will on me so what had to happen did happen. Let me say that I had the support, the silent support of all the New York Families. And the Tattaglia Family became my partners. If this quarrel continues, then the Corleone Family will stand alone against everyone. Perhaps if your father were well, it could be done. But the eldest son is not the man the Godfather is, no disrespect intended. And the Irish *Consigliori*, Hagen, is not the man Genco Abbandando was, God rest his soul. So I propose a peace, a truce. Let us cease all hostilities until your father is well again and can take part in these bargainings. The Tattaglia Family agrees, upon my persuasions and my indemnities, to forgo justice for their son Bruno. We will have peace. Meanwhile, I have to make a living and will do a little trading in my business. I do not ask your cooperation but I ask you, the Corleone Family, not to interfere. These are my proposals. I assume you have the authority to agree, to make a deal."

Michael said in Sicilian, "Tell me more about how you propose to start your business, exactly what part my Family has to play in it and what profit we can take from this business."

"You want the whole proposition in detail then?" Sollozzo asked.

Michael said gravely, "Most important of all I must have sure guarantees that no more attempts will be made on my father's life."

Sollozzo raised his hand expressively. "What guarantees can I give you? I'm the hunted one. I've missed my chance. You think too highly of me, my friend. I am not that clever."

Michael was sure now that the conference was only to gain a few days' time. That Sollozzo would make another attempt to kill the Don. What was beautiful was that the Turk was underrating him as a punk kid. Michael felt that strange delicious chill filling his body. He made his face look distressed. Sollozzo asked sharply, "What is it?"

Michael said with an embarrassed air, "The wine went right to my bladder. I've been holding it in. Is it all right if I go to the bathroom?"

Sollozzo was searching his face intently with his dark eyes. He reached over and roughly thrust his hand in Michael's crotch, under it and around, searching for a weapon. Michael looked offended. McCluskey said curtly, "I frisked him. I've frisked thousands of young punks. He's clean."

Sollozzo didn't like it. For no reason at all he didn't like it. He glanced at the man sitting at a table opposite them and raised his eyebrows toward the door of the bathroom. The man gave a slight nod that he had checked it, that there was nobody inside. Sollozzo said reluctantly, "Don't take too long." He had marvelous antenna, he was nervous.

Michael got up and went into the bathroom. The urinal had a pink bar of soap in it secured by a wire net. He went into the booth. He did it very quickly, then reached behind the enamel water cabinet until his hand touched the small, blunt-nosed gun fastened with tape. He ripped the gun loose, remembering that Clemenza had said not to worry about leaving prints on the tape. He shoved the gun into his waistband and buttoned his jacket over it. He washed his hands and wet his hair. He wiped his prints off the faucet with his handkerchief. Then he left the toilet.

Sollozzo was sitting directly facing the door of the toilet, his dark eyes blazing with alertness. Michael gave a smile. "Now I can talk," he said with a sigh of relief.

Captain McCluskey was eating the plate of veal and spaghetti that had arrived. The man on the far wall had been stiff with attention, now he too relaxed visibly.

Michael sat down again. He remembered Clemenza had told him not to do this, to come out of the toilet and blaze away. But either out of some warning instinct or sheer funk he had not done so. He had felt that if he had made one swift move he would have been cut down. Now he felt safe and he must have been scared because he was glad he was no longer standing on his legs. They had gone weak with trembling.

Sollozzo was leaning toward him. Michael, his belly covered by the table, unbuttoned his jacket and listened intently. He could not understand a word the man was saying. It was literally gibberish to him. His mind was so filled with pounding blood that no word registered. Underneath the table his right hand moved to the gun tucked into his waistband and he drew it free. At that moment the waiter came to take their order and Sollozzo turned his head to speak to the waiter. Michael thrust the table away from him with his left hand and his right hand shoved the gun almost against Sollozzo's head. The man's coordination was so acute that he had already begun to fling himself away at Michael's motion. But Michael, younger, his reflexes sharper, pulled the trigger. The bullet caught Sollozzo squarely between his eye and his ear and when it exited on the other side blasted out a huge gout of blood and skull fragments onto the petrified waiter's jacket. Instinctively Michael knew that one bullet was enough. Sollozzo had turned his head in that last moment and he had seen the light of life die in the man's eyes as clearly as a candle goes out.

Only one second had gone by as Michael pivoted to bring the gun to bear on McCluskey. The police captain was staring at Sollozzo with phlegmatic surprise, as if this had nothing to do with him. He did not seem to be aware of his own danger. His veal-covered fork was suspended in his hand and his eyes were just turning on Michael. And the expression on his face, in his eyes, held such confident outrage, as if now he expected Michael to surrender or to run away, that Michael smiled at him as he pulled the trigger. This shot was bad, not mortal. It caught McCluskey in his thick bull-like throat and he started to choke loudly as if he had swallowed too large a bite of the veal. Then the air seemed to fill with a fine mist of sprayed blood as he coughed it out of his shattered lungs. Very coolly, very deliberately, Michael fired the next shot through the top of his white-haired skull.

The air seemed to be full of pink mist. Michael swung toward the man sitting against the wall. This man had not made a move. He seemed paralyzed. Now he carefully showed his hands on top of the table and looked away. The waiter was staggering back toward the kitchen, an expression of horror on his face, staring at Michael in disbelief. Sollozzo was still in his chair, the side of his body propped up by the table. McCluskey, his heavy body pulling downward, had fallen off his chair onto the floor. Michael let the gun slip out of his hand so that it bounced off his body and made no noise. He saw that neither the man against the wall nor the waiter had noticed him dropping the gun. He strode the few steps toward the door and opened it. Sollozzo's car was parked at the curb still, but there was no sign of the driver. Michael turned left and around the corner. Headlights flashed on and a battered sedan pulled up to him, the door swinging open. He jumped in and the car roared away. He saw that it was Tessio at the wheel, his trim features hard as marble.

"Did you do the job on Sollozzo?" Tessio asked.

For that moment Michael was struck by the idiom Tessio had used. It was always used in a sexual sense, to do the job on a woman meant seducing her. It was curious that Tessio used it now. "Both of them," Michael said.

"Sure?" Tessio asked.

"I saw their brains," Michael said.

There was a change of clothes for Michael in the car. Twenty minutes later he was on an Italian freighter slated for Sicily. Two hours later the freighter put out to sea and from his cabin Michael could see the lights of New York City burning like the fires of hell. He felt an enormous sense of relief. He was out of it now. The feeling was familiar and he remembered being taken off the beach of an island his Marine division had invaded. The battle had been still going on but he had received a slight wound and was being ferried back to a hospital ship. He had felt the same overpowering relief then that he felt now. All hell would break loose but he wouldn't be there.

On the day after the murder of Sollozzo and Captain McCluskey, the police captains and lieutenants in every station house in New York City sent out the word: there would be no more gambling, no more prostitution, no more deals of any kind until the murderer of Captain McCluskey was caught. Massive raids began all over the city. All unlawful business activities came to a standstill.

Later that day an emissary from the Families asked the Corleone Family if they were prepared to give up the murderer. They were told that the affair did not concern them. That night a bomb exploded in the Corleone Family mall in Long Beach, thrown from a car that pulled up to the chain, then roared away. That night also two button men of the Corleone Family were killed as they peaceably ate their dinner in a small Italian restaurant in Greenwich Village. The Five Families War of 1946 had begun.

Unit 15

The Godfather

- Comprehension Questions
- Experiencing Fiction
- Discussion Guides
- Writing Exercise

COMPREHENSION QUESTIONS

For each of the following statements and questions, select the option containing the most complete or most accurate answer.

1. On the day of his meeting with Sollozzo and McCluskey, Michael
(c) receives a crash course from Clemenza in how to
    □ a. negotiate a deal.   □ c. speak Sicilian.
    □ b. commit murder.   □ d. wire explosives.

2. Clemenza wants Michael to wear a hat because "it gives witnesses an
(h) excuse to change their identification when we make them see the light."
    This statement implies that
    □ a. most witnesses cannot make a positive identification of a suspect.
    □ b. a hat obscures a criminal's face and makes positive identification difficult.
    □ c. the Family uses force and threats to scare off troublesome witnesses.
    □ d. witnesses sometimes change their identification when they see the suspect without a hat.

3. The plan to kill Sollozzo and McCluskey hinges upon one key piece of
(d) information, and that is
    □ a. what kind of guarantees Sollozzo will offer for the Don's safety.
    □ b. what role the Corleones will be offered in Sollozzo's new business.
    □ c. who will be driving the car carrying Sollozzo and McCluskey.
    □ d. where Sollozzo will take Mike for the meeting.

4. Michael says that the hardest part of knocking off Sollozzo and
(b) McCluskey is
    □ a. making up your mind to do it.
    □ b. catching them off guard.
    □ c. pulling the trigger.
    □ d. living with yourself afterwards.

5. Which of the following best defines *leery* as used in, "He must be
(l) *leery* as hell even with that police captain for his shadow"?
    □ a. Cool and fearless   □ c. Reckless and defiant
    □ b. Nervous and suspicious   □ d. Lax and careless

6. The fact that Captain McCluskey of the New York Police was accom-
(f) panying Sollozzo to this meeting leads the reader to conclude that
    □ a. the New York Police approve of Sollozzo and his business.
    □ b. Sollozzo and McCluskey are close friends.
    □ c. McCluskey is an undercover agent for the police.
    □ d. McCluskey is a crooked cop who is "on the take."

7. The business practices of the Corleones and the other Families are
(e) □ a. just barely within the law.
    □ b. like those of other corporations.
    □ c. often violent and lawless.
    □ d. like those of the average family.

8. Michael views his involvement in this whole affair with
(j) □ a. reluctance.   □ c. apprehension.
    □ b. a sense of duty.   □ d. a feeling of terror.

9. When Sonny asks Michael, "Did Clemenza tell you to be sure to drop
(k) the gun?" Michael answers, "A million times." Michael's reply is a
    figure of speech called
    □ a. meiosis (understatement).
    □ b. alliteration (first sounds are alike).
    □ c. simile (a direct comparison).
    □ d. hyperbole (exaggeration).

10. Tom Hagen notices an uncanny resemblance between
(a) □ a. Michael and his father.   □ c. Michael and Clemenza.
    □ b. Michael and his brother.   □ d. Sonny and Clemenza.

11. Tom Hagen is the *Consigliore*, or lawyer, for the Corleone family. His
(h) duties seem to consist of
    □ a. planning murders and disposing of the victims.
    □ b. advising the Corleones and making complex arrangements.
    □ c. doing the Family's dirty work.
    □ d. answering the telephone and running errands.

12. Tom Hagen is different from Michael, Sonny, Clemenza and Tessio in
(d) one important respect:
    □ a. he is much younger than any of them.
    □ b. he refuses to take part in murder.
    □ c. he is Irish, not Italian.
    □ d. he is not a trusted member of the Family.

13. In a speech to Tom Hagen, Michael singles out one factor which he
(c) claims is responsible for the Godfather's success, and that is
  □ a. he takes everything personally.
  □ b. he kills only when he has to.
  □ c. he never betrays his friends.
  □ d. luck is on his side.

14. Michael's attitude toward his father is
(g) □ a. hostile and rebellious.
  □ b. obedient, but resentful.
  □ c. loving, but disapproving.
  □ d. grateful and affectionate.

15. Which of the following best defines *irrevocable* as used in, "For if he
(c) believed what he said, then his life was set on an *irrevocable* course"?
  □ a. Unbearable   □ c. Unalterable
  □ b. Unprofitable   □ d. Unexciting

16. Michael's meeting with Sollozzo and McCluskey takes place
(a) □ a. on a crowded street.   □ c. in an automobile.
  □ b. in a restaurant.   □ d. in a deserted alley.

17. Don Corleone refused to join Sollozzo in his new line of business because
(h) □ a. he does not approve of it.
  □ b. he does not believe it will be profitable.
  □ c. he does not like Sollozzo.
  □ d. he wants the new business all to himself.

18. Sollozzo seems to greet Michael's request to go to the bathroom with
(g) □ a. annoyance.   □ c. ridicule.
  □ b. impatience.   □ d. suspicion.

19. In the moments before Michael pulls the trigger, Sollozzo's voice sounds
(i) like gibberish to Michael. "His mind was so filled with pounding blood
  that no word registered." In this scene, the author builds an atmosphere of
  □ a. trust.   □ c. hope.
  □ b. tension.   □ d. hostility.

20. As Michael turns to leave the restaurant, the other people there
(b) □ a. try to stop him from escaping.
  □ b. pull a gun on him.
  □ c. make no attempt to stop him.
  □ d. scream and run away in terror.

21. Michael's conduct and performance throughout this episode demon-
(j) strate that he is
    ☐ a. competent.   ☐ c. indifferent.
    ☐ b. cruel.   ☐ d. experienced.

22. In this chapter Michael undergoes a transformation from
(e) ☐ a. hero to coward.   ☐ c. obedient son to hired killer.
    ☐ b. loyal friend to traitor. ☐ d. law-abiding citizen to outlaw.

23. From his cabin in the freighter bound for Sicily, Michael "could see the
(k) lights of New York City burning like the fires of hell." This figure of
speech is called
    ☐ a. meiosis (understatement).
    ☐ b. alliteration (first sounds alike).
    ☐ c. simile (a direct comparison).
    ☐ d. personification (giving non-living things life).

24. Michael's mood on board the Italian freighter as it steams out of
(i) New York harbor is one of enormous
    ☐ a. guilt.   ☐ c. remorse.
    ☐ b. relief.   ☐ d. satisfaction.

25. The fact that Captain McCluskey's murder resulted in a crackdown on
(f) gambling and prostitution implies that
    ☐ a. Captain McCluskey had been a beloved member of the force.
    ☐ b. the police had not been aware of the Families' activities up till now.
    ☐ c. unlawful business activities were being "overlooked" by the police
        before this.
    ☐ d. there was probably a public outcry against social evils.

Comprehension Skills: a—isolating details; b—recalling specific facts; c—retaining
concepts; d—organizing facts; e—understanding the main idea; f—drawing a
conclusion; g—making a judgment; h—making an inference; i—recognizing tone;
j—understanding characters; k—appreciation of literary forms; l—knowledge of
word meanings.

EXPERIENCING FICTION

Practice Exercise A

Clemenza kept instructing him during the training session. "Drop the gun as soon as you've finished using it. Just let your hand drop to your side and the gun slip out. Nobody will notice. Everybody will think you're still armed. They'll be staring at your face. Walk out of the place very quickly but don't run. Don't look anybody directly in the eye but don't look away from them either. Remember, they'll be scared of you, believe me, they'll be scared of you."

1. If we had to give a title to Clemenza's "course," it might best be called
   - ☐ a. ballistics.
   - ☐ b. physical training.
   - ☐ c. psychology.
   - ☐ d. elements of business.

2. Clemenza counts on a special kind of reaction from witnesses that will assure Michael's safety. On the lines provided write the sentence from the second half of the passage which describes this reaction.

   _____

   _____

Practice Exercise B

For the second time he saw Michael Corleone's face freeze into a mask that resembled uncannily the Don's. "Tom, don't let anybody kid you. It's all personal, every bit of business. They call it business. OK. But it's personal as hell. You know where I learned that from? The Don. My old man. The Godfather. If a bolt of lightning hit a friend of his the old man would take it personal. He took my going into the Marines personal. That's what makes him great. The Great Don. He takes everything personal."

1. You may not experience the same feelings for your father as Michael, but you may apply a lesson here to success in business. What is the lesson?
   - ☐ a. Rub out the competition first or they will get you.
   - ☐ b. Greatness is as greatness does.
   - ☐ c. Business is a give-and-take proposition.
   - ☐ d. Everything that occurs must be regarded seriously.

2. One sentence indicates to an observer of the situation that Michael may be following in his father's footsteps. Write this sentence on the lines provided.

   _____

   _____

Practice Exercise C

The air seemed to be full of pink mist. Michael swung toward the man sitting against the wall. This man had not made a move. He seemed paralyzed. Now he carefully showed his hands on top of the table and looked away. The waiter was staggering back toward the kitchen, an expression of horror on his face, staring at Michael in disbelief. Sollozzo was still in his chair, the side of his body propped up by the table. McCluskey, his heavy body pulling downward, had fallen off his chair onto the floor. Michael let the gun slip out of his hand so that it bounced off his body and made no noise. He saw that neither the man against the wall nor the waiter had noticed him dropping the gun.

1. Imagine yourself as a participant in this scene. Which person would you probably act like?
   - ☐ a. The waiter
   - ☐ b. The man against the wall
   - ☐ c. Michael
   - ☐ d. Sollozzo

2. If you are deeply involved in the story, you will probably remember Clemenza's lesson when you read this passage (see Practice Exercise A). Circle the sentence from the second half of the passage which shows that Clemenza's lesson was a sound one.

Practice Exercise D

There was a change of clothes for Michael in the car. Twenty minutes later he was on an Italian freighter slated for Sicily. Two hours later the freighter put out to sea and from his cabin Michael could see the lights of New York City burning like the fires of hell. He felt an enormous sense of relief. He was out of it now. The feeling was familiar and he remembered being taken off the beach of an island his Marine division had invaded. The battle had been still going on but he had received a slight wound and was being ferried back to a hospital ship. He had felt the same overpowering relief then that he felt now. All hell would break loose but he wouldn't be there.

1. What you learn about the instincts of men in a combat situation from this passage is that
   - ☐ a. there is generally a feeling of elation.
   - ☐ b. they are filled with patriotic fervor.
   - ☐ c. they dislike cowards and traitors.
   - ☐ d. they want to escape from it.

2. Two sentences, one in the middle and one at the end of the passage, express both Michael's and the reader's feelings now that the shooting is over. Circle these two sentences.

THE GODFATHER

DISCUSSION GUIDES

Analyzing Fiction as an Experience

1. One of the things which you as a reader probably brought to the chapter was a preconceived notion of what kind of people gangsters are and what kind of lives they live. How does your reading support or contradict your original assumptions?

2. Michael says that when he shot Sollozzo, he saw "the light of life die in the man's eyes as clearly as a candle goes out." Chances are you have never seen a person die. How does this description make you feel as though you have?

Interpreting the Chapter

3. Clemenza says they should have stopped Hitler at Munich—they should never have let him get away with that. And Michael reflects that if the Families had been running the State Department there would never have been World War II. How do *you* feel about this original approach to international politics?

4. How do you explain Michael's belated decision to join the Family business after he had been to college, served in the Marines and could get a good job in the straight world?

5. Michael insinuates that his father, the Don, has no qualms about having people killed. Yet Sollozzo says that Don Corleone has "certain unrealistic scruples." Isn't this a contradiction? What kind of moral scruples can a killer have?

6. How would you compare Michael with his older brother, Sonny? How would you describe their relationship?

7. Reread Sollozzo's speech to Michael in the restaurant. What is he asking from Michael and what is he offering in return? Michael does not believe that Sollozzo is negotiating in good faith. What is your opinion?

8. Sollozzo is obviously a professional gangster who is shrewd, smart and confident, whereas Michael is an unseasoned amateur. What fatal error in judgment does Sollozzo make concerning Michael that leads to his death?

9. *The Godfather* has a reputation for being excessively violent, yet the episodes of violence—like the shooting of Sollozzo and McCluskey—are brief in comparison with the length of the book. What point do you think the author was most intent on getting across to the reader—the violent tactics which the Corleone Family used, or something else? Explain.

10. Captain McCluskey is shot while he is eating his veal and spaghetti. He chokes when the first shot hits him in the throat, "as if he had swallowed too large a bite of the veal." How do you think the author wants you to feel about Captain McCluskey's death?

WRITING EXERCISE

Read the following paragraphs from the beginning of Anton Chekhov's short story "The Bet." Then answer the questions which follow, using a few sentences or a short paragraph for each. The questions explore your personal response to the passage.

It was a dark autumn night. The old banker was pacing from corner to corner of his study, recalling to his mind the party he gave in the autumn fifteen years ago. There were many clever people at the party and much interesting conversation. They talked among other things of capital punishment. The guests, among them not a few scholars and journalists, for the most part disapproved of capital punishment. They found it obsolete as a means of punishment, unfitted to a Christian State and immoral. Some of them thought that capital punishment should be replaced universally by life-imprisonment.

"I don't agree with you," said the host. "I myself have experienced neither capital punishment nor life-imprisonment, but if one may judge *a priori*, then in my opinion capital punishment is more moral and more humane than imprisonment. Execution kills instantly, life-imprisonment kills by degrees. Who is the more humane executioner, one who kills you in a few seconds or one who draws the life out of you incessantly, for years?"

"They're both equally immoral," remarked one of the guests, "because their purpose is the same, to take away life. The State is not God. It has no right to take away that which it cannot give back, if it should so desire."

Among the company was a lawyer, a young man of about twenty-five. On being asked his opinion, he said:

"Capital punishment and life-imprisonment are equally immoral; but if I were offered the choice between them, I would certainly choose the second. It's better to live somehow than not to live at all."

1. Use your imagination to recreate the party—the atmosphere, the way the guests were dressed, the food they ate, and so on. Describe the scene as though you were there.

2. How would you have felt if you were a guest at the party?

3. Three views of punishment are presented in the passage. Which view comes closest to your own? Explain your answer in terms of your own values. (Some examples of personal values are a regard for life, a belief in revenge, a religious belief, a belief in the importance of protecting society, etc.)

4. After reading these opening paragraphs, do you have any interest in continuing the story? Explain your answer.

Answer Key

UNIT 1: RAGTIME

Comprehension Questions

1. c	6. c	11. d	16. c	21. d
2. b	7. d	12. b	17. d	22. c
3. d	8. a	13. c	18. a	23. b
4. a	9. b	14. b	19. b	24. c
5. b	10. d	15. a	20. a	25. b

Analyzing Setting

Practice Exercise A
1. b
2. the sun behind it now going down
   fir trees threw long shadows
   The shadows deepened.

Practice Exercise B
1. c
2. cold gray sky; snow; ice; overcoats

Practice Exercise C
1. a
2. The trucks were army Reo's with pagoda hoods and chain wheel drive.
   Steam drifted back from the engine like patches of fog.
   The bell quietly rang.

Practice Exercise D
1. c
2. emporium; satin toques; plumed with egret feathers

UNIT 2: ROOTS

Comprehension Questions

1. b	6. b	11. a	16. b	21. b
2. d	7. b	12. d	17. d	22. a
3. c	8. d	13. b	18. c	23. a
4. a	9. a	14. a	19. b	24. b
5. d	10. b	15. c	20. c	25. d

Recognizing Tone and Mood

Practice Exercise A
1. b
2. abruptly the Wolof spat out loudly enough to be heard across the entire hold

UNIT 2: ROOTS (Continued)

Practice Exercise B
1. c
2. a. with loathing
   b. like dogs

Practice Exercise C
1. b
2. they were no longer afraid, because they no longer cared whether they lived or died
   they had willed themselves to die

Practice Exercise D
1. a
2. sweat and gag; choke and vomit

UNIT 3: GREAT EXPECTATIONS

Comprehension Questions

1. b	6. b	11. a	16. c	21. b
2. d	7. d	12. c	17. a	22. a
3. c	8. a	13. d	18. d	23. c
4. a	9. c	14. b	19. b	24. b
5. c	10. b	15. d	20. c	25. c

Understanding Characterization

Practice Exercise A
1. c
2. a mortifying and penitential character ought to be imparted to my diet

Practice Exercise B
1. b
2. I had never thought of being ashamed of my hands before; but I began to consider them a very indifferent pair. Her contempt for me was so strong, that it became infectious, and I caught it.

Practice Exercise C
1. a
2. face; chest; voice; body; soul

Practice Exercise D
1. c
2. This gave me power to keep them back and to look at her

UNIT 4: HAWAII

Comprehension Questions

1. b	6. c	11. a	16. c	21. a
2. d	7. a	12. c	17. a	22. d
3. a	8. d	13. a	18. c	23. d
4. c	9. b	14. d	19. b	24. b
5. b	10. a	15. b	20. c	25. a

The Historical Novel

Practice Exercise A
1. b
2. "I understand perfectly that in the old days these kahunas accomplished much that was good. But God does not require kahunas."

Practice Exercise B
1. c
2. The girl is not an alii.
   Noelani is kapu alii.

Practice Exercise C
1. d
2. There was a long silence as this ugly accusation was digested, for the alii of Hawaii were proud people, desperately hungry for the world's approval.

Practice Exercise D
1. a
2. "But they are not alii," Malama insisted.

UNIT 5: DELIVERANCE

Comprehension Questions

1. c	6. a	11. a	16. b	21. b
2. b	7. c	12. c	17. d	22. a
3. a	8. b	13. b	18. d	23. c
4. d	9. d	14. a	19. a	24. d
5. b	10. c	15. d	20. c	25. b

Analyzing Conflict

Practice Exercise A
1. c
2. Suggested answers:
   I was the one who had to do the job.
                    or
   I was the one who had to scale the cliff.

UNIT 5: DELIVERANCE (Continued)

Practice Exercise B
1. a
2. And I swear to God that if you don't do exactly what I say I'll kill you myself.

Practice Exercise C
1. b
2. The wall was giving me nothing.

Practice Exercise D
1. d
2. harder than it was possible
I was up against a surface as smooth as monument stone, and I still believe that for a space of time I was held in the air by pure will, fighting an immense rock.

Writing Exercise

A. citizens of Poker Flat   versus   the outcasts
B. the outcasts   versus   the drunkard Billy
C. the outcasts   versus   the blizzard
D. instinct to survive   versus   responsibility to others

UNIT 6: AN AMERICAN TRAGEDY

Comprehension Questions

1. c	6. b	11. b	16. b	21. c
2. b	7. c	12. c	17. c	22. d
3. a	8. a	13. d	18. b	23. b
4. d	9. d	14. a	19. a	24. a
5. b	10. a	15. c	20. d	25. c

Analyzing Plot Structure and Development

Practice Exercise A
1. a
2. If one were slipping away at night or by day, who would encounter one here?

Practice Exercise B
1. c
2. an almost nebulous figure

Practice Exercise C
1. d
2. For now—now—in spite of himself, the long evaded and yet commanding moment.

UNIT 6: AN AMERICAN TRAGEDY (Continued)

Practice Exercise D
1. b
2. And then he, stirred by her sharp scream . . . rising and reaching half to assist or recapture her and half to apologize for the unintended blow

Writing Exercise

Step One

a. 4	d. 1	g. 12	j. 3	m. 5
b. 13	e. 7	h. 2	k. 6	
c. 8	f. 9	i. 10	l. 11	

Step Two

Exposition: d, h, j
Complication: a, m, k
Crisis: e, c, f
Climax: i, l
Resolution: g, b

UNIT 7: THE HOUND OF THE BASKERVILLES

Comprehension Questions

1. c	6. c	11. b	16. b	21. a
2. b	7. b	12. c	17. d	22. c
3. a	8. a	13. a	18. a	23. a
4. d	9. c	14. d	19. b	24. d
5. c	10. d	15. c	20. c	25. b

The Detective Novel

Practice Exercise A
1. a
2. You have presented an inch or two of it to my examination all the time that you have been talking.

Practice Exercise B
1. d
2. Barrymore, butler
Barrymore's wife, housekeeper
Dr. James Mortimer, friend and medical attendant
Murphy, gypsy horse-dealer
Mr. Henry Baskerville, next-of-kin, son of Sir Charles Baskerville's younger brother
Sir Charles Baskerville's younger brother

UNIT 7: THE HOUND OF THE BASKERVILLES (Continued)

Practice Exercise C
1. b
2. Yet you must admit that the footmark is material.
   The original hound was material enough to tug a man's throat out, and yet he was diabolical as well.

Practice Exercise D
1. a
2. He came of the old masterful Baskerville strain, and was the very image, they tell me, of the family picture of old Hugo.

UNIT 8: IN COLD BLOOD

Comprehension Questions

1. a	6. d	11. d	16. c	21. c
2. c	7. b	12. b	17. b	22. b
3. d	8. c	13. a	18. a	23. a
4. b	9. a	14. d	19. b	24. c
5. a	10. c	15. d	20. d	25. d

Psychological Aspects in Literature

Practice Exercise A
1. b
2. not your own fault *(also correct:* maybe a thing you were born with)
   If she'd ever had any luck at all

Practice Exercise B
1. d
2. It was an old half-dead mongrel, brittle-boned and mangy, and the impact, as it met the car, was little more than what a bird might make.

Practice Exercise C
1. a
2. Dear God! That poor family!

Practice Exercise D
1. c
2. It was a passable likeness, and the artist perceived one not very obvious aspect of the sitter's countenance—its mischief, an amused, babyish malice that suggested some unkind cupid aiming envenomed arrows.

UNIT 9: BABBITT

Comprehension Questions

1. b	6. a	11. b	16. b	21. b
2. a	7. d	12. d	17. b	22. a
3. d	8. c	13. a	18. d	23. a
4. c	9. b	14. c	19. c	24. c
5. c	10. a	15. b	20. a	25. d

Analyzing Figurative and Descriptive Language

Practice Exercise A
1. d
2. cheerful as the April dawn

Practice Exercise B
1. b
2. Socially it was almost as creditable as buying expensive cord tires.

Practice Exercise C
1. a
2. the pretentious tortoise-shell; the meek prince-nez

Practice Exercise D
1. c
2. sensational event

UNIT 10: WATERSHIP DOWN

Comprehension Questions

1. b	6. b	11. d	16. d	21. a
2. c	7. d	12. c	17. a	22. c
3. d	8. b	13. a	18. b	23. b
4. a	9. a	14. c	19. c	24. d
5. d	10. c	15. b	20. b	25. b

The Use of Allegory

Practice Exercise A
1. c
2. It was not long before his officers were asking to be allowed to lead patrols.

The General led an expedition against it and broke it up, the prisoners being brought back to Efrafa, where a few of them later rose to be Owsla members themselves.

UNIT 10: WATERSHIP DOWN (Continued)

Practice Exercise B
1. b
2. a. loss of respect for law and order
   b. birth control
   c. political unrest
   d. emigration
   e. political repression

Practice Exercise C
1. d
2. They are all names of plants.

Practice Exercise D
1. a
2. Woundwort was nonplused. He was no fool and it was, he could not help feeling, extremely odd that any right-minded rabbit should choose to walk into Efrafa of his own accord.

Writing Exercise

The following tells how Aesop completed the fables:

1. Shortly after this a wolf actually came, but this time the villagers thought the boy was deceiving them again and nobody came to his help.
2. Better beans and bacon in peace than cakes and ale in fear.
3. We often give our enemies the means of our own destruction.

UNIT 11: LORD OF THE FLIES

Comprehension Questions

1. b	6. d	11. a	16. d	21. c
2. d	7. a	12. d	17. b	22. b
3. a	8. b	13. b	18. c	23. d
4. b	9. a	14. c	19. a	24. c
5. c	10. c	15. a	20. d	25. a

The Use of Symbols

Practice Exercise A
1. b
2. We could experiment.

Practice Exercise B
1. c
2. "Listen all of you. Me and my hunters, we're living along the beach by a flat rock. We hunt and feast and have fun. If you want to join my tribe come and see us. Perhaps I'll let you join. Perhaps not."

UNIT 11: LORD OF THE FLIES (Continued)

Practice Exercise C
1. a
2. After the many brilliant speeches that had been made on this very spot Ralph's remarks seemed lame, even to the littluns.

Practice Exercise D
1. c
2. I'm part of you?

UNIT 12: HUCKLEBERRY FINN

Comprehension Questions

1. d	6. c	11. d	16. a	21. c
2. a	7. a	12. b	17. c	22. b
3. b	8. d	13. a	18. b	23. d
4. c	9. b	14. d	19. a	24. a
5. b	10. a	15. c	20. c	25. b

Identifying Themes in Literature

Practice Exercise A
1. b
2. lonesomeness; lazy

Practice Exercise B
1. d
2. sliding out; scatter out (also correct: get off)

Practice Exercise C
1. c
2. what you want, above all things, on a raft, is for everybody to be satisfied, and feel right and kind towards the others

Practice Exercise D
1. b
2. If I never learnt nothing else out of pap, I learnt that the best way to get along with his kind of people is to let them have their own way.

UNIT 13: BREAKFAST OF CHAMPIONS

Comprehension Questions

1. d	6. c	11. c	16. b	21. a
2. b	7. b	12. b	17. a	22. b
3. a	8. d	13. d	18. c	23. c
4. c	9. a	14. a	19. a	24. c
5. d	10. b	15. c	20. b	25. b

UNIT 13: BREAKFAST OF CHAMPIONS (Continued)

Analyzing Satire

Practice Exercise A
1. b
2. So, in the interests of survival, they trained themselves to be agreeing machines instead of thinking machines. All their minds had to do was to discover what other people were thinking, and then they thought that, too.

Practice Exercise B
1. c
2. This was because their English teachers would wince and cover their ears and give them flunking grades and so on whenever they failed to speak like English aristocrats before the First World War.

Practice Exercise C
1. d
2. war game

Practice Exercise D
1. c
2. Every person had a clearly defined part to play—as a black person, a female high school drop-out, a Pontiac dealer, a gynecologist, a gas-conversion burner installer.

Writing Exercise

1. education
2. success
3. congressman
4. worth it
5. funerals
6. economical

UNIT 14: MY LIFE AND HARD TIMES

Comprehension Questions

1. a	6. a	11. c	16. b	21. a
2. b	7. c	12. b	17. d	22. b
3. d	8. d	13. a	18. c	23. c
4. c	9. b	14. d	19. b	24. b
5. d	10. a	15. c	20. a	25. a

Understanding Humor

Practice Exercise A
1. b
2. He was sorry immediately, mother said. He was always sorry, she said, after he bit someone, but we could not understand how she figured this out.

UNIT 14: MY LIFE AND HARD TIMES (Continued)

Practice Exercise B
1. d
2. It was a foolhardy thing to do and the last time I saw my mother, about six months ago, she said she didn't know what possessed me. I don't either, except that I was pretty mad.

Practice Exercise C
1. c
2. So we tried it with every adjustment of the microscope known to man.

Practice Exercise D
1. d
2. "Button up your coat!"
   "You startled him!"
   "That won't help the situation!"

UNIT 15: THE GODFATHER

Comprehension Questions

1. b	6. d	11. b	16. b	21. a
2. c	7. c	12. c	17. a	22. d
3. d	8. b	13. a	18. d	23. c
4. a	9. d	14. d	19. b	24. b
5. b	10. a	15. c	20. c	25. c

Experiencing Fiction

Practice Exercise A
1. c
2. Remember, they'll be scared of you, believe me, they'll be scared of you.

Practice Exercise B
1. d
2. For the second time he saw Michael Corleone's face freeze into a mask that resembled uncannily the Don's.

Practice Exercise C
1. Reader's opinion
2. He saw that neither the man against the wall nor the waiter had noticed him dropping the gun.

Practice Exercise D
1. d
2. He felt an enormous sense of relief.
   He had felt the same overpowering relief then that he felt now.

BIBLIOGRAPHY

Adams, Richard. *Watership Down.* New York: Macmillan Publishing Co., 1972.

Capote, Truman. *In Cold Blood.* New York: Random House, 1965.

Dickens, Charles. *Great Expectations.* Originally published in 1861.

Dickey, James. *Deliverance.* Boston: Houghton Mifflin Co., 1970.

Doctorow, E. L. *Ragtime.* New York: Random House, 1974.

Doyle, A. Conan. *The Hound of the Baskervilles.* Originally published in 1902.

Dreiser, Theodore. *An American Tragedy.* New York: Boni and Liveright, 1925.

Golding, William. *Lord of the Flies.* New York: Coward, McCann & Geoghegan, 1954.

Haley, Alex. *Roots.* New York: Doubleday & Co., 1976.

Lewis, Sinclair. *Babbitt.* New York: Harcourt Brace Jovanovich, 1922, 1950.

Michener, James. *Hawaii.* New York: Random House, 1959.

Puzo, Mario. *The Godfather.* New York: G. P. Putnam's Sons, 1969.

Thurber, James. *My Life and Hard Times.* New York: Harper, 1933.

Twain, Mark. *Huckleberry Finn.* Originally published in 1884.

Vonnegut, Kurt, Jr. *Breakfast of Champions: Or Goodbye Blue Monday!* New York: Delacorte Press, 1973.

COMPREHENSION SKILLS

Use this graph to show the questions you get wrong. Starting at the bottom, put an *x* on the line above the appropriate letter every time you fail a question labeled with that letter. A line of *x*'s rising above the others indicates a specific comprehension weakness. The comprehension skills represented by the letters are given at the top of the graph. The numbers on the side show your total number of wrong answers for each comprehension skill. Consult your instructor if you fail ten questions in any one skill; this means you have discovered a comprehension weakness which must be corrected.

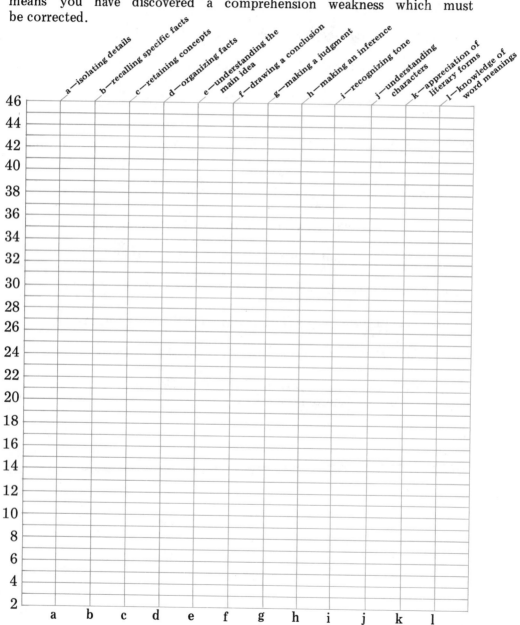

BEST-SELLING CHAPTERS

COMPREHENSION SCORES

Use this graph to plot your comprehension scores. The horizontal line represents the number of questions answered correctly. Put an x on the vertical line under each chapter title where it intersects the horizontal line. You should strive for scores of 80 percent or better (20 or more questions answered correctly). Connect the x's to form a graph of your comprehension. See the left side of the graph for percentages (scores), the right side for number of questions answered correctly. Consult your instructor if you consistently score below 80 percent.

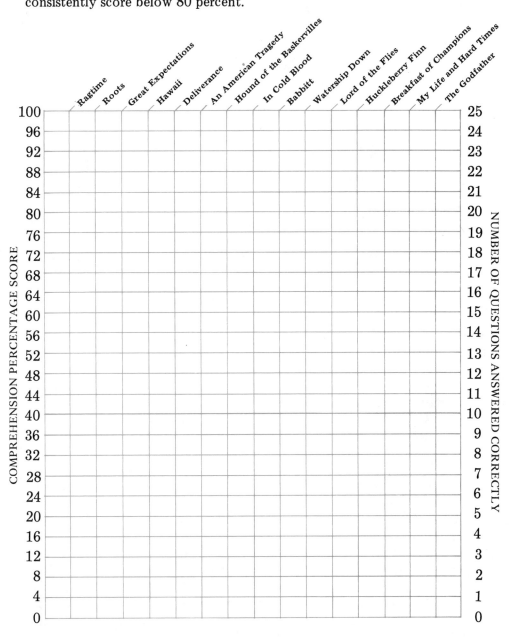